BLACKSTONE'S GUI

The Anti-Social Behaviour Act 2003

Jonathan Manning
Claire-Louise Manning
Victoria Osler

Great Clarendon Street, Oxford OX2 6DP

Oxford University Press is a department of the University of Oxford.
It furthers the University's objective of excellence in research, scholarship,
and education by publishing worldwide in

Oxford New York

Auckland Bangkok Buenos Aires Cape Town Chennai
Dar es Salaam Delhi Hong Kong Istanbul Karachi Kolkata
Kuala Lumpur Madrid Melbourne Mexico City Mumbai Nairobi
São Paulo Shanghai Taipei Tokyo Toronto

Oxford is a registered trade mark of Oxford University Press
in the UK and in certain other countries

Published in the United States
by Oxford University Press Inc., New York

© Jonathan Manning, Claire-Louise Manning, and Victoria Osler, 2004

The moral rights of the authors have been asserted
Database right Oxford University Press (maker)

First published 2004

Crown copyright material is reproduced under Class Licence
Number C01P0000148 with the permission of the Controller of
HMSO and the Queen's Printer for Scotland

All rights reserved. No part of this publication may be reproduced,
stored in a retrieval system, or transmitted, in any form or by any means,
without the prior permission in writing of Oxford University Press,
or as expressly permitted by law, or under terms agreed with the appropriate
reprographics rights organization. Enquiries concerning reproduction
outside the scope of the above should be sent to the Rights Department,
Oxford University Press, at the address above

You must not circulate this book in any other binding or cover
and you must impose this same condition on any acquirer

British Library Cataloguing in Publication Data
Data available

Library of Congress Cataloging-in-Publication Data

Manning, Jonathan.
Blackstone's guide to the anti-social behaviour Act 2003/Jonathan
Manning, Claire-Louise Manning, Victoria Osler.
p. cm.
Includes index.
ISBN 0-19-927316-2 (alk. paper)
1. Great Britain. Anti-social behaviour act 2003. 2. Breach of the
peace—England. 3. Police regulations—England. 4. Nuisances—England. I.
Title: Guide to the Anti-Social Behaviour Act 2003. II. Title: Anti-Social
Behaviour Act 2003. III. Manning, Claire-Louise. IV. Osler, Victoria. V.
Title.
KD8035.A31203M36 2004
344.4105—dc22

2004014380

1 3 5 7 9 10 8 6 4 2

Typeset by Hope Services (Abingdon) Ltd.
Printed in Great Britain
on acid-free paper by
Biddles Ltd., King's Lynn

HESC

BLACKSTONE'S GUIDE TO

The Anti-Social Behaviour Act 2003

BLACKBURN COLLEGE LIBRARY
01254 292120

Please return this book on or before the last date below

7 DAY LOAN
FINE = 10P PER DAY

13 FEB 2006
23 MAY 2006
09 JUN 2006
07 NOV 2006
4 MAY 2007

Preface

The Anti-Social Behaviour Act 2003 received royal assent on 15 November 2003 and is planned to come into force on various dates during 2004. It is arranged in nine parts (with three schedules) and legislates to control or prohibit a wide range of conduct, such as owning a property used for the manufacture, supply or use of Class A drugs, behaving in a manner capable of causing nuisance or annoyance to others, playing truant or being excluded from school, trespassing on land, carrying airguns or imitation firearms, not removing graffiti from one's own property, attending raves and demonstrations, or having a high hedge on one's land.

The legislative scheme employed by the Act, in relation to the majority of its parts, of merely amending pre-existing statutes makes it difficult to detect any overarching philosophy or themes behind the new legislation, but should not be allowed to conceal the many and various important measures which are contained within it. In this guide, we have sought to describe and explain those measures, setting them in their proper legal context and highlighting practical issues which are likely to arise. We have referred to the applicable ministerial guidance and Codes of Practice where these have been available at the time of writing.

We hope that this guide will prove to be a useful source of information to everyone—practitioner, student or lay adviser—who needs to get to grips with the provisions of the Act quickly, as well as to those who are studying its provisions from a more academic perspective. The law is stated as at 31 December 2003, although we have tried to take account of later developments where possible.

London
March 2004

Jonathan Manning
Claire-Louise Manning
Victoria Osler

BLACKBURN COLLEGE
LIBRARY
Acc. No. BB02317
Class No. HSC 344.05 MAN
Date 03/03/05

Contents—Summary

Contents

Table of Cases

Tables of Legislation

Secondary Legislation

Statutory Status Table

Section	SI	Commencement	Amendments	Notes
1	2003/3300	20.01.04		
2	2003/3300	20.01.04		
3	2003/3300	20.01.04		
4	2003/3300	20.01.04		
5	2003/3300	20.01.04		
6	2003/3300	20.01.04		
7	2003/3300	20.01.04		
8	2003/3300	20.01.04		
9	2003/3300	20.01.04		
10	2003/3300	20.01.04		
11	2003/3300	20.01.04		
12	NIF			
13	NIF			
14	NIF			
15	NIF			
16	NIF			
17	NIF			
18	2003/3300	27.02.04		
19	2003/3300	27.02.04		England Only
20	2003/3300	27.02.04		England Only
21	2003/3300	27.02.04		England Only
22	2003/3300	27.02.04		England Only
23	2003/3300	27.02.04		
24	2003/3300	27.02.04		England Only
25	2003/3300	27.02.04		
26	2003/3300	27.02.04		
27	2003/3300	27.02.04		
28	2003/3300	27.02.04		
29	2003/3300	27.02.04		
30	2003/3300	20.01.04		
31	2003/3300	20.01.04		
32	2003/3300	20.01.04		
33	2003/3300	20.01.04		
34	2003/3300	20.01.04		
35	2003/3300	20.01.04		
36	2003/3300	20.01.04		
37	2003/3300	20.01.04		
38	2003/3300	20.01.04		

39	2003/3300	20.01.04		s 39(1), (2), (4)–(6), and (3) in relation to: purchase, acquisition, manufacture, sale or transfer of prohibited weapon only
39	2003/3300	30.04.04		Remainder
40	2004/690	31.03.04	s 40(5)(a) amended by *Criminal Justice Act 2003*, *s 280(2)*, *Sch 26, para 59*	England Only
41	2004/690	31.03.04		England Only
42	2004/690	31.03.04		England Only
43	2004/690	31.03.04		England Only
44	2004/690	31.03.04		England Only
45	2004/690	31.03.04		England Only
46	2004/690	31.03.04		
47	2004/690	31.03.04		England Only
48	2004/690	31.03.04		Re: local authorities in England specified in The Anti-social Behaviour Act 2003 (Commencement No 2) Order 2004 (SI *2004/690, art 4(1)*) Remainder NIF
49	2004/690	31.03.04		Re: local authorities in England specified in The Anti-social Behaviour Act 2003 (Commencement No 2) Order 2004 (SI *2004/690, art 4(1)*) Remainder NIF
50	2004/690	31.03.04		Re: local authorities in England specified in The Anti-social Behaviour Act 2003 (Commencement No 2) Order 2004 (SI *2004/690, art 4(1)*) Remainder NIF
51				Re: local authorities in England specified in The Anti-social Behaviour Act 2003 (Commencement No 2) Order 2004 (SI *2004/690, art 4(1)*)

			Remainder NIF
52			Re: local authorities in England specified in The Anti-social Behaviour Act 2003 (Commencement No 2) Order 2004 (SI *2004/690, art 4(1)*) Remainder NIF
53	2003/3300	20.01.04	
54	2004/690	31.03.04	
55	2004/690	31.03.04	England Only
56	2004/690	31.03.04	England Only
57	2003/3300	20.01.04	
58	2003/3300	20.01.04	
59	2003/3300	20.01.04	
60	2003/3300	27.02.04	
61	2003/3300	27.02.04	
62	2003/3300	27.02.04	
63	2003/3300	27.02.04	
64	2003/3300	27.02.04	
65	NIF		
66	NIF		
67	NIF		
68	NIF		
69	NIF		
70	NIF		
71	NIF		
72	NIF		
73	NIF		
74	NIF		
75	NIF		
76	NIF		
77	NIF		
78	NIF		
79	NIF		
80	NIF		
81	NIF		
82	NIF		
83	NIF		
84	NIF		
85	Act	20.11.03	s 85(9)–(11) only
85	2003/3300	20.01.04	s 85(1)–(3), (7) and (4) re: Crime and Disorder Act 1998, s 1(10B) only
85	2003/3300	27.02.03	s 85(8) only
85	2004/690	31.03.04	s 85(4), (5)–(6) re: persons aged 18 yrs or over, (9)–(11) only

85			Remainder NIF
86	2003/3300	20.01.04	s 86(4)–(6) and (3) re: Crime and Disorder Act 1998, s 1(9B) and (9C) only
86	2004/690	31.03.04	Remainder
87	2003/3300	20.01.04	
88	NIF		
89	2003/3300	20.01.04	s 89(1)–(4), (6) and (7) only
89	2004/960	31.03.04	Remainder
90	NIF		
91	NIF		
92	2003/3300	20.01.04	
92	2004/690	31.03.04	See Sch 3
93	Act	20.11.03	
94	Act	20.11.03	
95	Act	20.11.03	
96	Act	20.11.03	
97	Act	20.11.03	
Sch 1	NIF		
Sch 2	NIF		
Sch 3		20.01.04	Repeals re: Firearms Act 1968; Prosecution of Offences Act 1985; Firearms (Amendment) Act 1988; Criminal Justice and Public Order Act 1994; Crime and Disorder Act 1998; Police Reform Act 2002 only Repeals re: *Noise Act 1996*, s 2(7) the words from 'and accordingly' to the end only NIF Remainder

Passage of Bill through Parliament

Date	House	Stage	Hansard vol	Cols
27.03.03	Commons	Bill Presented	402	462
08.04.03	Commons	Second Reading	403	136–240
24.06.03	Commons	Third Reading	407	895–992
18.07.03	Lords	Second Reading	651	1091–1156
11.09.03	Lords	Committee Stage	652	431–468 478–542
17.09.03	Lords	Committee Stage	652	951–979 993–1046
07.10.03	Lords	Committee Stage	653	224–282
23.10.03	Lords	Report Stage	653	1761–1769 1780–1840
17.11.03	Commons	Final	413	501–562

1

REMEDIES FOR ANTI-SOCIAL BEHAVIOUR

1.1. WHAT IS ANTI-SOCIAL BEHAVIOUR?

Anti-social behaviour is extremely difficult to define legally in any meaningful sense. Traditionally, it referred to conduct which was described in terms of causing a nuisance or annoyance to other people, usually neighbours.[1] 'Neighbours from hell' were anti-social and the conduct by which they were defined encompassed anything that might cause nuisance or annoyance to those living around them, be it joyriding, foul language and abuse, playing loud music, dealing drugs, allowing their children to run riot or not mowing the lawn sufficiently frequently. **1.1.1**

The first attempt at any statutory definition not derived from these tenancy-related concepts of good neighbourliness was made by the Protection from Harassment Act 1997 which, borrowing language from the Public Order Act 1986, ss 4A and 5, referred to 'harassment' in terms which included causing 'alarm' or 'distress'.[2] This was made the basis of the only statutory definition of the phrase 'anti-social behaviour', in s 1 of the Crime and Disorder Act 1998, namely conduct 'causing or likely to cause harassment, alarm or distress' to a person not of the same household as the perpetrator. **1.1.2**

In many ways, this made sense. The defining characteristic of anti-social behaviour was its effect on other people going about their business: it was the kind of behaviour which was likely to cause harassment, alarm or distress. While **1.1.3**

[1] See eg Housing Act 1985, Sch 2, Pt I, ground 2, the nuisance ground for possession, as originally enacted (ie prior to the amendments made by the Housing Act 1996, s 144).

[2] Protection from Harassment Act 1997, s 7(2).

not a million miles from the Housing Act formulation of conduct which was likely to cause nuisance or annoyance, it was a more complete and workable definition.

1.1.4 Of course it is wholly legitimate to argue that there is no need for a compendious definition of anti-social behaviour. People are anti-social in all manner of different ways which may not share any common features. The absence of an all-embracing definition should not stand in the way of taking effective action to combat the behaviour in question. There is a great deal of sense in such an approach. Definitions are not the be-all and end-all of good legislation.

1.1.5 What is important, however, is that with the governmental appetite for legislation in the field of anti-social behaviour showing no sign of abating, and in fact showing every sign of becoming ever more voracious,[3] regulation and prescription of the conduct of the private individual should not stray beyond the legitimate bounds of dealing with behaviour which can terrorize communities (or, even if not so extreme, make living or working in a particular locality—or even just travelling through it—a frightening, or dangerous, or distressing experience) and into the territory of the regulation of behaviour, not because it is inherently anti-social, but just because someone happens to find it eccentric or distasteful.

1.1.6 While constant warnings of the erosion of freedoms may frequently be overplayed, the fact remains that the conduct of minority groups (not necessarily racial or religious minorities) may be offensive to a number of people. That does not necessarily mean that such conduct should be condemned as 'anti-social' and made the subject of penal legislation. Without any definitions of what can and should legitimately be regarded as genuinely anti-social, we risk entering a world of legal relativism where any conduct is a legitimate target for government action.

1.1.7 The Anti-Social Behaviour Act 2003 does not limit itself by means of any conceptual or definitional limits. Its provisions range far and wide over the manifold different types of possible human behaviour, from carrying airguns or imitation firearms in public,[4] to not removing graffiti from one's property;[5] from having a high hedge[6] to not ensuring that one's children go to school;[7] from running a crack house[8] to gathering in a 'public assembly' of two people.[9] All of this conduct, and more, is impinged upon by the 2003 Act, not by way of many big new ideas (aside, perhaps, from Parts 1 (closure of crack houses), 2 (demotion of tenancies) and 8 (high hedges)—although the ideas in Parts 2 and 8 derive from other sources[10]) but by means of a succession of incremental amendments to a

[3] Pace the Crime and Disorder Act 1998, the Criminal Justice and Police Act 2001, the Police Reform Act 2002, the Anti-Social Behaviour Act 2003, the Criminal Justice Act 2003, and a new Housing Bill which has recently passed through its committee stage (24 February 2004).

[4] 2003 Act, Pt 5. [5] ibid, Pt 6. [6] ibid, Pt 8. [7] ibid, Pt 3. [8] ibid, Pt 1.

[9] ibid, Pt 7.

[10] Demotion of tenancies was suggested in the Law Commission Consultation Paper (No 162), *Renting Homes—1: Status and Security* (2001). The provisions of Pt 8 emanate from the Private Members' High Hedges (No 2) Bill.

panoply of other statutes. Beyond the fact that the Act legislates in respect of these matters and is termed an 'Anti-Social Behaviour Act', it is difficult to identify any unifying conceptual themes to its provisions so as to assist with any meaningful definition of what 'anti-social' behaviour actually comprises, beyond the platitudinous and generalistic assertions emanating from White Papers and consultation documents that it is conduct which makes other people's lives 'a misery'. That sort of definition could certainly encompass a whole range of human behaviour, much of it entirely legal.

Taking the implications of the Act to their logical conclusion, moreover, **1.1.8** everything which constitutes any kind of criminal offence or breach of civil obligation (or even which is wholly lawful but may be disruptive or inconvenient or simply upset someone)[11] could amount to anti-social behaviour. The breadth with which the legislative net is cast certainly gives the impression that the government's starting point was to make a list of things people do in any sphere of activity which may be considered (whether by individuals or indeed by government) socially undesirable, and then legislate to prohibit or restrict it in the Act. An example of this is the application of the powers of the police to place restrictions on public assemblies to groups of just two people, where previously only groups of 20 or more were included.[12]

Whether this renders the Act a long overdue attempt to restore order to soci- **1.1.9** ety as a whole and make life more bearable for those law-abiding citizens who have found the unlawful or unneighbourly activities of others disruptive to their daily lives, or whether it marks an increasingly authoritarian legislative trend may well depend, ultimately, on the individual's social, moral and political outlook, but it is not a matter of law.

It would seem that governments of all complexions are convinced that the **1.1.10** public supports and indeed demands ever tougher action against behaviour of the kind this Act seeks to prevent. This being so, the continuing flood of law to 'solve' the intractable social problems from which modern societies suffer is unlikely to abate, let alone dry up in the foreseeable future. Whether there will ever be enough law to achieve the aim of curing the problem of anti-social behaviour—indeed whether legislation can ever have such an effect—is certainly debatable, and almost certainly incapable of proof.

1.2. OTHER REMEDIES

In addition to the 2003 Act, a wide range of statutory provisions exists to deal **1.2.1** with the problem of anti-social behaviour. The availability of any specific provision will depend upon a number of factors, such as the identity, or legal status,

[11] Such as a 15 year old, walking alone to a nearby friend's house at 9.05 pm: s/he may now be liable to be taken home by a constable in uniform or community support officer: 2003 Act, s 30(6).

[12] ibid, s 57.

of the prospective claimant, and the criteria which the provision itself specifies must be satisfied before it may be invoked. A measure may, for example, stipulate the type of behaviour that it seeks to prevent or remedy, such as s 1(1) of the Crime and Disorder Act 1998, which may be relied upon where behaviour has caused or is likely to cause harassment, alarm or distress to one or more persons not of the same household as the perpetrator; or it may define its availability by reference to some other factor, such as the necessity for action to be taken in order to protect the interests of the community.[13]

1.2.2 Accordingly, it is necessary to analyse each of the main provisions in turn, in order to ascertain the circumstances in which they may be relevant.

Injunctions at common law

1.2.3 Landlords may seek to control anti-social behaviour by tenants, members of their households and their visitors by way of injunction, so long as they have a cause of action. Generally, in relation to tenants at least, this will not be a problem as most tenancy agreements contain covenants against nuisance on the part of both the tenant and members of his or her household and visitors. Accordingly, such behaviour will normally amount to a breach of the tenancy agreement and the cause of action will be in contract.

1.2.4 If the landlord's property is being damaged, moreover, as a result of such behaviour, the landlord may have a cause of action in nuisance or trespass. In practical terms, most injunction proceedings brought by social landlords will not rely on common law alone (or at all), but will be brought under one or more of the different statutory causes of action which now exist, and which are summarized below.

1.2.5 Other private citizens may seek injunctions based on private nuisance, trespass, interference with goods, and so on, if the relevant elements of the cause of action are established. They may also be able to institute a prosecution for statutory nuisance.[14]

Local Government Act 1972, s 222

1.2.6 This section states that: 'Where a local authority consider it expedient for the promotion or protection of the interests of the inhabitants of their area—they may prosecute or defend or appear in any legal proceedings and, in the case of civil proceedings, may institute them in their own name . . .'

1.2.7 This remedy is clearly only available to local authorities. In order for it to be exercisable, the authority must 'consider it expedient for the promotion or protection' of the interests of the inhabitants of their area. This has been held to

[13] See eg Local Government Act 1972, s 222.

[14] Environmental Protection Act 1990, ss 79 and 82.

mean *all* the inhabitants, not simply a section of them.[15] Since, however, it is in everybody's interest (particularly in urban areas) for an authority to do what it can to maintain, at the very least, the semblance of a law-abiding community, and what should be done to that end is for the authority to decide, s 222 is not merely applicable to the restraining of public nuisances. The local authority may use its discretion wherever it considers it is justified in doing so under the section.[16]

In using the power to restrain anti-social behaviour, it is necessary to establish **1.2.8** a cause of action, usually private nuisance, trespass to land and/or goods. The conduct complained of need not be criminal, nor is it necessary that criminal proceedings have been brought before recourse to the civil courts is permissible.[17] Accordingly, an injunction may be sought to restrain such conduct, whether without notice or on notice, and whether or not the criminal courts are also involved. Proceedings may be brought in the name of the authority; it is not necessary to join individual local residents as claimants.[18]

Race Relations Act 1976, s 71

By s 71: **1.2.9**

> . . . it shall be the duty of every local authority to make appropriate arrangements with a view to securing that their various functions are carried out with due regard to the need—
> (a) to eliminate unlawful racial discrimination; and
> (b) to promote equality of opportunity, and good relations, between persons of different racial groups.

This provision, too, only applies to local authorities and is a general, rather than **1.2.10** a specific duty.

Public Order Act 1986, ss 4A and 5

This Act creates, inter alia, the criminal offences of using threatening, abusive or **1.2.11** insulting words or behaviour, or disorderly behaviour; displaying any writing, sign or other visible representation which is threatening, abusive or insulting within the hearing or sight of a person likely to be caused harassment, alarm or distress thereby (s 5); and of causing another person harassment, alarm or distress, in any of the above ways, with intent to do so (s 4A, inserted by the Criminal Justice and Public Order Act 1994).

---

[15] *Stoke-on-Trent CC v B & Q (Retail) Ltd* [1984] Ch 1, CA, *per* Lawton LJ. The decision was upheld on appeal [1984] AC 754, HL.

[16] ibid. See also *Nottingham CC v Zain* [2001] EWCA Civ 1248; [2002] 1 WLR 607.

[17] *City of London Corporation v Bovis Construction Ltd* (1988) 86 LGR 660.

[18] By s 91 of the 2003 Act, it is possible to attach a power of arrest to a s 222 injunction in specified circumstances.

1.2.12 The normal prosecuting authority is the Crown Prosecution Service. Local authorities are also entitled, however, to institute criminal proceedings, and frequently do so in a range of criminal matters, such as unlawful eviction, harassment, trading standards, food safety and so on. Private prosecutions by other people are likely to be rare.

Criminal Justice and Public Order Act 1994

1.2.13 Part V of this Act introduced new police powers to remove trespassers on land[19] and to seize vehicles.[20] It also created the power to remove persons attending or preparing for raves,[21] and to prevent them from proceeding towards a rave.[22] The offence of 'aggravated trespass' was created and applies where a person does anything on land 'in the open air' intended to intimidate, obstruct or disrupt persons engaging in lawful activity on the land or adjoining land.[23] These provisions have been substantially amended by Part 7 of the 2003 Act.

Housing Act 1996, ss 152–153

1.2.14 These provisions are repealed and replaced by the 2003 Act, s 13. They are considered in full, together with the difficulties of implementing them, in Chapter 3 below. Briefly, however, s 152 confers jurisdiction upon the High Court or county court to grant an injunction, on application by a local authority, to prohibit a person from engaging or threatening to engage in conduct causing or likely to cause nuisance or annoyance to a person residing in, visiting or engaging in lawful activity in residential premises held under a secure or introductory tenancy or provided to a homeless person. An injunction may also be granted prohibiting a person from using or threatening to use such premises for illegal or immoral purposes or from entering, or being found in the locality of, such premises.[24] The injunction may relate to particular or general types of conduct, and to particular premises or a particular locality.[25]

1.2.15 The injunction may only be granted where the person had used or threatened violence against a resident, visitor or person engaging in lawful activity in the premises to which the section applies, and there is a significant risk of harm to that, or a similar, person if the injunction is not granted.[26] In order to assist enforcement, the court may attach a power of arrest to one or more of the provisions of an injunction made under this section.[27]

1.2.16 By s 153, the court may attach a power of arrest to an injunction which it intends to grant in relation to breaches or anticipated breaches of the terms of a tenancy, against a tenant or joint tenant of certain residential premises.[28] The

[19] Criminal Justice and Public Order Act 1994, s 61.
[20] ibid, s 62.
[21] ibid, ss 63–64.
[22] ibid, s 65.
[23] ibid, s 68.
[24] Housing Act 1996, s 152(1).
[25] ibid, s 152(4).
[26] ibid, s 152(3).
[27] ibid, s 152(6).
[28] ibid, s 153(1), (3).

power only applies where the applicant is a local authority, registered social landlord, housing action trust or charitable housing trust *and* is the respondent's landlord.[29]

The jurisdiction only applies to certain types of breach of the terms of the tenancy, namely, nuisance or annoyance, or using the premises for illegal or immoral purposes (whether by the tenant personally or by his allowing such conduct by a sub-tenant, lodger, other resident in or visitor to the premises).[30] As with s 152 injunctions, the court must be satisfied that violence has been used or threatened and that there is a significant risk of harm if the power of arrest is not granted.[31] **1.2.17**

Sections 154 and 155 contain ancillary provisions relating to the attachment of a power of arrest without notice, and to the arrest and remand of a person whom a constable has reasonable cause for suspecting to be in breach of the injunction or otherwise in contempt of court. In such a case, the court will need to be even more certain of the likelihood of harm if the power of arrest is not granted because of the fact that the respondent is not represented at the proceedings. **1.2.18**

The Housing Act 1996 also amended the provisions of the Housing Act 1985: **1.2.19**

(a) in relation to the taking of possession proceedings against tenants on the grounds of nuisance;
(b) by inserting new provisions relating to the service of notice of intention to seek possession (abolishing the 28 day period before proceedings may be commenced); and
(c) by creating a new ground for possession relating to domestic violence.[32]

Finally, the 1996 Act introduced 'introductory tenancies', ie probationary local authority tenancies lasting for a year before security of tenure is obtained.[33] **1.2.20**

The regime for possession proceedings taken in respect of anti-social behaviour has been substantially amended by Part 2 of the 2003 Act, and is discussed in more detail in Chapter 3, below. **1.2.21**

Noise Act 1996

This, largely ignored, legislation created a duty to secure that an officer of the authority took reasonable steps to investigate complaints, made by a person in a dwelling at night, that excessive noise was being emitted from another dwelling.[34] The duty was dependent, however, on the authority deciding to take it up, and so most authorities decided not to do so, due to the expense of providing officers on call 24 hours a day. **1.2.22**

[29] ibid, s 153(2).
[30] ibid, s 153(5).
[31] ibid, s 153(6).
[32] ibid, ss 144–149.
[33] ibid, Pt V, Ch 1.
[34] Noise Act 1996, s 2(1)–(2).

Protection from Harassment Act 1997

1.2.23 By s 1 of this Act, a person must not pursue a course of conduct which amounts to harassment of another and which he knows or ought to know amounts to harassment of that other person. Whether or not the person ought to know is considered objectively, the only valid excuses being that the person was pursuing the course of conduct in order to prevent or detect a crime, doing so in order to comply with the law, or that because of the specific circumstances of the case, the course of conduct was rendered reasonable. To harass another person contrary to s 1 is both a criminal offence and actionable by way of civil proceedings for an injunction and damages.[35] Causing 'harassment' includes causing alarm or distress.[36]

Crime and Disorder Act 1998

1.2.24 Sections 1–4 of this Act created two new types of order which may be made by the magistrates' court: the anti-social behaviour order and the sex offender order. Notwithstanding that they are made by the magistrates' court, they are civil orders and the making of them does not amount to a conviction. Breach of an order is, however, a criminal offence.[37] The provisions were substantially amended by the Police Reform Act 2002,[38] and are further amended by Part 9 of the 2003 Act.

1.2.25 Anti-social behaviour orders may be made where a person had engaged in anti-social behaviour, ie behaviour which has caused, or is likely to cause, harassment, alarm or distress to one or more persons not in the same household as the person against whom the order is sought. The minimum duration for such an order is two years. The relevant provisions of the Act came into force on 1 April 1999.[39]

1.2.26 Sex offender orders are similar to anti-social behaviour orders. The order requires the person against whom it is made to register under the Sex Offenders Act 1997. The minimum duration for such an order is five years.[40]

1.2.27 The 1998 Act also introduced the parenting order (s 8), which is designed to support parents in addressing the anti-social behaviour of children. To this end, a parenting order requires parents to undertake counselling or guidance for up to three months and/or imposes requirements encouraging them to take measures to control their children.[41] It may be made where the court makes a child safety order (see below), an anti-social behaviour or sex offender order; convicts a child or young person of a criminal offence; or convicts a person of an offence under ss 443 and 444 of the Education Act 1996. The court must also be satisfied that the making of such an order is in the interests of preventing further anti-

[35] Protection from Harassment Act 1997, ss 1–3.
[36] ibid, s 7(2).
[37] See further, Chapter 10 below.
[38] ss 61–65.
[39] Crime and Disorder Act 1998, s 1.
[40] ibid, s 2.
[41] ibid, ss 8–10.

social behaviour. Once the court is so satisfied, however, and makes an order against a parent, it is a criminal offence for that parent to fail to comply.

Child safety orders[42] relate to children under ten, and may be made on application by the social services department of a local authority. The power to make such an order exists if the child has committed an act which would have been an offence had he been above the age of criminal responsibility (ten years old); where an order would prevent anti-social behaviour; or where the child has contravened the terms of a curfew under s 14. The order places the child under the supervision of the responsible officer, and may last up to three months (or exceptionally up to 12 months). Failure to comply with an order entitles the court to discharge the order and replace it with a full care order. **1.2.28**

Further provisions relate to curfews,[43] truancy, the removal and seizure of face coverings worn by potentially violent offenders,[44] and racially and now religiously aggravated offences.[45] **1.2.29**

The Act also requires local authorities, the police and other agencies (such as health authorities and probation committees) to work together to implement strategies to reduce crime and disorder. Strategies will normally last for three years.[46] **1.2.30**

Many of these provisions are amended by the 2003 Act, Parts 2, 3, 4 and 9.[47] **1.2.31**

1.3. CONCLUSIONS

In the excitement of examining a new Act, it is frequently possible to ignore—or forget about—remedies that are already available and to concentrate exclusively on the novel powers that have been created. This is perhaps less of a danger in relation to the 2003 Act, as so many of its provisions amend pre-existing legislation rather than start from scratch. The existence of so many alternatives to action under the new Act perhaps underlines the difficulty—by reminding us of the previous attempts that successive governments have made—of finding a legislative solution to anti-social behaviour. **1.3.1**

Be that as it may, careful attention should be paid not only to the new provisions of the 2003 Act but also to the pre-existing statutory provisions that may well still provide a suitable remedy to a specific problem. **1.3.2**

[42] ibid, ss 11–13. [43] ibid, ss 14–15. [44] ibid, ss 25–27.

[45] ibid, ss 28–32 and 82. See the Anti-Terrorism, Crime and Security Act 2001.

[46] ibid, ss 5–7, 17.

[47] This is not an exhaustive list of alternative remedies: see also eg Environmental Protection Act 1990, Pt III; Noise and Statutory Nuisance Act 1993 etc.

2

AN OVERVIEW OF THE ANTI-SOCIAL BEHAVIOUR ACT 2003

2.1. INTRODUCTION

As stated in the previous chapter, there is little conceptual unity to be found in the Anti-Social Behaviour Act 2003. It is a wide-ranging measure making, with some exceptions, disparate amendments to pre-existing legislation in nine broad areas of law. Even within each area, much of the provision is piecemeal and technical. **2.1.1**

Accordingly, there are very few broad themes which can be drawn together in this chapter, and those that do exist are likely to be so broad as to be of little use in analysing the provisions. Having said this, two themes can be discerned running through many of the provisions of the Act. The first is the continuing trend towards the application of civil remedies to control breaches of the criminal law, primarily due to difficulties of proof which lie at the heart of the criminal justice system. By this route, it may be said that certain aspects of the criminal law are becoming 'civilized' even if the criminals themselves are not. **2.1.2**

Part 1 of the Act creates a civil remedy of closure notices and orders in respect of premises used for the production, supply or use of class A drugs associated with nuisance or disorder; Part 2 enhances the anti-social behaviour injunctions and powers of arrest available in the county courts, where such conduct has some effect on a social landlord's housing management functions; Part 3 creates parenting contracts and extends the availability of parenting orders to restrain truancy, criminal conduct and anti-social behaviour; Parts 4 and 7 extend police powers to remove people from, and prevent people attending, certain public places; Part 6 creates new powers for local authorities to require the owners of buildings and land to remove graffiti at their own expense; fixed penalty notices, **2.1.3** which permit a person to escape prosecution for an offence in return for payment of a financial penalty, are introduced in Parts 3, 6 and 9 in respect of Education Act, fly-posting, criminal damage and public order offences. Part 9 also extends the availability of anti-social behaviour orders and so on.

2.1.4 The second theme relates to controlling the behaviour of young people. Again, the provisions of Part 3 relating to parental responsibilities, of Part 4 creating the power to take home people under 16 in a public place after 9 pm, the increase in the minimum age for possession of certain airguns (Part 5), and sale of aerosol paints (Part 6), and extension of the anti-social behaviour order, curfew and supervision order and fixed penalty regimes all relate to the Act's broad focus on the behaviour of the young, and in a sense seek to intercept young people before they can misbehave.

2.1.5 These two themes can be discerned throughout the Act's rigid structure of nine substantive Parts, each of which provides new measures relating to a specific area of conduct which, it is considered, requires legislative intervention.

2.2. THE PROVISIONS OF THE ACT

2.2.1 The provisions of the Act are arranged as follows.

Part 1: Premises where drugs used unlawfully

2.2.2 Sections 1–11 create powers for the police to issue a closure notice, and then apply to the magistrates' court for a closure order, for the purpose of closing down premises that are being used for the supply, use or production of Class A drugs, where there is associated nuisance or disorder. The closure notice prohibits anyone other than a person who owns or lives in the premises from entering them. The closure order prohibits anyone entering them. Breach of either is a criminal offence.

Part 2 and Sch 1: Housing

2.2.3 This Part requires social landlords to formulate and publish their policies on anti-social behaviour (s 12); repeals the principal anti-social behaviour injunction-seeking powers of local authorities and other social landlords, in ss 152 and 153 of the Housing Act 1996, and replaces them with broader powers (s 13); introduces the concept of the 'demoted tenancy', under which social landlords may apply to the court to remove a tenant's security of tenure for a year on the ground of anti-social behaviour, rendering it much easier to evict them (ss 14–15); and 'structures' the decision-making of judges in deciding whether it would be reasonable to impose a possession order on the ground of anti-social behaviour, requiring them to have particular regard to the effect of the behaviour on others (s 16).

Part 3: Parental responsibilities

Sections 19 and 25 create the concept of the parenting contract, a voluntary document under which parents promise to comply with the requirements of the local education authority or the youth offending team with regard to their child's truancy or exclusion from school, or criminal conduct or anti-social behaviour. Sections 18, 20–22 and 26–28 extend and modify the provision for the making of parenting orders, and s 23 creates a new power to give fixed penalty notices to parents where their children truant from school. **2.2.4**

Part 4: Dispersal of groups

This Part creates new powers enabling the police to disperse groups of two or more people, where anti-social behaviour is a persistent problem in the locality, and to return children under 16 to their homes if they are out and not under the control of an adult between the hours of 9 pm and 6 am (s 30). It also extends the powers of community support officers and accredited persons to enable them to carry out these functions. **2.2.5**

Part 5: Firearms

Sections 37–39 prohibit the carrying of imitation firearms and certain air weapons in public places, and increase the lower age limit for air weapons generally from 14 to 17 (s 38). These should be read in conjunction with the provisions of the Criminal Justice Act 2003, which creates a system of minimum prison sentences (of five years) for carrying prohibited firearms,[1] including the air weapons referred to in s 39. **2.2.6**

Part 6: The environment

This Part creates a number of new powers. It makes general provision for local authorities to deal with noisy premises, amending the Noise Act 1996 as regards remedies for noise at night (s 42) and introduces a new power for the police to issue a closure order in relation to noisy premises (which are causing a public nuisance) (ss 40–41). **2.2.7**

It also creates new powers for local authorities to deal with fly-posting and graffiti (including the power to give fixed penalty notices—ss 43–47), to serve a notice upon the owner of a 'relevant surface' requiring the removal of graffiti from that surface at the owner's own expense (ss 48–52). The maximum fine for displaying advertisements in contravention of planning regulations is increased (s 53), the sale of aerosol paint to the under 16s is rendered a criminal offence **2.2.8**

[1] Firearms Act 1968, s 5.

(s 54), and new powers are created to enable local authorities to deal with litter and fly-tipping (ss 55–56).

Part 7: Public order and trespass

2.2.9 This group of sections extends the powers of the police to deal with public assemblies by redefining them as groups of two or more persons, where formerly the powers only applied to groups of 20 or more persons, and increases the conditions which may be imposed on such assemblies (s 57).

2.2.10 The powers available to deal with raves and aggravated trespass are also expanded, and their application extended from land in the open air to all land. Enhanced powers are provided to direct trespassers to leave the land and prohibit their return, including the seizure of the trespassers' property (ss 58–64).

Part 8: High hedges

2.2.11 Sections 65–84 create a new regime of control over high hedges, whereby a local authority may serve a notice requiring the owner of such a hedge to reduce its height to below two metres, failure to comply with which is a criminal offence and entitles the authority to carry out the works in default at the owner's expense.

Part 9: Miscellaneous powers

2.2.12 This, the last of the substantive parts, makes an assortment of amendments to the legislation concerning anti-social behaviour orders, expanding the authorities who can apply for them and enabling local authorities to prosecute breaches of them (ss 85–86); introduces fixed penalty notices for disorderly behaviour by 16–17 year olds (and the possibility of such notices for ten–15 year olds) (s 87); extends the powers of the criminal courts to impose curfew and supervision orders on young offenders (s 88); increases the powers of police civilians (community support officers and accredited persons) to give fixed penalty notices (s 89); confers a new power on criminal courts to ask local authorities to provide a report at bail hearings as to the availability of local authority accommodation (s 90); and creates a new power for the court to attach a power of arrest to a local authority injunction it is making under s 222 of the Local Government Act 1972, where the injunction is to restrain the use or threat of violence or there is a significant risk of harm (s 91).

Part 10: General

2.2.13 Sections 92–97 make provision for commencement and repeals etc.

Schedules 1–3

Schedule 1, in conjunction with ss 14–15, sets out the details of the demoted tenancy regime; Sch 2, in conjunction with s 88, extends the powers of the court with respect to curfew orders and supervision orders; Sch 3 deals with repeals. 2.2.14

3

PART 1 OF THE ACT: PREMISES WHERE DRUGS ARE USED UNLAWFULLY

3.1. INTRODUCTION

Part 1 of the Act makes new provision in relation to premises where Class A drugs[1] are produced, supplied or used unlawfully, and where the use of the premises is associated with disorder or serious nuisance to members of the public. **3.1.1**

In the White Paper *Respect and Responsibility, Taking a Stand Against Anti-Social Behaviour*,[2] the new measures are said to be aimed specifically at 'crack houses'. A crack house is a property used for the purpose of making and/or smoking crack cocaine. Because the equipment needed to produce crack is relatively basic, the operation is extremely mobile. The people who run the crack house are often unwanted guests of the legitimate occupier of premises, remaining there by threats or actual incidences of violence.[3] **3.1.2**

The White Paper states that, for some time, local authorities and the police have been 'frustrated by their lack of powers to close down' such premises.[4] **3.1.3**

> We have to close down these properties from which drug dealers operate, or new dealers will simply move in. These dealers are sophisticated and devious in their methods. They can prey on vulnerable people compelling them to give over their property whilst they deal and use drugs, and intimidate both the residents and neighbours, sometimes making them too frightened to speak out for fear of retribution.[5]

---

[1] Misuse of Drugs Act 1971, Sch 2. [2] Cm 5778, 2003, paras 3.12–3.14.
[3] House of Commons Research Paper 03/34, 4 April 2003, p 37.
[4] White Paper, para 3.12. [5] ibid, para 3.13.

3.1.4 The White Paper proposed that the police should be entitled to issue 'a notice of impending closure, ratified by a court, which will enable the property to be closed within 48 hours and sealed for a fixed period of up to six months. Drug dealers will be dealt with through the courts and the property will be recovered by the landlord.'[6]

3.1.5 Guidance issued by the Home Office[7] indicates the Government's intention that the new powers contained in Part I of the Act should be considered in their 'wider context'.[8] The police action contemplated by the Act is 'designed to "complete the loop" in action against serious criminality and drug supply'.[9] The Guidance suggests that a management protocol with the relevant local authority may be helpful but urges, even in the context of such an approach, that measures aimed at crack houses should be part of a wider initiative to combat the socio-economic conditions which led to them springing up in the first place in that location. This requires partnership working.[10]

3.1.6 The Guidance also advises that action should be co-ordinated against a number of premises and refers to another Home Office publication, *Disrupting Crack Markets*,[11] suggesting a 'systematic campaign' involving 'high visibility policing, designing out crime through neighbourhood renewal and environmental management and the use of intelligence to challenge the security of dealers'.[12]

3.1.7 Once premises have been closed, and dealers arrested, services for addicts with reduced access to drugs must be made available quickly if other dealers are to be prevented from moving into the area. This is not simply a question of treatment in a medical sense, but also requires involvement by housing and employment providers, counsellors and support workers. The assistance offered to displaced occupiers (not themselves dealers) is also critical if they are not to be preyed on again by dealers. Local authorities may be unwilling to house (or rehouse) people who have been involved in nuisance behaviour of this sort and/or with debts, but the support they are offered at this stage is crucial.[13] It is strongly recommended that a sub-group of the Drug Action Team or Crime Partnership work with the police to plan the strategic use of a wide range of powers including these new powers, but also those under the Misuse of Drugs Act 1971, relating to the prevention of illegally obtained utility supplies, housing management powers and policies, and drug treatment and support.

---

[6] White Paper, para 3.14.

[7] 'Anti Social Behaviour Act 2003, Closure of Premises used in connection with the production, supply or use of Class A drugs and associated with the occurrence of disorder or serious nuisance, Notes of Guidance, Premises where drugs used illegally', Home Office, January 2004.

[8] Guidance, para 12. [9] ibid, para 12.1. [10] ibid, para 12.2.

[11] HO, 2003. Reference is also made to 'Tackling Drugs in rented housing, a good practice guide' (HO/DTLR, 2002).

[12] Guidance, para 12.3. [13] ibid, paras 12.4–12.6.

3.2. LEGISLATIVE CONTEXT

The Misuse of Drugs Act 1971 (the '1971 Act') already provides a range of criminal offences in relation to the production, supply and possession of controlled drugs.[14] Section 8, moreover, creates an offence committed by occupiers, or persons concerned in the management, of premises who knowingly permit or suffer any of the activities listed in the section to take place there. **3.2.1**

Those activities are: **3.2.2**

(a) producing or attempting to produce a controlled drug, contrary to s 4(1);
(b) supplying or attempting to supply, or offering to supply, a controlled drug contrary to s 4(1);
(c) preparing opium for smoking; and
(d) smoking cannabis, cannabis resin or prepared opium.[15]

A person is the 'occupier' of premises if s/he is entitled to the exclusive possession of them, in that s/he possesses a degree of control over them enabling her/him to exclude from the premises those who might otherwise intend to carry on one of the activities forbidden by s 8.[16] An occupier can be guilty of an offence where s/he is aware that some other person is cultivating cannabis on the premises.[17] **3.2.3**

The alternative description of a person who may commit this offence, ie a person 'concerned in the management' of premises, includes a person who has no legal interest in the premises and who is not an occupier, but who is concerned in exercising control over the premises or in organizing them. This may even apply to a person who is on the premises unlawfully.[18] **3.2.4**

As originally enacted, permitting the use of a controlled drug on premises is only an offence under s 8, however, in respect of cannabis and opium. This reflects the mischief prevalent at the time the 1971 Act was enacted, and which the Act was aiming to prevent, namely the operation of opium dens. The rationale behind the distinction was that the smoking of opium or cannabis was considered to be readily detectable by owners and occupiers who could be certain that the use of such drugs was illegal, whereas other drugs consumed on the premises might be prescribed and thereby legitimate.[19] **3.2.5**

Accordingly, no criminal offence is currently committed by occupiers or managers of premises used as a crack house, although a prosecution could be brought for permitting the production or supply of any drugs including crack on their premises. The Criminal Justice and Police Act 2001 will extend the 'use' offence to cover all controlled drugs but has yet to be brought into force.[20] **3.2.6**

---

[14] 1971 Act, ss 3–7.
[15] ibid, s 8(a)–(d).
[16] *R v Tao* [1977] QB 141, CA; *Read v DPP* [1997] 10 CL 120, DC.
[17] *Taylor v Chief Constable of Kent* [1981] 1 WLR 606.
[18] *R v Josephs* (1977) 65 Cr App R 253, CA.
[19] House of Commons Research Paper 03/34, n 3 above, p 38.
[20] s 38.

3.3. THE PROVISIONS OF PART 1 OF THE ACT[21]

Introduction

3.3.1 What the 1971 Act does not provide, however, is a power to close down premises being used for the production, supply or use of controlled drugs. It is this perceived lacuna that Part 1 of the 2003 Act is designed to address. To this end, as stated above, it creates new powers for the police and courts to close down premises being used in connection with the production, supply or use of any Class A controlled drug, in circumstances where there is associated disorder or serious nuisance.

3.3.2 Part 1 prescribes a two-stage procedure for the closure of premises. The first stage is the issue and service of a 'closure notice' by the police, which prohibits 'access' to the premises in question by anyone who does not either own them or habitually reside there. The second stage is the making of a 'closure order' by the magistrates' court no more than 48 hours after the closure notice has been served. Provision is then made for enforcement and related matters.

What drugs?

3.3.3 By s 11(1) of the 2003 Act, references to a controlled drug and to the production or supply of such a drug (however expressed) must be construed in accordance with the 1971 Act. Section 11(2) provides that a Class A controlled drug is a drug that is a Class A drug within the meaning of Sch 2 to the 1971 Act. This includes heroin, cocaine, crack-cocaine, methadone, LSD, ecstasy, mescaline and opium. It does not include cannabis, amphetamine, or drugs such as diazepam and temazepam.

3.3.4 'Producing' is defined by s 37 of the 1971 Act as producing by manufacture, cultivation or other means while 'supply' has been held to mean to 'furnish to another the drug for the purpose of enabling the other to use it for his own purposes'.[22]

Guidance

3.3.5 The Home Office has issued 'Notes of Guidance' to this Part of the Act,[23] said to be 'designed principally for' the courts and the police who have responsibility to operate the legislation.[24] The courts, however, cannot be bound by the Secretary of State's view of the Act, nor even required to have regard to it save in so far as it promotes good practice. To the extent, therefore, that the Guidance suggests the meanings which should be given to statutory terms or the manner in which the Act should be applied by the courts, it would seem to have no effect

---

[21] These provisions came into force on 20 January 2004: Anti-Social Behaviour Act 2003 (Commencement No 1 and Transitional Provisions) Order 2003, SI 2003/3300.

[22] *R v Maginnis* [1987] AC 303.

[23] See n 7 above.

[24] ibid, Introduction, para 1.

save to the extent that the court considers it relevant and/or appropriate to take account of the Secretary of State's opinion. Ordinarily, however, a witness's view of the law is inadmissible and guidance can neither absolve nor prevent the court from reaching its own conclusions as to the meaning and application of the Act.

The closure notice

Preconditions for service

There are two types of precondition to the service of a closure order, under s 1 of the 2003 Act. The first of these relates to the premises themselves; the second stipulates procedural steps which must first have been taken. **3.3.6**

Premises

Section 1(1) provides for the issue and service of a 'closure notice' in respect of premises to which the section applies. Those premises are defined in terms of the use to which the police consider they are being (or have been) put. In other words, the closure notice procedure may be used in respect of premises if a police officer not below the rank of superintendent (the 'authorizing officer') has reasonable grounds for believing that: **3.3.7**

(a) at any time during the 'relevant period' (defined as the period of three months ending with the day on which the authorizing officer decides whether to issue a closure notice)[25] the premises have been used in connection with the unlawful use, production or supply of a Class A controlled drug; and
(b) the use of the premises is associated with the occurrence of disorder or serious nuisance to members of the public.[26]

'Premises' is defined in s 11 extremely broadly. There are two limbs to the definition which applies not just to buildings, given that it is expressed to include: **3.3.8**

(a) any land or other place (whether enclosed or not);
(b) any outbuildings which are or are used as part of the premises.

Accordingly, while the White Paper indicated that crack houses were the focus of the proposed new provisions, in principle the definition of premises would seem broad enough for this Part of the 2003 Act to apply to areas of waste ground, alleyways, walkways on housing estates, public parks and recreation grounds or even parts of the highway. It remains to be seen, of course, whether the courts will be prepared to give these provisions such a wide application, bearing in mind the effect that closing such areas would have on the general public. The Guidance indicates that the difficulty of securing such premises means that the power is unlikely to be appropriate for such locations.[27] **3.3.9**

[25] 2003 Act, s 1(10). [26] ibid, s 1(1)(a) and (b). [27] Guidance, para 2.7.3.

3.3.10 In this regard, however, it is noteworthy that the court has power to make provision to permit access to other parts of a building or structure of which the closed premises form part,[28] may decide to close only part of premises to which the closure notice applied,[29] and may only make a closure order if it is necessary to close the premises in question to prevent Class A drug-related disorder or serious nuisance.

3.3.11 The Secretary of State, moreover, may make regulations specifying premises or descriptions of premises to which s 1 does not apply.[30] At the time of writing (March 2004), no such regulations have been made. It is possible, however, that the Secretary of State may wish to exclude such premises as those used as 'safe injecting areas' to facilitate the rehabilitation of drug users within a regulated environment.[31]

3.3.12 The Notes of Guidance also refer specifically to the fact that garages, factories, shops, pubs, clubs, and other public buildings including schools and hospitals are included. While conceding that it would rarely be appropriate for the power to be exercised in respect of schools or hospitals, the Guidance emphasizes the discretion of the senior officer to do so in accordance with operational priorities (subject to any exempting regulations).[32]

3.3.13 *Use of premises* The use of the premises for a Class A drug-related purpose is not sufficient to engage the provisions of s 1. There must also be or have been disorder or serious nuisance to members of the public associated with the use. The wording of the section does not permit a notice to be issued on the basis that the drug-related use was 'likely to be associated' with disorder or serious nuisance, the formula used, for example, in the Crime and Disorder Act 1998 in relation to anti-social behaviour orders.[33] Accordingly, the authorizing officer would appear to need at least some evidence constituting reasonable grounds to believe both that the premises have been used in connection with the unlawful production, supply or use of controlled Class A drugs, and also that disorder and/or serious nuisance to members of the public associated with the use of the premises has actually occurred.

3.3.14 The Notes of Guidance suggest that 'it does not need to be demonstrated that the disorder or serious nuisance is associated or resultant from the drug use, production or supply, simply that both are present'.[34] This suggestion appears, however, to be inconsistent with the statutory wording of s 1(1)(a) and (b), which requires the authorizing officer to have reasonable grounds for believing that the premises are being or have been used for the production, supply or use of Class A drugs and that '*the use of* the premises is associated' with disorder or serious nuisance etc (emphasis supplied). In other words, it is not sufficient for the

[28] 2003 Act, ss 2(5) and 7. [29] ibid, s 2(8). [30] ibid, s 1(9).

[31] See House of Commons Research Paper 03/34, n 3 above, p 39.

[32] Guidance, paras 2.7.1–2.7.2.

[33] Crime and Disorder Act 1998, s 1(1) as amended. [34] Guidance, para 2.5.1.

premises themselves to be associated with disorder or serious nuisance; their use must be so associated.

Section 1(1), however, does not expressly provide that the drugs use must be the use which is associated with disorder or serious nuisance. If, therefore, the premises also had another use and that other use was the use associated with the disorder/nuisance, it is arguable that the provisions of the section would be made out. Even in this case, however, the authors believe that reading s 1(1)(a) and (b) together, the more natural construction of the words 'that the use is associated with' is that they refer to the drug use specified by s 1(1)(a). In either event, the suggestion in the Guidance that all that must be demonstrated is drug use and disorder/serious nuisance, whether or not the two are related, would appear to be dangerously simplistic. **3.3.15**

Disorder or serious nuisance There is no definition of disorder or serious nuisance. Disorder could be construed as meaning conduct of a type that would be contrary to the public order legislation.[35] Nuisance, in the context of other anti-social behaviour legislation, means an unreasonable interference with the ordinary comfort of those living, visiting or otherwise engaging in a lawful activity in the locality of the premises, and can include annoyance.[36] The concept of serious nuisance is a little nebulous but plainly raises the level of nuisance required above that of a mild disturbance (and this formulation may also be intended to spell out that mere annoyance will not suffice). The Guidance also suggests that the tortious concepts of public nuisance and what it describes as 'common nuisance' will be similar to those of disorder and/or serious nuisance. Statutory nuisances should also be considered potentially relevant.[37] **3.3.16**

The Guidance goes on to list certain examples of problems that are stated to be capable of constituting disorder or serious nuisance. It is also suggested that these examples 'should act as a guideline as to the level of nuisance to be considered serious in this context',[38] though, as noted above,[39] the court will not be bound by these examples and need not even consider them. The examples given are as follows:[40] **3.3.17**

- Intimidating and threatening behaviour towards residents
- A significant increase in crime in the immediate area surrounding the accommodation
- The presence or discharge of a firearm in or adjacent to the premises
- Significant problems with prostitution
- Sexual acts being committed in public
- Consistent need to collect and dispose of drugs paraphernalia and other dangerous items

[35] This may import the concept of an effect—or a likely effect—on a third party by means of the harassment, alarm or distress formulation used in that legislation. See, in particular, the Public Order Act 1986 and the Criminal Justice and Public Order Act 1994, both of which statutes are amended by this Act (see Chapter 9 below).

[36] See eg Housing Act 1996.

[37] Guidance, para 2.5.5.

[38] ibid, para 2.5.2.

[39] See para 3.3.5 above.

[40] Guidance, para 2.5.2.

- Violent offences and crime being committed on or in the vicinity of the premises
- Number counts of volume of people entering and leaving the premises over a 24 hour period and the resultant disruption they cause to residents
- Noise—constant/intrusive noise—excessive noise at all hours associated with visitors to the property

3.3.18 It is also unclear whether the words 'to members of the public' are intended to apply to 'serious nuisance' alone or also to disorder (ie does disorder, like serious nuisance, have to have been suffered by members of the public or is it sufficient if it occurred but did not affect anyone). In principle, a disjunctive construction would seem preferable. Unlike the concept of nuisance, which only has meaning in the sense of conduct which has had some detrimental effect on another person, disorder is a description of a type of behaviour; it is difficult to talk about disorder occurring *to* somebody.

3.3.19 Although s 1(1) refers to members of the public, it is unlikely that it will be necessary to show that more than one member of the public has suffered serious nuisance.[41] The Guidance refers to the evidence of residents and neighbours being given by professional witnesses in cases where the witnesses themselves fear recrimination.[42]

3.3.20 In practical terms, it is probable that, bearing in mind the purpose and aims of the Act, both terms will be given a broad common-sense meaning; whether or not a nuisance was serious would seem to be a question of fact and degree for the authorizing officer (and later the magistrates) with which the higher courts would only interfere on public law grounds.

3.3.21 *Timing* It is not necessary for the authorizing officer to have reason to believe that the premises are used for any of the prescribed purposes at the date of issue of the notice, only that s/he has reason to believe that they were being so used at any time during the three months preceding the decision whether or not to authorize the issue of the notice. It is not entirely clear whether much time will elapse between the decision to authorize the issue of a notice and its issue; nor indeed between issue and service, although there is no statutory time-limit for the service of a notice that has been issued (see further para 3.3.53 below).

3.3.22 It is nonetheless possible, in principle, that a notice may be served in relation to premises that have not been used in connection with Class A drugs for some considerable time. If that were to occur, the magistrates would then have to decide whether a closure order was appropriate. Given the test for the making of such an order—which includes a requirement that the court is satisfied that it is necessary to make an order to prevent the occurrence of disorder or serious nuisance related to the use of the premises (see below)—it would seem that, in

[41] By Interpretation Act 1978, s 6(c), the plural includes the singular and vice versa unless a contrary intention can be shown.

[42] Guidance, paras 2.5.3–2.5.4, 4.1.4.

principle at least, it may prove difficult to obtain an order unless there is at least some current evidence of drug-related use associated with disorder or serious nuisance.

Section 1(8) confirms that it is 'immaterial' to the exercise of the s 1 powers whether any person has been convicted of an offence relating to the use, production or supply of a controlled drug. **3.3.23**

Procedural requirements

By s 1(2) of the Act, the authorizing officer may authorize the issue of a closure notice if s/he is satisfied that: **3.3.24**

(a) the local authority for the area in which the premises are situated has been consulted; and
(b) reasonable steps have been taken to establish the identity of those living on the premises or who has control of, or responsibility for, or an interest in the premises.

Consultation Section 11(6) defines 'local authority', in England, as a district or London borough council, or a county council for an area for which there is no district council. The Common Council of the City of London in its capacity as a local authority and the Council of the Isles of Scilly are also included. In Wales, 'local authority' means a county council or a county borough council.[43] **3.3.25**

The Guidance fleshes out to some extent the requirements of consultation, by suggesting that, in addition to consulting the statutorily defined local authority, the police ought also to consult—where different—the relevant local social services authority. If the premises are owned or managed by a registered social landlord (RSL), consultation with them may also be appropriate.[44] The consultation should be addressed to the local authority/RSL's Chief Executive or Director of Housing.[45] In some cases, it may be appropriate to consult other bodies/individuals, such as local drug treatment services, private landlords and childcare teams. It is also important to contact social services departments.[46] The Guidance suggests that this is an operational issue, however, to be resolved as a matter of the authorizing officer's judgment.[47] **3.3.26**

The purpose of consultation, as emphasized by the Guidance, is to inform the consultees of police intentions and seek their views. They should be consulted as early as practicable. Consultees do not have a right of veto over action under this Part, although proper consideration must be given to their views.[48] **3.3.27**

In fact, the Guidance recommends that the police consider working together with local housing authorities/RSLs in an informal way, in addition to the **3.3.28**

[43] 2003 Act, s 11(7).
[44] Guidance, paras 2.6.1–2.6.3.
[45] ibid.
[46] ibid, para 2.6.4.
[47] ibid, paras 2.6.3, 2.6.6.
[48] ibid, paras 2.6.1–2.6.2. See also eg *R v Brent LBC, ex p Gunning* (1985) 84 LGR 168; *R v Secretary of State for Social Security, ex p Association of Metropolitan Authorities* (1993) 25 HLR 131.

formal consultation process. In this way, they can be alerted to the proposal to issue and serve a notice and their support may be gained. Information can also be exchanged, including the obtaining from them of evidence relating to the issue of disorder/serious nuisance, such as complaints from residents and information about the collection of drug paraphernalia.[49] Housing departments can also be alerted to the demands that may well be made of them if a closure order is granted (such as any specialist contractors that may be available to them to seal premises; the need to rehouse occupiers rendered homeless; social services and childcare requirements; and so on).[50]

3.3.29 Above all, the Guidance emphasizes that the use of this new power should be seen in the context of the existing powers available to the police and, more importantly, of the partnerships that already exist to provide an overall strategy for combating anti-social behaviour, drug abuse and crime generally, such as the local Drug Action Teams, Crime Reduction Partnerships and Local Strategic Partnerships.[51]

3.3.30 *Identifying residents, or others with an interest* Section 1(2)(b) does not require all (or any) such people actually to have been identified in order for the issue of a notice to be authorized; merely that the authorizing officer must be satisfied that 'reasonable steps' have been taken. What amounts to reasonable steps will depend on the circumstances, but it is plainly not a very high test.[52]

Authorizing the issue of a notice

3.3.31 The two sets of preconditions discussed above are intended to be applied in tandem. The police will identify potential premises used for drug-related purposes and associated with disorder or serious nuisance, and will then consult, or work together with, the relevant local authority and attempt to establish all those people who may live there or have some interest in, control of or responsibility for the premises (which it seems need not be pursuant to any legal right or obligation).

3.3.32 All of this must take place before the authorizing officer considers whether to authorize the issue of a notice, as that consideration has to include the issues of whether the premises have been used for a relevant purpose within the previous three months; whether disorder or serious nuisance is associated with that use of the premises; and whether the relevant procedural requirements have been complied with.

---

[49] There may be Data Protection Act 1998 implications in relation to this advice, and the exchange of information generally. On the other hand, the 1998 Act permits personal information to be disclosed for the purpose of law enforcement amongst other things. In addition, the local authority holding the information would be likely to seek the consent of the person who, for example, made a complaint about the premises in question before disclosing the information to the police. The provisions of s 115 of the Crime and Disorder Act 1998, permitting the sharing of information for the purposes of seeking an anti-social behaviour order, for example, do not apply.

[50] Guidance, para 2.6.5. [51] ibid, para 2.6.7. [52] ibid, para 3.2.2.

An authorization to issue a closure notice may be given orally or in writing, although if it is given orally the authorizing officer must confirm it in writing as soon as is practicable.[53] 3.3.33

The Act, unsurprisingly, does not specify how the decision to authorize the issue of a notice is to be made. The Guidance, however, goes into some detail on this topic, suggesting that the following specific factors should be taken into account: 3.3.34

- Whether the proposed actions will have the intended impact on the problem at hand
- The suitability of the powers, with all their implications
- The evidence about the level of disorder and nuisance and anti-social behaviour associated with the premises
- How this action is to be followed up ensuring the premises do not become re-occupied for similar purposes and how the closure can be followed up as part of a neighbourhood policing plan
- The views of the relevant local authority
- Any other powers that may be more suitable or achieve the same result without the need for the implications the closure power contains; or which can be used alongside the power to support the overall aim of reduction of nuisance.[54]

The Guidance also suggests that the police do not need forensic proof that the drugs used, produced or supplied are Class A drugs; there need only be a 'reasonable suspicion' to that effect.[55] This is not the test set out in s 1(1), however, which refers to the need for 'reasonable grounds to believe'. While it is important not to become overly semantic on the point, the statutory test is the one with which the police must comply (and which the courts would apply on appeal or judicial review). It is strongly arguable in law that 'reasonable grounds to believe' demands a higher standard of certainty than does 'reasonable suspicion', demanding that the authorizing officer hold a belief and that that belief is held on grounds that are themselves reasonable. 3.3.35

The Guidance also emphasizes that the existence of alternative powers and solutions to the problem should be considered as a matter of good practice when the authorizing officer is deciding whether or not to authorize the issue of a notice,[56] particularly where vulnerable people are involved. It is not necessary, however, to have attempted to resolve the problem using other powers before resort is had to the powers under this Part. The court, in deciding whether a closure order is 'necessary',[57] may, however, wish to know what other measures have been used and/or why such other measures were considered to be inappropriate or likely to be ineffective.[58] 3.3.36

[53] 2003 Act, s 1(3). [54] Guidance, para 4.1.3. [55] ibid, para 4.1.2.
[56] ibid, para 4.2. A list of alternative powers is given at Annex E to the Guidance.
[57] 2003 Act, s 2(3)(c). [58] Guidance, para 6.1.2.

Contents of the closure notice

3.3.37 Section 1(4) prescribes the contents of the closure notice. The notice must:

(a) give notice that an application will be made under s 2 for the closure of the premises (ie for a closure order from the magistrates' court);
(b) state that access to the premises by anyone other than a person who habitually resides in, or the owner of, the premises is prohibited;
(c) specify the date, time and place of the hearing at which the application to close the premises will be heard;
(d) explain the effects of a closure order under s 2;
(e) state that failure to comply with the notice is an offence; and
(f) give information about 'relevant advice providers'. This is defined as[59] information about the names and means of contacting persons and organizations in the area providing advice about housing and legal matters.

Information

3.3.38 The requirement to give information in the notice about the place, date and time of the application for a closure order (s 1(4)(c)) seems inconvenient, on its face, in that the application for a closure order is not made (s 2(1)) unless and until a closure notice has been issued. It would therefore seem that there will need to be a decision when the application to court will be made before the closure notice is issued. This may require some informal liaison between the police and the local magistrates' court. On this point, the Guidance confirms that court staff and police need to agree the date, time and place for the hearing before a notice has been served,[60] given that the notice as served must include the date, place and time for the hearing. The best course may be for the hearing to be fixed once the court is informed that the notice has been *issued*, and prior to service. In that way, a date can be arranged permitting service to take place within the statutory time-frame (see below).

Habitual residence

3.3.39 Section 1(4)(b) requires the notice to state that access to the premises is prohibited other than by a person who habitually resides in, or owns, the premises. Habitual residence is not the term used in s 1(2)(b) to describe the reasonable steps that the police must have taken prior to the decision to issue a notice, to discover who 'lives on' the premises (or controls, is responsible for or has an interest in them).

3.3.40 The term 'habitual residence' is a well-known concept, particularly in welfare legislation, meaning not merely residence, but 'habitual' residence, ie residence for an appreciable period of time that is likely to continue. The court will con-

[59] Guidance, para 6.1.2, s 1(11).

[60] Guidance, para 6.1.3.

sider not merely whether the person is voluntarily resident with an intention to remain permanently, but all the facts relevant to the particular case including whether the person has a right to reside there, has her/his possessions and/or family there, or has lasting ties with the premises or area in which it is situated. The period of time needed to turn residence into habitual residence is not fixed but is entirely dependent on the individual facts in each case.[61]

How the police are intended to know, for the purposes of enforcing the notice, whose residence is sufficiently prolonged and permanent to constitute 'habitual' residence as a matter of law, is not clear. This is a potentially very important issue, however, given that s 4(1) and (5) creates an arrestable offence of remaining on or entering premises in contravention of a notice. Individual police officers will therefore have to consider whether or not a person may be arrested if s/he asserts that s/he is habitually resident on the premises, and will be at risk of committing an unlawful arrest if they are wrong. **3.3.41**

In practical terms, then, these issues emphasize the importance of conscientious compliance with the requirement to take reasonable steps under s 1(2)(b) to identify who lives on the premises. **3.3.42**

If the Class A drug-related conduct is perpetrated solely by persons who all habitually reside in the premises, the closure notice will have no practical effect, as it does not prohibit occupiers from entering or remaining on the premises, although the closure order, if made, will close the premises to everyone, subject to limited exceptions. The notice will, however, give the occupiers a limited time to seek advice and/or find alternative accommodation prior to the court hearing. In theory, they could also stop using the premises in the manner which caused the notice to be issued and the order sought, and seek an adjournment of the court hearing in order to demonstrate that they have done so and that an order would not therefore be necessary. **3.3.43**

Service of the notice

A closure notice must be served by a constable.[62] There is no prescribed time within which service must take place following issue. Rather the Act imposes a 48 hour time-limit for the hearing of the closure order application triggered by service.[63] Accordingly, service must not take place more than 48 hours before the time which has (presumably[64]) already been fixed for the hearing. **3.3.44**

If, moreover, as seems probable, the closure procedure is engaged at the same time as application is made for search warrants in respect of the premises, the time-limits applicable to the warrants (which must usually be executed within 48 hours) will also be likely, for practical purposes, to determine the time-scale for **3.3.45**

[61] *Nessa v Chief Adjudication Officer* [1999] 1 WLR 1937, HL. See also *Swaddling v Adjudication Officer* [1999] All ER (EC) 217; *Gingi v Secretary of State for Work and Pensions* [2001] EWCA Civ 1685, [2002] 1 CMLR 20.

[62] 2003 Act, s 1(5).

[63] ibid, s 2(2).

[64] See para 3.3.38 above.

service of the notice (ie it would be logical to effect service at the time of execution of the warrants).

3.3.46 Service must be effected by the constable by *all* of the following means:

(a) fixing a copy of the notice to at least one prominent place on the premises;
(b) fixing a copy to each normal means of access to the premises;
(c) fixing a copy to any outbuildings which appear to the constable to be used with or as part of the premises;
(d) giving a copy of the notice to at least one person who appears to the constable to have control of or responsibility for the premises; and
(e) giving a copy to the persons who have been identified in accordance with the reasonable steps taken prior to the issue of the notice (s 1(2)(b)) and to any other persons appearing to the constable to fall within the same description, ie people who live on, or have control of, responsibility for or an interest in the premises.

3.3.47 A closure notice must also be served on any person who occupies any other part of the building or structure in which the premises are situated, if the constable reasonably believes, at the time of serving the notice, that that person's access to the part of the building or structure which s/he occupies will be impeded by the making of a closure order.[65]

3.3.48 It appears, then, to be the intention of the Act that the constable who effects service will simply attend the premises with a pile of notices and fix them to such parts of the premises as s/he considers to fall within the descriptions contained in s 1(6)(a)–(c), and give a copy to anyone who appears to fall within the descriptions set out at s 1(6)(d)–(e) and (7). The Guidance states that where enquiries as to the ownership of premises reveal only a letting agent, it is permissible to serve the letting agent.[66]

3.3.49 The Act does not make clear how service is to be effected on a person who is not present at the time the constable attends the premises but who has previously been identified as living there. It is not clear, for example, whether leaving a copy for each such person marked for her or his attention in a prominent place on the premises will satisfy the requirement. The Guidance suggests that service by post, though not desirable for reasons of speed, is permissible and sufficient if the owner or letting agent identified is not local.[67]

3.3.50 The Guidance gives the impression that it is not mandatory to serve every person referred to in s 1(6), stating that service can be effected by affixing the notice to the premises, although adding that 'effort should also be made to give a copy of the notice to any interested persons'.[68] It seems doubtful, however, whether this accurately reflects the terms of s 1(5)–(7) which provides that the notice 'must be served' and that 'service is effected by' the means set out in subs (6) which appear to be cumulative rather than alternative methods.

---

[65] 2003 Act, s 1(7). [66] Guidance, para 5.2.2. [67] ibid. [68] ibid.

On the other hand, a failure properly to effect service of the closure notice does not preclude the making of a closure order, nor does it appear to have any other consequences, save that not having been served may amount to a reasonable excuse for failing to comply with the notice, and thus a defence to the criminal offence that such a failure would otherwise comprise (see s 4(1) and para 3.3.54 below). A person who has an interest in the premises but who has not been served is nonetheless entitled to appeal against the making of a closure order.[69] **3.3.51**

Service starting time running

It is service under s 1(6)(a) alone, moreover, which triggers the commencement of a period of 48 hours within which the hearing of the application for the closure order must take place.[70] **3.3.52**

No provision is made for what happens to the closure notice if no application for a closure order is made, or if it is not heard within 48 hours of service (see paras 3.3.55–3.3.71 below). Presumably, however, on normal public law principles, the notice will fall after 48 hours if the application for an order has not come before the court by then. This construction is supported by the provisions of s 2(6) and (7), which confers on the court power to adjourn the hearing for up to 14 days, and states specifically that if the court exercises this power, it may order that the closure notice will remain in effect during the period of adjournment. **3.3.53**

Offences

Section 4(1) and (2)(a) creates two arrestable, summary offences[71] in relation to closure notices. The first is an offence of remaining on or entering premises in contravention of the notice (and so it will not apply to habitual residents or owners).[72] It is a defence to this offence that the person had a reasonable excuse for entering or being on the premises.[73] The second offence is of obstructing a constable acting under s 1(6)—ie serving the closure notice. There is, unsurprisingly, no defence of reasonable excuse in relation to this offence. The maximum penalties for these offences are six months' imprisonment or a fine not exceeding level 5 on the standard scale or both.[74] **3.3.54**

The closure order

Section 2(1) provides that once a closure notice has been issued, a constable must apply to the magistrates' court for the making of a closure order. No time-limit for the making of this application is given, though, as stated above, it must be heard within 48 hours of the principal method of service.[75] It is, accordingly, not necessary for the application to be made by—or in the name of—the authorizing officer. Nor is any form for the application specified; there is not even **3.3.55**

[69] 2003 Act, s 6(3)(b). [70] ibid, s 2(2). [71] ibid, s 4(3), (5). [72] ibid, s 1(4)(b). [73] ibid, s 4(4). [74] ibid, s 4(3). [75] ibid, ss 1(6)(a) and 2(2).

any requirement for it to be in writing. This informal procedure appears to be deliberate, and may be compared with the provisions of s 5(1) (extension or discharge of an order) which specifically requires that the application is to be made on complaint.

3.3.56 It would therefore appear that the constable can simply attend court and apply orally for a closure order. This is consistent with a number of features of these provisions, such as:

- the short time-scale (48 hours from service of the notice) for the hearing of the application;
- the requirement to state in the closure notice itself (ie prior to the application having been issued) the place, date and time at which the application will be heard, which clearly suggests that there will be no further process, such as a summons, prior to that hearing;
- the power of the court to adjourn the hearing of the application, on a limited basis, for up to 14 days if the application is contested.

3.3.57 The Guidance does not address this issue. It may be that different magistrates' courts will require different process from the police in their areas. The court's requirements in relation to application for a closure order are a matter which the police should discuss with the court in advance of service of the notice, ie before time for the hearing of the application starts running, and preferably before issuing the notice itself.

The test for making a closure order

3.3.58 By s 2(3), the court may make a closure order 'if and only if' it is 'satisfied' that each of the following paragraphs applies:

(a) the premises in respect of which the closure notice was issued have been used in connection with the unlawful use, production or supply of a Class A controlled drug;
(b) the use of the premises is associated with the occurrence of disorder or serious nuisance to members of the public; and
(c) the making of the order is necessary to prevent the occurrence of such disorder or serious nuisance for the period specified in the order.

3.3.59 By s 1(8), a closure order may be made in respect of all or any part of the premises in respect of which the notice was issued. It is noteworthy, however, that the matters set out in paragraphs (a) and (b) above, as to which the court must be satisfied before an order may be made, relate specifically to the premises in respect of which the closure notice was issued. The question therefore arises whether an order may be made, for example, closing part of the premises in respect of which a notice was issued, if the court is satisfied that that part, but not the whole of those premises served with the closure notice, was used for the use, production or supply of a Class A drug. This question can only be answered by the court.

On a related matter, it would appear that s 2(8) does not permit the court, where a closure notice has only been issued in relation to part of a building, to order the closure of the whole, or a greater part, of the building. The Guidance does not address either point. 3.3.60

Burden and standard of proof

Section 2 does not specify any burden or standard of proof on the basis of which the court must be satisfied as to matters that must be proved, but merely states that the court may make the order 'if and only if' it is so satisfied.[76] The requirement of satisfaction is not explained further, though s 2(9) provides that it is 'immaterial' whether any person has been convicted of an offence relating to the use, production or supply of a controlled drug. 3.3.61

It would seem unlikely that Parliament intended the court to require satisfaction to the criminal standard, given the structure and intention of Part 1 and, in particular, the speed with which this remedy is apparently intended to be invoked. The closure order is plainly intended to be a civil order rather than a criminal offence; and there seems little doubt that, as a matter of domestic law, this intention has been achieved. This is not the end of the matter, however, because a measure may be criminal in nature for the purposes of European law,[77] whatever its classification in domestic law. Europe looks to the substance of the measure and, in particular, whether it is punitive in nature, in which case it is likely to be criminal, or merely preventative.[78] 3.3.62

The primary significance of this distinction relates to whether a criminal standard of proof will be demanded and whether hearsay evidence should be admissible under the Civil Evidence Act 1995, and the Magistrates' Courts (Hearsay Evidence in Civil Proceedings) Rules 1999.[79] 3.3.63

It may be arguable that no burden or standard of proof is required by the Act at all. It is simply a question of whether or not the court is 'satisfied' as to the statutory requirements. This is the position in other classes of proceeding before the magistrates' court, such as bail cases.[80] Bearing in mind the nature and effect of the closure order, however, it is likely that the courts will require the police to prove their case, and prove it to either the civil or criminal standard. The Guidance suggests that it is the civil standard (balance of probabilities) that is applicable.[81] 3.3.64

Guidance, of course, cannot resolve this issue. It is a matter that can only be determined by the court. Even if the Guidance is correct, moreover, it does not follow that the civil standard requires only a bare balance of probabilities (ie 51 per cent). This issue has already been played out in the context of anti-social behaviour orders.[82] In that context, the House of Lords decided, in *R (McCann)* 3.3.65

---

[76] 2003 Act, s 2(3). [77] eg Human Rights Act, Sch 1, Art 6.

[78] See eg *R (McCann) v Manchester Crown Court* [2002] UKHL 39; [2003] 1 AC 787, and the European cases cited therein.

[79] SI 1999/681. [80] Bail Act 1976, s 4 and Sch I, para 2. [81] Guidance, para 6.2.2.

[82] Crime and Disorder Act 1998, s 1.

v Manchester Crown Court,[83] that while such orders were civil in nature, the civil standard of proof (balance of probabilities) was a flexible standard, requiring a higher or lower level of proof depending on the severity of the allegations made and the remedy sought. In anti-social behaviour order cases, the court would therefore require proof to a civil standard indistinguishable from the criminal standard, ie beyond reasonable doubt.[84]

3.3.66 It may be observed that Parliament might well have been surprised, when legislating for the creation of the anti-social behaviour order, to discover that the courts would, in effect, impose a criminal standard of proof on these civil remedies. The arguments, however, in relation to the remedy of the closure order are finely balanced and different from those arising under s 1 of the Crime and Disorder Act. That Act, for example, specifically stated that the allegations must be 'proved',[85] whereas s 2 of the 2003 Act simply refers to the court being satisfied. The effect of a closure order, on the other hand, evicting lawful occupiers from their homes because of their conduct, and preventing owners of property using that property, again because of past conduct on the premises, bears more of the hallmarks of a punitive remedy than could be said of the anti-social behaviour order.

3.3.67 All that can be said at this stage is that the issue is ripe for litigation, and that it is by no means clear that the courts will accept the view of the Home Secretary, as stated in the Guidance, to the effect that only a civil (balance of probabilities) standard of proof, lower than the criminal standard, is required.

Adjournment of the proceedings

3.3.68 By s 2(7), the court may adjourn the hearing for up to 14 days to allow certain categories of person, namely: (a) the occupier of the premises; (b) the person with control of or responsibility for the premises; or (c) any other person with an interest in the property, to show why an order should not be made.[86] No such adjournment may therefore be granted at the request of any other person who may have been served with the closure notice, such as a person occupying any other part of the building, whose access will be impeded by the making of the order (although the court can take account of issues of access in making an order: s 2(8)).[87]

3.3.69 Examples of situations where an adjournment may be appropriate can be easily imagined:[88] the owner may not have been aware of the use of the premises and may wish to be given time to bring them under proper control or to evict non-secure occupiers; the police evidence may be disputed and time needed to bring forward contrary evidence and witnesses etc; it may be claimed that the use of the premises for drug-related purposes has stopped and that a short adjournment would demonstrate this and so on. The court may order that the closure notice continue to have effect during the period of adjournment (s 2(7)).

[83] See n 78 above.
[84] See n 78 above.
[85] Crime and Disorder Act 1998, s 1(4).
[86] 2003 Act, s 2(6).
[87] See paras 3.3.59 and 3.3.95–3.3.99.
[88] And see Guidance, para 6.3.

The Guidance states that the Government does not intend that cases will routinely be adjourned, as this would defeat the object of the new power (ie speed), and suggests that a person seeking an adjournment will need to demonstrate reasonable grounds why it is needed.[89] While no test of 'reasonable grounds' is provided in the Act itself—and cannot be imposed upon the court by mere guidance—it would seem a matter of common sense that the court will not grant an adjournment where the person asking for it cannot demonstrate any reasonable ground for supposing that s/he requires it. **3.3.70**

The Guidance also suggests that while the options before the court are, formally, to grant, refuse or adjourn the application for a closure order, 'in practice the ability to vary the length of the order gives the court flexibility to deal with different circumstances where a shorter order may be appropriate, bring immediate relief whilst the landlord and police deal with the problem, but not leading to extended and costly closure'.[90] Thus the court could refuse an adjournment but grant a closure order for only a few weeks, enabling the owner to take the steps s/he has promised to take and leaving the police free to apply for an extension to the order[91] if those steps do not prove effective. **3.3.71**

Effect and enforcement of closure order

The closure order closes the premises completely, to owners and residents and visitors alike, for such period as the court decides, which may not exceed three months.[92] The order may make such provision as the court thinks appropriate for access to any part of the building or structure of which the premises form part, such as the stairways or common parts in a block of flats, the other rooms in a house in multiple occupation, and so on.[93] As stated above, it may be made in respect of all or any part of the premises in respect of which the closure notice was issued.[94] **3.3.72**

Where an order is made, a constable or 'authorised person' (defined as a person 'authorised by the chief officer of police for the area in which the premises are situated'[95] may enter the premises and do anything reasonably necessary to secure them against entry by any person,[96] using reasonable force if necessary.[97] These are the only persons who are permitted to enter the premises. A constable or authorized person seeking entry for this purpose must, if asked to do so by or on behalf of an owner, occupier or person in charge of the premises, produce evidence of her/his identity and authority before entering the premises.[98] **3.3.73**

Entry may also be effected at any time while the order is in force for the purpose of carrying out essential maintenance or repairs to the premises.[99] **3.3.74**

The Guidance suggests that entering the premises to enforce the order should be undertaken with extreme caution, as occupants may be armed and resistant **3.3.75**

[89] ibid, para 6.3.2.
[90] ibid, para 6.2.4.
[91] 2003 Act, s 5(1).
[92] ibid, ss 2(4) and 3(2).
[93] ibid, s 2(5).
[94] ibid, s 2(8).
[95] ibid, s 3(6).
[96] ibid, s 3(2).
[97] ibid, s 3(3).
[98] ibid, s 3(4).
[99] ibid, s 3(5).

to leaving. Accordingly a risk assessment must be undertaken and substantial operational—including armed—support may be needed. The premises should also be searched thoroughly for hidden drugs or money. Authorized persons should not be permitted to enter the premises until safety issues have been addressed and the property has been cleared.[100]

Offences

3.3.76 Section 4(2)(b) and (c) creates summary, arrestable offences[101] of remaining on or entering premises subject to a closure order, although it is a defence if a person has a reasonable excuse for entering or being on the premises.[102] A further summary, arrestable offence[103] is created (s 4(2)(a)) of obstructing a constable or authorized person entering, or securing against entry, premises in respect of which an order has been made. There is, unsurprisingly, no defence of reasonable excuse to this offence.

3.3.77 The maximum penalty on summary conviction of any of the above offences is a fine not exceeding level 5 on the standard scale (currently £5,000) and/or a term of imprisonment of up to six months.[104]

Extension and discharge of closure order

3.3.78 At any time before the end of the period for which a closure order is made, or previously extended, a constable may apply, by way of a complaint, to an 'appropriate'[105] justice of the peace for an extension or further extension of the period for which the order has effect.[106] It is noteworthy that the application for an extension must be made by complaint, whereas no such procedure is specified for the application for the original closure order.[107]

3.3.79 Be that as it may, an application—although it may be made by a constable—must be authorized by a police officer of not below the rank of superintendent who:

(a) has reasonable grounds for believing that it is necessary to extend the period for which the closure order has effect for the purpose of preventing the occurrence of disorder or serious nuisance to members of the public, and
(b) is satisfied that the local authority has been consulted about the intention to make the complaint.[108]

3.3.80 If a complaint is made, the court may issue a summons requiring the persons to whom it is directed to attend the court to answer the complaint. The summons, if issued, is directed to the following classes of people:

---

100 Guidance, paras 7.2.2–7.2.3.
101 2003 Act, s 4(3) and (5).
102 ibid, s 4(4).
103 ibid, s 4(3) and (5).
104 ibid, s 4(3).
105 ie a justice of the peace acting for the petty sessions area in which the premises subject to the closure order are situated: ibid, s 5(10).
106 ibid, s 5(1).
107 See paras 3.3.55–3.3.57 above.
108 2003 Act, s 5(2).

(a) people on whom the closure notice was served under s 1(6)(d) or (e) and (7) (ie those living on or having control of, responsibility for, or an interest in the premises, and those whose access to other parts of the building may be impeded by the closure order);
(b) any other person who appears to the justice to have an interest in the closed premises but on whom the closure notice was not served.[109]

If a summons is issued for the complaint to be answered, a notice giving the date, time and place of the hearing of the complaint must be served on the persons to whom the summons is directed, and on a constable as the court considers appropriate (unless he is the complainant) and the local authority.[110] **3.3.81**

It is a feature—whether intentional or otherwise—of this mechanism (ie that the summons and notification of the hearing are only served on persons who were either served with the closure notice or who have an interest in the closed premises but were not so served) that a person who occupies part of a building, another part of which has been closed, and who therefore ought to have been served with the closure notice under s 1(7) is not included in these summons and notice provisions if service of the closure notice did not actually take place. **3.3.82**

This seems a little unfortunate, bearing in mind that service of the closure notice will potentially be a little 'hit-and-miss'; the obligation to serve is dependent on the constable effecting service reasonably believing that her/his access to the part of the building s/he occupies 'will be impeded' if a closure order is made. Parliament considered a person served under s 1(7) to have a sufficiently legitimate and important interest in the question of whether an order should be extended that s/he should be summonsed to attend the hearing. On that basis, it might be thought that a person who ought to have been served but was not should also be summonsed, especially bearing in mind that other categories of person who ought to have been, but were not, served (those with an interest in the closed premises) are included in the summons procedure. **3.3.83**

Be that as it may, if the court is satisfied that the extension is necessary to prevent the occurrence of disorder or serious nuisance, it may extend the order for a further period not exceeding three months. A closure order, however, must not have effect for more than six months (including the period for which the original order had effect).[111] Accordingly, the extension procedure may be invoked as many times as the police consider necessary, but subject to the conditions that no individual order or extension may take effect for more than three months, and that the aggregate period for which the original order and any subsequent extension(s) may have effect is six months. **3.3.84**

Discharge of closure order

Application by complaint to an 'appropriate justice'[112] may also be made for an order that the closure order be discharged.[113] Such an application may be made **3.3.85**

---

[109] ibid, s 5(3).
[110] ibid, s 5(9)(a), (c) and (d).
[111] ibid, s 5(4) and (5).
[112] See n 105 above.
[113] 2003 Act, s 5(6).

by a constable, the local authority, a person on whom the closure notice was served and any other person with an interest in the closed premises but who was not served with the notice.[114] It seems that the application may be made at any time.

3.3.86 If the discharge application is not made by a constable, the court may summon such constable as it considers appropriate to appear before the court to answer the complaint. As in the case of a summons issued on an application to extend the closure order,[115] where a summons is issued on a discharge application, a notice stating the place, date and time at which the complaint will be heard must also be served on the following people: those persons (except the complainant) on whom the closure notice was served or who have an interest in the closed premises but were not served;[116] such constable as the court thinks appropriate (unless he is the complainant); the local authority (unless it is the complainant).[117]

3.3.87 The court only has power to make an order discharging the closure order if it is satisfied that the closure order is no longer necessary to prevent the occurrence of disorder or serious nuisance to members of the public.[118]

3.3.88 The Guidance encourages the early discharge of orders where possible, on the application of the police or local authority, on the basis that properties should not remain empty longer than necessary. Assuming the owner of the property is co-operative, the Guidance suggests that once a possession order (or orders) has been obtained against the tenant(s) of the premises, or they have surrendered their tenancies, there is no reason why the building should not be brought back into use and re-let quickly. Where it is not clear that the owner/landlord will be able to prevent the same pattern of use re-establishing itself, however, the court should be more circumspect. Similarly, where the tenant or other legal occupier, or a private sector landlord—whether or not suspected of complicity in the original conduct—seeks the discharge of the order, the Guidance suggests that the court will require 'much more evidence' that measures are in place that will prevent a return to the previous use of the property and associated conduct.[119]

Appeals

3.3.89 A right to appeal to the Crown Court is provided against the making of a closure order or an order extending or discharging a closure order, or against a decision not to make any such orders.[120] An appeal must be brought within 21 days, beginning with the day on which the order or decision is made.[121]

[114] 2003 Act, s 5(6).

[115] See para 3.3.81 above.

[116] A person who falls within the service requirements under s 1(7) but was not served is not included: see paras 3.3.82–3.3.83 above.

[117] 2003 Act, s 5(9)(b), (c) and (d).

[118] ibid, s 5(8).

[119] Guidance, paras 10.4.1–10.4.4.

[120] 2003 Act, s 6(1).

[121] ibid, s 6(2).

If the appeal is against the making or extension of a closure order, it may be brought by a person on whom the closure notice was served under s 1(6)(d) or (e) or by a person who has interest in the closed premises but on whom the closure notice was not served.[122] This excludes from the right of appeal a person who is served with the closure notice under s 1(7)—ie a person who occupies another part of the building or structure in which the closed premises are situated and whose access to her/his own property will be impeded by the order. Such people, however, have a right to apply to the court under s 7.[123] 3.3.90

Conversely, if the appeal is brought against a decision not to make a closure order or not to extend it may be brought by a constable or the local authority.[124] 3.3.91

Unhelpfully, while s 6(1) states that the right of appeal applies to the making or refusal of an order under ss 2 or 5 of the Act, which includes a decision to discharge or not to discharge a closure order under s 5(8), s 6 makes no further reference to discharge and does not specify who may appeal against the discharge of, or the refusal to discharge, an order. Nor does the Guidance mention the issue. Presumably this was a mere legislative oversight, but it raises the interesting question whether the courts will construe s 6 not to apply to discharge decisions, or to enable a wider class of appellant against such decisions, that class not being limited by any provision of the section. 3.3.92

In particular, while s 6(4) excludes the right of appeal against the making or extension of an order by a person who occupies adjacent property and whose right of access is impeded by the order, it is strongly arguable that such a person should have a right of appeal in relation to discharge decisions, in relation to which s/he could (s 5(6)(c)) have been the complainant seeking discharge of the order, and would have been entitled to take part in the discharge hearing in any event (s 5(9)(b)). 3.3.93

On an appeal the Crown Court may make such order as it thinks appropriate. Grounds of appeal are not specified by s 6, and so such grounds may in principle raise issues relating to the current necessity of the order in addition to arguments that the order was wrongly made (or refused) at the time.[125] 3.3.94

Access applications

Any person who occupies or owns a part of the building or structure in which the closed premises are situated, but which is not itself closed, may apply to the court at any time while the closure order remains in force for an order under s 7 of the 2003 Act.[126] This right does not depend on the person having been served with a closure notice under s 1(7), presumably because such service is likely to be idiosyncratic, the officer effecting service only being obliged to serve those 3.3.95

[122] ibid, s 6(3). [123] See paras 3.3.95–3.3.99 below. [124] 2003 Act, s 6(4).

[125] See also Guidance, para 10.3, though it does not add a great deal to the sum of human knowledge.

[126] 2003 Act, s 7(1) and (2).

people whom he reasonably believes at the time of service will have their access to their own part of the building impeded if a closure order is made.

3.3.96 Strangely, s 7 does not explicitly state what is the purpose of such an application, giving only a clue by providing, in s 7(4), that:

> (4) On an application under this section the court may make such order as it thinks appropriate in relation to access to any part of a building or structure in which closed premises are situated.

3.3.97 It is thereby made tolerably clear that while generally excluded from a right to appeal the making, extension or refusal of a closure order, occupiers of other parts of the same building as the closed premises may seek the assistance of the court to retain or regain their rights to access their own property. The Guidance states that the intention of s 7 is to allow persons access to the common parts of buildings, such as stairwells, and to permit the variation of orders to facilitate this.[127]

3.3.98 Application is made to the magistrates' court in relation to a closure order or extension, and to the Crown Court concerning an order made on appeal.[128] It is immaterial whether any provision for access was included (s 2(5)) on the making of the closure order.[129]

3.3.99 Notice of the date, time and place of the hearing of the application must be given to a constable, the local authority, those served with the closure notice under ss 1(6)(d) and (e) and 1(7) (ie including occupiers of other parts of the same building whose rights of access are affected, at least one of whom will be the applicant), and any person who has an interest in the closed premises but who was not served with the closure notice.[130] There is no obligation, however, to notify persons who should have been served under s 1(7) but were not, even though such persons can apply for an order under s 7 themselves.

Compensation costs and damages

Reimbursement of costs

3.3.100 The court which made the closure order has power, on the application of a police authority or local authority, to make such order as it thinks appropriate for the owner of the closed premises to reimburse all or some of the expenditure incurred by the applicant authority in clearing, securing or maintaining the premises while the order has effect.[131]

3.3.101 The court may not entertain such an application, however, unless it is made within three months of the date on which the closure order ceased to have effect.[132]

3.3.102 An application made by a local authority must be served on the police authority for the area in which the premises are situated. Likewise, an application made

[127] Guidance, para 9.1.
[128] 2003 Act, s 7(2).
[129] ibid, s 7(5).
[130] ibid, s 7(3), applying s 5(6).
[131] ibid, s 8(1)–(2).
[132] ibid, s 8(3).

by a police authority must be served on the local authority. The owner of the premises must be served in all cases regardless of the applicant's identity.[133]

The Act does not make specific provision for the situation where the police authority and the local authority each incur expenditure which they wish to recoup from the owner of the premises. Presumably, each authority must make its own application and serve it on the other. The two applications should plainly be heard together, so that the court—and indeed the owner—is given the opportunity to consider in the round the total sums claimed and reach a conclusion as to the appropriate order to make on all the information. **3.3.103**

Damages

Section 9 confers a partial exemption from liability in damages for the police in carrying out their functions under Part 1 of the Act.[134] The exemption covers the liability of a constable for acts done or omitted to be done by him in performance or purported performance of his functions under Part 1. It also covers the liability of a chief officer of police for anything done or omitted to be done by a constable under his direction or control in the performance or purported performance of his functions under the Part. **3.3.104**

The exemption only extends to liability for 'relevant damages', however, which are defined as 'damages in proceedings for judicial review or for the tort of negligence or misfeasance in public duty',[135] the latter presumably being intended to refer to the tort of misfeasance in public office. It does not affect any other exemption from liability whether at common law or otherwise.[136] The definition of 'relevant damages' does not exclude liability for other torts (such as wrongful arrest, false imprisonment, malicious prosecution, assault). **3.3.105**

Nor does the exemption extend to acts or omissions shown to have been committed in bad faith, or in respect of acts which are unlawful by virtue of s 6(1) of the Human Rights Act 1998, ie which amount to an act by a public authority incompatible with a person's human rights listed in Sch 1 to that Act.[137] **3.3.106**

Compensation

A person who has suffered financial loss in consequence of the service of a closure notice or a closure order having effect may apply to the magistrates' court which considered the application for the closure order or the Crown Court if the closure order was made or extended on appeal.[138] An application under this section must be made within three months, starting on the later of: **3.3.107**

(a) the day the court decides not to make a closure order;
(b) the day the Crown Court dismisses an appeal against a decision not to make a closure order; or
(c) the day a closure order ceases to have effect.[139]

---

[133] ibid, s 8(4). [134] ibid, s 9(1) and (2). [135] ibid, s 9(5). [136] ibid, s 9(4).
[137] ibid, s 9(3). [138] ibid, s 10(1)–(2). [139] ibid, s 10(3).

3.3.108 The court may order the payment of compensation from central funds[140] where it is satisfied that:

(a) the person had no connection with the use of the premises for the production, supply or use of Class A controlled drugs;
(b) if s/he is the owner or occupier of the premises, that s/he took reasonable steps to prevent that use;
(c) s/he has suffered financial loss as referred to above; and
(d) it is appropriate in all the circumstances to order a payment of compensation in respect of that loss.[141]

[140] See 2003 Act, s 10(5) for the definition of 'central funds'.

[141] ibid, s 10(4).

4

PART 2 OF THE ACT: HOUSING

4.1. INTRODUCTION

History

Most of the measures currently available to combat anti-social behaviour originate in one form or another from action that local authorities began to take in the early 1990s, either by way of injunction or for breach of tenancy agreement, to remedy conduct that amounted to a nuisance or annoyance to neighbours and to seek to reclaim and regenerate housing estates, in particular, that were sliding into lawlessness and violence, wrecking the lives of those law-abiding people who still lived there and costing authorities a fortune in repairing damaged property and foregoing rents on the huge numbers of empty flats and houses which no one—not even homeless families—was willing to rent.[1] **4.1.1**

Prior to the enactment of the Housing Act 1996, authorities' options were somewhat limited. Possession proceedings were available against tenants for breach of the tenancy agreement or under the specific nuisance ground for possession,[2] but such proceedings could not provide a remedy where no member of the perpetrator's household was a council tenant, and they came to be seen as an imperfect remedy, to be used only as a last resort, in that they risked penalizing innocent family members, and merely moved the problem on elsewhere, possibly into the private sector where far fewer remedies were available. Moreover, **4.1.2**

---

[1] See eg s 222 of the Local Government Act 1972; the nuisance ground for possession under Ground 2 of Sch 2 to the Housing Act 1985.

[2] Housing Act 1985, Sch 2, Ground 2. In its form prior to the Housing Act 1996 amendments, the ground for possession was in terms that 'the tenant or a person residing in the dwelling-house has been guilty of conduct which is a nuisance or annoyance to neighbours or has been convicted of using the dwelling-house or allowing it to be used for immoral or illegal purposes'.

since the explosion of the right to buy, the private sector rented accommodation to which a family moved could easily be on the very estate from which they had just been evicted.

4.1.3 Alternatively, an authority could seek an injunction to prevent the continuation of the conduct under s 222 of the Local Government Act 1972, which provides that an authority may institute proceedings in its own name where it considers it expedient to do so to promote or protect the interests of the inhabitants of its area.[3] In a series of cases, the courts held that authorities were entitled to use this power to obtain injunctive relief to prevent conduct that was also criminal in nature, but where the civil remedy was more convenient.[4]

4.1.4 Registered social landlords (RSLs) enjoyed even fewer options. They had a similar right to seek possession under the Housing Act 1988,[5] but the disadvantages of possession proceedings have already been discussed. As they were not local authorities, s 222 of the 1972 Act was not available.

4.1.5 Other common law causes of action for an injunction were also available, at the instance of local authorities, RSLs and others. A person could be restrained, for example, from entering council or RSL offices, such as a neighbourhood housing office, by an injunction sought in trespass. Shopping centre owners succeeded in obtaining an injunction to keep troublemakers out of the shopping centre at night.[6] An injunction could also be granted against a tenant, on the basis of enforcing the nuisance covenants in the tenancy agreement.

4.1.6 Like possession proceedings, however, injunctions were not without disadvantages. There was no particularly effective means of protecting witnesses because no power of arrest could be attached to a s 222 or other common law injunction. The penalty for breach of the injunction, moreover, depended on the court's contempt of court jurisdiction, under which the only available penalties were committal to prison for a maximum period of two years,[7] a fine and/or sequestration of assets. Imprisonment was not available in respect of a defendant under the age of 18,[8] and neither a fine nor sequestration would be much of a deterrent for a young person with no money (indeed a financial penalty could even lead to further anti-social conduct if the defendant decided to steal something or rob someone in order to pay it). The Court of Appeal, moreover, had held that an injunction should not be imposed unless there was a realistic means of enforcing it and that the remedy was not therefore generally available against minors.[9]

---

[3] This means all the inhabitants, not merely a section of them: *Stoke-on-Trent CC v B & Q Retail Ltd* [1984] Ch 1, CA (approved by the House of Lords at [1984] AC 754).

[4] *City of London Corp v Bovis Construction Ltd* [1992] 3 All ER 697, CA; *Nottingham CC v Matthew Zain* [2001] EWCA Civ 1248, [2002] 1 WLR 607; *Stoke-on-Trent CC v B & Q Retail Ltd*, ibid.

[5] Housing Act 1988, Sch 2, Ground 14.

[6] See *CIN Properties v Rawlins* [1995] 2 EGLR 130, CA.

[7] Contempt of Court Act 1981, ss 9 and 14; see also CCR Ord 29 (now CPR Sch 2 CCR 29).

[8] Criminal Justice Act 1982, s 1.

[9] See *Wookey v Wookey* [1991] Fam 121, CA.

The Housing Act 1996, Part V, sought to assist local authorities and, to a more limited extent, other social landlords, by introducing the concept of the local authority 'introductory tenancy',[10] broadening the nuisance ground for possession[11] and streamlining the notice procedure in nuisance possession cases,[12] adding a new ground for possession based on domestic violence,[13] and introducing new injunctions, to which powers of arrest may be attached, in respect of perpetrators of conduct likely to cause a nuisance or annoyance to people residing in or visiting residential accommodation let by the local authority or engaging in a lawful activity in the locality of such accommodation.[14] **4.1.7**

The new injunctions were not available to RSLs.[15] The courts were, however, also given power to attach a power of arrest to injunctions they proposed to grant to enforce the terms of a tenancy agreement in proceedings brought by a wider class of social landlords.[16] These powers are considered in more detail below,[17] but could not be combined with a possession order to prohibit a person from returning to the area from which s/he had been evicted, because once possession was granted, there were no tenancy terms that could be enforced.[18] **4.1.8**

Neither s 152 nor s 153 specifically addressed the issue of obtaining a remedy against minors, and although the Court of Appeal indicated that the s 152 injunction may be available against a minor, as may the power of arrest,[19] more recent authority suggests that the court may be reluctant to grant injunctions and powers of arrest against minors where there is no realistic means of enforcing them.[20] The problem of what to do about conduct perpetrated by non-tenants in a locality other than that of local authority housing also remained and, as more housing authorities transferred their stock to RSLs, started to become more significant. **4.1.9**

In 1998, the Crime and Disorder Act 1998 created the anti-social behaviour order (ASBO). An order may be made by a magistrates' court (or, in certain circumstances, a county court) prohibiting specified types of conduct where it is proved that a person has acted in a manner causing, or likely to cause, harassment, alarm or distress to another person not of the same household as himself, and where the court considers that such an order is necessary to prevent further such acts. The order must last for a minimum period of two years. **4.1.10**

Although proceedings to obtain an ASBO are civil, breach of any of its terms is a criminal offence, triable either way. Because of this, the problem of seeking an order against minors is overcome. So long as the minor is over the age of criminal responsibility (ie ten years old), the ASBO can, in principle anyway, be **4.1.11**

[10] Housing Act 1996, ss 124–132.
[11] ibid, ss 144 and 148.
[12] ibid, ss 147 and 151.
[13] ibid, ss 145 and 149.
[14] ibid, s 152.
[15] ibid, s 152(1).
[16] ibid, s 153.
[17] See paras 4.2.3–4.2.5 below.
[18] *Medina Housing Association v Case* [2002] EWCA Civ 2001, [2003] 1 All ER 1084.
[19] *Enfield LBC v B* [2000] 1 WLR 2259, CA; *Re H (A Child) (Occupation Order: Power of Arrest)* [2001] 1 FLR 641, CA.
[20] *Harrow LBC v G* [2004] EWHC 17, QBD, relying on *Wookey v Wookey* [1991] Fam 121, CA.

enforced, although in practical terms there is little that can be done to a ten year old who refuses to comply with the terms of an ASBO.

4.1.12 The remedy was not without its problems, however, particularly prior to amendments made in 2002.[21] It was not available to RSLs but only to local authorities or the police. Witnesses could not be properly protected because the court had no power to make any form of interim order pending trial (this has now been remedied[22]). Delay could be substantial, particularly where there were numerous defendants, as busy courts did not have sufficient time to set aside, and enforcement had to be handed over to the Crown Prosecution Service which meant that the necessary continuity between obtaining the order and enforcing it could easily be lost. The lack of any procedural rules, moreover, led to numerous procedural disputes, causing further delay and expense.

4.1.13 The ASBO, however, while in many ways cumbersome, inconvenient and expensive to obtain, is a useful addition to the armoury of remedies available to combat housing-related anti-social behaviour, particularly in relation to perpetrators who are under 18.

Proposals for reform

4.1.14 By 2002, Government statistics appeared to show that while crime of an anti-social nature had been falling during the last few years, fear of crime had fallen much less significantly. Anti-social behaviour continued to cause problems for a significant number of people, particularly those living in social housing, ranging from noise nuisance to intimidatory, abusive and/or violent behaviour, from litter to graffiti, vandalism and the use and sale of drugs. The White Paper *Respect and Responsibility—Taking a Stand Against Anti-Social Behaviour*[23] set out the Government's position on housing-related anti-social behaviour:

> As with everything in tackling anti-social behaviour, it is vital that perpetrators understand that keeping their home is dependent on their behaviour not ruining whole communities . . . We intend to take action to make the perpetrators deal with their behaviour or they will be evicted themselves. Proper contractual agreements should be put in place as with good social or private sector landlords, which make it the norm whatever the tenure, for landlords and tenants to behave in a civilised fashion.

4.1.15 To this end, it was proposed that:

- all social landlords should be obliged to publish their policies and procedures on anti-social behaviour;
- the scope of the s 152 injunction should be extended and made available to other social landlords;
- anti-social tenants should lose their security of tenure;

[21] Amendments made by Police Reform Act 2002, ss 61–65.
[22] Police Reform Act 2002, s 65 inserting a new s 1D into the Crime and Disorder Act 1998.
[23] Cm 5778, 2003, p 59.

- courts should have to consider, in anti-social behaviour cases, the impact of such behaviour on the victim, witnesses and the community;
- the working between the various agencies involved in dealing with such behaviour (including housing and social services departments, the police and private sector landlords) should be improved;
- there should be consultation on whether those who behave anti-socially should suffer 'housing benefit sanctions', ie have payments of their housing benefit withheld.

The Law Commission

The reference to depriving anti-social tenants of their security of tenure derived 4.1.16
from a proposal made by the Law Commission in their consultation paper on the reform of housing law, *Renting Homes—1: Status and Security*, also published in 2002.[24] That paper proposed, amongst other things, a system of demoting tenancies in cases of anti-social behaviour, suspending their security of tenure and thus rendering straightforward the eviction of the tenants. 'Structured' decision-making in anti-social behaviour possession cases was also proposed,[25] so that the court would either have to decide whether it was reasonable to make a possession order by reference to an explicit statutory set of criteria, or would even be obliged to make such an order unless the case fell within one of a number of statutory exceptions.

A general duty to deal with anti-social behaviour?

Local authorities and other landlords owe no general duty to their tenants or, in 4.1.17
the case of authorities, to the inhabitants of their areas to take steps to prevent or to deal with anti-social behaviour, unless such an obligation is in some way accepted voluntarily, for example by a clause in the tenancy agreement, which is extremely uncommon. Thus no liability could be established by a claimant living next door to a property in which the local authority accommodated a family known to have a history of nuisance,[26] nor where an authority failed to take possession proceedings against a nuisance family,[27] nor where people caused damage to the property of local shopkeepers by throwing stones from a housing estate.[28]

During consultation prior to the Act it was canvassed that a general duty 4.1.18
should be placed on local authorities to deal with anti-social behaviour as, it was argued, the variable responses of social landlords to tackling such behaviour

---

24 Law Commission Consultation Paper No 162.

25 ibid, paras 12.11–12.22.

26 *Smith v Scott* [1973] Ch 314.

27 *Islington LBC v O'Leary* (1982) 9 HLR 81, CA; *Wandsworth LBC v Mowan* (2001) 33 HLR 56, CA.

28 *Hussain v Lancaster CC* [2000] QB 1, CA.

were in part due to the absence of a specific duty.[29] This proposal was not included in the Act, apparently due to fears from social landlords, perhaps heightened by their experiences with the specific duty to repair, that the imposition of such a duty would lead to 'ambulance chasing' for legal work and leave local authorities open to challenge.[30]

4.1.19 Local authorities are subject to a duty, however, under the Crime and Disorder Act 1998,[31] to exercise their functions having due regard to the need to prevent crime and disorder, and under a further duty, pursuant to the Local Government Act 2000, to prepare a strategy to promote the economic, social and environmental 'well-being' of their areas.[32]

4.1.20 This Part of the 2003 Act enhances the remedies of local authorities and RSLs in respect of anti-social behaviour in a housing context.[33] The new remedies themselves, and their prospective effect, are considered below.

4.2. LEGISLATIVE CONTEXT

4.2.1 Much of the general legislative context of the new measures introduced by this Part of the 2003 Act has already been discussed above. The new measures fall into two principal categories: injunctions and possession proceedings.

Injunctions

4.2.2 Injunctions are available at common law and by statute. Common law causes of action include trespass, breach of implied licence to enter land,[34] and of course private or (in the case of enforcement by a local authority) public nuisance.[35] Statutory powers available to local authorities included the ability to bring proceedings under Local Government Act 1972, s 222 (with the possibility of utilizing the Race Relations Act 1976 and the 'incidental' powers of Local Government Act 1972, s 111). These powers had not been designed to deal with the major problem of anti-social behaviour to which their use came to be adapted (not entirely satisfactorily). In particular, no power of arrest was available for dealing with people who breached the terms of an injunction.[36]

---

[29] See Law Commission Consultation Paper No 162, n 24 above, paras 13.23–13.33.

[30] See House of Commons Research Paper 03/34, 4 April 2003, p 43, citing the National Housing Federation response to *Tackling Anti-Social Tenants*, DETR Consultation Paper, April 2002.

[31] s 17(1).

[32] s 4.

[33] A little reported amendment introduced in the House of Lords and to be found in Pt 9 of the Act (s 91) is, ironically, one of the most significant provisions of the Act in this regard, and will be considered in more detail below, see paras 11.2.78–11.2.80.

[34] See eg *CIN Properties v Rawlins* [1995] 2 EGLR 130, CA.

[35] *Nottingham CC v Zain* [2001] EWCA Civ 1248, [2002] 1 WLR 607 (and see the other cases referred to above).

[36] See now, 2003 Act, s 91.

Accordingly, ss 152–158 of the Housing Act 1996 were introduced, conferring new powers on local authorities to seek injunctions with powers of arrest against those who behaved anti-socially in the locality of local authority housing (the 's 152 injunction'), and granting additional powers to other social landlords to attach powers of arrest to injunctions enforcing the terms of their tenancy agreements (the 's 153 power of arrest'). For a s 152 injunction or a power of arrest under either section to be available, anti-social conduct amounting to violence or threats of violence and a significant risk of harm had to be shown[37] to a person residing in, visiting or otherwise engaging in a lawful activity in the locality of the local authority housing relied on (or, under s 153, the locality of the property subject to the tenancy whose terms were being enforced).[38] 4.2.3

The difficulties encountered in relation to these provisions did not derive from those provisions themselves, but from the judicial interpretation of them in three cases: *Enfield LBC v B*,[39] *Nottingham CC v Thames*,[40] and *Manchester CC v Lee*.[41] In those cases, the court held that: 4.2.4

(a) to be protected by an injunction, a person must reside in local authority housing in the locality, be a visitor to such accommodation, or be engaging in a lawful activity in such accommodation or in its locality. It was not sufficient to reside in the locality, or to visit the locality;
(b) even a person engaging in a lawful activity in the locality would not be protected unless there was a nexus or connection between that activity (and/or the person engaging in it) and the local authority housing itself.

Thus a local authority was not entitled to protect its staff who were attacked in an office only a few hundred yards from a council estate, because there was no nexus between the activities of the staff in the office and the estate.[42] Nor could an authority obtain an injunction to protect a right-to-buy freehold owner-occupier living on a council estate who was attacked by his next-door-neighbour's grandson as he walked up the street outside his home.[43] 4.2.5

Possession proceedings

Secure tenancies

Meaning

A secure tenancy is defined in the Housing Act 1985 ('the 1985 Act') in the following terms: a 'tenancy under which a dwelling-house is let as a separate dwelling is a secure tenancy at any time when the conditions described in sections 80 and 81 as the landlord condition and the tenant condition are satisfied'.[44] The landlord condition[45] is that the landlord under the tenancy is: a local 4.2.6

[37] 1996 Act, ss 152(3) and 153(6).
[38] ibid, s 152(1).
[39] [2000] 1 WLR 2259, CA.
[40] [2002] EWCA Civ 1098, [2003] HLR 14.
[41] [2003] EWCA Civ 1256, [2004] 1 WLR 349.
[42] *Enfield LBC v B* [2000] 1 WLR 2259, CA.
[43] *Manchester CC v Lee* [2003] EWCA Civ 1256, [2004] 1 WLR 349.
[44] Housing Act 1985, s 79.
[45] ibid, s 80.

authority; the Commission for new towns; a New Town development corporation; the Housing Corporation or Housing for Wales; the Development Board for Rural Wales; and, in relation to a tenancy granted before 15 January 1989, a charitable housing trust. The tenant condition[46] is that the tenant is an individual who occupies the dwelling-house (which may be a house or part of a house or land let together with a dwelling-house other than agricultural land) as his only or principal home. If the tenancy is a joint tenancy, then at least one of the tenants must be an individual and at least one must be in occupation as his/her only or principal home.[47]

Termination

4.2.7 The termination procedure in respect of secure tenancies is governed by ss 82–85 of the 1985 Act. A secure tenancy cannot be terminated other than by a court order.[48] For a court order to be obtained, the landlord must serve a notice of seeking possession (unless the court considers it just and equitable to dispense with the notice)[49] and then establish one of the grounds for possession provided in Sch 2 to the Act. Even if such a ground is made out, moreover, an order will only be made on the basis of anti-social behaviour if the court considers it reasonable to do so.[50] The court may make an outright order, or an order suspended on terms, or may adjourn the proceedings. It may also stay or suspend the execution of any possession order at any time until physical possession is actually given up.[51]

Introductory tenancies

4.2.8 One of the innovations of the Housing Act 1996 was the creation of a new, probationary form of tenancy for local authorities and housing action trusts: the introductory tenancy. The key feature of this tenancy is that it does not attract security of tenure until the first anniversary of its grant. Accordingly, while possession cannot be recovered without obtaining a possession order, the court has no jurisdiction to refuse such an order if, within the probationary period, the landlord serves a notice of proceedings, setting out (amongst other things) the reasons for the decision to terminate the tenancy, and begins possession proceedings.[52] In such a case, the tenancy remains introductory, even after the first anniversary of the grant of the tenancy, pending the resolution of the proceedings.[53]

---

[46] Housing Act 1985, s 81.

[47] Whether the dwelling-house is the tenant's 'principal home' is a question of fact for the judge to decide. If the tenant has left the property for a period of time the judge must consider the tenant's actions and intentions objectively and decide whether he intended to return to the property but not focus on fleeting changes of mind: *Crawley BC v Sawyer* (1988) 20 HLR 98; *Hammersmith and Fulham LBC v Clarke* (2000) 33 HLR 77, CA.

[48] 1985 Act, s 82.

[49] ibid, ss 83–83A.

[50] ibid, s 84.

[51] ibid, s 85.

[52] 1996 Act, ss 127–128.

[53] ibid, s 130.

The tenant has a right to request a review of the decision to evict, within 14 days of the service of the notice of proceedings. The review must be carried out and the result notified prior to the date specified in the notice of proceedings as the date after which proceedings may be brought.[54] A failure to comply with the review procedures does not, however, enable the tenant to defend any possession proceedings brought or entitle the court to refuse to make a possession order. The tenant's only remedy is to seek to adjourn or stay the possession proceedings pending an application for judicial review of the decision to evict and/or the conduct of (or the failure to conduct) the review process.[55] **4.2.9**

For introductory tenancies to be granted, the landlord must have resolved to operate an introductory tenancy regime. If this decision is made, then every 'allocation', ie new grant of a tenancy to someone who was not already a tenant of a social landlord, will take effect as an introductory tenancy.[56] The purpose of the introductory tenancy regime is to enable landlords to assess the suitability of tenants before they acquire security of tenure, thus facilitating their speedy eviction where the landlord concludes that they are not suitable. **4.2.10**

Assured tenancies

Meaning and termination

The regime for assured tenancies is contained in Part I of the Housing Act 1988, the basic principles of which are akin to those concerning secure tenancies, referred to above. Assured tenancies confer security of tenure principally in the private sector and, since 15 January 1989, on tenancies granted by RSLs. A tenant condition must be met.[57] As with secure tenancies, the tenancy may only be terminated by an order of the court,[58] following the giving of a notice of seeking possession[59] and the proof of a ground for possession.[60] In the case of anti-social behaviour, the court must also consider it reasonable to order possession.[61] Outright and suspended orders for possession may be made, and the court has power to suspend or stay the execution of any order.[62] **4.2.11**

Assured shorthold tenancies

There is no exact equivalent to the introductory tenancy, but a species of the assured tenancy which is similar in effect is the assured shorthold tenancy.[63] This is an assured tenancy, but operates so that once any contractual term of the tenancy has expired, the landlord may recover possession by serving a notice specifying that possession is required. Two months' notice must be given,[64] but on the expiry of the notice, the court has no power to refuse to make a possession order.[65] **4.2.12**

---

[54] ibid, s 129.
[55] *Manchester CC v Cochrane* [1999] 1 WLR 809, CA.
[56] 1996 Act, ss 124–126.
[57] 1988 Act, s 1(1).
[58] ibid, s 5.
[59] ibid, s 8.
[60] ibid, s 7 and Sch 2.
[61] ibid, s 7(4). The requirement of reasonableness does not apply to all grounds for possession (see s 7(3), (5A) and (6), and Sch 2, Pt 1).
[62] ibid, s 9.
[63] ibid, s 20.
[64] ibid, s 21.
[65] ibid.

During the currency of the contractual term, the landlord may only recover possession in the normal way applicable to assured tenancies. Where there is no contractual term, the tenancy being periodic, a possession order may not take effect during the first six months of the tenancy.[66]

The 2003 Act

4.2.13 The measures introduced by the 2003 Act fall essentially into four categories:

(a) they require social landlords to prepare and publish policies on anti-social behaviour;[67]
(b) they repeal and replace the provisions of ss 152 and 153 of the Housing Act 1996, enacting a modified scheme for injunctions of wider scope and available to a wider class of social landlord;[68]
(c) they introduce a new form of tenancy, the 'demoted tenancy', under which security of tenure may be suspended by the court in the case of anti-social behaviour;[69] and
(d) they create a specific requirement that, in considering whether it is reasonable to make a possession order in nuisance possession cases, the court must have particular regard to the impact of the anti-social behaviour on the community, and the effect of its continuation and/or repetition.[70]

4.3. THE PROVISIONS OF PART 2 OF THE ACT

Landlord's policies and procedures

4.3.1 Section 12 of the 2003 Act inserts a new s 218A into the Housing Act 1996. In essence it obliges local housing authorities, housing action trusts and RSLs[71] to prepare, publish and keep under review policies and procedures on anti-social behaviour, and to make them—and summaries of them—available to the public. Anti-social behaviour in this context has the same meaning as in new ss 153A and 153B of the Housing Act 1996 (inserted by s 13 of the 2003 Act).[72] Accordingly, it means conduct:

(a) which is capable of causing nuisance or annoyance to any person and which directly or indirectly relates to or affects the housing management functions of a relevant landlord; or
(b) which consists of or involves using or threatening to use housing accommodation owned or managed by a relevant landlord for an unlawful purpose.

4.3.2 This requirement is not innovative in principle; similar requirements exist in other areas of activity, such as that of publishing homelessness strategies imposed

[66] 1988 Act, s 21(5). [67] 2003 Act, s 12. [68] ibid, s 13. [69] ibid, ss 14–15.
[70] ibid, s 16. [71] 2003 Act, s 12(1) inserting new s 218(A)(1) into the Housing Act 1996.
[72] Housing Act 1996, s 218A(8).

by the Homelessness Act 2002,[73] and the obligation, which these new provisions closely resemble, imposed on authorities to publish their housing allocation schemes, and make summaries of them available to the public.[74] The aim is to inform tenants and members of the public about the measures that these landlords will use to address anti-social behaviour issues in relation to their stock.[75]

Specifically, the new provision requires the landlord to prepare a policy in relation to anti-social behaviour and procedures for dealing with occurrences of such behaviour.[76] A statement of these policies and procedures must then be published not later than six months after s 12 of the 2003 Act comes into force.[77] From time to time, the landlord must then keep the policy and procedures under review and, when it thinks appropriate, publish a revised statement.[78] A summary of the policy and procedures must also be prepared[79] (and presumably, though the section does not so state, revised as and when revisions are made to the policy and procedures themselves). 4.3.3

In preparing and reviewing the policy and procedures, regard must be had to guidance issued, in the case of local authority and housing action trusts, by the Secretary of State or, for RSLs, by the 'relevant authority', ie in England, the Housing Corporation, and in Wales, the National Assembly for Wales.[80] 4.3.4

A copy of the published statement or revised statement must be available for inspection at all reasonable hours at the landlord's principal office, and must be provided on payment of a reasonable fee to any person who requests it. A copy of the summary must be provided without charge to any person who requests it.[81] 4.3.5

Anti-social behaviour injunctions

Section 13 of the Act repeals ss 152 and 153 of the 1996 Act and replaces them with five new sections: ss 153A–E, which confer similar, but not identical powers on a wider range of social landlords to apply to the county court for injunctions against anti-social behaviour. 4.3.6

Meaning of anti-social behaviour

The new sections apply to the types of conduct described in ss 153A(1) and 153B(1), namely conduct: 4.3.7

[73] s 1(1)(b).

[74] Housing Act 1996, s 168.

[75] See explanatory notes to the Anti-Social Behaviour Bill 2003, para 25.

[76] Housing Act 1996, s 218A(2).

[77] ibid, s 218A(3). The section is expected to come into force in June or July 2004.

[78] ibid, s 218A(4).

[79] ibid, s 218A(6)(a).

[80] ibid, s 218A(7). By subs (9), 'relevant authority' has the same meaning as in Pt I of the 1996 Act. Section 12(2) of the 2003 Act amends s 36(2) of the 1996 Act which sets out the functions of the Housing Corporation relating to guidance, and the corresponding functions in Wales, by inserting a new sub-para (i), which adds, as a matter about which the Corporation should issue guidance: 'the policy and procedures a landlord is required under section 218A to prepare and from time to time revise in connection with anti-social behaviour'.

[81] ibid, s 218A(6)(b).

(a) which is capable of causing nuisance or annoyance to any person and which directly or indirectly relates to or affects the housing management functions of a relevant landlord; or
(b) which consists of or involves using or threatening to use housing accommodation owned or managed by a relevant landlord for an unlawful purpose.

4.3.8 In addition, s 153D provides for prohibitions that may, if certain conditions are satisfied, be included in an injunction granted, on the application of a relevant landlord, to enforce the nuisance clauses of a tenancy agreement which have been breached, or breach of which is anticipated.[82] This is considered further below.[83]

Definitions

Relevant landlord

4.3.9 A 'relevant landlord' is a local housing authority within the meaning of the Housing Act 1985, a housing action trust or an RSL.[84]

Housing management functions

4.3.10 The 'housing management functions' of a relevant landlord include functions conferred by or under any enactment and the powers and duties of the landlord as the holder of an estate or interest in housing accommodation.[85]

Housing accommodation

4.3.11 This includes flats, lodging-houses, and hostels and any yard, garden, outhouses and appurtenances belonging to the accommodation or usually enjoyed with it. In relation to a neighbourhood, it includes the whole of the housing accommodation owned or managed by a relevant landlord in the neighbourhood and any common areas used in connection with the accommodation.[86]

Owned or managed

4.3.12 A landlord 'owns' housing accommodation for these purposes if either:

(a) he is a person (other than a mortgagee not in possession) who is for the time being entitled to dispose of the fee simple in the premises, whether in possession or reversion; or
(b) he is a person who holds or is entitled to the rents and profits of the premises under a lease which (when granted) was for a term of not less than three years.

In other words, a flat of which a long lease has been granted under the right to buy provisions of the Housing Act 1985[87] is still, for these purposes, owned by the relevant landlord. A right to buy transfer of the freehold of a house, however, deprives the landlord of ownership under these provisions.

---

[82] Housing Act 1996, s 153D(1)–(3). [83] See paras 4.3.49–4.3.53.
[84] Housing Act 1996, s 153E(7). [85] ibid, s 153E(11). [86] ibid, s 153E(9).
[87] Housing Act 1985, Pt V.

Some of the results of this difference could be somewhat odd. Illegal user of a right to buy flat could be the subject of an anti-social behaviour injunction application, but not such user of a right to buy house unless it could be argued that the local authority still 'managed' the house, which seems unlikely (though this may well depend on the terms of the transfer, including any covenants which were entered into between the authority and the purchaser). Other possible anomalies have been resolved, by means of amendments to the Bill during its progress through the House of Lords.[88] 4.3.13

'Managed' is not defined. 4.3.14

What conduct?

Conduct of the kind referred to at para 4.3.7 above need not have actually taken place prior to the injunction application being made. It is sufficient—consistent with the language of s 153B(1) and, indeed, the terms of the old s 152—that the person against whom an injunction is sought 'threatens' to engage in such conduct.[89] Thus, in theory anyway, an injunction could be obtained against a person who threatens to engage in conduct capable of causing annoyance to any person. Put in this way, the breadth of the new provision can clearly be seen. Almost all conduct is capable of annoying *someone*, and the defendant does not even have to have caused any annoyance. 4.3.15

In purely practical terms, it may be difficult for a landlord to know who might be threatening to engage in anti-social behaviour, but there are some circumstances in which the possibility of relief on this basis will be useful; if, for example, the landlord discovers that a tenant is proposing to hold a series of all-night parties with amplified music, or to start a car repair business from her/his property. 4.3.16

Similarly, it appears that the conduct need not be continuing at the time of the injunction application, as it is sufficient to show that the defendant 'is engaging' or 'has engaged' in it.[90] If the conduct complained of has ceased before the hearing, it may still be reasonable to make an injunction forbidding future recurrences of the behaviour.[91] 4.3.17

Although the conduct in question need only be capable of causing nuisance to any person, for an injunction to be obtained, it needs to be shown that the conduct was capable of causing a nuisance or annoyance to a person with at least one of four qualifying characteristics related to where they live, their employment or the activity they themselves are engaging in.[92] 4.3.18

---

[88] eg the introduction of s 153A(4)(b), which removed the anomaly (arising, on the original drafting, from the wording of s 153(4)(a)) that an injunction could protect a right to buy leaseholder but not a right to buy freeholder.

[89] Housing Act 1996, s 153A(3).

[90] ibid.

[91] This principle applies to nuisance possession cases: the mere fact that the nuisance has stopped by the date of the hearing does not of itself dictate that it cannot be reasonable for the court to order that possession of the premises be given up: see eg *Newcastle CC v Morrison* (2000) 32 HLR 891, CA.

[92] ibid, s 153A(4). See further paras 4.3.27–4.3.39 below.

4.3.19 The terminology of 'nuisance or annoyance' in s 153A(1) renders this new provision consistent with those relating to possession proceedings on nuisance grounds[93] and, indeed, with the previous s 152. The use of the formula 'conduct which is capable of causing' such nuisance or annoyance is, apparently, a deliberate widening of the language of s 152 which referred to conduct causing or 'likely to cause' nuisance or annoyance. Whether the effect of this will be significant in practical terms is open to doubt: injunction proceedings do not often turn on whether the conduct was likely or only capable of causing a nuisance.

4.3.20 More important, in terms of extending the conduct in respect of which an injunction may be sought, is the omission of any requirement from s 153A that the anti-social conduct must involve violence or threats of violence, which was one of the jurisdictional preconditions of the former s 152. For an injunction to contain an exclusion zone which the defendant may not enter or to have attached to it a power of arrest, violence or threatened violence and a significant risk of harm will, however, still need to be proved.[94]

4.3.21 A less significant change of statutory wording, when compared to its statutory predecessor,[95] is the provision by s 153B(1) of unlawful, but not immoral, user of premises as a ground for seeking an injunction. The use of premises for illegal or immoral purposes is a ground for possession of premises,[96] and immoral as well as illegal user was within the scope of the old s 152. It is doubtful whether the omission of immorality is material, however. If the putatively immoral conduct is not also illegal, there is considerable doubt whether an injunction ought to be—it is no part of the role of social landlords to police the morality of their tenants or, indeed, anyone else unless that conduct is also capable of causing some nuisance to others or is illegal. The use of premises for drug use or dealing, prostitution and/or handling stolen goods is, of course, currently illegal.

4.3.22 Section 153B is a useful provision in a situation where no evidence can be brought forward that anyone suffered or was capable of suffering any nuisance or annoyance from the activities. If, for example, a tenant was using her/his home to store goods s/he regularly stole from commercial premises, or was abstracting electricity, or growing cannabis in the garden, the neighbours might very well not even know about it.

4.3.23 It is important to note that s 153B(1) does not require that the housing accommodation used for illegal purposes be accommodation in which the person accused of the conduct resides or has any right to reside or occupy. Accordingly, where, for example, a person uses a friend's flat—or an empty flat—owned or managed by a relevant landlord to store his stolen goods, or his drugs, an injunction may be granted against that person as well as against the tenant (if any) personally.

---

[93] Housing Act 1985, Sch 2, Ground 2; Housing Act 1988, Sch 2, Ground 14.

[94] ibid, s 153C(1)–(2). See further paras 4.3.45–4.3.49 below.

[95] ibid, s 152(1)(b).

[96] Housing Act 1985, Sch 2, Ground 2(b).

The conduct must also directly or indirectly relate to or affect the relevant landlord's housing management functions. This requirement for the grant of an injunction is new, but seems to be premised on the same sorts of considerations that moved the courts to attempt to limit the effect of s 152 (albeit rather haphazardly) in the *Enfield*, *Nottingham* and *Manchester* cases, namely that a power contained in a public housing Act (or here a housing part of a general Act) entitling a body to restrict the activities of the citizen on pain of arrest and imprisonment must require its exercise to be connected in some way with housing if it is not to be unacceptably wide. Having said this, however, the formulation of conduct which directly or indirectly relates to or affects housing management provides, it seems deliberately, a very low threshold test.[97] 4.3.24

Section 153A: conditions to be satisfied

For an injunction to be made restraining conduct capable of causing nuisance or annoyance under s 153A (but not for the grant of an injunction relating to illegal user under s 153B), two additional conditions must be satisfied.[98] 4.3.25

The first condition is that the person against whom the injunction is sought 'is engaging, has engaged or threatens to engage in conduct to which this section applies'.[99] As already noted, the conduct need not already have taken place. 4.3.26

The second condition is that the conduct is capable of causing nuisance or annoyance to any of the following categories of person: 4.3.27

(a) a person with a right (of whatever description) to reside in or occupy housing accommodation owned or managed by the relevant landlord;
(b) a person with a right (of whatever description) to reside in or occupy other housing accommodation in the neighbourhood of the housing accommodation mentioned in (a);
(c) a person engaged in lawful activity in or in the neighbourhood of the housing accommodation mentioned in (a);
(d) a person employed (whether or not by the relevant landlord) in connection with the exercise of the relevant landlord's housing management functions.

Categories of protection

Section 152 offered protection for people 'residing in, visiting or otherwise engaging in a lawful activity in residential premises to which this section applies [ie properties let on secure or introductory tenancies, or provided to the homeless] or in the locality of such premises'. The courts interpreted this statutory formulation in terms that residents in or visitors to such premises were protected, but not those residing in or visiting the locality of it. People engaging in a lawful activity in such premises were also protected, but those engaging in such an activity in the locality of such premises were only protected if the activity itself had a nexus or connection with the residential premises in the locality. 4.3.28

---

[97] See Explanatory notes to the Bill, para 34.
[98] Housing Act 1996, s 153A(2).
[99] ibid, s 153A(3).

4.3.29 This gave rise to all manner of absurd anomalies, of which the following are only a few examples. The school child walking through the housing estate to get to school, or to go to the local sweet shop, was not protected. Nor was the child who went to visit her school friend whose parents had exercised the right to buy, though she would be protected when visiting her other friend whose parents had not done so. If the gang of youths threw a stone at the owner-occupier's window and broke it, the repair man replacing the window would not be protected. If the youths had missed with the stone and happened to break the window of the secure tenant's house next door, the repair man would be protected. Housing officers were not protected even where they worked on the housing estate itself, their presence on the estate not having sufficient nexus with the housing stock, as the housing office did not need to be situated on the estate.[100]

4.3.30 The new provisions have sought to ameliorate some of these absurdities, and have recast the qualifying characteristics of those who are protected. Residents of (and those with a right to occupy) housing accommodation owned or managed by the landlord (including tenants, licensees and long leaseholders) are included, as before, within the protection of s 153A.[101]

4.3.31 People residing in or with any kind of right to reside in or occupy other housing accommodation in the neighbourhood of housing accommodation owned or managed by the relevant landlord are now included, reversing the effect of the *Enfield*, *Nottingham* and particularly the *Manchester* cases. In *Manchester*, the Court of Appeal held that a right to buy freeholder attacked by his neighbour's grandson in the street outside his house due to a neighbour dispute was not protected by s 152 because the act of walking up the street did not enjoy any nexus with the local authority housing through which he was walking.

4.3.32 Interestingly, in s 153A(4)(b), the word 'neighbourhood' has been used instead of 'locality'—the terminology of s 152. This was a late amendment to the Bill,[102] 'locality' having been the word originally used. The significance of this change is discussed further below.[103]

4.3.33 Both s 153A(4)(a) and (b) refer to a right to reside in or occupy. The word 'reside' has a specific and established meaning in housing law, developed in the context of security of tenure under the Rent Acts.[104] In this context, however, it is a little hard to see what the concept of residence adds to that of occupation—in other words, it is not clear why Parliament considered it necessary to include the more restrictive word 'reside' if it was also content to protect those who fell within the less restrictive formulation 'occupy' (nor is it obvious who is protected by use of the words 'reside in' who would not also be protected by the word

[100] *Nottingham CC v Thames* [2002] EWCA Civ 1098, [2003] HLR 14.

[101] Housing Act 1996, s 153A(4)(a).

[102] Introduced in the House of Lords, at report stage, amendment no 16, 23 October 2003.

[103] See paras 4.3.35–4.3.36.

[104] See eg *Brickfield Properties v Hughes* (1988) 20 HLR 108, CA; *Tickner v Hearn* [1960] 1 WLR 1406, CA.

'occupy')—unless it is simply to make clear that occupation includes persons whose right to occupy is less than a right to reside (ie the courts might have construed 'occupy' as limited to residing if the concept of residence were not also included).

There is perhaps some indication from the terms of s 153D(5), however, that the explanation may be rather less arcane. That section provides, in the context of injunctions to restrain breach of a tenancy agreement, that 'tenancy agreement' includes any agreement for the occupation of residential accommodation owned or managed by the relevant landlord. Accordingly, it may simply be that the draftsman of s 153A(4)(a) and (b) used 'reside' to refer to occupation by tenants and 'occupy' to refer to occupation by licensees.[105] **4.3.34**

Visitors are no longer specifically mentioned. Instead, they are subsumed within the third category: people engaged in lawful activity in or in the neighbourhood of housing accommodation owned or managed by a relevant landlord. The explanatory notes to the Bill[106] make it clear that the Government's intention was to avoid the pitfalls arising from the courts' interpretation of who was protected under s 152. This new category is therefore the most difficult to assess. The change of the word 'locality' to 'neighbourhood' at the eleventh hour (bearing in mind that *Manchester*, which was decided just as the Bill was introduced into the House of Lords, made reference to the same problems of construction arising under the new provisions—as then drafted)[107] seems likely to have been a further attempt to distance the new provisions from their statutory predecessor. It is hard to think of any other reason for the change from one word to another which means exactly the same thing.[108] **4.3.35**

It is therefore to be hoped that the concept of nexus will play no part in the construction of s 153A(4)(c), and that the courts will accept this change of language as indicative of Parliament's intention to break with the construction of the old s 152, and the requirement of the conduct having at least some indirect effect on the landlord's housing management functions as providing a limitation on the breadth of the powers, the achievement of which had been the court's aim (however misguidedly it accomplished it) in inventing the doctrine of nexus. **4.3.36**

The final category of persons who can be protected is another new category: people employed (whether or not by the relevant landlord itself) in connection with the exercise of the relevant landlord's housing management functions.[109] The statutory definition of housing management functions has been discussed **4.3.37**

---

[105] The explanatory notes to the Act do not bear out such a distinction, however, referring only to tenants: see para 36.

[106] See especially para 31, though these notes were drafted at a stage when the wording of s 153A was significantly different.

[107] [2003] EWCA Civ 1256, [2004] 1 WLR 349 *per* Pill LJ at [22].

[108] This Government amendment was introduced by Baroness Scotland of Asthal without explanation or comment: see *Hansard*, HL Vol 653, col 1797 (23 October 2003).

[109] Housing Act 1996, s 153A(4)(d).

above.[110] The explanatory notes to the Bill stated that the term 'housing management' should be interpreted broadly and would include activities such as regeneration, mediation, tenant training and participation, welfare rights advice to tenants and supported housing.[111]

4.3.38 The term would also seem to be sufficiently wide to reverse the specific results of the *Enfield* and *Nottingham* cases, which decided that housing officers were not protected when assaulted in their offices, because there was no nexus between the officers and the housing estate in the locality of which their housing office was situated. Utility company employees, milkmen, postmen, road repairers etc will not be covered, but will continue to need to rely on the 'engaging in lawful activity in the neighbourhood' basis of protection.

4.3.39 There is, in relation to this category, the additional feature that both the conduct of the perpetrator and the employment of the person protected must have some, though not necessarily the same, connection with the relevant landlord's housing management functions.[112]

Location of the conduct

4.3.40 It is immaterial where the conduct occurs.[113] It need not occur in the neighbourhood of any housing accommodation owned or managed by the relevant landlord, but it must still in some direct or indirect way relate to or affect the relevant landlord's housing management functions. This provision confirms the essence of the High Court decision in *Manchester CC v Ali*,[114] in which the judge held that for the purposes of old s 152 there did not have to be what he described as a 'geographical nexus' between the locality of the relevant residential premises and the conduct complained of, for otherwise a person could lie in wait for her or his victim just outside the locality of the residential accommodation, knowing that the victim was thereby unprotected by the provisions of that section.

Who may apply for an injunction?

4.3.41 The relevant landlords who may apply are local housing authorities, housing action trusts and RSLs.[115] This is a deliberate extension of the housing providers who have access to injunctions of this type. The s 152 powers were available only to local authorities.

Terms of the injunction

4.3.42 If the conduct referred to under s 153A(1) is established, and the two conditions made out, an injunction may be granted prohibiting the person in respect of whom it is granted from engaging in the conduct to which that section applies: ie conduct that is capable of causing nuisance or annoyance to any person and

---

110 See para 4.3.10 above.
111 Explanatory Notes at paras 33–34.
112 Housing Act 1996, s 153A(1) and (4)(d).
113 ibid, s 153A(5).
114 [2003] HLR 11, QBD.
115 Housing Act 1996, s 153E(7).

which directly or indirectly relates to or affects the relevant landlord's housing management functions.[116] Similarly, if the conduct specified in s 153B(1) is proven, the court may grant an injunction prohibiting the person from engaging in conduct to which that section applies: conduct that consists of or involves using or threatening to use housing accommodation owned or managed by the relevant landlord for illegal purposes.[117]

As a matter of good practice, it would seem desirable that the injunction should in fact be far more specific about the conduct that is prohibited. An injunction order which merely stated that the defendant was prohibited from engaging in any conduct capable of causing nuisance or annoyance to any person, or even to any person of a description referred to in s 153A(4), would be likely to find it difficult to enforce such an injunction. It is a fundamental principle of law that a person should not be committed for breach of an order unless that person clearly understood what may and what may not be done under the terms of the order.[118] Accordingly, the conduct prohibited (which may include a general 'sweeping up' provision) should be clearly specified on the face of the order.[119] **4.3.43**

If an injunction under any of the provisions of ss 153A–D is to be expressed to protect someone who has not taken part in the proceedings, or a class of persons, the judge should make a finding of fact that there is a significant risk of harm to such persons.[120] **4.3.44**

Exclusion orders and powers of arrest

If the court is proposing to grant either of the above kinds of injunction, it may also, if either of two further conditions are met, include an exclusion order—which is a provision prohibiting the person from entering or being in any premises specified in the injunction and/or any area specified in the injunction—and/or attach a power of arrest to 'any provision of the injunction', which appears to include a provision that by itself could not have attracted a power of arrest, ie because the conduct, while sufficient to trigger ss 153A and/or 153B, did not fall within either of the additional conditions specified in s 153C. **4.3.45**

Those additional conditions are that the court 'thinks' that either: **4.3.46**

(a) the conduct in question consists of or includes the use or threatened use of violence; or
(b) there is a significant risk of harm to a person mentioned in s 153A(4).[121]

---

[116] ibid, s 153A(6).

[117] ibid, s 153B(2). The housing accommodation need not be accommodation which the enjoined person occupies or in respect of which s/he has any right of occupation.

[118] And see *Manchester CC v Lee* [2003] EWCA Civ 1256, [2004] 1 WLR 349, *per* Chadwick LJ at [48]–[54].

[119] The Court of Appeal has recently reaffirmed this principle in the context of ASBOs—see *R v P* [2004] EWCA Crim 287, *per* Henriques J at [34].

[120] ibid, *per* Mummery LJ at [38]–[39].

[121] Housing Act 1996, s 153C(1).

4.3.47 'Harm' includes serious ill-treatment or abuse, whether physical or not.[122] Such harm could include emotional or psychological harm. As stated in the explanatory notes to this section, the definition could apply, for example, in cases of racial or sexual harassment.[123]

4.3.48 An exclusion order is permitted to have the effect of excluding a person from his normal place of residence.[124] The court has asserted a right to make an order excluding a person from an area including his home even at common law, but it has always been regarded as an unusual order.[125] It is not clear whether this express provision will alter the court's approach in this regard, but it is by no means inevitable that this will be the case.

Enforcing tenancy conditions—exclusion orders and powers of arrest

4.3.49 Section 153D provides for the inclusion of an exclusion order in, and/or the attaching of a power of arrest to, an injunction granted to enforce the terms of a tenancy agreement which have been breached, or of which a breach is anticipated by the relevant landlord.[126] The relevant landlord (which term, under this section, includes a charitable housing trust which is not an RSL)[127] must apply for the injunction in respect of a breach or anticipated breach of the tenancy terms on the grounds that the tenant is either:

(a) engaging or threatening to engage in conduct capable of causing nuisance or annoyance to any person; or
(b) allowing, inciting or encouraging any other person to engage in or threaten to engage in such conduct.[128]

4.3.50 The second of these limbs is new, and extends the circumstances in which the powers of the court are available, compared with the provisions of the former s 153. In order to fall within s 153D, the allowing, inciting or encouraging relied on must also amount to a breach or anticipated breach of the terms of the tenancy. Most modern tenancy agreements render the tenant responsible for the behaviour of members of the tenant's household and visitors. In this sense, the new limb may not be as broad a provision as it would appear at first sight.

4.3.51 To add an exclusion order or power of arrest, the court must also be satisfied (cf s 153C(1) under which the court need only 'think') that either the conduct includes the use or threatened use of violence or there is a significant risk of harm to any person. The exclusion order may, as stated above, have the effect of excluding the person from his normal place of residence.[129] Under s 153D, there are no protected categories of person as under s 153A(4). Accordingly, where the words 'any person' are used, they apparently mean *any* person.

---

[122] Housing Act 1996, s 153E(12).
[123] Explanatory notes, para 35.
[124] Housing Act 1996, s 153E(2)(b).
[125] See eg *Liburd v Cork* The Times, 4 April 1981; *Islington LBC v Bowry* (Clerkenwell County Court, 19 April 1996).
[126] Housing Act 1996, s 153D(3).
[127] ibid, s 153E(8).
[128] ibid, s 153D(1).
[129] ibid, s 153E(2)(b).

The now repealed provisions of s 152(3) and 153(6) of the 1996 Act provided that in order to make a s 152 injunction (with or without power of arrest) or to attach a s 153 power of arrest, the applicant had to show that violence had been used or threatened against a protected person *and* that there was a significant risk of harm to that person or a person of a similar description. There was no power to make an exclusion order under the old provisions of s 153. 4.3.52

It is therefore clear that the new provisions in ss 153C(1) and 153D(3) are considerably wider, as an exclusion order and power of arrest can now be included where *either* violence has been used or threatened *or* there is a significant risk of harm to protected persons. Accordingly, a power of arrest will now be available in cases where there is a significant risk of harm even if there has been no actual or threatened violence. 4.3.53

When a power of arrest should be attached

There is some fairly old family law authority for the proposition that a power of arrest should not be regarded as a routine remedy, but should be granted only in exceptional circumstances, for example when there is persistent disobedience to orders,[130] and that the power should rarely be used where the incidents justifying it occurred some time prior to the application.[131] More recently, the Court of Appeal held—again in a family context—that a power of arrest could be attached to the provisions of an injunction made against a minor, even where it was unclear what measures could be taken against the minor to enforce the injunction.[132] 4.3.54

It is not clear that an identical approach to powers of arrest is necessarily called for in anti-social behaviour and family cases. The question only arises in the context of the 2003 Act either where violence has been used or threatened, or where there is a significant risk of harm. If either test is made out, the court will need to consider whether it is appropriate to attach a power of arrest. In principle, there seems no reason why it should not do so, although it is probably correct that a power of arrest should be viewed as offering protection additional to, rather than comprising part of, that provided by the injunction itself. 4.3.55

A recent High Court decision,[133] moreover, renders it doubtful whether in most cases an injunction or power of arrest will be available in respect of a minor, as it was held that an injunction should not be made where it cannot be enforced because the defendant is too young to be imprisoned for contempt of court and has no resources with which to pay a fine and/or no assets that can be sequestered. No consideration appears to have been given to the cases that have held, albeit in other contexts, that the enforceability of an injunction is not relevant to the question whether to grant it.[134] 4.3.56

---

130 *Lewis v Lewis* [1978] Fam 60, CA.

131 *Horner v Horner* [1982] Fam 90, CA.

132 *Re H* [2001] 1 FLR 641, CA.

133 *Harrow LBC v G* [2004] EWHC 17, QBD, relying on *Wookey v Wookey* [1991] Fam 121, CA.

134 See *Re H* [2001] 1 FLR 641, CA; *Hampshire Waste Services Ltd v Intending Trespassers upon Chineham Incinerator Site* [2003] EWHC 1738, [2003] 42 EGCS 126.

Length of injunction

4.3.57 Injunctions, exclusion orders and powers of arrest may be made for a specified period or until varied or discharged.[135] This is akin to the equivalent provision of s 152(4).

Discharge or variation

4.3.58 The person against whom the injunction (whether or not including an exclusion order) was made, or the relevant landlord, may apply to vary or discharge the injunction.

Injunctions without notice to the respondent

4.3.59 An application for an injunction, or an application to vary an injunction, may be made without notice to the respondent. The court may grant—or vary—the injunction where notice has not been given if it 'thinks it just and convenient' to do so.[136] If an injunction is granted or varied on this basis, the court must give the person against whom the injunction has been made or varied an opportunity to make representations in relation to the injunction as soon as it is practicable for him/her to do so.[137]

4.3.60 It is likely that applications will be heard on a without notice basis either where there is particular urgency that requires an injunction to be obtained immediately or where the relevant landlord considers that the giving of notice is likely to prove a trigger for anti-social conduct, in particular where neighbours have come forward as witnesses and require some kind of interim protection. In other cases, it may often be preferable to seek to abridge time and allow the person against whom the application is made the opportunity to attend on short notice.[138]

4.3.61 It is only former ss 152 and 153 that have been repealed. The provisions of ss 154–158 are amended[139] to ensure that they refer to the new ss 153A–D rather than the previous provisions, but are otherwise unaltered.

Demotion of tenancies

The demotion order

4.3.62 The other new concepts introduced by Part 2 of the 2003 Act are those of the 'demotion order' and 'demoted tenancy'. The former is an order that the court may make in proceedings brought by certain landlords[140] of secure or assured tenants on the basis of anti-social behaviour, essentially as an alternative to granting either an outright or a suspended possession order. The effect of a

[135] Housing Act 1996, s 153E(2)(a). [136] ibid, s 153E(4). [137] ibid, s 153E(5).

[138] See eg *Wookey v Wookey* [1991] Fam 121, CA, *per* Butler-Sloss LJ at 131.

[139] Housing Act 1996, s 153E(2)–(7).

[140] Local authorities, RSLs and housing action trusts: 2003 Act, s 14(1).

demotion order is to demote the defendant's secure or assured tenancy to a 'demoted tenancy'[141] for a period of 12 months during which the landlord may obtain an order for possession without establishing a ground for possession.

Section 14(2) inserts a new s 82A into the 1985 Act, which confers upon local authorities, housing action trusts and RSLs the power to apply to the county court for a demotion order.[142] Section 82 of the Housing Act 1985 is also amended so as to include the demotion order amongst the court's powers on hearing possession proceedings. The amendments to the Housing Act 1985 only apply, of course, to permit the demotion of a secure tenancy. Since 15 January 1989, RSLs have not generally been able to grant secure tenancies,[143] but have granted assured tenancies instead. Accordingly, so far as such tenancies are concerned, s 14(4) amends the Housing Act 1988, inserting a new s 6A, so as to enable an RSL to seek demotion from an assured to a demoted assured shorthold tenancy.[144] 4.3.63

The amendments to the 1988 Act are not, however, entirely analogous to those to the 1985 Act and they are considered separately. Section 5 of the 1988 Act, which is equivalent to s 82 of the 1985 Act, is not amended, and the notice requirements before an application for a demotion order can be made are different, as are the consequences of demotion in terms of the means of terminating the demoted tenancy and the remedies available to the tenant. These issues are considered further below. 4.3.64

Conditions for making a demotion order

Before the court may make a demotion order, it must be satisfied that the tenant, or another resident of, or visitor to, the tenant's dwelling-house, has engaged in or threatened to engage in conduct to which s 153A or 153B applies, ie conduct capable of causing nuisance or annoyance that directly or indirectly relates to or affects the housing management functions of a relevant landlord; or conduct amounting to the use or threatened use of the dwelling-house for unlawful purposes. The court must also be satisfied that it is reasonable to make the order.[145] 'Dwelling-house' is defined as a house or part of a house. Land let together with a dwelling-house is treated, for the purposes of Chapter 1A, as part 4.3.65

---

[141] By Sch 1, para 1 to the 2003 Act, a new Ch 1A is inserted into Pt V of the Housing Act 1996. Chapter 1A includes a new s 143A which defines 'demoted tenancy', for the purposes of local authority and housing action trust landlords, as a periodic tenancy in relation to which the landlord is a local authority or housing action trust, the tenant condition set out in s 81 of the Housing Act 1985 is satisfied, and the tenancy has been created by virtue of a demotion order under s 82A of the Housing Act 1985. See also n 144 below.

[142] Housing Act 1985, s 82A(1) and (2).

[143] Housing Act 1988, ss 34–38.

[144] s 15 of the 2003 Act inserts a new s 20B into the Housing Act 1988, subs (1) of which defines a demoted assured shorthold tenancy as a tenancy created by virtue of a demotion order made by the court under s 82A of the Housing Act 1985 or s 6A of the Housing Act 1988, where the landlord is a RSL.

[145] Housing Act 1985, s 82A(4); Housing Act 1988, s 6A(4).

of the dwelling-house unless it is agricultural land which would not be treated as part of a dwelling-house for the purposes of Part IV of the Housing Act 1985.[146]

4.3.66 Accordingly, the Act imports the concept of reasonableness in relation to demotion orders that already apply in relation to the making of a possession order, whether outright or suspended, on the grounds of nuisance or annoyance (amongst other grounds), and it is suggested that the case law relating to reasonableness in the context of possession orders will also be applicable in the case of demotion orders.[147]

Notice requirements

4.3.67 In cases where demotion is sought of an assured tenancy, the court may not entertain the proceedings unless the landlord has served the requisite notice on the tenant under the new s 6A(6) of the Housing Act 1988, or the court thinks it just and equitable to dispense with the requirement for such a notice.[148] A notice under s 6A(6) must give particulars of the conduct in respect of which the demotion order is sought, state that the proceedings will not be brought before the date specified in the notice (which must not be before the end of the period of two weeks beginning with the date of service of the notice),[149] and state that the proceedings will not be commenced after 12 months from the date of service of the notice.[150]

4.3.68 The reason for this provision, which is not repeated in relation to the demotion of secure tenancies where the matter of notice is dealt with differently, is not obvious. The notice of seeking possession must be served prior to the taking of possession proceedings, so that if a landlord wished to seek possession and, in the alternative, demotion, it would be necessary to serve a notice under s 8 and s 6A(6) in respect of the different orders sought.

4.3.69 This causes a further anomaly. Where anti-social behaviour is the ground on which possession is sought,[151] possession proceedings may be begun immediately following the service of the s 8 notice.[152] Where, however, a landlord wished to ask the court to consider both possession and demotion, the demotion proceedings cannot be started less than two weeks from the service of the notice.[153] Accordingly, the landlord in this situation would appear to have three not entirely satisfactory options:

(a) wait two weeks before issuing the proceedings together, which may be impracticable where an interim injunction is required as a matter of urgency;

[146] 1996 Act, s 143O.

[147] The case law is too extensive to refer to compendiously here. See eg *Cummings v Danson* [1944] 2 All ER 653, CA; *Newcastle CC v Morrison* (2000) 32 HLR 891, CA; *Lambeth LBC v Howard* [2001] EWCA Civ 468, (2001) 33 HLR 58; *Canterbury CC v Lowe* (2001) 33 HLR 53 for some general statements of the principles to be applied to the exercise of the reasonableness jurisdiction in anti-social behaviour possession cases. It appears that the amendments made to the 'reasonableness' discretion in the context of possession proceedings, by s 16 of the 2003 Act, do not apply in demotion cases.

[148] Housing Act 1988, s 6A(5). [149] ibid, s 6A(7). [150] ibid, s 6A(6).

[151] ibid, Sch 2, Ground 14. [152] ibid, s 8(4). [153] ibid, s 6A(7).

(b) issue the possession proceedings immediately, issue the demotion proceedings two weeks later (incurring another court fee) and then seek an order for the consolidation of the two sets of proceedings; or
(c) issue the two sets of proceedings together immediately on service of the notices and seek the dispensation of the court under s 6A(5)(b) in relation to the failure to give two weeks' notice of the demotion proceedings.

The court may well be sympathetic to an application to dispense with the requirements of the s 6A(6) notice, on the basis that the application for a possession order could be commenced immediately following service of the s 8 notice. Demotion is a less draconian remedy than outright possession and there appears to be no real purpose to be served—and no real protection for the tenant provided—by the s 6A(7) requirement that two weeks' notice is given of the demotion proceedings in cases where possession is also sought. **4.3.70**

Different provision is made with respect to notice of seeking demotion of a secure tenancy. Section 14(3) of the 2003 Act amends s 83 of the Housing Act 1985 (possession proceedings in respect of a secure tenancy may not be entertained unless a notice of seeking possession has been served) so as to apply the requirements of that section to both possession and demotion proceedings. Thus the notice must be in the prescribed form, specify the ground on which the order is sought, and give particulars of that ground.[154] By a new s 83(4A), if the proceedings are for demotion, the s 83 notice must specify the date after which the proceedings may be started and the notice ceases to be in force 12 months after the date so specified. The date specified must not be earlier than that on which the landlord could have terminated the tenancy by notice to quit but for the fact that such notices have no effect under the 1985 Act. This would normally mean that 28 days' notice ending on the last day of a period of the tenancy must be given.[155] **4.3.71**

Where possession is sought on the ground of anti-social behaviour,[156] possession proceedings may be commenced immediately following the service of the s 83 notice.[157] The issue raised at para 4.3.69 above therefore arises in relation to proceedings for possession and/or demotion of secure tenancies, but in a slightly different form from that concerning assured tenancies. Unlike the position relating to assured tenancies, the position appears to be that the same s 83 notice can seek possession and demotion of the tenancy. By s 83(2)(b) as amended by the 2003 Act, the notice must specify the ground for seeking possession or demotion of the tenancy; the word 'ground' is used to describe both the ground for possession[158] and also the reason for seeking demotion. **4.3.72**

Given that, by s 83(3), where the anti-social behaviour ground for possession is 'one of the grounds specified in the notice' for any order under s 82(1A), ie a **4.3.73**

[154] Housing Act 1985, s 83(2).
[155] Protection from Eviction Act 1977, s 5.
[156] Housing Act 1985, Sch 2, Ground 2.
[157] ibid, s 83(3)(a).
[158] This is the statutory term used throughout Pt IV of, and Sch 2 to, the Act to refer to the potential bases for claiming possession listed in Sch 2.

possession order or a demotion order, the proceedings may be begun immediately, the argument must be available for landlords that proceedings claiming possession and demotion in the alternative can be begun immediately notwithstanding s 83(4A) and (5), in the same way that they may be begun immediately where anti-social behaviour and one or more other ground(s) are relied on to claim possession.

4.3.74 If that is the correct analysis, then the landlords of secure tenancies will be able to issue proceedings claiming both remedies without encountering the problems identified in relation to assured tenancies above.[159] If this is not accepted by the courts, however, then the same issue will arise. Possession proceedings can be commenced immediately on service of the notice but demotion proceedings cannot be commenced until 28 days later. The options available to landlords would, in that event, appear to be identical with those suggested at para 4.3.69 above.

Effect of demotion on secure tenancies

4.3.75 The effect of a demotion order is to terminate the pre-existing tenancy and create a new demoted tenancy. As with demotion procedure, however, the precise effects of a demotion order differ between secure and assured tenancies. More than this, demoted secure tenancies are not all treated identically. A demoted RSL secure tenancy is in a different position to any other kind of tenancy, whether secure or assured, in that it is treated—in terms of some of the effects of demotion—as if it were an assured tenancy and, therefore, differently from demoted secure tenancies of local authorities or housing action trusts.[160]

All secure tenancies

4.3.76 In the case of any secure tenancy, the demotion order terminates the secure tenancy with effect from the date specified in the order. If the tenant remains in occupation of the premises after that date, a 'demoted tenancy' is created with effect from that date. Any rent arrears or credits on the former secure tenant's rent account are to be transferred across to the rent account of the new demoted tenancy.[161]

4.3.77 The parties to the old secure tenancy, the period of that tenancy, and the amount of the rent and the dates on which it is payable are statutorily preserved and imported into the demoted tenancy, with the exception that if the secure tenancy was for a fixed term, the demoted tenancy will be a weekly periodic tenancy, otherwise the purpose of demotion would be defeated as a fixed term demoted tenancy would not be determinable other than for cause prior to the term's expiration.[162]

---

[159] See paras 4.3.69–4.3.70 above.

[160] By Housing Act 1985, s 82A(8), Sch 1 to the 2003 Act inserting a new Ch 1A into Pt V of the Housing Act 1996 does not apply to RSL secure tenancies but only to local authority and housing action trust secure tenancies. RSL secure tenancies are instead governed by the new s 20B of the Housing Act 1988, inserted by s 15(1) of the 2003 Act.

[161] Housing Act 1985, s 82A(3).

[162] ibid, s 82A(5)–(6).

The landlord may also serve on the tenant a statement of other express terms of the secure tenancy that are to apply to the demoted tenancy. This would appear to be the anticipated normal course. The landlord would presumably wish many of the tenant's covenants contained in the former secure tenancy to apply to the demoted tenancy although not all of the tenant's rights. It would, for example, not be appropriate to provide for the right to buy, or the right to exchange or succeed to a tenancy, particularly as these matters are dealt with statutorily in relation to demoted (former secure) tenancies.[163] Repairing obligations on the landlord implied by s 11 of the Landlord and Tenant Act 1985 will continue.[164] It would appear that the landlord cannot include a term in a statement of terms served on the tenant which was not a term of the former secure tenancy. **4.3.78**

Local authority and housing action trust demoted tenancies only

Section 14(5) of the 2003 Act applies the provisions of Sch 1 to the demoted secure tenancy regime. Schedule 1 itself inserts a new Chapter 1A into Part V of the Housing Act 1996 (Conduct of Tenants). The location there of these new provisions is not accidental. The pre-existing Chapter 1 of Part V made provision for 'introductory' tenancies (12-month probationary tenancies for new tenants) upon which provisions the detailed demoted tenancy regime has plainly been modelled. This regime applies to 'demoted tenancies' which fall within new s 82A(8) of the Housing Act 1985[165] and new s 143A of the 1996 Act,[166] namely periodic tenancies in relation to which the landlord is a local authority or housing action trust, the tenant condition set out in s 81 of the Housing Act 1985 is satisfied,[167] and the tenancy has been created by virtue of a demotion order under s 82A of the Housing Act 1985. **4.3.79**

Duration of demoted tenancy A demoted tenancy will normally remain demoted for a period of one year from the date on which the demotion order takes effect (the 'demotion period'), following which it will become a secure tenancy, except in any of the following circumstances: **4.3.80**

(a) either the landlord ceases to be a local authority or a housing action trust, or the tenant ceases to satisfy the tenant condition in s 81 of the Housing Act 1985. This could occur, for example, on a local authority stock transfer to a housing association, or if the tenant moved out of the premises so that it was no longer his/her only or principal home;
(b) the demotion order is quashed; or
(c) the tenant dies and there is no one entitled to succeed to the tenancy.[168]

---

[163] See ibid, ss 143G–143M. See also 2003 Act, Sch 1, para 2.

[164] A demoted tenancy is still a tenancy and qualifies as a short lease for the purposes of the covenant implied by s 11.

[165] Inserted by 2003 Act, s 14(2).

[166] Inserted by ibid, s 14(5) and Sch 1.

[167] ie the tenant is an individual and occupies the dwelling as his only or principal home; or, where the tenancy is a joint tenancy, each of the joint tenants is an individual and at least one of them occupies the dwelling as his only or principal home: Housing Act 1985, s 81.

[168] Housing Act 1996, s 143B(2). See also paras 4.3.96–4.3.110 below.

4.3.81 Conversely, if the landlord serves a notice of proceedings for possession of the dwelling during the demotion period, the tenancy remains demoted, even after the end of the demotion period, until the notice is withdrawn by the landlord, the possession proceedings are determined in favour of the tenant, or six months elapses from the date of service of the notice and no proceedings for possession have been brought.[169]

4.3.82 A tenancy does not come to an end merely because it ceases to be a demoted tenancy.[170] Accordingly, it is necessary to consider each scenario in which a tenancy ceases to be a demoted tenancy in order to ascertain the status of the tenancy. Where the demotion order is quashed, for example,[171] it would seem that the former secure tenancy will revive as the order demoting it will, ex hypothesi, have been removed and so will provide no lawful authority for the removal of the security of tenure. Where the tenant dies and there is no one entitled to succeed,[172] the tenancy will become a bare contractual tenancy that may be determined by notice to quit served on the Public Trustee Office. This will also be the position if the tenant ceases to satisfy the tenancy condition under s 81 of the Housing Act 1985.[173] Where a notice of possession proceedings is served but withdrawn or no proceedings are brought within six months, or such proceedings are resolved in favour of the tenant, the tenancy will mature into a new secure tenancy following the end of the demotion period, as usual.[174]

4.3.83 *Change of landlord* The status of the demoted tenancy on a change of landlord depends on the status of the new landlord. If the new landlord is also a local authority or housing action trust, the tenancy remains demoted[175] and will therefore become secure on the expiration of the demotion period unless action to terminate it before then has been taken. If the new landlord is not an RSL and satisfies the landlord condition in s 80 of the Housing Act 1985,[176] the tenancy will become secure.[177] Section 143C(2)–(3) provides that if the new landlord is an RSL or a person who does not satisfy the landlord condition in s 80 of the 1985 Act, the tenancy becomes an assured shorthold tenancy. The section does not, however, specify whether this is a demoted assured shorthold tenancy, ie one that will become assured after the 12 month demotion period,[178] or simply a periodic assured shorthold tenancy under Chapter II of the Housing Act 1988 which will remain an assured shorthold until termination.

---

[169] Housing Act 1996, s 143B(3)–(4). [170] ibid, s 143B(5). [171] ibid, s 143B(2)(b).
[172] ibid, s 143B(2)(c). [173] ibid, s 143B(2)(a). [174] ibid, s 143B(1), (3)–(4).
[175] ibid, s 143C(1).
[176] The landlord condition specified in s 80(1) of the 1985 Act is that the landlord is: (a) a local authority; (b) a new town corporation; (c) a housing action trust; (d) an urban development corporation; or (e) a housing co-operative within the meaning of s 27B of the 1985 Act (agreements under certain superseded provisions) where the dwelling-house in question is comprised in a housing co-operative agreement within the meaning of that section. See also s 4 of the 1985 Act for further definitions of these bodies.
[177] ibid, s 143C(3). [178] Housing Act 1988, s 20B(2).

It would appear that the former possibility most probably represents the intention of Parliament, given that (a) the transfer of the landlord's interest to one of the other categories of new landlord specified in s 143C either restores full security of tenure immediately or else preserves the right to the restoration of security on the expiry of the demotion period (there seems to be no reason of principle why transfer to an RSL or other landlord not satisfying the landlord condition should be different in this respect); and (b) it is a deliberate feature of this new statutory scheme for demotion of tenancies that the tenancy does not remain demoted forever. It would be surprising if Parliament had intended to make an exception to that principle solely in cases of local authority or housing action trust former secure tenancies where, during the demotion period, the interest of the landlord happens to be transferred to one specific type of new landlord. **4.3.84**

Terminating a local authority or housing action trust demoted tenancy

Sections 143D–143F of the 1996 Act prescribe the procedure by which a demoted tenancy may be terminated. In essence, the court has very limited discretion to refuse a possession order if one is sought by a landlord, and may only do so if it considers that the landlord has failed properly to follow the procedure set out in ss 143E (requirement to serve a notice of proceedings) and 143F (requirement to carry out a review of decision to seek possession). This procedure is plainly based on that for determining introductory tenancies[179] but with one key difference: the court can refuse to award possession of a dwelling held under a demoted tenancy (but not under an introductory tenancy[180]) if the landlord has not properly followed the procedure for reviewing the decision to terminate the tenancy, if requested by the tenant to carry out such a review.[181] **4.3.85**

Notice of proceedings Proceedings may not be brought for a possession order unless a notice of proceedings in accordance with s 143E has been served on the tenant.[182] The notice must comply with the following requirements,[183] namely it must: **4.3.86**

(a) state that the court will be asked to make an order for the possession of the dwelling-house;
(b) set out the reasons for the landlord's decision to apply for the order;
(c) specify the date after which proceedings for possession of the dwelling-house may be begun;
(d) inform the tenant of his/her right to request a review of the landlord's decision and of the time within which the request may be made;
(e) state that if the tenant needs help or advice about the notice, or about what to do about it, s/he must immediately take the notice to a Citizens' Advice Bureau, a housing aid centre or a solicitor.[184]

---

179 Housing Act 1996, Pt V, Ch 1.
180 ibid, s 127(2).
181 ibid, s 143D(2).
182 ibid, s 143E(1).
183 ibid, s 143E(2).
184 ibid, s 143E(5).

4.3.87 The date specified as that after which possession proceedings may be begun must not be earlier than the date on which the tenancy could be brought to an end by a notice to quit given by the landlord on the same date as the notice of proceedings, ie 28 days and ending on the last day of a period of the tenancy.[185] If proceedings are begun before that date, the court is not permitted to entertain them.[186]

4.3.88 *Review of decision to seek possession* The tenant has 14 days from the date of service of the notice of proceedings to request the landlord to review its decision to seek possession of the property.[187] If such a request is made, the review must be carried out in accordance with the procedure set out in regulations that may be made by the Secretary of State. That procedure will include provisions that the decision on review must be made by a person of appropriate seniority who was not connected with the original decision, and as to the circumstances in which the tenant may be entitled to attend an oral hearing, with or without representation.[188] The decision on the review and the reasons for that decision must be notified to the tenant.[189]

4.3.89 The review must have been carried out and the decision and reasons notified to the tenant before the date specified in the notice of proceedings as the date after which possession proceedings may be begun.[190] The Act does not state the consequences of a failure by the landlord to comply with this requirement. In particular, if only 28 days' notice of the issue of proceedings is given in the notice, and if a request for a review is not received until the end of the 14 day period allowed, and if an oral hearing with representation is to be held, it is highly unlikely that the requirement for the review to be completed and the result notified to the tenant prior to the date specified in the notice will be met.

4.3.90 It seems unlikely that a failure to carry out and notify the decision on the review will invalidate subsequent possession proceedings, so long as the proceedings are not commenced prior to the conclusion of the review process. The purpose of the requirement to complete the review process prior to the date specified in the notice as the date after which proceedings may be commenced is to prevent the issue of proceedings before the review process—which may cause the landlord to change its mind—has been concluded. Where that purpose is complied with, and the proceedings are not issued until after the review has been determined and the result notified to the tenant, the court hearing any subsequent possession proceedings would be likely to regard the requirement to complete the review process prior to the date specified in the notice as a merely 'directory' rather than a 'mandatory' requirement, failure to comply with which

[185] Housing Act 1996, Pt V, Ch 1, s 143E(3).
[186] ibid, s 143E(4).
[187] ibid, s 143F(1).
[188] ibid, s 143F(2)–(4).
[189] ibid, s 143F(5).
[190] ibid, s 143F(6).

had not caused any prejudice to the tenant and which would not invalidate the proceedings.[191]

It is the county court that will determine this issue, not the Administrative Court in judicial review proceedings. Judicial review is not appropriate to challenge decisions on review or the failure to comply with any other aspect of the review procedure, as the county court hearing possession proceedings has expressly been conferred with jurisdiction to deal with them, unlike the position concerning introductory tenancies. This is made clear by s 143D(2) which provides that the court is not obliged to make an order for possession if it thinks that the review procedure has not been followed, and is confirmed by s 143N(1) which provides that the county court has jurisdiction, inter alia, to determine questions arising under Chapter 1A of Part V of the 1996 Act. Indeed, costs penalties are applied if a person takes proceedings in the High Court that he could have taken in the county court; no costs may be recovered in such circumstances.[192] **4.3.91**

The effect of possession proceedings It will be recalled that if a landlord served a notice of proceedings within the 12 month demotion period, the tenancy remains demoted until the notice is withdrawn, the possession proceedings are determined in favour of the tenant, or six months pass after the service of the notice without proceedings being issued.[193] **4.3.92**

If proceedings are issued, but the demotion period ends or the tenancy ceases to be a demoted tenancy for one of the other reasons set out at s 143B(2),[194] the landlord may continue the proceedings. **4.3.93**

The right to buy If, while possession proceedings are pending, the tenancy ceases to be a demoted tenancy and becomes a secure tenancy,[195] the tenant is not entitled to exercise the right to buy unless and until the proceedings are finally determined and the tenant is not required to give up possession of the dwelling-house. Proceedings are 'finally determined' if they are withdrawn, any appeal is abandoned or the time for appealing has expired without an appeal having been brought.[196] **4.3.94**

Once a demoted tenancy has matured into a secure tenancy, following the expiration of the demotion period, the right to buy will be available to the **4.3.95**

[191] See, for cases concerning mandatory and directory requirements, eg *London & Clydeside Estates v Aberdeen DC* [1981] 1 WLR 182, HL, *per* Lord Hailsham of St Marylebone at 189–190; *Secretary of State for Trade and Industry v Langridge* [1991] 3 All ER 591, CA; *Haringey LBC v Awaratife* (1999) 32 HLR 517, CA. For an introduction to the issues of public law invalidity including 'mandatory' and 'directory' requirements, see Manning, *Judicial Review Proceedings, A Practitioners' Guide* (2nd edn, LAG, 2004).

[192] 1996 Act, s 143N(4).

[193] ibid, s 143B(4).

[194] ie the landlord ceases to be a local authority or housing action trust, or the tenant condition ceases to be satisfied, or the tenant dies without there being any successor.

[195] ie under s 143C(4).

[196] 1996 Act, s 143G(4)–(5).

tenant once again, but time spent as a demoted tenancy does not count either towards the right to buy qualifying period or towards the discount.[197]

Rights of succession

4.3.96 *Tenant already a successor* New ss 143H–143J of the 1996 Act provide a set of rules concerning rights of succession to a demoted local authority or housing action trust tenancy.

4.3.97 If the tenant under the demoted tenancy was himself a successor (either to the secure tenancy which was demoted or to the demoted tenancy itself) the tenancy ceases to be demoted but does not become a secure tenancy.[198] In other words, the tenancy continues as a contractual tenancy which may be terminated by the landlord by notice to quit, and the possibility of the tenancy becoming secure is lost, as the tenancy ceases to be demoted. This reflects the position as regards secure tenancies where, if the secure tenant was already a successor, there is no further right to succeed to the tenancy.[199]

4.3.98 A person is treated as a successor to a secure tenancy if:

(a) the tenancy vested in him by virtue of s 89 of the Housing Act 1985 (ie as a secure tenancy) or s 133 of the Housing Act 1996 (ie as an introductory tenancy) or under the will or intestacy of the preceding tenant;[200] or
(b) the tenancy arose under s 86 of the Housing Act 1985 (automatic periodic tenancy arising on expiration of fixed term) and the original fixed term tenancy was granted to another person or to him jointly with another person;[201] or
(c) he became a tenant by taking an assignment of the tenancy, unless the assignment was made in matrimonial proceedings[202] and neither he nor the other party to the marriage was a successor;[203] or
(d) he became the tenant on an assignment under s 92 of the Housing Act 1985 (assignment by way of mutual exchange) if he was a successor to the tenancy which he assigned in exchange.[204]

4.3.99 A person is a successor to a demoted tenancy if the tenancy vested in him by virtue of the provisions of s 143H(4) or (5), as to which, see below.[205] A joint tenant who, on the death of another joint tenant, has become a sole tenant under the right of survivorship is also a successor.[206]

4.3.100 *Qualification to succeed* If the tenant under the demoted tenancy was not a successor, then a right of succession exists to a person qualified to succeed to the

[197] 2003 Act, Sch 1, para 2(5), inserting a new para 9A into Sch 4 to the Housing Act 1985.
[198] 1996 Act, s 143H(2).
[199] Housing Act 1985, ss 87–88.
[200] Housing Act 1996, s 143J(2) and (3).
[201] ibid, s 143J(2) and (4).
[202] ie under ss 23A or 24 of the Matrimonial Causes Act 1973 (property adjustment orders in connection with matrimonial proceedings); or s 17(1) of the Matrimonial and Family Proceedings Act 1984 (property adjustment orders after overseas divorce etc).
[203] Housing Act 1996, s 143J(2) and (5).
[204] ibid, s 143J(2) and (6).
[205] ibid, s 143J(7). See para 4.3.106 below.
[206] 1996 Act, s 143J(8).

tenancy. A person is qualified to succeed if all three of the following conditions are satisfied:

(a) the person occupied the dwelling-house as his only or principal home[207] at the time of the tenant's death;
(b) he is a member of the tenant's family; and
(c) he has resided with the tenant throughout the period of 12 months ending with the tenant's death.[208]

'Member of the tenant's family' is defined so as expressly to include gay and lesbian and unmarried partners in an enduring family relationship with the deceased tenant and, importantly, places them in a position equivalent to that of a spouse so that, if there is more than one family member qualified to succeed, they will take automatic priority.[209] Stepchildren, half-blood relations and those related by marriage are also included as family members. By s 143P(1), a person is a member of another person's family if: 4.3.101

(a) he is the spouse of that person;
(b) he and that person live together as a couple in an enduring family relationship, but he does not fall within para (c);
(c) he is that person's parent, grandparent, child, grandchild, brother, sister, uncle, aunt, nephew or niece.

For the purposes of (b) above, it is immaterial that two persons living together in an enduring family relationship are of the same sex.[210] For the purposes of (c) above, a relationship by marriage must be treated as a relationship by blood; a relationship of the half-blood must be treated as a relationship of the whole blood; and a stepchild of a person must be treated as a child.[211] 4.3.102

The requirement that, to be qualified to succeed, a person must have resided with the tenant throughout the period of 12 months ending with the tenant's death, reflects that applicable to the succession of non-spouses to secure tenancies under s 87 of the 1985 Act. In relation to demoted tenancies, however, as distinct from secure tenancies,[212] even a spouse must establish that s/he satisfies the residence qualification. 4.3.103

'Residing with' has been held, albeit in the slightly different context of succession to a Rent Act statutory tenancy, to mean more than 'living or staying at' the premises, although not necessarily so much as residing permanently or indefinitely.[213] In this context, however—in common with the provisions 4.3.104

[207] See para 4.2.6 above.
[208] ibid, s 143H(3).
[209] See para 4.3.106 below. In the unusual situation where the deceased tenant had a spouse and one or more other partners, all of whom lived together in an enduring relationship for the 12 months prior to the tenant's death, the spouse would be entitled to succeed to the tenancy in preference to the unmarried partner. (Whether the court would be prepared to construe 'enduring family relationship' to include all the partners in the above scenario remains to be seen.)
[210] 1996 Act, s 143P(2).
[211] ibid, s 143P(3).
[212] 1985 Act, s 87.
[213] *Swanbrae v Elliott* (1987) 19 HLR 86.

concerning secure tenancies—the requirement is that the residence must have been 'throughout' the 12 month period, which entails something closer to permanent residence. The 12 months' residence must have been with the deceased tenant but not necessarily for all of that period in the property succession to the tenancy of which is sought.[214]

4.3.105 A period of absence has also been held not necessarily to break the continuity of residence, but the nature and extent of the continuing connection with the premises throughout the period of absence and the quality of the intention to return will plainly be relevant.[215] Normal periods of absence, however, such as for a holiday, will not result in the loss of the right to succeed. Whether an absence is such as to preclude the prospective successor establishing the residence condition would appear to be a matter of fact and degree for the court.[216]

4.3.106 *Someone qualified to succeed* If only one person is qualified to succeed, the tenancy vests in him by virtue of s 143H of the 1996 Act.[217] If more than one person is qualified to succeed, the tenancy will vest, by virtue of the section, in the tenant's spouse or, if the tenant had no spouse, the person with whom he lived as a couple in an enduring family relationship and who is not a parent, grandparent, child, grandchild, brother, sister, uncle, aunt, nephew or niece, in preference to any other potential successor.[218]

4.3.107 Otherwise, if there are two or more other members of the tenant's family qualified to succeed, none of whom is a spouse or enduring partner, the successor may be chosen by the agreement of all the potential successors or, if they cannot agree, selected by the landlord.[219]

4.3.108 *No one qualified to succeed* If the demoted tenant dies and no one is qualified to succeed, the tenancy ceases to be demoted if it is vested or otherwise disposed of in the course of the administration of the tenant's estate unless the vesting or other disposal is in pursuance of an order under:

(a) ss 23A or 24 of the Matrimonial Causes Act 1973 (property adjustment orders in connection with matrimonial proceedings);
(b) s 17(1) of the Matrimonial and Family Proceedings Act 1984 (property adjustment orders after overseas divorce, etc); or
(c) Sch 1, para 1 to the Children Act 1989 (orders for financial relief against parents).[220]

4.3.109 The tenancy also ceases to be demoted if it is known that, when the tenancy is vested or otherwise disposed of in the course of the administration of the tenant's estate, it will not be in pursuance of an order under one of the provisions referred to above.[221] This provision appears to have been inserted so as to

[214] *Waltham Forest LBC v Thomas* [1992] 2 AC 198, HL.

[215] *Camden LBC v Goldenburg* [1997] 1 FLR 556, CA.

[216] See the authorities referred to in the previous two footnotes.

[217] ibid, s 143H(4).

[218] ibid, ss 143H(5)(a) and 143P(1)(b)–(c).

[219] ibid, s 143H(5)(b).

[220] ibid, s 143I(3).

[221] ibid, s 143I(4).

permit the landlord to terminate the tenancy by notice to quit (it having ceased to be demoted) and recover possession of it without needing to wait for its disposal in the course of the administration of the tenant's estate, if it is known beforehand that any such disposal will not be made under any of the types of property adjustment order in family proceedings, referred to above, which will preserve the demoted status of the tenancy.

If the tenancy ceases to be demoted due to the death of the tenant and the absence of any qualifying successor, it cannot subsequently become secure.[222] **4.3.110**

Miscellaneous provisions

Assignment A demoted tenancy, like a secure tenancy, is not capable of being assigned save in specific circumstances.[223] Those circumstances are even more limited in the case of a demoted tenancy, however, than as regards a secure tenancy; the only permissible assignment being where it is made in pursuance of a court order made in specified matrimonial or family proceedings.[224] Accordingly, no assignment is permissible, as would be the case if the tenancy were secure, by way of mutual exchange or to a person who would be qualified to succeed.[225] **4.3.111**

Right to repair Section 96 of the 1985 Act confers power on the Secretary of State, by regulations, to permit secure tenants of local housing authorities to require their landlords to carry out certain 'qualifying' repair works within a prescribed period, failing which, the tenant may require the landlord to appoint a different contractor and to pay compensation. This power has been exercised by the Secretary of State, in the Secure Tenants of Local Authorities (Right to Repair) Regulations 1994.[226] New s 143L of the 1996 Act enables the Secretary of State, by regulations, to apply those provisions to demoted tenants as they apply to secure tenants. He does not have power to make different provision in relation to demoted and secure tenancies.[227] **4.3.112**

Provision of information A local housing authority and housing action trust landlord of a demoted tenancy must publish from time to time, and so far as reasonably practicable keep up to date,[228] information about the demoted tenancy 'in such form as it thinks best suited to explain in simple terms and so far as it considers appropriate' the effect of: **4.3.113**

(a) the express terms of the tenancy;
(b) the provisions of Chapter 1A of Part V of the 1996 Act;
(c) the landlord's implied repairing obligations under ss 11–16 of the Landlord and Tenant Act 1985.[229]

---

[222] ibid, s 143I(5).
[223] ibid, s 143K.
[224] Matrimonial Causes Act 1973, s 24; Matrimonial and Family Proceedings Act 1984, s 17(1); Children Act 1989, Sch 1, para 1: see 1996 Act, s 143K(2).
[225] 1985 Act, ss 91–94.
[226] SI 1994/133.
[227] 1996 Act, s 143L.
[228] ibid, s 143M(3).
[229] ibid, s 143M(1)–(2).

4.3.114 The landlord must supply the tenant with a copy of such information and a written statement of terms of the tenancy which are not expressed in the lease or written tenancy agreement, nor implied by law. The statement must be supplied on the grant of the demoted tenancy or as soon as practicable afterwards.[230]

4.3.115 *County court jurisdiction* Section 143N provides that the county court has jurisdiction to:

(a) determine questions arising under Chapter 1A;
(b) entertain proceedings brought under the Chapter;
(c) determine claims (for whatever amount) in connection with a demoted tenancy;[231] and
(d) entertain proceedings as to whether a written statement of the terms of the tenancy, which has been supplied to the tenant under s 143M(4)(b), is accurate,[232] and it is immaterial that no relief other than a declaration is sought.[233]

4.3.116 If a person brings proceedings in the High Court which he could have brought in the county court, he is not entitled to recover any costs.[234]

4.3.117 As stated above,[235] and as s 143N also shows, the scheme of these provisions is clearly to require issues arising under them to be litigated in the county court rather than, as is the case with introductory tenancies, by way of judicial review in the High Court. Indeed, in proceedings for possession of a property held under a demoted tenancy—as distinct from such proceedings concerning a property let under an introductory tenancy[236]—the county court may entertain a defence by the tenant that the review procedure set out in s 143F was not followed.[237]

4.3.118 This raises the issue whether the county court may also entertain a defence that although the procedural requirements were followed, the result of the review was wrong. It appears that the provisions do not go this far, as to permit the county court to entertain a defence that, on the merits, the landlord should have decided not to seek possession because, for example, it ought to have rejected further allegations of anti-social behaviour, would be to deprive the demoted tenancy regime of its principal effect—namely that the landlord does not have to establish a ground for possession in order to recover possession of the property.

4.3.119 If, on the other hand, the tenant wished to raise a defence alleging that the landlord's decision and/or review process was flawed as a matter of public law, whether because it was perverse or because, for example, the landlord was acting for improper purposes, failed to take account of relevant considerations, took account of irrelevant ones, breached the principles of procedural fairness

[230] 1996 Act, s 143M(4)–(5). [231] ibid, s 143N(1). [232] ibid, s 143N(2).
[233] ibid, s 143N(3).
[234] ibid, s 143N(4). This mirrors the provisions of 1985 Act, s 110(3) as regards secure tenancies.
[235] See paras 4.3.91–4.3.92. [236] See 1996 Act, s 127. [237] ibid, s 143D.

etc, it would seem that, in principle, such matters could be raised by way of defence, given:

(a) the construction of s 143N (including the costs penalties for bringing High Court proceedings);
(b) the construction of Chapter 1A as a whole, including, specifically, the differences between its provisions concerning the court's powers and those of Chapter 1 (which immediately precedes it) relating to introductory tenancies; and
(c) the principles of public law in cases such as *Anisminic v Foreign Compensation Commission*,[238] which established the principle that all public law errors will take a body outside its jurisdiction, and *Wandsworth LBC v Winder*,[239] which held that a public law defence linked to a private law defence on the merits may be raised in private law proceedings. In this context, the court may refuse a possession order—and so enable the tenant to retain his/her home—if it thinks that the requirements of notice and review provided in the Act have not been followed.

Each of the factors referred to above would seem to make it possible to distinguish the demoted tenant's position from that of the introductory tenant who, as held by the Court of Appeal in *Manchester CC v Cochrane*,[240] may not raise such issues as a defence to the possession proceedings, but can only seek to have them adjourned pending an application for judicial review. **4.3.120**

The Lord Chancellor (or, presumably, the Secretary of State for Constitutional Affairs) is given power to make rules and directions to give effect to the county court's jurisdiction, including for its exercise by a district judge and/or in private.[241] **4.3.121**

Consequential amendments Various consequential amendments are made to the Housing Act 1985. Section 105 of that Act is amended so that the requirement to consult secure tenants on housing management issues is extended to include demoted tenants.[242] Schedule 1 is amended to include demoted tenancies among the list of tenancies that cannot be secure tenancies,[243] and the right to buy and preserved right to buy provisions are amended so that a period of demotion does not count towards qualification for the right to buy or the calculation of discount,[244] and a person ceases to have a preserved right to buy if his tenancy becomes a demoted tenancy.[245] **4.3.122**

---

[238] [1969] 2 AC 147, HL. [239] [1985] AC 465, HL. [240] [1999] 1 WLR 809, CA.

[241] 1996 Act, s 143N(5)–(6). The rules and directions-making power must be exercised by statutory instrument using the negative resolution procedure.

[242] 2003 Act, Sch 1, para 2(2), inserting a new s 105(7) into the 1985 Act.

[243] ibid, Sch 1, para 2(4), inserting a new para 1B into Sch 1 to the 1985 Act.

[244] ibid, Sch 1, para 2(5), inserting a new para 9A into Sch 4 to the 1985 Act.

[245] ibid, Sch 1, para 2(3), inserting a new s 171B(1A) into the 1985 Act.

Registered Social Landlord secure tenancies

4.3.123 Demoted RSL secure tenancies are treated in the same way as demoted RSL assured tenancies. New s 20B of the Housing Act 1988, inserted into that Act by s 15 of the 2003 Act, applies to both types of demoted tenancy.[246]

Effect of demotion on assured tenancies

4.3.124 As is the case with a demotion order made in respect of a secure tenancy, a demotion order brings the assured tenancy to an end on the date specified in the order. If the tenant remains in occupation after that date, a new demoted tenancy is created with effect from that date.[247] Any rent arrears or credits existing at the termination of the assured tenancy are to be transferred to the new demoted tenancy.[248]

4.3.125 Likewise, the parties to the tenancy, the period of the tenancy, the amount of the rent and the dates on which it is payable are statutorily preserved and imported into the demoted tenancy, with the exception that if the secure tenancy was for a fixed term, the demoted tenancy will be a weekly periodic tenancy, otherwise the purpose of demotion would be defeated as a fixed term demoted tenancy would not be determinable other than for cause prior to the term's expiration.[249]

4.3.126 If the landlord of the demoted tenancy serves on the tenant a statement of any express terms of the assured tenancy which are to apply to the demoted tenancy then such terms will become terms of the demoted tenancy.[250] A formerly assured demoted tenancy is a tenancy to which new s 20B of the 1988 Act applies.[251]

4.3.127 Section 15 of the 2003 Act inserts a new s 20B into the 1988 Act which makes equivalent (though not identical) provision to the new Chapter 1A of the 1996 Act,[252] concerning the issues discussed above in relation to secure tenancies (see paras 4.3.81–4.3.94).

4.3.128 If the landlord is an RSL, a tenancy demoted by virtue of an order of the court under either s 82A of the 1985 Act or s 6A of the 1988 Act becomes a 'demoted assured shorthold tenancy', usually for a period of one year. At the end of that period, it ceases to be an assured shorthold tenancy and becomes an assured tenancy unless, before the end of the demotion period, the landlord has given notice of proceedings for possession of the dwelling-house (ie under s 21(4) of the 1988 Act).[253]

4.3.129 It seems, from the scheme of ss 14 and 15 of the 2003 Act, that a secure RSL tenancy, if demoted, does not at the end of the demotion period become a secure tenancy but an assured tenancy. It is clear from new s 82A(8)(b) of the 1985 Act[254]

---

[246] See 1985 Act, s 82A(8)(b), so far as demoted RSL secure tenancies are concerned; 1988 Act, s 6A(11), concerning assured tenancies.

[247] 1988 Act, s 6A(3)(a) and (b).

[248] ibid, s 6A(3)(c)–(d). See para 4.3.76 above in relation to secure tenancies.

[249] ibid, s 6A(8)–(9).

[250] ibid, s 6A(10). See para 4.3.78 above. The giving of a statement of terms is likely to be important.

[251] ibid, s 6A(11).

[252] Inserted into that Act by 2003 Act, Sch 1, para 1.

[253] 1988 Act, s 20B(2)–(3) and 2003 Act, s 15(3).

[254] Inserted by 2003 Act, s 14.

that an RSL secure tenancy, when demoted, becomes an assured shorthold tenancy. Such a tenancy is described in the new s 20B(1) of the 1988 Act as 'an assured tenancy' which 'is an assured shorthold tenancy to which this section applies'. Section 15(3) of the 2003 Act inserts a new para 5A into Sch 2A to the 1988 Act so as to include within the category of assured tenancies that are not shorthold tenancies 'an assured tenancy which ceases to be an assured shorthold tenancy by virtue of section 20B(2) or (4)'.

This would seem to accord with the feature of demotion that the demoted tenancy is a new tenancy and not a continuation of the former secure or assured tenancy. As a new tenancy granted by an RSL, it would not normally be capable of taking effect as a secure tenancy after 15 January 1989,[255] and so would generally be an assured tenancy of some description. Thus by means of demotion, it appears that the tenant will fall out of the 1985 Act scheme of security of tenure permanently; if and when security of tenure is reapplied to the tenancy, it will be under the 1988 Act, which may well constitute a less favourable regime for the tenant. **4.3.130**

Terminating a demoted assured shorthold tenancy

If notice of proceedings is served by the landlord during the demotion period, the tenancy continues to be a demoted assured shorthold tenancy until either the one year demotion period expires or, if later, one of the following occurs: **4.3.131**

(a) the notice is withdrawn;
(b) the proceedings are determined in favour of the tenant;
(c) the period of six months since the service of the notice comes to an end without any possession proceedings having been brought.[256]

Section 15(2) of the 2003 Act inserts new s 21(5A) into the 1988 Act. The effect of this is to disapply the normal rule[257] that a possession order granted on the basis that the landlord has given notice under s 21(4) of the 1988 Act cannot take effect within the first six months of the tenancy. **4.3.132**

What can be seen is that the demoted tenant whose tenancy was assured, or the demoted tenant of an RSL whether the tenancy was assured or secure, does not have the right that is granted to a demoted tenant of a local housing authority or housing action trust,[258] ie to seek a review of the decision to seek possession of the property. Although some RSLs may include a contractual right of review in their tenancy agreement, or operate a voluntary review process, formally under the Act, the position is that once the notice under s 21 of the 1988 Act has been properly served, the tenant has no means of resisting a possession order in the county court. The court has no power to refuse a possession order where the premises possession of which is sought is let on an assured shorthold **4.3.133**

[255] 1988 Act, s 38.
[256] ibid, s 20B(4).
[257] ibid, s 21(5) (inserted by 1996 Act, s 99).
[258] See 1996 Act, s 143D–F.

tenancy. Nor is it yet clear that judicial review would be available to challenge a decision of an RSL to take possession in these circumstances.[259]

Discretion in possession proceedings: anti-social behaviour

4.3.134 Schedule 2 to the 1985 Act sets out the grounds upon which a landlord under a secure tenancy may seek an order for possession against a secure tenant. Ground 2 (as amended by s 144 of the 1996 Act) provides a ground for possession where a tenant or any member of the tenant's household, or a visitor to the property, has:

(a) been guilty of conduct which is, or is likely to cause a nuisance or annoyance to a person residing, visiting or otherwise engaging in lawful activity in the locality, or
(b) . . . been convicted of:
  (i) using the dwelling-house or allowing it to be used for immoral or illegal purposes, or
  (ii) an arrestable offence committed in, or in the locality of, the dwelling-house.

4.3.135 Such conduct also amounts to a ground for possession against assured tenants, specified in Ground 14 of Sch 2 to the 1988 Act.

The court's discretion

4.3.136 Section 16 of the 2003 Act introduces identical new ss 85A and 9A into, respectively, the 1985 and the 1988 Acts to oblige the court, when considering whether it is reasonable to grant an order for possession on Ground 2 or, under the 1988 Act, Ground 14,[260] to consider, in particular:

(a) the effect that the nuisance or annoyance has had on persons other than the person against whom the order is sought;
(b) any continuing effect the nuisance or annoyance is likely to have on such persons;
(c) the effect that the nuisance or annoyance would be likely to have on such persons if the conduct is repeated.

4.3.137 This attempt to impose a structure on the exercise of the court's reasonableness jurisdiction adds, in one sense, little to the obligations of the court in any event. These considerations are plainly central to the balancing exercise carried out by the court when deciding whether or not to grant a possession order, and

---

[259] Although an RSL may be judicially reviewable in relation to some of its activities (see *Poplar HARCA v Donoghue* [2001] EWCA Civ 595, [2002] QB 48), the *Poplar* decision turned on a number of features particular to the constitution and functions of the RSL in that case. The Court of Appeal commented that the mere provision of accommodation by an RSL would be unlikely to involve public law issues.

[260] But apparently not when considering reasonableness in the context of demotion: s 16(1).

a court which failed to take them into account, and give them appropriate weight, would be failing properly to exercise its discretion.

The purpose of the new provisions appears, however, to go further than to ensure that the court takes these factors into account. The requirement that the court has regard to them 'in particular', coupled with the absence of any reference to the factors to be weighed in the balance on the side of the tenant—for example, the effect of eviction on the tenant's family, including members of the family who may be entirely innocent of the conduct complained of, the needs of any children, issues arising under the Disability Discrimination Act 1995,[261] etc—would appear to indicate an attempt to 'weight' the factors relevant to the exercise of the discretion so that more weight must be given to those that support the making of a possession order. **4.3.138**

Wales

Section 17 of the 2003 Act ensures that all functions of the Secretary of State arising from the amendments to the Housing Acts 1985, 1988 and 1996 that have been discussed above, so far as they are exercisable in relation to Wales, are to be carried out by the National Assembly for Wales. All references to those Acts in Sch 1 to the National Assembly for Wales (Transfer of Functions) Order 1999 are to be treated as references to those Acts as amended by Part 2 of the 2003 Act. **4.3.139**

[261] See eg *North Devon Homes Ltd v Brazier* [2003] EWHC 574, (2003) 6 CCLR 245.

5

PART 3 OF THE ACT: PARENTAL RESPONSIBILITIES

5.1. INTRODUCTION

Parenting contracts

The creation of parenting contracts has been fuelled by a generally widely held belief amongst agencies working with children and young people and their families in relation to disruptive behaviour in school, truancy, criminal conduct, anti-social behaviour and so on, that a structured, early intervention can be crucial in resolving these issues. It has been acknowledged that an imposed solution for families is often not the most effective, a finding of the recent National Evaluation of the Youth Justice Board's Parenting Programme. **5.1.1**

There is, however, an uneasy tension within the professional community between the desire, on the one hand, to see a structured, early intervention, and—on the other—the parenting contract as it appeared in the Anti-Social Behaviour Bill and now appears in statute. The decision to introduce parenting contracts was not without controversy. The Children's Society published a response to the proposals on behalf of the Society and other agencies working in the same field, stating that: **5.1.2**

> we have a number of serious reservations about the status of parenting contracts . . . we are concerned about the coercive nature of these measures.

Liberty, in its response to the proposals, did not voice the same concerns, stating: 'Liberty agrees that the introduction of Parenting Contracts may well be of benefit in addressing problems with truancy before the need for a Parenting Order arises'. **5.1.3**

5.2. CONTEXT

Parenting contracts

5.2.1 Parenting contracts are clearly modelled on acceptable behaviour contracts (ABCs), which were first introduced by Islington LBC in North London as a voluntary measure to deal with young people aged between ten and 17. They constitute an agreement between the local authority or the police, or even a school and the person whose behaviour is causing concern. Unlike parenting contracts themselves, ABCs are not statutory creations and are flexible in terms of content and format. The perpetrator must be prepared voluntarily to admit his anti-social behaviour and agree to abide by a set of terms to prevent that behaviour recurring. An ABC usually lasts for a year although the period may be extended or reduced depending on the circumstances.

5.2.2 ABCs often contain very similar, or even identical, terms to anti-social behaviour orders (ASBOs). They have no legal effect, however, and no sanctions attach to non-compliance. If a contract is breached, the only remedy available may be to apply for an ASBO. The Guidance recommends that, where an ABC is selected as the best option to pursue, it should contain a statement that the continuation of unacceptable behaviour may lead to an application for an ASBO and that where a contract is broken it should be used as evidence in the application for an ASBO. It may also be possible to use evidence of anti-social behaviour that was originally collected for the ABC in any subsequent ASBO application.

5.2.3 The ABC may come with an offer of support to assist the perpetrator in complying with the agreement. ABCs have proved effective in encouraging young people, and sometimes adults, to refrain from such activities as graffiti and verbal abuse.

Parenting orders

5.2.4 Parenting orders are not a new concept. They were introduced by the Crime and Disorder Act 1998, ss 8 and 9, as an order that would assist parents with the improvement of their parenting skills and which could be 'bolted on' to other remedies and sentences granted in respect of anti-social behaviour by children and young people.

5.2.5 By s 8 of the 1998 Act, a parenting order may be made where a child or young person has been convicted of an offence, made subject to an ASBO or a child safety order, or if the parent of the child has been convicted of failing to ensure the regular attendance of the child or young person at school, or to ensure compliance with the terms of an attendance centre order.[1] The court must be sat-

[1] Crime and Disorder Act 1998, s 8(1)(a)–(d).

isfied that the conditions set out in s 8(6) of the 1998 Act are satisfied before exercising its discretion to make such an order, ie it must be satisfied that the order is desirable to prevent the recurrence of the conduct or the commission of further offences.

Section 9 of the 1998 Act requires the court to make a parenting order where a child or young person under the age of 16 is convicted of an offence and the court considers the s 8(6) conditions to be fulfilled (see above). **5.2.6**

Section 324 of and Sch 34 to the Criminal Justice Act 2003 amend these provisions in several respects, primarily relating to the relationship between the imposition of a referral order on a child or young person convicted of an offence, and a parenting order. In cases where the court is considering making both a referral order in respect of a child convicted of an offence and a parenting order, the court must consider a report by an appropriate officer relating to the proposed requirements of the parenting order and why it is considered that they would be desirable in the interests of preventing further offending by the child or young person, together with consideration of the family's circumstances and the effect on those circumstances of making the order.[2] **5.2.7**

The Powers of the Criminal Courts (Sentencing) Act 2000 is also amended,[3] so that the youth court now has power to make a parenting order where, in the context of a referral order, a parent has been ordered to attend meetings of a youth offender panel[4] but has failed to do so.[5] **5.2.8**

Fixed penalty notices

The Criminal Justice and Police Act 2001[6] introduced the fixed penalty notice which could be administered for a range of low-level, nuisance-type offences such as cycling on footpaths, throwing stones at trains, trespassing on the railway, buying a drink for a minor in licensed premises, wasting police time by making a false report, knowingly giving a false alarm to the fire brigade, consuming alcohol in public and so on. The rationale for and effect of such notices are that, if a financial penalty is paid within a specified period, usually 14 days,[7] no criminal proceedings will be brought against the defendant and so s/he will not acquire a criminal record.[8] **5.2.9**

[2] Criminal Justice Act 2003, Sch 34, para 2, amending Crime and Disorder Act 1998, s 9.

[3] ibid, Sch 34, esp para 6.

[4] Powers of the Criminal Courts (Sentencing) Act 2000, s 20.

[5] ibid, Sch 1, paras 9–9F.

[6] s 1(1). Offences may be added to or removed from the list by order of the Secretary of State: 2001 Act, s 1(2).

[7] Anti-Social Behaviour Act 2003, s 43(4)(b).

[8] See also Criminal Justice and Police Act 2001, s 5(2), for notices under which the specified period is 21 days.

5.3. THE PROVISIONS OF PART 3 OF THE ACT

Structure of the Part

5.3.1 Part 3 of the 2003 Act contains 12 sections (ss 18–29). Its subject matter does not, however, follow a numeric sequence. Instead, its provisions deal with three main concepts in which parental responsibility is extended by the Act: parenting contracts, parenting orders and fixed penalties. This chapter will consider each of these concepts in turn.

Aim of the Part

5.3.2 As the title to this Part would suggest, ss 18–29 of the Act provide a package of measures that Parliament intends to be available to those with responsibility for young people who behave anti-socially (in the broadest sense). These measures range from assistance by way of intervention, to coercive penalties, applied by way of punishment. To achieve this range, a voluntary framework of parenting contracts[9] is created, designed to be used where a lesser degree of intervention is appropriate, and/or in certain specified circumstances where voluntary parental co-operation is likely to be forthcoming.

5.3.3 Although the provisions of the Part relating to parenting orders begin before those relating to parenting contracts, and are littered throughout it, it is important that practitioners and courts alike keep in mind the incremental approach here; that contracts are likely to be the first step, followed by orders if they are unsuccessful. The positioning of the parenting order provisions probably reflects, if subconsciously, government's impatience with voluntary models for reducing anti-social behaviour by children and young people by improving the parenting skills of those with care of them, and indeed with the reluctance hitherto of both the courts and local education authorities to make parenting orders in school attendance prosecutions, notwithstanding the fact that they have been available to the courts since June 2000.

5.3.4 Be that as it may, it is essential that courts, practitioners and agencies alike remember that parenting contracts are voluntary arrangements, and are not imposed like orders. Conversely, parenting orders are imposed, with criminal sanctions for breach.[10] That is not to say that the potential for the court to be invited to rely on a parent's earlier refusal to engage with the contract process (whether by not complying with the terms of such a contract or by simply refusing to enter into one) when considering an application for a parenting order (s 27) has not caused concern.

5.3.5 Both the Home Office and the Department for Education and Skills have now issued their final guidance as to parenting contracts and orders. These sets of

---

[9] 2003 Act, ss 19–25. [10] 1998 Act, s 9(7).

guidance appear in Appendix 3, but they were unfortunately issued too late for the text of this chapter to assimilate their provisions fully, although we have commented on them where possible.

Parenting contracts

Sections 19 and 25 of the 2003 Act introduce a new statutory concept: the parenting contract.[11] The making of such a contract can be triggered by one of two sets of conditions: exclusion from school or truancy,[12] or criminal conduct and anti-social behaviour.[13] The specific statutory purpose in making it is set out in each of these sections, though the format of the contract is the same. At the time of writing, no *pro forma* is suggested within the draft Home Office Guidance on parenting orders and contracts. **5.3.6**

The first set of trigger conditions are to be found in s 19. A parenting contract can be made in cases where a pupil has been excluded from a 'relevant school'[14] on disciplinary grounds, either permanently or for a fixed period.[15] In such a case the statutory purpose of the contract is to improve the behaviour of the pupil.[16] **5.3.7**

A parenting contract can also be made where a child of compulsory school age has failed to attend regularly at a relevant school of which he is a registered pupil, ie where the child has truanted from school.[17] Here, the statutory aim of the order is to ensure that the child attends regularly at the relevant school at which he is a registered pupil.[18] **5.3.8**

A parenting contract under s 19 of the 2003 Act is a document entered into between the local education authority or the school governing body and the parent of the pupil or child.[19] The term 'parent' is defined differently in relation to the two types of parenting contract. In relation to a s 19, school-related, parenting contract, 'parent' is defined to include a person who is not a parent of the child in question but has parental responsibility for, or care of, him. A person does not constitute a parent, however, for the purposes of this Act, if he is not an individual.[20] **5.3.9**

The document contains two statements: a statement by the parent that he agrees to comply with the requirements specified in the document for such period as is also specified in the document, and a statement by the local education authority **5.3.10**

[11] These are not to be confused with youth offender contracts, made as a result of a referral order: Powers of the Criminal Courts (Sentencing) Act 2000, ss 16–17.

[12] ibid, s 19.

[13] ibid, s 25.

[14] Defined in s 24 as either a qualifying school within the meaning of Education Act 2002, s 1(3) or a pupil referral unit as defined in Education Act 1996, s 19(2).

[15] 2003 Act, s 19(1).

[16] ibid, s 19(6)(a).

[17] ibid, s 19(2).

[18] ibid, s 19(6)(b).

[19] ibid, s 19(3).

[20] A parent is to be construed in accordance with Education Act 1996, s 576, as amended by School Standards and Framework Act 1998, Sch 30, para 180, but does not include a person who is not an individual: ibid, s 24.

or school governing body that it agrees to provide support to the parent for the purpose of complying with those requirements,[21] which may include a requirement to attend a counselling or guidance programme.[22] The contract must be signed by the parent and on behalf of the local education authority or governing body,[23] but creates no binding obligations on either party that could be enforced in contract or tort.[24] Local education authorities and governing bodies must have regard to any guidance issued by the Secretary of State[25] in carrying out their functions in relation to parenting contracts.[26]

5.3.11 The second type of trigger condition for the making of a parenting contract is that the child[27] or young person[28] has been referred to a youth offending team (ie in respect of criminal conduct or anti-social behaviour).[29] The youth offending team (YOT) may enter a parenting contract with a parent of the child or young person if a member of that team has reason to believe that the child or young person has engaged, or is likely to engage, in criminal conduct or anti-social behaviour.[30] The statutory purpose of this type of parenting contract is to prevent the child or young person from engaging in criminal conduct (or further criminal conduct) or anti-social behaviour (or further such behaviour).[31]

5.3.12 In this context, 'parent' is defined differently from the definition applicable to the s 19 parenting order. Here, parent is defined simply to include 'guardian'.[32]

5.3.13 As with the s 19 contract, however, the parenting contract is a document containing a statement from the parent of his agreement to be bound by the requirements specified in the document for the period of time which is also specified. The second statement, this time, is made by the YOT, agreeing to support the parent for the purpose of complying with those requirements[33] (which may include a requirement to attend a counselling or guidance programme).[34] The document is signed by the parent and on behalf of the YOT,[35] but creates no legally binding obligations.[36] The YOT must have regard to guidance from the Secretary of State in carrying out its functions in relation to parenting contracts.[37]

---

[21] 2003 Act, s 19(4). [22] ibid, s 19(5). [23] ibid, s 19(7). [24] ibid, s 19(8).

[25] Or the National Assembly for Wales: ibid, s 24. [26] ibid, s 19(9).

[27] By s 29, 'child' has the same meaning as in s 117 of the Crime and Disorder Act 1998, ie a person under 14 years of age.

[28] By s 29, 'young person' has the same meaning as in s 117 of the Crime and Disorder Act 1998, ie a person who has attained the age of 14 and is under 18.

[29] 2003 Act, s 25(1).

[30] ibid, s 25(2). Anti-social behaviour is defined in s 29 in common with its definition in Crime and Disorder Act 1998, s 1.

[31] ibid, s 25(5).

[32] ibid, s 29. 'Guardian' has the same meaning as in s 107 of the Children and Young Persons Act 1933, ie it includes any person who, in the opinion of the court having cognisance of any case in relation to the child or young person or in which the child or young person is concerned, has for the time being the care of the child or young person.

[33] ibid, s 25(3). [34] ibid, s 25(4). [35] ibid, s 25(6). [36] ibid, s 25(7).

[37] ibid, s 25(8).

As has been seen, in each case, a parenting contract will contain two statements: the parent's agreement to comply with the requirements contained within the document for the duration of the contract, and the authority's agreement to support the parent. The requirements specified in a contract will presumably have to serve the relevant statutory purpose (see para 5.3.11 above). There is nothing in these provisions, however, requiring anything specific to be included in the document: Parliament appears to have left it open to the appropriate body, for example, to draft a requirement that the parent agree to abide by such directions as he may be given from time to time by the local education authority or YOT, etc, for the purpose of giving effect to the statutory purpose. This is akin, in some ways, to bail conditions requiring defendants to 'comply with such instructions as they might receive from Probation for the purposes of preparing a pre-sentence report' or to 'live as directed by social services'. **5.3.14**

Presumably, as with the type of bail condition referred to above, so long as there is sufficient certainty that those bound to comply fully understand the nature of what they are required to do or not do then this would be acceptable. It is after all inherent in the nature of these contracts that the parties reach a flexible agreement based on what will work in the circumstances of the particular case, rather than simply inserting the authority's 'standard' requirements in all cases. Common sense, too, dictates that a degree of flexibility must exist. **5.3.15**

It is, then, in effect a judgment call for the YOT, having regard to the criteria set out in s 25(2) and (5), as to whether such a contract should be considered, the aim being, it seems, for the *parent*, with support, to prevent the young person either from offending or behaving anti-socially for the first time (it is sufficient for a contract to be made that the YOT has reason to believe that the child or young person is likely to engage in criminal conduct or anti-social behaviour) or from repeating such conduct or behaviour. It is perhaps a little ironic that preventing offending by children and young people (rather than supporting others to prevent it) is already supposed to be the role of the YOT and indeed the principal statutory aim of the youth justice system.[38] It would be more ironic still if a consequence of the wholesale adoption of parenting contracts was to shift the focus of responsibility for any failure to prevent offending or re-offending on to the parent rather than the criminal justice system (whether in the form of the YOT or otherwise). **5.3.16**

Whatever the specific terms, however, the fact that signatories to such a contract must not be set up to fail through a lack of clarity as to what is required of them is a live issue for both agencies working in the field and, it appears, for the Home Office. **5.3.17**

The drafting of ss 19(4) and 25(4), and in particular the differences between, on the one hand, the specificity of ss 19(4)(a) and 25(4)(a) in relation to the obligations of the parent, and, on the other, the generality of ss 19(4)(b) and 25(4)(b) **5.3.18**

[38] Crime and Disorder Act 1998, s 37.

as to the obligations of the authority, suggests that while detailed requirements will be imposed on the parent (whether such requirements are included within that statement or annexed to the contract, as is commonly the case with ABCs), the second 'support' statement can contain just a brief and general statement of intent.

5.3.19 Curiously perhaps, although the contract creates no binding obligations on either party, a sanction for non-performance is indirectly imposed on the parent, in that the court can take account of a refusal to enter into, or a failure to comply with the requirements of, a contract in deciding whether to make a parenting order.[39] There is no enforcement mechanism, however, to ensure that the promised support actually materializes in concrete (or any other) form. If a parent, for example, feels that the local education authority or YOT has failed to offer any or appropriate support, the parent is provided with no remedy under the Act. Judicial review may, in principle, be available but would undoubtedly be costly and, even if funding could be obtained, time-consuming. It would also be unlikely to foster warm relations with the authority, at a time when the parent concerned is likely to be anxious not to appear antagonistic.

5.3.20 When contrasted with the parenting order, it is clear that the intention behind the parenting contract is to provide a support mechanism for parents of children whose behaviour is a cause for concern. On prosecutions brought against parents under the Education Act 1996, however, it is not uncommon for the parent to tell the court that they were entirely confused about what they should be doing: with the school saying one thing, the local education authority another, and the social worker yet another. If the format of the contract with specific and defined requirements adds clarity to parents' understanding of what is expected of them, this may well mark an improvement on the current position.[40]

5.3.21 Home Office Guidance on Part 3 gives some general guidance to YOTs in relation to parenting contracts. The Guidance is extremely generalistic, however, and significant areas, particularly concerning protocols for inter-agency working, have not been covered. Whilst in one sense this is understandable as practical issues such as resources will vary from region to region, affecting how work will be shared by different agencies, it is also unhelpful as a national consistency of approach may prove elusive.

Parenting orders

5.3.22 The first, and perhaps most modest, amendment to the existing regime of parenting orders[41] is effected by s 18 of the 2003 Act. This amends s 8(4) and (5) of

---

[39] Crime and Disorder Act 1998, ss 21(1) and 27(1).

[40] Annex C to the Home Office guidance provides a specimen contract, the terms of which appear to be intended to be short and not especially complex (given the space provided on the form).

[41] Crime and Disorder Act 1998, ss 8–9.

the 1998 Act by removing the restriction that where an order requires a parent to attend a counselling or guidance programme, he cannot be required to attend such a programme more than once a week.[42]

Section 18 also provides that a counselling or guidance programme can include or consist of a residential course, but only if the court is satisfied that the attendance of the parent at a residential course is likely to be more effective than his attendance at a non-residential course in preventing the repetition of the child's behaviour or the commission of a further offence, and that any interference with family life likely to result from the attendance at a residential course is proportionate in all the circumstances.[43] 5.3.23

Other than these amendments, the parenting order remains in its 1998 Act form. 5.3.24

Parenting orders in school exclusion cases

Section 20 of the 2003 Act extends the circumstances in which a parenting order can be made to cases of exclusions from school and truancy, adding to the original situations set out in s 8(1) of the 1998 Act. A local education authority may now apply for a parenting order in respect of a parent of a pupil who has been excluded from school on disciplinary grounds either permanently or for a fixed period and where any conditions prescribed by the Secretary of State[44] are satisfied.[45] An order could already be made under s 8(1)(d) of the 1998 Act in truancy cases. 5.3.25

The court may grant the application if it is satisfied that the making of such an order would be desirable in the interests of improving the behaviour of the pupil.[46] The order requires the parent:[47] 5.3.26

- to comply, for a period not exceeding 12 months, with the requirements specified in the order; and
- to attend, for a concurrent period not exceeding three months, such counselling or guidance programme as may be specified in directions given by the officer specified as the 'responsible officer', save that a parenting order need not include such a requirement where a previous parenting order (under any enactment) has been made in respect of the parent.[48] The provisions referred to at para 5.3.22, relating to such programmes consisting of or including a residential course, are repeated.[49]

Requirements specified in, and directions given under, a parenting order must avoid, as far as practicable, any conflict with the parent's religious beliefs, and any interference with the times, if any, at which he normally works or attends an educational establishment.[50] 5.3.27

42 2003 Act, s 18(2) inserting a new s 8(4) and (5) into the 1998 Act.

43 ibid, s 18(3) inserting a new s 8(7A) into the 1998 Act.

44 Or in Wales the National Assembly for Wales: ibid, s 29.

45 ibid, s 20(1). The application is made to the magistrates' court on complaint; see the form set out in Annex C of the Home Office guidance.

46 ibid, s 20(3). 47 ibid, s 20(4). 48 ibid, s 20(5). 49 ibid, s 20(6)–(8).

50 1998 Act, s 9(4), applied by 2003 Act, ss 21(3) and 27(3).

Parenting orders for criminal conduct and anti-social behaviour

5.3.28 Section 26 of the 2003 Act permits a member of a YOT to apply for a parenting order where a child has been referred to it. It is worth repeating that the definition of 'parent' that applies to s 26 is different from that applicable to s 20.[51] A referral to a YOT may have happened in one of several ways—for example, the child or young person may have received a police warning[52] in respect of offending behaviour, in which circumstances the police have a statutory duty to refer the child or young person to a YOT as soon as is practicable,[53] or the child or young person may have come before the youth court and been made the subject of either a mandatory or discretionary referral order,[54] and so on.

5.3.29 As with the s 25 parenting contract, it is a matter for the YOT whether to seek a parenting order under s 26.[55] The only criterion for such an application being made is that the child or young person has been referred to the YOT.[56] Unlike the parenting contract, however,[57] an order may not be made unless some criminal conduct or anti-social behaviour has actually been engaged in by the child or young person in question. The court may make such an order if satisfied that:

(a) the child or young person has engaged in criminal conduct or anti-social behaviour; and
(b) making the order would be desirable in the interests of preventing the child or young person from engaging in further criminal conduct or anti-social behaviour.[58]

5.3.30 The provisions concerning the form and requirements of the order are identical to those referred to above, in relation to s 20 parenting orders.[59]

Common issues

5.3.31 Sections 21 and 27 contain a number of further provisions that the court must take into account when deciding whether or not to make a parenting order under either s 20 or s 26, namely:

(a) any refusal by the parent to enter into a parenting contract under ss 19 or 25;[60] or
(b) if the parent has entered into a contract, any failure by the parent to comply with its requirements.[61]

5.3.32 The court must also, before making a parenting order in the case of a child under the age of 16, obtain and consider information about the pupil, child or young person's family circumstances and the likely effect of the order on those

[51] See 2003 Act, ss 24 and 29. [52] Crime and Disorder Act 1998, s 65. [53] ibid, s 66.
[54] Powers of the Criminal Courts (Sentencing) Act 2000, Pt III.
[55] The application is made to the magistrates' court on complaint; see the form set out in Annex C of the Home Office guidance.
[56] 2003 Act, s 26(2). [57] ibid, s 25(2). [58] ibid, s 26(3).
[59] See paras 5.3.25–26 above, and ibid, ss 26(4)–(8) and 27(3).
[60] ibid, ss 21(1)(a) and 27(1)(a). [61] ibid, ss 21(1)(b) and 27(1)(b).

circumstances.[62] In practice, this information is most likely to take the form of a report from the YOT itself, although there is no statutory requirement that the information must be in the form of a report, oral or written. The Home Office Guidance makes reference to a report but does not specify a format for any such report. This requirement cannot be dispensed with, unlike the position with regard to sentencing.[63]

It may well be expedient for YOTs to adopt the oral report procedure frequently used when informing the court as to a young offender's remand situation or compliance with bail packages or sentences. Practice is likely to vary from court to court, taking account of such factors as the resources and time available to the YOT. If the parenting order application is a 'stand-alone' application, there will clearly be more time before any hearing for the relevant information to be gathered and put into a comprehensible form than if an order is sought at the conclusion of proceedings in the youth court. The Home Office Guidance to YOTs[64] suggests that applications for 'stand-alone' parenting orders should be reserved for cases where attempts to obtain voluntary parental co-operation (for example, in the form of a parenting contract) have failed. Whilst technically it is of course possible for a stand-alone order to be sought without any prior attempt to obtain a parenting contract, courts may well be reluctant to use the parenting order as the first form of intervention, a view realistically acknowledged by the Home Office Guidance on the point.[65] 5.3.33

Standard of proof

The 2003 Act does not, in relation to either new parenting order, specify a standard of proof. The court must simply be 'satisfied' that the relevant factual criteria are met (be it exclusion, truancy, anti-social behaviour, or criminal conduct) and that the making of an order is desirable to meet the statutory goal of improving the child's behaviour or attendance at school. As to the first of these limbs, this appears to be a lower test than that applicable for an ASBO under s 1 of the Crime and Disorder Act 1998, which requires that the applicant prove that anti-social behaviour has been committed. Parliament's intention would seem to be that any burden of proof need only satisfy the court to the civil standard, but whether the court will accept this as accurate, should it ever be challenged, is a separate issue: see *R (McCann) v Manchester Crown Court*,[66] in relation to the standard of proof for anti-social behaviour orders. 5.3.34

As to the second limb, that the court is satisfied that it is desirable to make a parenting order, this too requires a lower standard of proof than applies to ASBO applications, where the court must be satisfied that it is 'necessary' to make an order.[67] It would seem, however, that the House of Lords' approach 5.3.35

[62] ibid, ss 21(2) and 27(2).
[63] Powers of the Criminal Courts (Sentencing) Act 2000, s 81.
[64] Home Office guidance, paras 5.3–5.4.
[65] ibid, para 5.4.
[66] [2002] UKHL 39, [2003] 1 AC 787. As to the standard of proof in relation to the making of an ASBO, see Chapter 11 below.
[67] Crime and Disorder Act 1998, s 1.

to that issue in *McCann* applies equally to the question of the desirability of making a parenting order; ie that whether an order is necessary is not an issue to which a standard of proof attaches, rather it is an exercise of judgment or evaluation.[68]

5.3.36 In any event, the balancing exercise required by the interest of justice test, perhaps the test most familiar to summary courts, does not feature in this scheme of legislation. Nor is there any reference to the welfare principle. The test is, on any view, however, likely to be subject to the umbrella of proportionality under the Human Rights Act 1998, which will embrace most of these principles in one form or another.

Logistics

5.3.37 Little consideration appears to have been given to the logistics of the YOT making 'stand-alone' applications for parenting orders in the magistrates' court. Given that the usual listing arrangements in magistrates' courts is for the YOT to attend on the day(s) when a youth court is sitting, whereas stand-alone parenting orders are made by the adult court, there would seem to be a potential difficulty that the YOT officers will not normally be present at courts where a parenting order could be made.

5.3.38 Two possible solutions present themselves, however. Arrangements could be made for YOT officers to make applications (perhaps in bulk) at hearings specifically listed for that purpose—akin perhaps to other non-CPS lists such as prosecutions for non-compliance with community orders—so as to reduce impact on remand lists. It remains to be seen, however, if there will be a sufficient volume of these applications to merit a stand-alone court to deal with them. The normal 'welfare' principles should, additionally, still apply to cases dealing with children and young people, so that delay in hearing such cases purely for the convenience of the court would be inappropriate.

5.3.39 Alternatively, justices and district judges could be asked to reconvene as adult courts at the conclusion of youth court sittings (and possibly vice versa) in order to deal expeditiously with stand-alone applications.

5.3.40 One further consideration is the right of the public and the press to be present when adult court sittings take place. It is not clear why such stand-alone applications cannot be considered by the youth court, although the obvious explanation would seem to be that the parent is likely to be an adult and therefore would ordinarily appear in an adult court. When the court considers whether or not to make an order, however, the criteria to be applied involve considering potentially detailed evidence about the child or young person (and the likely effect on her or him of the order being made on his/her parent) and not specifically about the parent to anything like the same degree.

[68] *McCann*, n 61 above, *per* Lord Steyn at [37].

Courts and practitioners will have to remember the issue of publicity, although it is not clear that s 39 of the Children and Young Persons Act 1933 will apply in such cases, as the child is not, or at least is not likely to be, either a party to or a witness in the stand-alone parenting order proceedings. **5.3.41**

Further problems may arise if applications are listed in the magistrates' court on non-youth court sitting days, as this could easily result in the justices hearing these applications not being members of a specialist youth panel, and therefore having experience neither of dealing with young people, save in remand situations, nor of the specialist sentences and practices of the youth court. The guidance is silent on this issue. Courts will have to negotiate with YOTs to establish list time and additional attendance by YOTs at such applications. **5.3.42**

Meaning of criminal conduct

It is also worthy of note that, so far as s 26(3) is concerned, the court needs to be satisfied merely that the child or young person has engaged in criminal conduct: a conviction for an offence is not necessary. In this context, it is not entirely clear what is meant by the language of 'criminal conduct'. By s 29, the phrase is defined as conduct which: (a) constitutes a criminal offence, or (b) in the case of conduct by a person under the age of ten, would constitute a criminal offence if the person in question had attained the age of criminal responsibility, ie ten. **5.3.43**

This does not resolve the issue entirely, as it does not make it clear whether the use of the phrase is intended merely to include within the conduct that can be considered offences in relation to which final warnings or reprimands were given, or whether criminal conduct has a less restrictive meaning. It is conceivable, for example, that it could mean either conduct that is criminal in the sense that it could have given rise to a prosecution in the case of the particular child or young person, or alternatively criminal 'in principle' as it were (ie where the *actus reus* of an offence is made out but not the *mens rea*). **5.3.44**

It is not the case where the *actus reus* of an offence could be made out that conduct would also amount to anti-social behaviour in any event, because 'anti-social behaviour' is defined in s 1 of the Crime and Disorder Act 1998 as behaviour causing or likely to cause harassment, alarm or distress to a person not of the same household as the defendant. There are numerous criminal offences the commission of which would not satisfy this test. **5.3.45**

Supplementary provisions

Before making a parenting order, a court must explain to the parent in ordinary language: the effect of the order and of the requirements proposed to be included in it; the consequences of failing to comply with any of those requirements (ie that failing to comply is a summary offence punishable by a fine on level 3 of the standard scale);[69] and that the court has power[70] to review the order on the application either of the parent or of the responsible officer.[71] **5.3.46**

69 1998 Act, s 9(7).

70 ibid, s 9(5).

71 ibid, s 9(3) applied by 2003 Act, ss 21(3) and 27(3).

5.3.47 The Secretary of State[72] may make provision by regulations as to how the costs associated with the requirements of parenting orders under s 20—ie those obtained by local education authorities and governing bodies—(including the costs of providing counselling and guidance programmes) are to be borne.[73] No equivalent provision is made in relation to parenting orders under s 26, presumably because, in the case of applications by YOTs, the costs will be borne in the normal way.

Appeals, variation and discharge

Appeals

5.3.48 Sections 22 and 28 make identical provision, creating a right of appeal against the making of a parenting order under s 20 or s 26. There is a right to appeal to the Crown Court against the making of a parenting order.

5.3.49 On such an appeal, the Crown Court has power to make whatever orders are necessary to give effect to its determination of the appeal; and make any incidental or consequential orders as appear to it to be just. Any order of the Crown Court on appeal (other than one directing that an application be re-heard by a magistrates' court) is, moreover, for the purposes of the provisions of s 9 of the 1998 Act governing variation and discharge of parenting orders,[74] treated as if it were an order of the magistrates' court.[75]

Variation and discharge

5.3.50 Either the responsible officer for the parenting order or the parent may apply to the court that made the parenting order, while it is still in force, for the order to be varied or discharged. If it appears to the court that it is appropriate to do so, the court may discharge the parenting order, or vary it:

(a) by cancelling any provision included in it; or
(b) by inserting into it (in addition to or in substitution for any of its provisions) any provision that could have been included in the order when it was made.[76]

5.3.51 Where an application for the discharge of a parenting order is dismissed, no further application for its discharge can be made other than with the consent of the court that made the order.[77]

Breach

5.3.52 It is a summary offence to fail to comply with any of the requirements of a parenting order, punishable with a fine on level 3 of the standard scale.[78]

72 In Wales, the National Assembly for Wales: 2003 Act, s 24.
73 In Wales, the National Assembly for Wales: 2003 Act, s 21(4).
74 ie 1998 Act, s 9(5)–(6).
75 2003 Act, ss 22(2) and 28(2), applying in part the provisions of 1998 Act, s 10(2)–(3). See also, Home Office guidance on Pt 3, para 9.9.
76 2003 Act, ss 21(3) and 27(3) applying 1998 Act, s 9(5)–(6).
77 ibid.
78 ibid, applying 1998 Act, s 9(7).

Fixed penalty notices

Section 23 of the 2003 Act amends the provisions of the Education Act 1996, to insert new ss 444A and 444B. These confer power on an 'authorised officer' to serve a fixed penalty notice on a person, where the officer has reason to believe that the person has committed an offence under s 444(1) of the Education Act 1996 (ie that he has failed to secure the attendance at school of a registered pupil) and that the school is a relevant school in England.[79] In relation to Wales, the National Assembly for Wales is given power to apply the provisions of ss 444A and 444B to Wales.[80] 5.3.53

An 'authorised officer' is: 5.3.54

(a) a constable;
(b) an officer of a local education authority in England who is authorized by the authority to give penalty notices; or
(c) an 'authorised staff member', which term is itself defined as a head teacher or a member of the staff of a relevant school in England who is authorized by the head teacher of the school to give penalty notices.[81]

A chief officer of police may also designate community support officers and accredited persons to give penalty notices for this offence, and (in the case of a community support officer) to detain a person until a constable arrives and (in the case of an accredited person) to require a person to give his name and address.[82] 5.3.55

A 'relevant school' is a maintained school, a pupil referral unit, an academy, a city technology college or a city college for the technology of the arts.[83] 5.3.56

A 'penalty notice' is a notice offering a person the opportunity of discharging any liability to be convicted of the offence under s 444(1) of the Education Act 1996, by payment of a penalty in accordance with the notice.[84] Where a person is given a penalty notice, proceedings for the offence to which the notice relates (or a related offence arising out of the same circumstances)[85] may not be instituted until after the end of the prescribed period for paying the penalty under the notice.[86] If the person pays the penalty in accordance with the notice, he cannot be convicted of the offence to which it relates (or the related offence arising out of the same facts).[87] Penalties are payable to the local education authority, and sums received by them may be used by the authority for the purposes of any of their functions that may be specified in regulations.[88] 5.3.57

New s 444B confers power on the Secretary of State to make regulations as to the details of the form and content of penalty notices, including as to the amount of the penalty (which may include different amounts in different cases or 5.3.58

[79] Education Act 1996, s 444A(1), inserted by 2003 Act, s 23(1).
[80] 2003 Act, s 23(9)–(10).
[81] Education Act 1996, s 444B(4), inserted by 2003 Act, s 23(1).
[82] 2003 Act, s 23(3)–(8).
[83] Education Act 1996, s 444B(4).
[84] ibid, s 444A(2).
[85] ibid, s 444(1A).
[86] ibid, s 444A(3).
[87] ibid, s 444A(4).
[88] ibid, s 444A(5)–(6).

circumstances[89]), the methods by which it may be paid, the officers who may be authorized to give penalty notices, codes of conduct in relation to giving penalty notices, and the consequences of failure to pay the penalty in accordance with the notice.[90] Local education authorities, head teachers and authorized officers must have regard to any guidance published by the Secretary of State.[91]

5.3.59 It need not be established that such an offence has actually been committed in the sense of establishing it beyond a reasonable doubt. All that is necessary is that the officer 'has reason to believe' that this is so. Accordingly, as with all fixed penalty notices, if the commission of the offence is disputed, the recipient's only course is to refuse to comply with the notice and (if proceedings are thereafter instituted against him) to contest the trial.

[89] Education Act 1996, s 444B(2). [90] ibid, s 444B(1). [91] ibid, s 444B(3).

6

PART 4 OF THE ACT: DISPERSAL OF GROUPS

6.1. INTRODUCTION

To the extent that any broad themes are evident in this Act, one of them is the extension of police powers to deal with groups of people, especially young people. Such people may assemble on public land or private premises, whether their own or other people's. Part 1 (closure of premises where drugs are unlawfully used); Part 6 (the environment including the closure of noisy premises); Part 7 (public assemblies, groups trespassing on private land) all have this feature in common to a greater or lesser extent and, indeed, seem to be premised on the belief that anti-social conduct would be less prevalent if people could be prevented from congregating together. **6.1.1**

Part 4 of the Act shares this theme, conferring new police powers to disperse groups and, more controversially, take under 16 year olds home. **6.1.2**

Equally controversial is the decision to permit the police to designate that the powers conferred by this Part may be exercised by community support officers, ie civilians employed by the police who are not trained police officers. While community support officers have existed since the Police Reform Act 2002, their role has (with some exceptions) hitherto been far more limited than that envisaged by this legislation which contemplates constitutionally significant police powers being given to civilian support staff to interfere with the freedom of the citizen to assemble with even one other person in public, which in some cases is likely to involve difficult and potentially dangerous situations. **6.1.3**

6.2. LEGISLATIVE CONTEXT

6.2.1 The powers introduced by this Part are themselves new, but should still be considered in the context of pre-existing legislation. Some of this legislation, such as the Public Order Act 1986 and the Criminal Justice and Public Order Act 1994, are considered in more detail elsewhere, in the context of the provisions of Part 7 of this Act.[1]

Dispersal of groups

6.2.2 The 2003 Act's provisions relating to the dispersal of groups are similar to those contained in the Criminal Justice and Public Order Act 1994 ('the 1994 Act') concerning the removal of trespassers. Section 61 of the 1994 Act empowers the senior police officer present at a scene to direct trespassers to leave land, and to remove any vehicles and property they have with them, if he reasonably believes, inter alia, that any of the trespassers has caused damage to the land or property on the land or has threatened, abused or insulted the occupier of the land, or his family, employees or agents.

6.2.3 Section 61(4) creates an offence if a person who knows a direction has been given that applies to him fails to leave the land, or enters it again as a trespasser within three months of the giving of the direction.

6.2.4 Similarly, under s 68(1) of the 1994 Act,[2] a person commits the offence of aggravated trespass if he trespasses on land and does anything intended to intimidate, obstruct or disrupt the lawful activities of any other people who are on that or adjoining land.

6.2.5 There is some overlap between this offence and an offence under s 5 of the Public Order Act 1986 which applies to trespassers who engage in conduct with intent to intimidate people engaged in a lawful activity, to obstruct them or disrupt them from their activity. A defence of reasonable conduct is available under s 5; no such defence is available under the 1994 Act.

Curfews and removal home of children under 16

6.2.6 Sections 14 and 15 of the Crime and Disorder Act 1998 ('the 1998 Act')[3] make provision for 'local child curfew schemes'. The procedure under the 1998 Act (to some extent replicated by the provisions of this Part) is that the local authority or a chief officer of police may make a scheme, following consultation, and then, after further consultation, may give a curfew notice, if this is considered necessary for the purpose of maintaining order. The curfew notice may impose, for a

[1] See Chapter 9 below. [2] As amended by 2003 Act, s 58. See paras 9.3.14–9.3.15 below.
[3] As amended by the Criminal Justice and Police Act 2001, ss 48 and 49.

period not exceeding 90 days, a ban on children under 16 years old[4] from being in a public place within a specified area between the hours of 9 pm and 6 am unless under the effective control of a parent or responsible person over 18.[5]

Where a constable has reasonable cause to believe that a child is in contravention of a ban imposed by a notice, he must inform the local authority of this as soon as practicable, and may remove the child to her or his place of residence unless he has reasonable cause to believe that if he does so, the child would be likely to suffer significant harm.[6] **6.2.7**

Community support officers

Section 38 of the Police Reform Act 2002 ('the 2002 Act') allowed the creation of community safety accreditation schemes that enable chief officers of police to designate police authority civilian employees under their direction and control to have certain powers conferred on them. **6.2.8**

A chief officer can designate civilians to perform functions in four kinds of role: community support officer; investigating officer; detention officer; and escort officer. Powers are conferred on such officers by means of the chief officer, in the designation itself, applying specific paragraphs of Sch 4 to the 2002 Act (which contain the powers) to the civilian in question. Accordingly, there is nothing to stop a chief officer of police conferring different powers on different civilians. **6.2.9**

The powers available to be conferred on community support officers[7] include, in this context, the power to issue a range of fixed penalty notices relating to anti-social behaviour (for example, dog fouling or cycling on the pavement); the power to request a name and address from a person committing a fixed penalty offence or an offence that causes injury, alarm, distress or damage to another; and the power to detain for a limited period (awaiting the arrival of a constable) a person who fails to comply with the request to give their name and address. Other powers are less restrictive, such as the power to stop and search vehicles under the provisions of the Terrorism Act 2000. **6.2.10**

6.3. THE PROVISIONS OF PART 4 OF THE ACT[8]

Dispersal of groups and removal home of under 16 year olds

Section 30 of the Act introduces two new police powers: to disperse groups of two or more people of any age, and to return home young people under 16 who are unsupervised in public places between 9 pm and 6 am. **6.3.1**

---

[4] As originally enacted, the power existed in relation to children under ten years old.

[5] Crime and Disorder Act 1998, s 14(1)–(3A).

[6] ibid, s 15(1)–(3).

[7] 2002 Act, Sch 4, Pt 1.

[8] These provisions came into force on 20 January 2004: Anti-Social Behaviour Act 2003 (Commencement No 1 and Transitional Provisions) Order 2003, SI 2003/3300. The Secretary of State has also issued guidance on this Part, contained in Home Office Circular 04/2004.

Dispersal of groups

6.3.2 By s 30(4) a constable in uniform may, if he has reasonable grounds for believing that the presence or behaviour of a group of two or more people in a public place in the relevant locality[9] has resulted or is likely to result in any members of the public being intimidated, harassed, alarmed or distressed, give one or more of the following directions:

(a) a direction requiring the persons in the group to disperse (either immediately or by such time as he may specify and in such way as he may specify);
(b) a direction requiring any of those persons whose place of residence is not within the relevant locality to leave the relevant locality or any part of the relevant locality (either immediately or by such time as he may specify and in such way as he may specify); and
(c) a direction prohibiting any of those persons whose place of residence is not within the relevant locality from returning to the relevant locality or any part of the relevant locality for such period (not exceeding 24 hours) from the giving of the direction as he may specify.

6.3.3 A direction may be given orally, to any person individually or to two or more persons together and may be withdrawn or varied by the person who gave it.[10]

6.3.4 These provisions may be more draconian than would first appear, particularly given their application to groups as small as two in number, and in relation to those whose place of residence is not within the relevant locality.[11] Such a person may be required not only to leave the locality but not to return for up to 24 hours. A person, for example, who was employed or was at school or college in a locality, but did not live there, could find her or himself unable to attend work/school etc the next day. The same could plainly apply to medical appointments, complying with probation requirements, etc.

Exceptions

6.3.5 No direction under this section may be given in respect of a group of people who are engaged in lawful industrial action, or in a public procession in respect of which written notice has either been given or is not required under s 11 of the Public Order Act 1986.[12]

Enforcement

6.3.6 A person who knowingly contravenes a direction to disperse under s 30(4) commits an arrestable, summary offence, punishable with a term of three months' imprisonment and/or a fine on level 4 of the standard scale.[13]

---

[9] Defined in 2003 Act, s 36 to mean the same as in s 30(1); as to which see para 6.3.11 below.
[10] ibid, s 32(1).
[11] Defined in ibid, ss 36 and 30(1)(a); see further para 6.3.11 below.
[12] ibid, s 30(5).
[13] ibid, s 32(2).

Returning children home

If a constable in uniform finds, between the hours of 9 pm and 6 am, a person in any public place in the 'relevant locality',[14] and has reasonable grounds for believing that the person is under the age of 16 and is not under the effective control of a parent or responsible person aged 18 or over, he may 'remove the person to the person's place of residence' unless he has reasonable grounds for believing that, if taken home, the person would be likely to suffer significant harm.[15] **6.3.7**

Any local authority whose area includes any part of the relevant locality must be notified if a person has been removed and taken home pursuant to the s 30(6) powers.[16] **6.3.8**

It should be noted that this provision operates whether the young person is engaging in anti-social conduct or helping old people across the road. The mere presence of the young person (even if s/he is not in fact under the age of 16, but is reasonably believed to be by the officer) is sufficient to trigger the power to 'remove' her or him back home. **6.3.9**

The requirement of authorization

A little of the draconian effect is taken out of these provisions by the fact that the new powers will not be generally available to the police throughout the country on the coming into force of Part 4 of the Act, without more. They will not be available at all, in fact, unless and until the 'relevant officer', ie an officer of at least the rank of superintendent,[17] gives an authorization that they are to be exercisable for a period specified in the authorization which may not exceed six months.[18] **6.3.10**

Meaning

The relevant officer may give an authorization where the statutory preconditions are satisfied, namely that s/he has reasonable grounds for believing that: **6.3.11**

(a) any members of the public have been intimidated, harassed, alarmed or distressed as a result of the presence or behaviour of groups of two or more persons in public places in any locality in the police area—the 'relevant locality'; and
(b) anti-social behaviour is a significant and persistent problem in the relevant locality.[19]

It can be seen that this test is likely to be applicable to large areas of many towns and cities in England and Wales. Neither the authorization provisions nor **6.3.12**

[14] Defined in ibid, ss 36 and 30(1)(a); see further para 6.3.11 below.
[15] ibid, s 30(6). [16] ibid, s 32(4). [17] ibid, s 36.
[18] ibid, s 30(2). [19] ibid, s 30(1).

the substantive powers conferred by s 30 require that the person to whom a direction is given or the under 16 year old who is removed home need to have been in any way implicated in the significant or persistent anti-social behaviour that gave rise to the authorization itself. For a direction to be given, the constable must have reasonable grounds for believing that the mere presence or the behaviour of a group of two or more persons has resulted or is likely to result in any members of the public being intimidated, harassed, alarmed or distressed. This does not mean every member of the group: a reference to the presence or behaviour of a group must be read as including a reference to the presence or behaviour of any one or more of the people in the group.[20]

6.3.13 How this is to be applied is not entirely clear. Some members of the public, particularly elderly people, may find a group of young people in the street intimidating or alarming of itself, even if none of its members was behaving anti-socially. Does this entitle a constable to direct the group to disperse? No definition of group is given, moreover. An additional question therefore arises where, for example, a crowd of people is waiting for a bus or queuing for a club or a cinema, formed from a number of smaller groups that do not know each other, whether the presence or behaviour of one or two members of that crowd could entitle a constable to direct the whole crowd to disperse.

6.3.14 These issues of construction will have to be resolved by the courts, although by the time a case could be heard (presumably on judicial review), the practical effect of the direction will long have come to an end. Questions of the appropriate balance to be struck between the competing rights of some members of society to meet freely in public places and other members of society to feel protected in such places is of course a matter for Parliament to decide. These issues are constitutionally important in the context of human rights and freedoms.

Form of and procedure for authorization

6.3.15 The procedure by which an authorization is made, and the form of the authorization itself, is set out in s 31 of the 2003 Act. The authorization must be in writing, signed by the relevant officer giving it, and specify the relevant locality, the grounds on which the authorization is given and the period during which the powers contained in s 30(3)–(6) are exercisable.[21]

6.3.16 An authorization may not be given unless each local authority whose area includes any part of the relevant locality consents to it.[22] It is noteworthy that this is not a consultation requirement, but a requirement that consent is given; a right of veto.

6.3.17 Before the period specified in the authorization commences,[23] moreover, it must be publicized by either (or both) publishing it in a newspaper circulating in the relevant locality and/or posting an authorization notice in some conspicuous place or places within the relevant locality.[24] An authorization notice is a notice

[20] 2003 Act, s 30(7). [21] ibid, s 31(1). [22] ibid, s 31(2). [23] ibid, s 31(5).
[24] ibid, s 31(3).

that states that the authorization has been given; specifies the relevant locality; and specifies the period during which the s 30 powers are exercisable.[25]

Withdrawal of authorization

An authorization may be withdrawn by the relevant officer who gave it or by any other relevant officer whose police area includes the relevant locality and who is of the same rank as, or a higher rank than, the officer who gave it.[26] Before it is withdrawn, however, any local authority whose area includes any part of the relevant locality must be consulted (though their consent to the withdrawal does not, it seems, have to be obtained).[27] The withdrawal of an authorization does not affect the exercise of any power pursuant to it that occurred prior to its withdrawal, nor does it prevent the giving of a further authorization in respect of a locality that includes all or part of the relevant locality to which the withdrawn authorization related.[28] **6.3.18**

Exercise of constable's powers by other officers

Community support officers

As stated above, the Police Reform Act 2002 sets out a list of the powers some or all of which a chief officer of police may confer on a community support officer designation.[29] Section 33 of the 2003 Act adds to the list of such powers by inserting three new provisions into Part I of Sch 4 to the 2002 Act. **6.3.19**

The effect of this is that a chief officer of police may confer on a community support officer the power: **6.3.20**

(a) to detain a person for an offence under s 32(2) of the 2003 Act (knowingly contravening a direction);[30]
(b) to exercise the powers of a constable in uniform under s 30(3)–(6) (ie to give directions to disperse groups and remove a person under 16, between 9 pm and 6 am, to her/his place of residence);[31] and
(c) to exercise the powers of a constable under s 15(3) of the Crime and Disorder Act 1998 (ie to remove a child under 16, between 9 pm and 6 am, to her/his place of residence if the officer has reasonable cause to believe that the child is in breach of a curfew notice). The requirement to inform the local authority as soon as practicable, if the power is exercised, applies to the community support officer, as to the constable.[32]

---

[25] ibid, s 31(4). [26] ibid, s 31(6). [27] ibid, s 31(7); cf s 31(2). [28] ibid, s 31(8)–(9).
[29] Police Reform Act 2002, s 38, and Sch 4, Pt I.
[30] 2003 Act, s 33(2); inserting a new Sch 4, para (2)(6)(aa) into the Police Reform Act 2002.
[31] ibid, s 33(3) inserting a new Sch 4, para (4A) into the Police Reform Act 2002.
[32] ibid, s 33(3) inserting a new Sch 4, para (4B) into the Police Reform Act 2002.

British Transport Police

6.3.21 Section 35 of the Act applies the powers conferred by this Part upon the British Transport Police Force with minor consequential amendments.

Code of practice

6.3.22 Relevant to some of the issues referred to above is the power conferred on the Secretary of State to issue, and revise from time to time, a code of practice concerning the giving or withdrawal of authorizations and the exercise of the s 30(3)–(6) powers.[33] A code of practice may make different provision for different cases.[34] Any code issued and any revisions to it must be laid before Parliament.[35]

6.3.23 If a code of practice is issued, and it is the intention of the Government to issue one,[36] although at the time of writing (March 2004) it is not available, even in draft form, regard must be had to it by a relevant officer in giving or withdrawing an authorization, and by a constable in uniform or community support officer in exercising the s 30(3)–(6) powers.[37]

[33] 2003 Act, s 34(1)–(2). [34] ibid, s 34(6). [35] ibid, s 34(3).

[36] The National Centre for Policing Excellence has been asked to produce this following consultation: see Home Office Circular 04/2004, para 24.

[37] ibid, s 34(4)–(5).

7

PART 5 OF THE ACT: FIREARMS

7.1. INTRODUCTION

Part 5 of the Act aims to tackle the misuse of air weapons and imitation firearms by introducing a number of amendments to the Firearms Act 1968 ('the 1968 Act'). Many of these amendments were recommended by the House of Commons Home Affairs Select Committee report *Controls over Firearms*.[1] In particular, stricter controls are introduced concerning specially dangerous air weapons. **7.1.1**

The firearms page of the Home Office 'Crime & Policing' website makes plain the Government's concern regarding the availability of firearms: **7.1.2**

> In some areas, gun crime is a major cause of fear and distress. Most worrying is the rise in the number of young people carrying firearms, either to boost their image, or from a misguided idea about self-protection. Last year 97 lives were lost to gun crime. This is unacceptable, and the police will soon organise a crackdown.[2]

Recent initiatives attempting to control the number of firearms available on the street have included the 'Gun Amnesty—Get Guns Off the Streets'. Between 31 March and 30 April 2003, the amnesty encouraged people to hand in illegally-held guns and ammunition at local police stations without being charged. A total of 43,908 guns and 1,039,358 rounds of ammunition were handed in. The items included: 6,529 prohibited firearms (including 5,734 handguns), 10,513 shotguns, 13,974 air weapons, 9,480 imitations, 3,412 assorted rifles and other guns.[3] While the Government, arguably with some justification, considers the **7.1.3**

---

[1] Home Affairs Committee, *Controls over Firearms* (HC 95 1999–2000) 6 April 2000.

[2] Additional information concerning these issues is available on the Home Office website, at *www.homeoffice.gov.uk/crimeandpolicing/firearms.*

[3] Additional information concerning these issues is available on the Home Office website, at *www.homeoffice.gov.uk/crimeandpolicing/firearms.*

amnesty to have been a success, the large number of weapons handed in indicates the extent of the firearms problem.

7.2. LEGISLATIVE CONTEXT

Firearms Act 1968

7.2.1 The Firearms Act 1968 contains a wide range of provisions relating to the possession, handling and distribution of firearms and ammunition for firearms.

7.2.2 A firearm is defined as any lethal barrelled weapon of any description from which a shot, bullet or other missile can be discharged, including any 'prohibited weapon' whether or not it is a lethal weapon, any component of a lethal or prohibited weapon, and any accessory to any such weapon designed or adapted to diminish the noise or flash caused by firing the weapon.[4]

7.2.3 A 'lethal weapon' is one which, when misused, is capable of causing injury from which death may result.[5] It is irrelevant whether or not the instrument was designed to cause injury or death.[6]

7.2.4 The provisions in the 1968 Act do not apply to an antique firearm that is sold, given away, bought or possessed as an ornament.[7]

Previous amendments

7.2.5 A new s 16A was inserted into the 1968 Act by s 1 of the Firearms (Amendment) Act 1994, creating a further offence in relation to the use of imitation firearms. It provides that it is an offence for a person to have in his possession any firearm or imitation firearm with intent (a) by means thereof to cause, or (b) to enable another person by means thereof to cause, any person to believe that unlawful violence[8] will be used against him or another person.

Suggestions for further reform

7.2.6 In its White Paper, *Respect and Responsibility, Taking a Stand Against Anti-Social Behaviour*, the Government focused on the menace of imitation firearms:

> . . . the misuse of replica firearms has also resulted in considerable alarm. In inner city areas the police estimate that 50% of call-outs of armed police result from the sighting of an imitation firearm. There is a real risk that the person carrying the imitation will be shot if they appear to threaten the police or members of the public. There is also evidence that replica firearms are used to threaten victims and that some young people, particularly in inner city areas, have taken to carrying replica firearms as fashion accessories and to intimidate

[4] 1968 Act, s 57(1).
[5] *R v Thorpe* [1987] 1 WLR 383, CA.
[6] *Read v Donovan* [1947] KB 326, DC.
[7] 1968 Act, s 58(2).
[8] ie violence not justified by self-defence etc.

others. This cannot be ignored and we intend to combat it by introducing a new offence of having an imitation firearm in a public place without lawful authority or reasonable excuse. As with air weapons, this offence will have a power to arrest and to seize attached to it.[9]

The Home Affairs Select Committee considered, in its report *Controls over Firearms*,[10] that: **7.2.7**

. . . the main mischief involving the misuse of firearms by young people is in the unsupervised misuse of airguns.

During the 2001/02 parliamentary session, three Private Members' Bills were introduced that attempted to tackle the use of airguns by minors.[11] None of these Bills, however, even achieved a second reading. The most recent was Jonathan Shaw's Air Weapons Bill,[12] introduced as a 'ten minute rule' Bill on 29 October 2002. During the first reading, which was unopposed, he stated that his Bill sought: **7.2.8**

. . . to amend the Firearms Act 1968, by raising the age for unsupervised possession and use of air weapons from 14 to 17 years. That would bring the legislation relating to air weapons into line with other gun control legislation. My Bill will not have an effect on youngsters under 17 using air weapons in registered clubs.[13]

Although the Bill did not become law, the Government took up its theme in the White Paper, promising to tackle the dangers of airguns: **7.2.9**

[S]ome people use airguns to break windows, hurt pets and even shoot people. This conduct is wholly unacceptable and we are determined to deal with it. For this reason, we have decided to increase the age at which young people can own an air weapon from 14 to 17 and to tighten up on when they can be used without adult supervision.

The White Paper also expressed concern that air weapons using self-contained gas cartridge systems have, because of their realistic appearance: **7.2.10**

. . . become popular with certain criminals and have been used in a number of serious crimes including seven homicides. No viable way has been found of making these weapons less easily convertible. We intend, therefore, to ban the importation, sale and manufacture of these weapons.[14]

This concern was repeated in the explanatory notes to the Anti-Social Behaviour Bill,[15] stating that such weapons can easily be converted to fire conventional ammunition and have been increasingly used in gun crime. **7.2.11**

The provisions of Part 5 of the 2003 Act focus on reforming the position concerning imitation firearms,[16] the possession of air weapons by minors, and the prohibition of certain types of air weapon. **7.2.12**

[9] Cm 5778, 2003, paras 3.17–3.18.
[10] Cm 4864, October 2000, p 10.
[11] See House of Commons Research Paper 03/34, 4 April 2003, pp 86–87.
[12] Bill 198, 2001–2002.
[13] *Hansard*, HC col 685 (29 October 2002).
[14] Cm 5778, 2003, para 3.19.
[15] 2003 Act, Explanatory Notes, para 99.
[16] Defined by Firearms Act 1968, s 57(4). See also para 7.3.4.

7.3. THE PROVISIONS OF PART 5 OF THE ACT[17]

Possession of air weapons or imitation firearms in public places

7.3.1 In its form before the amendments effected by the 2003 Act (and until those amendments come into force), s 19 of the Firearms Act 1968 provided:

> 19. A person commits an offence if, without lawful authority or reasonable excuse (the proof whereof lies on him) he has with him in a public place a loaded shot gun or loaded air weapon, or any other firearm (whether loaded or not) together with ammunition suitable for use in that firearm.[18]

7.3.2 'Public place' includes any highway and any other premises or place to which, at the material time, the public have or are permitted to have access whether on payment or otherwise.[19] To prove that a person has a firearm 'with him', it is necessary to show more than mere possession: some form of close physical link and immediate control must be demonstrated.[20]

7.3.3 Section 19 is amended by s 37 of the 2003 Act, so that the prohibition it provides now extends to air weapons and imitation firearms.[21] Accordingly, it will be an offence to carry an air weapon (whether loaded or not) or an imitation firearm in a public place without lawful authority or reasonable excuse.[22] The new wording of the section is as follows:

> 19. A person commits an offence if, without lawful authority or reasonable excuse (the proof whereof lies on him) he has with him in a public place
> (a) a loaded shot gun,
> (b) an air weapon (whether loaded or not),
> (c) any other firearm (whether loaded or not) together with ammunition suitable for use in that firearm, or
> (d) an imitation firearm.

7.3.4 'Imitation firearm' is defined to include anything that has the appearance of being a firearm whether or not it is capable of discharging a shot, bullet or other missile.[23]

---

[17] In force from 20 January 2004, except s 39 which came into force on 20 January 2004 and 30 April 2004: Anti-Social Behaviour Act 2003 (Commencement No 1 and Transitional Provisions) Order 2003, SI 2003/3300. See also the Secretary of State's guidance contained in Home Office Circular 01/2004.

[18] Prevention of Crime Act 1953, s 1 provides a similar offence relating to offensive weapons.

[19] Firearms Act 1968, s 57(4).

[20] *R v Kelt* [1977] 3 All ER 1099.

[21] s 37 came into force on 20 January 2004.

[22] By s 37(2), consequential amendments are made to Sch 6, Pt I of the 1968 Act, dealing with modes of prosecution, maximum punishment and powers of the court on conviction of firearms offences.

[23] Firearms Act 1968, s 57(4). A weapon designed or adapted for the discharge of any noxious liquid, gas or other thing, within s 5(1)(b), is not an imitation firearm.

The contrast between s 16A of the 1968 Act[24] and the new s 19 is clear. The former requires proof of intent to use the imitation firearm to threaten unlawful violence. The new offence requires no proof of any intent; it is sufficient that the person has the imitation firearm with her/him in a public place, without reasonable excuse.[25] 7.3.5

The new offences in respect of air weapons and imitation firearms are arrestable for the purposes of the Police and Criminal Evidence Act 1984.[26] They are summary offences only, the maximum penalty on summary conviction being a term of six months' imprisonment, and/or a fine not exceeding the statutory maximum (currently £5,000).[27] 7.3.6

Age limits for air weapons

The intentions set out in the White Paper, which closely followed the Air Weapons Bill referred to above,[28] are given legislative form in s 38 of the 2003 Act.[29] Section 38(2) amends s 22(4) and repeals s 22(5) of the 1968 Act (concerning the acquisition and possession of firearms by minors), to increase the age at which a young person may own any air weapon from 14 to 17, subject to certain exceptions. 7.3.7

The exceptions are set out in s 23 of the 1968 Act, which section is also amended. Current exceptions continue, allowing a person over the age of 14 to have with him an air weapon or ammunition while under the supervision of a person over the age of 21,[30] and when he is engaging in target shooting as a member of an approved rifle or miniature rifle club, or in a shooting gallery where only air weapons or miniature rifles are used.[31] 7.3.8

A new exception is also created, by means of a new s 23(3) and (4)[32] permitting 14 year olds and above to have an air weapon with them unsupervised on private premises and with the consent of the occupier. The new s 23(4) makes it a summary offence, however, to fire any missile beyond the boundaries of those premises, punishable by a fine not exceeding level 3 on the standard scale.[33] It is also an offence to give an air weapon or ammunition to a person under the age of 17,[34] or, unless 7.3.9

---

[24] See para 7.2.5 above.

[25] Guidance issued in Home Office Circular 01/2004 suggests that, in the absence of a statutory definition of 'reasonable excuse', it will be for police officers to exercise discretion as to what action to take in individual cases. It is not intended to penalize legitimate activities, such as theatrical work or historical re-enactment (para 6).

[26] 2003 Act, s 37(3), inserting a new para 5A into Sch 1A to the Police and Criminal Evidence Act 1984.

[27] ibid, s 37(2), amending Sch 6, Pt 1.

[28] See paras 7.2.8–7.2.9 above.

[29] In force 20 January 2004.

[30] But where he is on premises in circumstances where the only reason an offence is not committed is this very exception, it is an offence for the person—and for the supervising person to permit the person—to use the weapon beyond those premises: 1968 Act, s 23(1).

[31] ibid, s 23(2).

[32] Inserted by 2003 Act, s 38(3).

[33] Currently £1,000.

[34] Formerly, the age was 14.

by s 23 of the 1968 Act he is not prohibited from having it with him, to part with possession of such a weapon or ammunition to a person under 17.[35]

Prohibition of certain weapons

7.3.10 Section 39(3) of the Act extends the provisions of s 5 of the 1968 Act, which imposes a general prohibition on purchasing, acquiring, manufacturing, selling, transferring or having in one's possession the weapons listed in that section, to include air weapons that use the self-contained gas cartridge system. As stated above, the Government has become concerned that such weapons are vulnerable to conversion to fire conventional ammunition and have been increasingly used in gun crime.[36] Accordingly, a new s 5(1)(af) is inserted, relating to:

> any air rifle, air gun or air pistol which uses, or is designed or adapted for use with, a self-contained gas cartridge system.[37]

7.3.11 Consequently, these weapons cannot be possessed, purchased, acquired, manufactured, sold or transferred without the authority of the Secretary of State.

7.3.12 These new prohibitions are not retrospective, however, in that they do not remove the right of people who already own such weapons to retain them. By s 39(4) of the Act, the general prohibition contained in s 5(1) of the 1968 Act does not prevent a person's continued possession of such a weapon, but an existing owner will now be required to obtain a firearms certificate for it from the police.[38] The requirement for a firearms certificate does not apply, however, to possession by authorized dealers.[39]

7.3.13 It should be noted that the Criminal Justice Act 2003 makes fresh provision for the procedures for prosecuting firearms offences, including breaches of the general prohibition imposed by s 5(1) in respect of the new category of air weapons now set out at s 5(1)(af), and for the sentences that may be imposed on conviction, including the imposition of a minimum term of imprisonment of five years for a defendant who is over 18 and three years for a defendant who is under 18. These offences have now been made triable only on indictment.[40]

---

[35] See 2003 Act, s 38(4) and (5), making consequential amendments to 1968 Act, s 24(4) and Sch 6, Pt I.

[36] See para 7.2.11 above.

[37] 2003 Act , s 39(3). A consequential amendment is made to s 1(3)(b) of the 1968 Act by s 39(2). Section 39 came into force on 20 January 2004, except for the offence of possession of a self-contained gas cartridge gun, which came into force on 30 April 2004.

[38] ibid, s 39(4)(b), applying s 1 of the 1968 Act. The police will not be able to refuse or revoke or partially revoke a certificate (as they normally can) on the basis that the owner does not have a good reason for having the weapon in his possession, but the other grounds for refusal will still be available: see 1968 Act, Pt II and in particular, ss 27(1)(b), 30A(4) and 30B(2).

[39] 2003 Act, s 39(5) and 1968 Act, s 8.

[40] Criminal Justice Act 2003, ss 287–288.

Specially dangerous weapons

Section 39(6) of the Act amends s 1(4) of the Firearms (Amendment) Act 1988, which enables the Secretary of State, by order, to include further prohibited weapons and ammunition under s 5(1) of the 1968 Act, to enable the Secretary of State to use this power to prohibit an air rifle, air gun, or air pistol that appears to be 'specially dangerous'. **7.3.14**

A new s 1(4A), inserted by s 39(6)(b) of the 2003 Act, provides that the Secretary of State's order may apply any other provision of the 1968 Act with or without modification or exception to any newly prohibited weapon; impose conditions on any application, modification or exception provided by the order (including a requirement to obtain a firearms certificate); make provision generally or by reference to a particular purpose or circumstance; confer a function on the Secretary of State or any other specified person; and make transitional, consequential or incidental provision. **7.3.15**

8

PART 6 OF THE ACT: THE ENVIRONMENT

8.1. INTRODUCTION

Graffiti, noise and litter were matters referred to in the Government's Sustainable Development Strategy[1] as symptomatic of urban decline and likely to lead to further degradation of an area: **8.1.1**

Dirty and dangerous places encourage graffiti, vandalism and anti-social behaviour, which in turn undermine public confidence in them and leads people to avoid them . . . A high quality local environment is a big influence in making people visit a place, spend money and invest in it. Conversely, a low quality environment can lead to places becoming stigmatized and drive people, businesses and investment away.

Part 6 of the 2003 Act seeks to address some of these issues. **8.1.2**

Noise

In its 2002 *Pollution Handbook*, the National Society for Clean Air and Environmental Protection describes noise in the following terms. **8.1.3**

In its widest sense, neighbourhood noise might be defined as any unwanted sound in the vicinity of the home or its locality. That definition might embrace industrial noise, noise from transport as well as noise from domestic premises, which is the biggest source of noise nuisance complaints.

---

[1] *Living Places, Cleaner, Safer, Greener*, Office of the Deputy Prime Minister, October 2002.

8.2. LEGISLATIVE CONTEXT

Noise

8.2.1 Sections 2–9 of the Noise Act 1996 ('the 1996 Act') enabled local authorities to adopt powers to deal with night-time noise, and in particular the power to issue a fixed penalty notice to 'noise offenders'. It was hoped that these powers would allow local authorities to short-cut the often time-consuming judicial process involved in serving abatement notices and pursuing statutory nuisance proceedings under Part III of the Environmental Protection Act 1990 ('the 1990 Act').

8.2.2 If an authority wished to take up the powers conferred by the 1996 Act, it was necessary to notify the Secretary of State that they were doing so and also to provide 24 hour noise patrols. Because of the drain on resources that this would entail, and the other potential costs of the scheme, only 14 local authorities took up the powers on offer.

Litter, graffiti and fly-posting

8.2.3 Part IV of the 1990 Act confers on local authorities the power to deal with litter, but does not extend to graffiti or fly-posting. The 1990 Act makes littering an offence (with fixed penalty notice) and gives local authorities, educational institutions, designated statutory undertakers and other public bodies a duty to clear litter and refuse from their local land and highways, to designate litter control areas and to issue litter abatement notices if relevant land is not kept clear of litter.

8.2.4 Sections 91–92 of the 1990 Act entitle a member of the public to seek a litter abatement order.

8.3. PROVISIONS OF PART 6 OF THE ACT[2]

Noise

Closure of noisy premises

8.3.1 Section 40 of the 2003 Act creates a new power to close down certain premises that are causing a noise nuisance. The premises which may be closed are (a) licensed premises; and (b) premises in respect of which a temporary event notice has effect.[3] A temporary event notice[4] is a notice given by the owner of premises

[2] ss 40–45, 47, 55 and 56 came into force in England only on 31 March 2004. Sections 46 and 54 came into force generally on the same date. Sections 48–52 (graffiti removal notices) came into force in 12 pilot areas in England on the same date: Anti-Social Behaviour Act 2003 (Commencement No 2) Order 2004, SI 2004/690.

[3] 2003 Act, s 40(2).

[4] ibid, s 41(3) states that the term is to be treated as having effect in accordance with s 170(6) of the Licensing Act 2003. There is, however, no such provision; s 170 of the Licensing Act 2003 has

who is intending to use the premises for a temporary activity (not exceeding 96 hours and not involving more than 500 people) for which a licence would otherwise be required. Part V of the Licensing Act 2003 permits certain activity ('temporary permitted activity') where a temporary event notice is in force and the requirements of the licensing authority and police have been met.[5]

The chief executive officer[6] of the relevant local authority[7] may make a closure order in respect of such premises if he reasonably believes that: **8.3.2**

(a) a public nuisance is being caused by noise coming from the premises; and
(b) the closure of the premises is necessary to prevent that nuisance.[8]

The chief executive of the authority does not have to exercise this function personally. He may authorize an environmental health officer[9] of the same authority to do so, either generally or in relation to specific premises.[10] If he does so, the authorized environmental health officer must reasonably believe that public nuisance is caused by noise from the premises and that it is necessary to close the premises.[11] **8.3.3**

A closure order is an order that requires the premises it specifies to be kept closed during a period that is also specified in the order. That period may not exceed 24 hours and begins at the time a manager of the premises in question receives written notice of the order.[12] Unusually, therefore, it seems that the notice itself does not have to be served on the manager but that written notice of the order is sufficient. The 'manager' of the premises, for this purpose, is defined as: **8.3.4**

(a) a person who holds a premises licence in respect of the premises;
(b) a designated premises supervisor under a premises licence in respect of the premises;
(c) the premises user in relation to a temporary event notice that has effect in respect of the premises; and
(d) any other person who works at the premises in a capacity (paid or unpaid) that enables him to close them.[13]

---

only five subsections. That section confers on the police an exemption from liability for damages if they enforce a closure order in respect of licensed premises made under Pt 8 of that Act.

5 See Licensing Act 2003, Pt 5 and in particular ss 98–102.

6 ie the Head of Paid Service under s 4 of the Local Government and Housing Act 1989: 2003 Act, s 41(3).

7 Meaning the local authority that has statutory functions for the area in which the premises are situated in relation to minimizing or preventing the risk of pollution of the environment or of harm to human health: 2003 Act, s 41(3).

8 ibid, s 40(1).

9 Defined as an officer authorized by the authority for the purpose of exercising a statutory function in relation to pollution of the environment or harm to human health: ibid, s 41(3).

10 ibid, s 41(2)(a). 11 ibid, s 41(2)(b). 12 ibid, s 40(3). 13 ibid, s 41(3).

8.3.5 On making the order, notice of it must be given as soon as reasonably practicable to the licensing authority for the area in which the premises are situated.[14]

8.3.6 It is a summary offence to permit premises to be kept open in contravention of a closure order. The maximum penalty on conviction of this offence is three months' imprisonment and/or a fine not exceeding £20,000.

8.3.7 The chief executive or authorized environmental health officer[15] may cancel the closure order before the end of the specified period by notice in writing to the manager of the premises.[16] The order must, in fact, be cancelled as soon as reasonably practicable if he believes (which need not be a reasonable belief) that it is no longer necessary to prevent a public nuisance being caused by noise from the premises.[17]

Noise at night

8.3.8 The other noise-related provisions of Part 6 relate to noise at night, and operate by amending the unsuccessful and largely ignored powers created by the Noise Act 1996.[18]

8.3.9 A new s 1 is inserted into the 1996 Act by s 42(2) of the 2003 Act, applying the (amended) provisions of ss 2–9 of the 1996 Act to the area of every local authority in England and Wales, where previously those provisions only applied if an authority had made a resolution to that effect.

8.3.10 The amendments to ss 2–9 of the 1996 Act render those provisions—now applicable to all English and Welsh local authorities—rather less onerous in their effect. A new s 2(1), inserted by s 42(3) of the 2003 Act, downgrades to a power the previous duty to secure that an officer of the authority takes reasonable steps to investigate complaints, made by a person in a dwelling at night, that excessive noise is being emitted from another dwelling.[19]

8.3.11 Section 9(4) of the 1996 Act is also amended in relation to the use that may be made of the proceeds of a fixed penalty notice. If a person continues to make a noise exceeding a permitted limit notwithstanding the service on him of a warning notice, he commits a criminal offence.[20] The authority may, however, give him a fixed penalty notice offering him the chance to discharge any liability he would otherwise have to be convicted of that offence, by paying a penalty in accordance with the terms of the notice (within 14 days).[21] By s 9(4) of the 1996 Act as originally enacted, the proceeds of all such notices had to be paid to the Secretary of State.

---

[14] 2003 Act, s 41(1)(c). [15] ibid, s 41(2). [16] ibid, s 41(1)(a). [17] ibid, s 41(1)(b).

[18] See paras 8.2.1–8.2.2 above.

[19] Noise Act 1996, s 2(1)–(2). Section 42(4) makes amendments to s 2(7) of the 1996 Act consequent on the extension of the application of these sections to all authorities in England and Wales, omitting the words that had been inserted to clarify that the power of an authority to act in relation to a property in another authority's area applied even where the other authority had not taken up the powers itself.

[20] 1996 Act, s 4. [21] ibid, s 8.

Section 42(5) inserts new s 9(4)–(4F), entitling an authority to retain any sums it receives by way of fixed penalties, and to use them for the purposes of their 'qualifying functions'.[22] Qualifying functions are functions under the 2003 Act and functions of a description specified in regulations made by the Secretary of State, which may have the effect that an authority may use its receipts for the purposes of any of its functions.[23] Regulations may also make provision for what authorities are to do with their penalty notice receipts pending their use for a qualifying function, and what they are to do with such receipts if they have not been used for a qualifying function within a time limit specified in the regulations, which may include paying them to another person including the Secretary of State. Such regulations may also specify accounting arrangements for such receipts.[24] Before making regulations, the Secretary of State must consult the local authorities to which the regulations apply and any other person he considers appropriate.[25] 8.3.12

Authorities must supply the Secretary of State with such information as he may require about their use of penalty notice receipts.[26] 8.3.13

Penalty notices for graffiti and fly-posting

Sections 43–47 of the Act introduce a new power for local authorities to give fixed penalty notices to offenders who have perpetrated acts of graffiti or fly-posting. 8.3.14

Circumstances in which a notice may be given

If an authorized officer[27] of a local authority[28] has reason to believe that a person has committed a 'relevant offence' in that authority's area, he may—subject to certain exceptions—give that person a fixed penalty notice, which has the effect of offering him the opportunity of discharging any liability to conviction for that offence by payment of a penalty in accordance with the notice.[29] 8.3.15

The 'relevant offences', all graffiti and fly-posting type offences otherwise prosecutable under the various enactments listed below, and usually prosecuted under the Criminal Damage Act 1971, are as follows: 8.3.16

---

[22] 1996 Act, s 9(4) as amended. [23] ibid, s 9(4A)–(4B). [24] ibid, s 9(4D)–(4E).

[25] ibid, s 9(4F).

[26] ibid, s 9(4C). 2003 Act, s 42(6) and (7) makes a minor consequential amendment to s 11 (interpretation) of the 1996 Act and deems the reference to the 1996 Act in the National Assembly for Wales (Transfer of Functions) Order 1999, SI 1999/672 to be a reference to that Act as amended by s 42.

[27] Defined as an officer of a local authority who is authorized in writing by the authority for the purpose of giving notices under s 43(1): 2003 Act, s 47(1).

[28] 'Local authority' means a litter authority for the purposes of Environmental Protection Act 1990, s 88, ie an English county council or joint board, the Broads Authority and a 'principal litter authority' which is none of the above.

[29] 2003 Act, s 43(1).

(a) an offence under s 54, para 10, of the Metropolitan Police Act 1839 (affixing posters etc);
(b) an offence under s 20(1) of the London County Council (General Powers) Act 1954 (defacement of streets with slogans etc);
(c) an offence under s 1(1) of the Criminal Damage Act 1971, which involves only the painting or writing on, or the soiling, marking or other defacing of, any property by whatever means;
(d) an offence under s 131(2) of the Highways Act 1980, including as applied by the Countryside Act 1968, s 27(6) (damaging the highway, including obliteration of a traffic sign) which involves only an act of obliteration;
(e) an offence under s 132(1) of the Highways Act 1980 (painting or affixing things on structures on the highway etc); and
(f) an offence under s 224(3) of the Town and Country Planning Act 1990 (displaying an advertisement in contravention of regulations).

Form of notice

8.3.17 A penalty notice must be in the form prescribed by an order made by the 'appropriate person', ie in England, the Secretary of State, and in Wales, the National Assembly for Wales.[30] Apart from this, it must contain such details of the circumstances alleged to constitute the offence as are necessary to give reasonable information of the offence.[31] It must also state the period during which proceedings will not be instituted for the offence, the amount of the penalty and the person to whom and address at which the penalty can be paid.[32] Without prejudice to any other means of paying the penalty, payment may be made by posting a stamped letter containing the amount of the penalty in cash or otherwise, to that person at the address specified.[33] Where this is done, the payment is deemed to have been made at the time when the letter would have been delivered in the ordinary course of post.

8.3.18 The amount of the penalty payable is £50, but the appropriate person may, by order, substitute a different amount.[34]

Effect of notice

8.3.19 If a penalty notice is given to a person in respect of an offence, the person has 14 days in which to pay the penalty. No prosecution for any relevant offence arising out of the circumstances in which the notice was given may be instituted within that period. If he pays the penalty in accordance with the notice, within the 14 day period, he cannot be convicted of the offence.

8.3.20 In any proceedings, a certificate that purports to be signed by, or on behalf of, the person responsible for the financial affairs of a local authority, and which

[30] 2003 Act, ss 43(9) and 47(1). [31] ibid, s 43(5). [32] ibid, s 43(6).
[33] ibid, s 43(7).
[34] ibid, s 43(10)–(11) and see s 47(1) (and para 8.3.17) for the definition of 'appropriate person'.

states that the payment of a penalty under s 43(1) either was or was not received by a date specified in the certificate, is evidence of the facts stated.[35] The certificate is not stated, however, to be conclusive evidence of the facts contained in the certificate, nor even to raise a rebuttable presumption of the truth of those facts. Accordingly, it would seem to remain open to the defendant in the normal way to contend that the payment was made in accordance with the terms of the notice and that therefore he cannot be convicted of the offence.

Exceptions to the power to give a notice

Where the relevant offence is an offence under s 224(3) of the Town and Country Planning Act 1990 (displaying an advertisement in contravention of regulations),[36] a penalty notice may not be given to a person unless the authorized officer has reason to believe that the person personally affixed to or against, or placed the advertisement[37] on, the land or object on which it was displayed.[38] Accordingly, in the case of fly-posting, the person whose goods or services are advertised will not be liable to a fixed penalty (unless he or she also affixed the advertisement). **8.3.21**

The other statutory exception to the power to give a fixed penalty relates to the seriousness of the offence. No penalty notice may be given in respect of an offence if the officer considers that the offence is motivated by racial or religious hostility. Specifically, a notice may not be given if the authorized officer considers that: **8.3.22**

(a) the relevant offence in question arises under s 44(1)(c) (ie an offence under s 1(1) of the Criminal Damage Act 1971, which involves only the painting or writing on, or the soiling, marking or other defacing of, any property by whatever means) and also involved the commission of racially aggravated criminal damage for the purposes of s 30 of the Crime and Disorder Act 1998; or
(b) the offence is any of the other relevant offences and was motivated even in part by hostility towards a person based on his membership or presumed membership of a racial or religious group,[39] or towards members of a racial or religious group based on their membership of that group.[40]

[35] ibid, s 45(2).

[36] ibid, s 44(1)(f).

[37] 'Advertisement' and 'land' are defined by s 47(1) to have the meanings given to them by s 336(1) of the Town and Country Planning Act 1990, ie 'advertisement' means any word, letter, model, sign, placard, board, notice, device or representation, whether illuminated or not, in the nature of, and employed wholly or partly for the purposes of, advertisement, announcement or direction, and (without prejudice to the previous provisions of this definition) includes any hoarding or similar structure used, or adapted for use, for the display of advertisements, and references to the display of advertisements shall be construed accordingly; 'land' means any corporeal hereditament, including a building.

[38] 2003 Act, s 43(3).

[39] Defined to have the meanings given to them by s 28(4) and (5) of the Crime and Disorder Act 1998, ie 'racial group' means a group of persons defined by reference to race, colour, nationality (including citizenship) or ethnic or national origins; 'religious group' means a group of persons defined by reference to religious belief or lack of religious belief.

[40] 2003 Act, s 43(2).

Penalty receipts

8.3.23 Penalties payable under s 43(1) are payable to the local authority.[41] As with noise nuisance penalty receipts, receipts from fixed penalty notices given under s 43(1) may be retained by the local authority but may only be used for 'qualifying functions' of the authority.[42]

8.3.24 Qualifying functions are functions under s 43 of the 2003 Act (ie giving penalty notices) and functions of a description specified in regulations made by the 'appropriate person',[43] which may have the effect that an authority may use its receipts for the purposes of any of its functions.[44] Regulations may also make provision for what authorities are to do with their penalty receipts pending their use for a qualifying function, and what they are to do with such receipts if they have not been used for a qualifying function within a time limit specified in the regulations, which may include paying them to another person including the appropriate person.[45] Such regulations may also specify accounting arrangements for such receipts.[46] Before making regulations, the Secretary of State must consult the local authorities to which the regulations apply and any other person he considers appropriate.[47]

8.3.25 Authorities must supply the appropriate person with such information as he may require about their use of penalty notice receipts.[48]

Powers of police civilians

8.3.26 As discussed elsewhere,[49] the Police Reform Act 2002 ('the 2002 Act') provided for the creation of community safety accreditation schemes that enabled chief officers of police to designate civilians under their direction and control to exercise powers and undertake duties in carrying out specified functions. Civilians employed by a police authority may be designated 'community support officers';[50] civilians employed by other people with whom a chief officer of police has an arrangement in respect of the carrying out of community safety functions may be accredited as 'accredited persons'.[51]

8.3.27 Section 46(1) of the 2003 Act amends Sch 4 to the 2002 Act to extend the powers of community support officers to include the issue of penalty notices under s 43(1).[52] Schedule 5 to the 2002 Act is similarly amended to allow 'accredited persons' to issue such penalty notices.[53]

Graffiti removal notices

8.3.28 Where a local authority[54] is satisfied that a 'relevant surface' in an area has been defaced by graffiti, and that the defacement is detrimental to the amenity of the

[41] 2003 Act, s 45(1). [42] ibid, s 45(3). [43] See ibid, s 47(1) and para 8.3.17 above.
[44] ibid, s 45(5). [45] ibid, s 45(7)–(8). [46] ibid, s 45(7)(b). [47] ibid, s 45(9).
[48] ibid, s 45(6). [49] See Chapters 6 and 11. [50] 2002 Act, s 38 and Sch 4.
[51] 2002 Act, s 41 and Sch 5. [52] Inserting a new Sch 4, para 1(2)(ca).
[53] 2003 Act, s 46(2) inserting a new Sch 5, para 1(2)(ba) into the 2002 Act.
[54] Meaning a local litter authority for the purposes of the Environmental Protection Act 1990, s 88: 2003 Act, s 48(12). For the definition of 'litter authority', see n 28 above.

area, or is offensive, it may serve a 'graffiti removal notice' upon any person who is responsible for the surface that has been defaced. A notice requires that the defacement must be removed, cleared or otherwise remedied within the period specified in the notice, beginning with the day on which the notice is served, which must be at least 28 days.[55] If the requirement is not complied with, the authority or any person authorized by it may remove, clear or otherwise remedy the defacement, and may enter the land to the extent reasonably necessary for that purpose.[56]

Relevant surface

A 'relevant surface' is any of the following surfaces, which may be internal or external, open to the air or not. **8.3.29**

The relevant surface first described is the surface of any street that is public land or of any building, structure, apparatus, plant or other object in or on any street that is public land.[57] **8.3.30**

Other relevant surfaces are: **8.3.31**

(a) the surface of any land owned, occupied or controlled by a statutory undertaker or of any building, structure, apparatus, plant or other object in or on any such land; and
(b) the surface of any land owned, occupied or controlled by an educational institution (including its governing body) or of any building, structure, apparatus, plant or other object in or on any such land;

but only if the land is public land, or the surface is visible from public land or it is otherwise visible to members of the public using the services or facilities of the statutory undertaker or educational institution in question or any other statutory undertaker or educational institution.[58]

Definitions

Graffiti

Graffiti includes painting, writing, soiling, marking or other defacing by whatever means.[59] **8.3.32**

Statutory undertaker

A 'statutory undertaker' is a body so defined by s 98(6) of the Environmental Protection Act 1990, namely: **8.3.33**

(a) any person authorised by any enactment to carry on any railway, light railway, tramway or road transport undertaking;
(b) any person authorised by any enactment to carry on any canal, inland navigation, dock, harbour or pier undertaking; or

---

[55] 2003 Act, s 48(3). [56] ibid, s 48(4)–(5). [57] ibid, s 48(9)(a) and (10)(a).
[58] ibid, s 48(9)(b)–(c) and (10)(b). [59] ibid, s 48(12).

(c) any relevant airport operator (within the meaning of Part V of the Airports Act 1986).[60]

Educational institution

8.3.34 Likewise, 'educational institution' has the meaning given by s 98(2) of the Environmental Protection Act 1990, as amended, namely:

(a) the Open University;
(b) any institution that provides higher education or further education (or both) which is full-time education being an institution which—
  (i) is maintained by grants made by the Secretary of State under s 485 of the Education Act 1996;
  (ii) is maintained by a local education authority;
(c) any institution within the higher education sector within the meaning of s 91(5) of the Further and Higher Education Act 1992;
(d) any institution within the further education sector within the meaning of s 91(3) of the Further and Higher Education Act 1992;
(e) any city technology college or city college for the technology of the arts or academy;
(f) any community, foundation or voluntary school; or
(g) any community or foundation special school.

Person responsible for the surface

8.3.35 The person responsible for the surface is, where the surface in question is the surface of any land, including a street, a person who owns, leases, occupies, controls, operates or maintains the land. Where the surface is the surface of anything else, the person responsible for the surface is a person who owns, leases, occupies, controls, operates or maintains the thing.[61]

8.3.36 The notice is served on any person responsible for the surface.[62] Service should be effected at the proper address of the recipient.[63]

8.3.37 If, after reasonable enquiry, the local authority is unable to ascertain the name or proper address of any person responsible, it may affix a notice to the surface affected and enter the land to the extent reasonably necessary for that purpose. If it takes this course, the notice is treated as having been served on a person responsible for the surface.[64] Given the terms of an exemption from liability for any damage this may cause, it is likely that the authority will instruct an officer rather than a contractor to undertake this exercise, where it is necessary (see s 52(2)(b) and para 8.3.47 below).

8.3.38 These service provisions give rise to a question as to the position where the local authority is itself the person responsible for the relevant surface.

[60] 2003 Act, s 48(12). [61] ibid, s 48(11). [62] ibid, s 48(2).
[63] ibid, s 48(7), applying the provisions of s 160 of the Environmental Protection Act 1990; see para 8.3.39 below.
[64] ibid, s 48(8).

In *R v Cardiff CC, ex p Cross*,[65] the Court of Appeal held that the repair notice provisions of (then) the Housing Act 1957, Part II, under which the relevant local authority served notice on the person managing or controlling the building requiring repairs to be effected, did not apply where the local authority was itself the manager/controller of the building, as it was legal nonsense for a person to serve a notice upon himself. It would seem strongly arguable that the same legal principle would apply to the serving of any notice by a local authority on itself, particularly a notice so similar in concept as a graffiti removal notice. Accordingly, local authority owned and controlled surfaces may be immune from this procedure.

Contents of the notice

The notice must explain that if its requirements are not complied with within the permitted time, the authority may enter the land and remedy the defacement itself. It must also explain that if it does exercise that power, it may recover from the person responsible for the surface the expenditure it reasonably incurs in doing so, so long as it first serves a notice on that person setting out the amount and details of the expenditure it intends to recover. The effect of s 160 of the Environmental Protection Act 1990, which has effect in relation to graffiti removal notices, must also be explained.[66] The notice must, finally, explain that a person on whom a graffiti removal notice is served has a right to appeal against it to the magistrates' court within 21 days of the date of service, and explain the grounds on which such an appeal may be brought (see further paras 8.3.42–8.3.44 below).[67] **8.3.39**

Recovery of expenditure

As stated above, if a graffiti removal notice is not complied with and the authority exercises its power to take the requisite action itself, it may, after serving a notice setting out the amount and details of the expenditure it proposes to recover, recover its reasonable expenses incurred in taking the remedial action from the person on whom the graffiti removal notice was served.[68] As with the graffiti removal notice itself, the notice may be validly served by delivering it to the recipient or by leaving it at the recipient's proper address, or by sending it by post to that address.[69] **8.3.40**

Guidance

The Secretary of State must issue guidance to local authorities in England, and the National Assembly for Wales must issue guidance to local authorities in Wales, **8.3.41**

[65] (1982) 6 HLR 6, CA.

[66] ie that the notice may be properly served by delivering it to the recipient or by leaving it at the recipient's proper address, or by sending it by post to that address.

[67] ibid, s 48(6), requiring an explanation of the effects of ss 48(4)–(5), 49 and 51.

[68] ibid, s 49.

[69] ibid, s 49(3), applying s 160 of the Environmental Protection Act 1990.

for the purposes of ss 48 and 49 of the 2003 Act, as to the exercise of the powers those sections create. Local authorities must have regard to such guidance.[70]

Appeals

8.3.42 Any person on whom a graffiti removal notice is served may, within 21 days of service, appeal against the notice to a magistrates' court on any of the following grounds:

(a) that the defacement is neither detrimental to the amenity of the area nor offensive;
(b) that there is a material defect or error in, or in connection with, the notice;
(c) that the notice should be served on another person.[71]

8.3.43 Where an appeal is brought, the graffiti removal notice is of no effect pending the final determination or withdrawal of the appeal.[72]

8.3.44 On determination of the appeal, the court must quash the notice, modify it or else dismiss the appeal. If it takes either of the latter two options, it may extend the period specified in the notice for compliance with the requirements it specifies.[73]

Appeal against recovery of expenses

8.3.45 A person on whom a notice is served in respect of the proposed recovery of expenditure may appeal to the magistrates' court, within 21 days of service of the notice, on the grounds that the expenditure that the local authority seeks to recover is excessive.[74] On determination of the appeal the court must either confirm that the amount that the authority is proposing to recover is reasonable, or else substitute a lower amount as the amount that the authority is entitled to recover.[75]

Exemptions from liability

8.3.46 The Acts confer a broad exemption from liability (for damages or otherwise; at common law or otherwise) on a person responsible for a relevant surface,[76] arising out of anything done or not done in the exercise or purported exercise of the power to take remedial action in default of compliance with a notice, or of the power to enter land and affix a notice, in circumstances where the person responsible cannot be found.[77]

---

[70] The obligation to have regard to guidance does not mean that the authority must necessarily follow it: see *De Falco v Crawley BC* [1980] QB 460, CA, *per* Lord Denning MR at 478; see also *R v Islington LBC ex p Rixon* [1998] 1 CCLR 119, *per* Sedley J at 123J–K; and most recently, *R (M) v Islington LBC* [2003] HLR 1129, *per* Wilson J at [31]–[33].

[71] 2003 Act, s 51(1)–(2).

[72] ibid, s 51(3).

[73] ibid, s 51(4)–(5).

[74] ibid, s 51(6).

[75] ibid, s 51(7).

[76] Defined by ibid, s 48(11); see s 52(5).

[77] ibid, s 52(1).

The exemption is conferred, in respect of default action, on a local authority and any of its employees, and upon any person, and any employer or employee of his, authorized by an authority for the purpose of taking remedial action in default of compliance with the requirements of a notice.[78] In respect of service of a notice by entering the land and affixing it there, the exemption is conferred on the local authority and any employee of the authority.[79] This is a clear indication that authorities would be well advised to instruct their own officers to effect service of a notice in the manner prescribed by s 48(8), rather than engage a contractor to do so, where such action is necessary. **8.3.47**

The exemption will not apply, however, if the act or omission complained of is shown to have been in bad faith, or the liability arises out of a failure to exercise due care and attention, or so as to prevent an award of damages made in respect of an act or omission on the ground that it was unlawful by virtue of s 6(1) of the Human Rights Act 1998.[80] The exemption does not affect any other exemption from liability that may apply at common law or otherwise.[81] **8.3.48**

Display of advertisements in contravention of regulations

Section 53 of the Act amends s 224(3) of the Town and Country Planning Act 1990, by substituting a fine at level 4 of the standard scale as the maximum punishment for the offence that section creates, in place of the previous maximum fine, which was at level 3 on the standard scale. **8.3.49**

Sale of aerosol paints to children

Section 54 of the 2003 Act creates a new summary criminal offence committed by a person if he sells an aerosol paint container to a person under the age of 16.[82] The offence as originally drafted referred to a person under 18. An 'aerosol paint container' is a device that: **8.3.50**

(a) contains paint stored under pressure, and
(b) is designed to permit the release of the paint as a spray.83

The offence is to 'sell', not to 'supply' an aerosol paint container, and so the legitimate supply by businesses or schools to under 16s who may, for example, use such paints for art projects or in their employment would seem to fall outside the scope of the Act. **8.3.51**

The maximum penalty on conviction of the offence is a fine not exceeding level 4 on the standard scale, currently £2,500.[84] **8.3.52**

It is a defence, however, for the defendant to prove that he took all reasonable steps to determine the purchaser's age and reasonably believed that the purchaser was not under 16.[85] It is also a defence for a defendant charged with the offence **8.3.53**

[78] ibid, s 52(2)(a). [79] ibid, s 52(2)(b). [80] ibid, s 52(3). [81] ibid, s 52(4).
[82] ibid, s 54(1). [83] ibid, s 54(2). [84] ibid, s 54(3). [85] ibid, s 54(4).

in relation to a sale effected by another person to prove that the defendant took all reasonable steps to avoid the commission of the offence.[86] Thus where a shop-owner is prosecuted for a sale made by an employee, he will need to demonstrate the reasonableness of the systems he had in place, and the employee training he had provided (for example, instructing staff to require age identification from the purchaser before making a sale) to avoid sales to under 16s.

Waste and litter

8.3.54 Under the Control of Pollution (Amendment) Act 1989 ('the 1989 Act') local authorities were given powers to carry out 'spot-checks' on vehicles carrying waste, to fine them if they were not registered carriers, and to seize vehicles that had been used to commit the offence.[87] This power was transferred to the Environment Agency upon its creation in 1996.[88]

8.3.55 The 2003 Act extends the powers of local authorities in their waste management role, redesignating them 'waste regulation authorities'[89] to assist them to deal with the problem of fly-tipping. The 1989 Act is amended by s 55 of the 2003 Act to give waste collection authorities under the Environmental Protection Act 1990[90] in England and Wales the powers to stop, search and seize a vehicle they suspect of being used for the unlawful deposit of waste. Waste collection authorities are also regulation authorities.[91]

8.3.56 Section 55(4) amends the Environmental Protection Act 1990 by inserting a new s 59A, which gives the Secretary of State the power to issue statutory directions to clarify the roles and responsibilities of the Environment Agency and waste collection authorities when exercising their powers with regard to requiring the removal of illegally deposited waste under s 59 of the Environmental Protection Act, and to set out categories of waste that should be given priority for the purposes of exercising those powers; the specified categories may be different in different areas. Consequential amendments are also made entitling the Secretary of State to require authorities to provide him (or someone designated by him) with information concerning their use of their s 59 or other powers in respect of illegally deposited waste.[92]

---

[86] 2003 Act, s 55(5).

[87] Control of Pollution (Amendment) Act 1989, ss 5–6.

[88] Environment Act 1995, s 2(1)(b)(i).

[89] Control of Pollution (Amendment) Act 1989, s 7(1) as amended by 2003 Act, s 55(2).

[90] ie in England, district councils, London borough councils, the Common Council of the City of London, the Sub-Treasurer and Under-Treasurer, respectively, of the Inner and Middle Temples; in Wales, county or county borough councils: Environmental Protection Act 1990, s 30(3).

[91] 2003 Act, s 55(3), inserting a new s 9(1A) into the Control of Pollution (Amendment) Act 1989.

[92] ibid, s 55(5), amending Environmental Protection Act 1990, s 71, by inserting a new subs (4). Section 71 confers power on local authorities and the Secretary of State, for the purpose of the discharge of any of their functions under Pt II of that Act (entitled 'Waste on Land'), to serve notices requiring any person to provide them, in a specified form and within a specified time, with information that they reasonably consider to be needed. In Wales, the National Assembly for Wales assumes the Secretary of State's functions.

Section 55(6)–(8) amends various definitions in s 108 of the Environment Act 1995 (which confers powers of entry and investigation, and local pollution control functions on an 'enforcing authority'[93]), the effect of which is to include waste collection authorities within the definition of 'enforcing authority' for certain purposes, so as to confer on them the s 108 powers for the purpose of investigating incidents of unlawfully deposited waste. **8.3.57**

Litter

Section 56 of the Act replaces s 92(10) of the Environmental Protection Act 1990 and inserts new subss (11) and (12), so as to remove the restriction imposed by s 92(10) in its original form preventing local authorities from entering Crown land or land owned by statutory undertakers to deal with litter, if a litter abatement notice is not complied with. Under the new provisions, the only Crown land exempt from the local authority's powers is land occupied for naval, military or air force purposes.[94] The Secretary of State may, however, specify by order land of a statutory undertaker which will remain exempt, if it is requisite or expedient in the national interest that such local authority powers should not apply.[95] **8.3.58**

[93] Defined in Environment Act 1995 , s 108(15) as the Secretary of State, the Environment Agency and a 'local enforcing authority' as defined in 1995 Act, s 113(5).

[94] 2003 Act, s 56(1), inserting a new s 92(11) into the Environmental Protection Act 1990.

[95] ibid, s 56(1), inserting a new s 92(12) into the Environmental Protection Act 1990.

9

PART 7 OF THE ACT: PUBLIC ORDER AND TRESPASS

9.1. INTRODUCTION

9.1.1 Legislation to combat public disorder has tended, over the last 20 years, to respond to specific issues, perceived or real. The Public Order Act 1986 sought to deal with the public processions and assemblies in the wake of the miners' strike of 1984, and with the behaviour of youths in the streets; the Criminal Justice and Public Order Act 1994 was intended to combat the social menace of the rave, together with the much publicized tendency of 'new-age travellers' to invade farmers' land and set up encampments there, causing damage and behaving threateningly.

9.1.2 The measures introduced in the Anti-Social Behaviour Act 2003 are intended to deal with the threats to public order considered by the Government to be the most current (or at least the best publicized by the press), such as the protesters' interference with genetically modified crops, buildings where vivisection is practised and so on.

9.1.3 The new provisions increase the powers of the police to control the conduct of the citizen whether or not, in many circumstances, he or she is acting unlawfully. Most controversially, the powers of the police applicable to public assemblies and processions of 20 or more people now apply to groups of just two people, whatever those people may be doing.

9.2. LEGISLATIVE CONTEXT

Assemblies and processions

9.2.1 The Public Order Act 1986 ('the 1986 Act'),[1] Part II (ss 11–16), establishes controls over the holding and conduct of public assemblies, public processions and trespassory assemblies.[2]

9.2.2 The 1986 Act defines a 'public assembly' as 'an assembly of 20 or more persons in a public place which is wholly or partly open to the air'.[3] A 'public procession' is defined as 'a procession in a public place'.[4] A trespassory assembly is not defined, but comprises an assembly intended to be held at a place on land to which the public has no, or only a limited, right of access, and which is likely to be held without the permission of the occupier of the land or to conduct itself in such a way as to exceed the limits of any such permission or of the public's right of access to the land, and which may result in serious disruption to the life of the community or, in certain circumstances, significant damage.[5]

9.2.3 A 'public place' is defined as meaning any highway or any place to which at the material time the public or any section of the public has access, on payment or otherwise, as of right or by virtue of express or implied permission.[6] Roads, bridges and subways, for example, would all be included within the definition of 'public place'.

Public assemblies

9.2.4 Section 14 of the 1986 Act confers power upon the 'senior police officer'[7] to give directions imposing conditions on people organizing or taking part in a public assembly. Such conditions may relate to the place at which the assembly is to be (or is being) held, the maximum duration of the assembly and the maximum number of people who may attend it.[8]

9.2.5 This power is only available, however, where the senior police officer reasonably believes, having regard to the time at, or place and other circumstances in, which the assembly is being or is intended to be held, that it may result in serious public disorder, serious damage to property or serious disruption to the life

[1] As amended by the Criminal Justice and Public Order Act 1994, ss 70–71 and Sch 10.

[2] The Public Meetings Act 1908 still governs conduct at public meetings.

[3] 1986 Act, s 16.

[4] ibid.

[5] ie where the land or a building or monument on it is of historical, architectural, archaeological or scientific importance, significant damage to the land, building or monument: 1986 Act, s 14A(1)(b)(ii), as amended.

[6] ibid, s 16.

[7] Meaning, where the assembly is actually in the course of being held, the most senior officer present at the scene; where the assembly is intended to be held, the chief officer of police: ibid, s 14(2). The chief officer of police may delegate his functions to an assistant chief constable: s 15(1).

[8] ibid, s 14(1).

of the community, or that the purpose of the people organizing a demonstration is the intimidation of others with a view to compelling them not to do something they have a right to do or to do something they have no right to do.[9]

A person organizing or taking part in a public assembly who knowingly fails 9.2.6
to comply with a condition commits an arrestable offence, as does a person who incites a person taking part in the assembly to commit the offence of failing to comply described above. The organizing and incitement offences carry a maximum penalty, on summary conviction, of three months' imprisonment and/or a fine not exceeding level 4 on the standard scale. The taking part offence carries a maximum penalty on summary conviction of a fine not exceeding level 3 on the standard scale.[10]

Raves

Section 63 of the Criminal Justice and Public Order Act 1994 ('the 1994 Act') 9.2.7
provides powers to the police to remove persons attending or preparing for a rave. A rave is described as:

(1) . . . a gathering on land in the open air of 100 or more persons (whether or not trespassers) at which amplified music is played during the night (with or without intermissions) and is such as, by reason of its loudness and duration and the time at which it is played, is likely to cause serious distress to the inhabitants of the locality; and for this purpose

(a) such a gathering continues during intermissions in the music and, where the gathering extends over several days, throughout the period during which amplified music is played at night (with or without intermissions); and
(b) 'music' includes sounds wholly or predominantly characterised by the emission of a succession of repetitive beats.

If a police officer, of at least the rank of superintendent, reasonably believes 9.2.8
that two or more people are making preparations on land in the open air for the holding there of a rave, and/or that ten or more persons are waiting there for a rave to begin, and/or that ten or more persons are attending a rave there which is in progress, he may give directions to those people and any other people who attend there for the same purposes that they are to leave the land and remove any vehicles or other property which they have with them on the land. It is a criminal offence to fail to leave the land in accordance with a direction or to enter the land again within seven days of the direction.[11]

Aggravated trespass

By s 68(1) of the 1994 Act a person commits the offence of aggravated trespass 9.2.9
if he trespasses on land in the open air and, in relation to any lawful activity

[9] ibid. [10] ibid, s 14(4)–(6).
[11] Criminal Justice and Public Order Act 1994, s 63(2), (7).

which persons are engaging in or are about to engage in on that or adjoining land, does anything that is intended by him to have the effect of intimidating any of the persons so as to deter them from engaging in that activity, or of obstructing or disrupting the activity.

9.2.10 The senior police officer present at the scene may, if he reasonably believes that a person is committing, has committed or intends to commit aggravated trespass, or that two or more persons are trespassing on land in the open air with the common purpose of intimidating persons to deter them from engaging in a lawful activity or to disrupt or obstruct such activity, direct those persons to leave the land.[12]

9.2.11 It is a criminal offence to fail to leave the land as soon as practicable, or to enter the land again as a trespasser within three months of the date on which the direction was given.[13] The offence is summary only, but is arrestable.[14] The maximum penalty, on conviction, is three months' imprisonment and/or a fine at level 4 of the standard scale.

9.2.12 There is some overlap between these provisions and the offence created by s 5 of the Public Order Act 1986 which applies to trespassers who engage in conduct with intent to intimidate people engaged in a lawful activity, to obstruct them or disrupt them from their activity. A defence of reasonable conduct is available under s 5; no such defence is available under the 1994 Act.

Power to remove trespassers

9.2.13 Section 61 of the 1994 Act provides a power for the senior police officer present at a scene to direct two or more persons to leave land with their vehicles and other property, where he reasonably believes that they are trespassing on the land with the intention of residing there for any period. He must also reasonably believe that the occupier of the land has taken reasonable steps to ask them to leave, that any of the trespassers has caused damage to the land or property on it, or has used threatening or abusive words or behaviour towards the occupier or his family or employees or agents, and that the trespassers have between them six or more vehicles on the land. If the persons are reasonably believed by the police officer not originally to have been trespassers, he must reasonably believe that these conditions are satisfied after the time that they became trespassers.[15]

9.2.14 This power was introduced to combat what was seen as a wave of so-called 'new-age travellers' entering farmland without permission, causing damage, being abusive and refusing to leave.

9.2.15 If a direction is given, it is an offence to fail to leave the land as soon as reasonably practicable or, having left, to re-enter the land as a trespasser within three months of the direction having been given. The offence is summary only,

[12] Criminal Justice and Public Order Act 1994, s 69(1).
[13] ibid, s 69(3).
[14] ibid, s 68(4).
[15] ibid, s 61(1)–(2).

but is arrestable, and punishable by a term of three months' imprisonment and/or a fine not exceeding level 4 on the standard scale.[16] It is a defence for the defendant to show that he was not trespassing on the land or that he had a reasonable excuse for failing to leave the land as soon as reasonably practicable or for re-entering as a trespasser.[17]

9.3. PROVISIONS OF PART 7 OF THE ACT

Public assemblies

9.3.1 As stated above, s 16 of the 1986 Act defined an assembly as 'an assembly of 20 or more persons in a public place which is wholly or partly in the open air'. Accordingly, the police powers to make directions imposing conditions on assemblies only applied to groups of 20 or more people.[18]

9.3.2 Section 57 of the 2003 Act amends this definition of 'public assembly' referred to above, by reducing the number of people who must be in attendance for the assembly to qualify from '20 or more persons' to '2 or more persons'.

9.3.3 This is plainly a very important provision, significantly extending the scope of police control of assemblies, whether or not they amount to demonstrations and protests, and curtailing the rights of small groups of people to gather in public as they see fit. An assembly of two or more people may be thought to be a very different kind of assembly from one involving 20 or more people (the previous threshold for the exercise of these powers), posing considerably fewer problems for policing or indeed for issues of safety and inconvenience to members of the general public, and representing an extremely limited risk of serious public disorder, serious damage to property or serious disruption of the life of the community.

9.3.4 The explanatory notes to the Act make the point that peaceful picketing by members of a trade union at their place of work will not be affected by this new provision, as picketing is protected by s 220 of the Trade Union and Labour Relations (Consolidation) Act 1992 which makes it lawful to engage in certain activities done for the purpose of peacefully obtaining or communicating information or of peacefully persuading a person to work or not work.[19]

Raves

9.3.5 Section 58 makes a number of changes to s 63 of the Criminal Justice and Public Order Act 1994, aimed at increasing the powers of the police in relation to smaller gatherings and those taking place in buildings as well as on open land.

[16] ibid, s 61(4)–(5). [17] ibid, s 61(6). [18] See paras 9.2.2 and 9.2.4 above.
[19] Explanatory notes, para 124.

9.3.6 Section 58(2) amends s 63 of the 1994 Act so that the s 63 powers to direct people to leave the land with their vehicles and property now apply to gatherings not of 100 or more people, as previously required by s 63, but of 20 or more people.

9.3.7 In addition to this amendment, s 58(3) inserts a new subs (1A) into s 63 of the 1994 Act, which applies s 63 to gatherings taking place on land (including buildings) that is not 'in the open air'.[20] A gathering must be of 20 or more persons who are trespassing on the land and, but for the fact that it is not taking place on land in the open air, otherwise fall within the definition of a rave provided by s 63(1). Consequential amendment is made to s 63(2), so that the power to give directions no longer applies only to land in the open air.[21]

9.3.8 Section 58(6) of the 2003 Act inserts new s 63(7A) and (7B) into the 1994 Act, creating a new, broader criminal offence. The original offence, under s 63(6), is committed by a person who, knowing that a direction has been given which applies to him, fails to leave the land with his vehicles and property or returns within seven days. This plainly does not apply to a person who was not on the land when the direction was given.

9.3.9 New s 63(7A) creates an offence, committed by a person who, knowing that a direction has been given that applies to him:

> . . . makes preparations for or attends a gathering to which this section applies within the period of 24 hours starting when the direction was given.[22]

In other words, it is no longer necessary for a person to have been on the land when the direction was made. It is now sufficient that a person, not on the land when the direction is given, knows about that direction and prepares for or attends the gathering.

9.3.10 It is not clear whether this new offence is committed by a person who, with knowledge of the direction, prepares for the gathering but does so without actually attending the land in respect of which the direction was given. It seems that this is not the case, however, because by s 63(2), the direction that may be given is framed in terms that the persons already on the land 'and any other persons who *come* to prepare or wait for or attend the gathering' (emphasis added) are to leave the land. Thus where a person makes preparations for a gathering without attending the land, the direction given would seem not to apply to him as he has not *come* to prepare, and thus the first precondition of the offence (that the person knows that a direction has been given which applies to him) is not made out.

9.3.11 The offence under new s 63(7A) is arrestable[23] but summary only, the maximum penalty being a term of three months' imprisonment and/or a fine not exceeding level 4 on the standard scale.

---

[20] The explanatory notes to cl 60 of the Bill (now s 59 of the 2003 Act), para 141, explain that the Interpretation Act 1978 defines land so as to include buildings. This also appears to be the Government's thinking in relation to the drafting of s 58(3) and (4).

[21] 2003 Act, s 58(4).

[22] ibid, s 58(7) inserting a new s 63(7A) into the 1994 Act.

[23] 1994 Act, s 63(8).

The creation of this new offence is, perhaps, not as significant as it may first seem. Section 65 of the 1994 Act already contained a power for a constable to stop a person he reasonably believes to be on his way to a gathering to which s 63 applies and in respect of which a direction is in force. The constable may direct the person not to proceed in the direction of the gathering and it is an arrestable, summary offence to fail to comply with the constable's direction, the maximum penalty being a fine on level 3 of the standard scale. **9.3.12**

The s 65 power may only be exercised within five miles of the boundary of the site of the gathering, however, and so the principal effect of the new offence appears to be to make it unlawful (and arrestable) to travel to a gathering in respect of which it is known that a direction under s 63(2) has already been made, without the need for a constable physically to stop each and every person, within five miles of the site, and direct her or him to turn back. **9.3.13**

Aggravated trespass

Section 59 of the 2003 Act amends the provisions of the 1994 Act relating to the offence of aggravated trespass. The effect of this amendment is that the offence may now be committed on any land (including buildings), and not just 'land in the open air'.[24] This amendment is therefore akin to that made by s 58(3) in relation to raves.[25] Accordingly, s 68(1) of the 1994 Act is amended by omitting the words 'in the open air' immediately after the words '[a] person commits the offence of aggravated trespass if he trespasses on land . . .'. **9.3.14**

Section 69(1) of the 1994 Act is similarly amended, removing references to land 'in the open air' so that the police powers to direct people to leave the land will now apply to any land or buildings. The explanatory notes to the Bill suggested, by way of example, that these amended provisions might be used in respect of activists who invade the building of a targeted company with the intention of conducting an intimidating and disruptive protest.[26] **9.3.15**

Power to remove trespassers

Sections 60–64 of the 2003 Act insert new ss 62A–62E into the 1994 Act so as to create a new statutory regime for the removal from public or private land of trespassers who intend to 'reside on land for any period'. These measures would therefore appear to be aimed at travellers or protesters who take up occupation of land. **9.3.16**

New s 62A, inserted into the 1994 Act by s 60 of the 2003 Act, provides a power for the senior police officer present at a scene to direct any person in relation to whom the conditions for the exercise of the power are satisfied to leave the land and to remove any vehicle or other property he has with him on the **9.3.17**

[24] See n 15 above. [25] See para 9.3.7 above. [26] Explanatory notes, para 140.

land.[27] Such a direction may be communicated to the person to whom it applies by any constable at the scene.[28]

Conditions

9.3.18 The conditions for the exercise of this power are as follows.[29] The senior police officer at the scene must reasonably believe that:

(a) the person in respect of whom the officer is considering the exercise of his powers, and one or more other people, are trespassing on the land;
(b) the trespassers have between them at least one vehicle[30] on the land;
(c) the trespassers are present on the land with the common purpose of residing there for any period;[31]
(d) if it appears to the officer that the person in respect of whom he is considering exercising his powers has one or more caravans in his possession or under his control on the land, that there is a suitable pitch on a 'relevant caravan site' for each caravan; and
(e) the occupier of the land (or someone acting on her/his behalf) has requested the police to remove the trespassers from the land.

9.3.19 Where condition (d) above applies, the police officer must consult each local authority[32] within whose area the land is situated as to whether there is in fact a suitable pitch for each caravan on a relevant caravan site within the area of the local authority in question.[33] In other words, although the section does not specifically so state, it would seem that the power to remove a traveller with one or more caravans is dependent on there being a suitable pitch on a caravan site in the same local authority area as the land on which the traveller is trespassing: if the police officer is required to consult the relevant local authorities and is told that no suitable pitch is available, it would be difficult for the officer to hold the requisite reasonable belief that that condition was satisfied.

Relevant caravan site

9.3.20 The term 'relevant caravan site' is defined[34] as a caravan site that is situated in the area of a local authority within whose area the land is situated and managed by a relevant site manager. 'Relevant site manager'[35] means either a local authority or a registered social landlord, although the Secretary of State may, by order, amend this definition by adding a person or description of person.[36]

---

[27] 1994 Act, s 62A(1). [28] ibid, s 62A(3). [29] ibid, s 62A(2).
[30] Defined in s 61(8); see s 62E(7).
[31] By s 62E(8), a person may have a purpose of residing in a place even if he has a home elsewhere.
[32] Defined in s 62E(4) as meaning (a) in Greater London, a London borough or the Common Council of the City of London; (b) in England outside Greater London, a county council, district council or the Council of the Isles of Scilly; (c) in Wales, a county or county borough council.
[33] 1994 Act, s 62A(4)–(5). [34] ibid, s 62A(6). [35] ibid. [36] ibid, s 62A(7)–(8).

Offences

New s 62B of the 1994 Act[37] creates an offence of failing to comply with a direction given under s 62A. By s 62B(1)–(2), a person commits an offence if he knows that such a direction has been given which applies to him, and he: 9.3.21

(a) fails to leave the land as soon as is reasonably practicable; or
(b) enters any land as a trespasser (ie whether the land he left or any other land) in the area of the relevant local authority, within three months of the day on which the direction was given, with the intention of residing there.

The offence is summary only but arrestable. The maximum penalty, on conviction, is three months' imprisonment and/or a fine on level 4 of the standard scale.[38] 9.3.22

It is a defence, however, if the defendant can show that: 9.3.23

(a) he was not trespassing on the land on which the offence is alleged to have been committed; or
(b) he had a reasonable excuse for failing to leave the relevant land[39] as soon as reasonably practicable, or for entering that or any other land in the area of the relevant local authority[40] with the intention of residing there; or
(c) he was under 18 and residing with his parent or guardian at the time the direction under s 62A was given.

Seizure of vehicles

New s 62C of the 1994 Act[41] confers power upon a constable to seize and remove a vehicle if he reasonably suspects that the person to whom a s 62A direction applies has, without reasonable excuse, either: 9.3.24

(a) failed to remove the vehicle that is on the relevant land and which appears to the constable to belong to him or be in his possession or under his control; or
(b) entered any land in the area of the relevant local authority (ie committing an offence under s 62B(1)(b)), within three months of the day on which the direction was given, as a trespasser and with the intention of residing there.

The provisions of s 67(1) of the 1994 Act are applied, entitling the police to retain and charge for the storage of any seized vehicles in accordance with regulations prescribed by the Secretary of State.[42] 9.3.25

---

[37] Inserted by 2003 Act, s 61.
[38] 1994 Act, s 62B(3)–(4).
[39] Defined in s 62E(5) to mean the land the subject of the direction under s 62A(1).
[40] Defined in s 62E(6) to mean (a) if the relevant land is situated in the area of more than one local authority (not in the Isles of Scilly) the district council or county borough council within whose area the relevant land is situated; (b) if the relevant land is situated in the Isles of Scilly, the Council of the Isles of Scilly; (c) in any other case, the local authority in whose area the relevant land is situated.
[41] Inserted by 2003 Act, s 62.
[42] 2003 Act, s 62(2). See the Police (Retention and Disposal of Vehicles) Regulations 1995, SI 1995/723.

Land

9.3.26 New s 62D[43] makes consequential provision in relation to common land. In the case of such land, ss 62A–C have effect with modifications. References to trespassers and trespassing have effect as if they were references to acts constituting a trespass against the occupier (ie where the public have a right of access to the land, the local authority and any commoner; where there is no public right of access, any commoner) or an infringement of the commoners' rights.[44] This does not require that any action be taken by more than one occupier, nor does it render a person a trespasser against one commoner or the local authority, if he has the permission of another occupier to be there.[45]

Interpretation

9.3.27 New s 62E is an interpretation section.[46] Unlike the s 61 definition of 'land' which defines land so as not generally to apply to highways, s 62E(2) contains no equivalent limitation.

---

43 Inserted by 2003 Act, s 63.
44 1994 Act, s 62D(2)–(3).
45 ibid, s 62D(4).
46 Inserted by 2003 Act, s 64.

10

PART 8 OF THE ACT: HIGH HEDGES

10.1. INTRODUCTION

The problem with hedges

Part 8 of the 2003 Act, which was not included in the Bill as originally published, but was only introduced at a comparatively late stage of its progress through the House of Lords,[1] introduces a local authority administered procedure for dealing with complaints regarding high hedges. The issue of high hedges has received considerable media attention in recent years, as rapid-growth, evergreen hedges have become increasingly popular as a method of screening neighbouring properties from each other. **10.1.1**

The notorious Leyland Cyprus (*X Cupressocyparis leylandii*), more widely known as the Leylandii, has caused particular concern to those living under its shadow. It is a rapid evergreen hybrid with a growth rate of one metre per year, capable of reaching a height of 30 metres. It is not the only species, however, that has this effect. Other evergreen species with great growth capacity include the Lawson Cyprus (ultimate height of 20 metres), the Thuja (25 metres) and even the privet hedge (13 metres). **10.1.2**

The growth rate and potential of these species mean that if the owner fails to trim the hedge at least bi-annually, considerable problems for neighbours can arise.[2] This may not be because the owner is unwilling to behave in a neighbourly fashion: neglect may be caused by the owner's inability to afford the cost of a tree surgeon to carry out the necessary trimming. **10.1.3**

---

[1] Pt 8 began life as a private members' Bill, the High Hedges (No 2) Bill. It was decided by the Government to adopt its provisions and bring them within the Anti-Social Behaviour Bill as a new Pt 9. It became Pt 8 on the re-ordering of the provisions that occurred at the Bill's final reading.

[2] DETR, *High Hedges: possible solutions. A consultation paper covering England and Wales*, November 1999; *www.wildlife-countryside.detr.gov.uk/consult/highhedges/index.htm*.

10.1.4 According to Hedgeline, an organization founded in 1998 by members of the public concerned about this issue, the problems most commonly associated with high hedges are that they:

(a) threaten roofs, guttering and drains;
(b) deprive people of light in their houses;
(c) deprive them of the right to use their gardens in the way they choose; and
(d) prevent owners of small gardens from growing the plants they wish to grow.[3]

10.1.5 Government consultation[4] on the issue found the following problems as the most likely to give rise to complaints:

(a) the reduction in light;
(b) the blocking of views;
(c) damage to drains and nearby structures;
(d) concerns such as the effect on people's mental and physical health.

10.1.6 By analysing data concerning the 5,200 complaints received by approximately 30 per cent of local authorities in the year 1998–99, the Department of the Environment, Transport and the Regions (DETR) (as it then was) estimated that there were probably around 17,000 problem hedges in England and Wales.

Proposals for change—planning law

10.1.7 House of Commons Research Paper 99/35[5] discussed the possibility of amending planning law to require planning permission for high hedges, given that it is already required for fences. A planning application must be submitted if a fence next to a highway used by vehicular traffic is more than one metre in height, or if 'the height of any other gate, fence, wall or means of enclosure erected or constructed would exceed two metres above ground level'.[6]

10.1.8 A significant problem with this proposal, however, was that planning permission can only be required in respect of the development of land, and 'development' is defined, by s 55(1) of the Town and Country Planning Act 1990, in the following terms:

> 'development' means the carrying out of building, engineering, mining or other operations in, on, over or under land, or the making of any material change in the use of any building or other land.

10.1.9 This definition makes it clear that the growing of a hedge is not development and so cannot require planning permission, whereas the erection of a fence

---

[3] Hedgeline, *Some thoughts on the subject of hedge tyranny,* September 1997.

[4] DETR, *High Hedges,* n 2 above.

[5] 25 March 1999, p 11.

[6] Town and Country Planning (General Permitted Development) Order 1995, SI 1995/418, Sch 2, Pt 2, Class A. See also House of Commons Research Paper 99/35, p 13.

requires permission because it does amount to development. Thus while the rule for fences may, in principle, seem suitable for hedges, the s 55(1) definition of development would require amendment to include high hedges within its compass.

Proposals for change—the Crime and Disorder Bill 1998

As early as 1998, there were calls for the Crime and Disorder Bill (as it then was) **10.1.10**
to include provisions to deal with hedges that had become a nuisance to neighbouring owners or occupiers. It was suggested that anti-social behaviour orders could be made against those whose high hedges were causing severe problems for neighbours. This suggestion was rejected.

Five years later, however, Yvette Cooper, Minister for Regeneration at the **10.1.11**
Office of the Deputy Prime Minister, said:

> High hedges can block out the light from neighbours' homes and gardens and make their lives a real misery. This is anti-social behaviour, just as much as graffiti and noisy neighbours, and it isn't fair on those who have to suffer as a result. That is why we want to take action through the Anti-social Behaviour Bill so that local authorities will have the power to sort out high hedge disputes and where necessary to chop those hedges back.

Part 8

Part 8 of the Act, therefore, creates a new regime for dealing with this problem. **10.1.12**
Local authorities are given powers to determine complaints by owners or occupiers of residential property adversely affected by evergreen hedges more than two metres in height. If an authority considers a complaint about such a hedge to be justified, it may issue a 'remedial notice' requiring the owner or occupier of the land on which the hedge is situated to carry out works to remedy the problem and prevent its recurrence. The local authority also has default powers to enter the land and undertake the necessary work. Failure to comply with a remedial notice is a criminal offence.

The structure of the Part will be familiar to environmental and housing **10.1.13**
lawyers. The statutory concept of the notice requiring action to be taken with a right of appeal followed by a time to comply with the notice's requirements in default of which the authority may do the work itself at the expense of the defaulter appears to be derived from public health and fitness provisions of earlier legislation. For example, it is particularly reminiscent of the powers conferred on local authorities under Parts VI and XI of the Housing Act 1985 to enforce housing conditions in private tenancies and houses in multiple occupation; Part III of the Environmental Protection Act 1990 (statutory nuisance abatement notices); Part I of the Prevention of Damage by Pests Act 1949 (requiring steps to be taken to prevent rats and mice resorting to land) and so on.

Unlike those provisions, however, and more redolent of planning legislation, **10.1.14**
the right of appeal enjoyed by the recipient of a notice is not to the county court,

but to the Secretary of State (or, in Wales, the National Assembly), who may appoint a person to hear and determine the appeal on his/its behalf. Criminal offences are created where a person does not comply with the requirements of a notice within the stated time. The authority, and the appeal authority, are also granted powers to enter land for the purposes of their functions.

10.2. LEGISLATIVE CONTEXT

10.2.1 As acknowledged in the explanatory notes[7] to the previous Bills aiming to tackle the menace of high hedges (the High Hedges Bill[8] and the High Hedges (No 2) Bill[9]): '[w]here neighbours do not co-operate, there is little that the person affected by the hedge can do to obtain relief'.[10]

Nuisance

10.2.2 Section 79 of the Environmental Protection Act 1990 ('the 1990 Act') obliges local authorities to investigate complaints about potential statutory nuisance occurring on premises which include land. If, following such an investigation, an authority concludes that a statutory nuisance exists, or that one is likely to occur or recur, it must serve an abatement notice on the person responsible for the nuisance.[11]

10.2.3 A person is entitled to make a formal complaint to the local authority's Environmental Health Department regarding any hedge on neighbouring land which they consider to be a statutory nuisance. A person may also institute a prosecution in the magistrates' court, by complaint, against the person responsible for a statutory nuisance. The court may make a nuisance order if satisfied that the nuisance exists at the date of the hearing, requiring steps to be taken for the abatement (or to prevent the recurrence) of the nuisance.[12]

10.2.4 The difficulty with attempting to apply nuisance legislation in this context, however, is that there is no specific category of nuisance, as defined in s 79 of the 1990 Act, relating to high hedges. Accordingly, it would be necessary to seek to adapt a category to cover the situation. House of Commons Research Paper 01/20[13] suggests that, in the absence of a court ruling establishing that a high hedge can constitute a nuisance, local authority environmental health officers are often unwilling to act. A complainant will face the same problem bringing a prosecution in the magistrates' court: to obtain a nuisance order, considerable

---

[7] High Hedges (No 2) Explanatory Notes, Bill 13-EN, High Hedges Bill Explanatory Notes, Bill 28-EN.

[8] Introduced into the House of Commons on 17 January 2001 (Bill 13).

[9] Introduced into the House of Commons on 11 December 2002 (Bill 28).

[10] High Hedges Bill Explanatory Notes, Bill 28-EN, paras 5–6.

[11] Environmental Health Act 1990, s 80.

[12] ibid, s 82. See also *Coventry CC v Doyle* [1981] 1 WLR 1325, DC.

[13] 7 March 2001, p 10.

costs will be expended, public funding not being available, on an outcome that is far from certain. It is perhaps unsurprising, then, that the law of statutory nuisance is as yet untested with regard to high hedges.

The Control of Hedgerows Bill[14] proposed the insertion of an additional category of nuisance into s 79 to cover: 'any residential hedgerow in such a place, or maintained in such a manner, as to be prejudicial to health or a nuisance'. **10.2.5**

The principal advantage of this proposal was that the 1990 Act already provides a scheme for local authority investigation of complaints and service of notices where a problem complained of constitutes a statutory nuisance. The perceived disadvantage, however, was that the owner of a hedge the subject of an abatement notice would have been required to take positive action at a potentially high cost. It may also have been necessary to issue repeated abatement notices and/or to take repeated court action if an owner simply refused to continue to maintain the hedge at a reasonable height. The Bill did not receive Government support and consequently failed to obtain a second reading.[15] **10.2.6**

Common law nuisance

An interference with light may be actionable as a nuisance. Whether there has been an interference with light amounting to an actionable nuisance will be a matter of fact and degree.[16] The interference with the claimant's land would, however, need to be significant: the damage suffered must be such as materially to interfere with the ordinary comfort of human existence.[17] There is then the question of whether the court would be willing to grant an injunction or only damages. **10.2.7**

Rights to light

There is no right to light at common law, given that it is an overriding common law principle that an owner of land is free to use it as he wishes even if that use interferes with the light that would otherwise reach neighbouring land. Accordingly, absent statutory intervention, a right to light can only be acquired as an easement. **10.2.8**

Easements for light are difficult to obtain, and must relate to specific windows; for example, it will not be possible to sustain a general claim for light over the entirety of a piece of land.[18] To be able to claim for the loss of light, moreover, **10.2.9**

---

[14] Bill 61 of 1998/1999.

[15] Baroness Gardner of Parkes introduced the Statutory Nuisance (Hedgerows in Residential Areas) (HL Bill 10 of 1999/2000) in the House of Lords. This Bill proposed that the 1990 Act be amended by adding to the existing list of possible nuisances 'boundary hedges between two private dwellings prejudicial to health or nuisance'. The Bill reached report stage in the House of Lords.

[16] See also House of Commons Research Paper 99/35, p 11.

[17] *St Helen's Smelting Co Ltd v Tipping* (1865) 11 HL Cas 642; *City of London Brewery Co Ltd v Tenant* (1837) LR 9 Ch App 212.

[18] *Colls v Home & Colonial Stores* [1904] AC 179.

the amount lost must be very significant, as the principles applied in such cases derive from the rule in nuisance—stated above—that the damage suffered must be such as materially to interfere with the ordinary comfort of human existence.[19] A more modest diminution in the amount of light reaching the affected property is not, therefore, likely to be sufficient.

10.2.10 The Prescription Act 1832 ('the 1832 Act') may have offered some assistance to those whose light was detrimentally affected by high hedges. Section 3 of that Act provides that if the 'use of light' to 'any dwelling-house, workshop or other building' has been 'actually enjoyed . . . for the full period of 20 years without interruption, the right thereto shall be deemed absolute and indefeasible'. In practice, however, this Act appears to have done little to help those affected by high hedges.

Overhanging branches

10.2.11 At common law, a person affected by overhanging branches from neighbouring land is entitled to cut the branches back to the boundary line of the neighbouring land (but must return to the owner, for example, by throwing them back over the fence, the branches that have been cut back). Common law does not, however, permit the person affected by the branches to reduce the height of a neighbouring hedge and is therefore of limited utility to those suffering the adverse effects of high hedges.

10.3. THE PROVISIONS OF PART 8 OF THE ACT

Complaints

10.3.1 The scheme of Part 8 is that local authorities investigate complaints about high hedges and, if they are justified, serve a remedial notice on the owner or occupier of the land on which the hedge is situated, referred to as the 'neighbouring land',[20] requiring steps to be taken to abate the problem.

10.3.2 Not just anyone can complain about a high hedge. Section 65 specifies the two categories of complaint that will have effect to invoke the Part 8 procedure to which the Act applies:

(a) complaints made by an owner or occupier of domestic property alleging that his reasonable enjoyment of that property is being adversely affected by the height of a high hedge situated on land owned or occupied by another person (the 'neighbouring land'[21]);[22] and

[19] See para 10.2.7 above. See also *St Helen's Smelting Co Ltd v Tipping* (1865) 11 HL Cas 642; *City of London Brewery Co Ltd v Tenant* (1837) LR 9 Ch App 212.

[20] 2003 Act, s 65(5).

[21] See para 10.3.1 above, and 2003 Act, s 65(5).

[22] ibid, s 65(1).

(b) complaints made by an owner of unoccupied domestic property alleging that the reasonable enjoyment of that property by a prospective occupier of that property would be adversely affected by the height of a high hedge situated on neighbouring land.[23]

The Part 8 procedure does not apply to complaints about the effects of the roots of a high hedge.[24] 10.3.3

Domestic property

The complainant must be the owner or occupier of 'domestic property', which is defined as a dwelling or a garden or yard which is used and enjoyed wholly or mainly in connection with a dwelling.[25] The relevance of this second part of the definition is not so much that it enables owners of gardens or yards to make complaints even if they do not own or occupy the dwelling with which the garden or yard is wholly or mainly enjoyed, but rather that it relates to the provision that references to 'reasonable enjoyment of domestic property' include reasonable enjoyment of part of the property.[26] In other words, it is not necessary for the complainant's reasonable enjoyment of the whole of his land to be affected, rather it is enough that his enjoyment of part of the property—such as the garden or the yard—is affected. 10.3.4

'Dwelling' means any building or part of a building occupied, or intended to be occupied, as a separate dwelling.[27] 10.3.5

High hedge

A 'high hedge', for the purposes of Part 8, is defined so as not to include the whole of a hedge. Instead, the term is defined[28] in two ways meaning 'so much of a barrier to light or access' as: 10.3.6

(a) is formed wholly or predominantly by a line of two or more evergreens (which means an evergreen tree or shrub, or semi-evergreen tree or shrub);[29] and
(b) rises to a height of more than two metres above ground level.

A single tree or shrub is therefore not included, nor is a barrier to light or access formed by trees or shrubs that are not evergreen or semi-evergreen. Any part of a barrier to access or light that exists between ground level and two metres above ground level is also not included—the definition only includes 'so much of' the barrier as rises to a height of more than two metres from ground level. 10.3.7

A line of evergreens is not to be regarded as forming a barrier to light or access at all, if the existence of gaps significantly affects its overall effect as a barrier at heights of more than two metres above ground level.[30] 10.3.8

[23] ibid, s 65(2). [24] ibid, s 65(4). [25] ibid, s 67(1). [26] ibid, s 67(3).
[27] ibid, s 67(2). [28] ibid, s 66(1). [29] ibid, s 66(3). [30] ibid, s 66(2).

10.3.9 This is clearly a narrow definition, which informs many of the other provisions of Part 8, particularly those relating to the action, by way of remedial notice, that the local authority may require to be taken by the owner of the hedge. A remedial notice may not, for example, require or involve the reduction in the height of a hedge to less than two metres above ground level.[31] Nor may it require the removal of the hedge.[32]

The complainant

10.3.10 By s 65(5) the 'complainant' is defined as a person by whom a complaint is made or, if every person who made the complaint ceases to be an owner or occupier of the domestic property specified in the complaint, any other person who is for the time being an owner or occupier of that property. References to a complainant include references to more than one complainant.[33]

10.3.11 The complainant must be an owner or occupier of domestic property. 'Occupier' is defined to mean, in relation to any land, a person entitled to possession of the land by virtue of an estate or interest in it.[34] It therefore seems that the occupier does not actually have to live or stay in the domestic property itself, although he or she must be able to demonstrate that his or her reasonable use of it is affected. 'Owner' is defined to mean, in relation to any land, a person (other than a mortgagee not in possession) who, whether in his own right or as trustee for any person, is entitled to receive the rack rent of the land or, where the land is not let at a rack rent, would be so entitled if it were let.[35] This is an ancient formulation, first found in the Public Health Act 1875, and is frequently used in the context of local authority enforcement of private sector housing conditions.[36]

10.3.12 If, notwithstanding its being unoccupied, the owner of unoccupied domestic property could nonetheless assert that his own reasonable enjoyment of the property was being adversely affected, it would seem that his complaint would be made under s 65(1) rather than s 65(2).

Neighbouring land

10.3.13 Although the land on which the high hedge is situated is referred to in Part 8 as the 'neighbouring land',[37] there is nothing in these provisions that requires that land to be adjacent to the land of the person who makes the complaint; the hedge may apparently be situated on any land, so long as it can properly[38] be alleged that the hedge is adversely affecting the reasonable enjoyment of the complainant's property.

10.3.14 The definition of 'high hedge' and/or the scope of complaints relating to high hedges to which Part 8 applies may be amended by regulations made, in

[31] See para 10.3.1 above, and 2003 Act, s 69(3)(a). [32] ibid, s 69(3)(b).
[33] ibid, s 65(5). [34] ibid, s 82. [35] ibid, s 82.
[36] See eg Housing Act 1985, ss 207, 398; Public Health Act 1936, s 343(1).
[37] 2003 Act, s 65(5).
[38] Frivolous or vexatious complaints may be rejected by the authority: ibid, s 68(2)(b).

England, by the Secretary of State and, in Wales, by the National Assembly for Wales.[39]

Complaints procedure

Section 68 of the 2003 Act sets up a procedure whereby the 'relevant' local authority, ie the local authority for the area where the land on which the high hedge stands is situated,[40] which may not be the local authority for the complainant's 'domestic property', must receive and consider complaints falling within Part 8, although authorities may charge a fee for this function.[41] **10.3.15**

Form of complaint

The Act does not prescribe any form of complaint. Indeed, it appears that Parliament intended the process of making a complaint to be informal. It does not even seem that a complaint needs to be made in writing. What does seem clear, however, from the provisions of s 68(3)(a) of the 2003 Act, is that the complaint must contain certain critical information, namely it must: **10.3.16**

(a) specify the high hedge to which it relates; and
(b) specify the domestic property that the complainant owns or occupies.[42]

It does not appear to be necessary, however, though it would plainly be advisable, to specify the manner in which the high hedge is adversely affecting the reasonable enjoyment of the complainant's property. Whether the high hedge is having this effect is a matter that the authority has to decide,[43] as is the question whether any remedial action should be taken and, indeed, whether the complaint falls within Part 8 at all, and for all of these purposes the authority is given power to enter the neighbouring land.[44] There is no requirement, however, that the complainant must address these matters—which may turn on technical issues such as whether it is the part of the hedge rising above two metres that is causing the adverse effect—in the complaint. **10.3.17**

The complainant must, however, before complaining, have taken any steps that it would be reasonable to take to resolve the problem amicably or, at any event, without resorting to the Part 8 procedure, or the local authority will be entitled simply to refuse to proceed with the complaint.[45] **10.3.18**

---

[39] ibid, s 83. Regulations may also make consequential amendments to Pt 8 as the maker considers appropriate: s 83(3).

[40] ibid, s 65(5). In England, 'local authority' means a district council, a county council for a county in which there are no districts, a London borough council, or the Common Council of the City of London. In Wales, it means a county council or a county borough council.

[41] ibid, s 68(1)(b).

[42] See ibid, s 68(3)(a).

[43] See ibid, s 68(3)(a).

[44] ibid, s 74(1)(a) and (b).

[45] ibid, s 68(2)(a).

Dealing with a complaint

10.3.19 Complaints must be made to the relevant authority and must be accompanied by any fee that the authority has determined to charge. The fee must not exceed the amount prescribed in regulations made by the Secretary of State (if the high hedge is in England) or the National Assembly for Wales (if it is in Wales).[46] The January 2001 briefing by the (then) DETR concerning the High Hedges Bill[47] indicated that the maximum fee would be set at approximately £100, although the cost to local authorities of actually administering the regime was estimated at about £200 per complaint.[48] Fees may be refunded in such circumstances and to such extent as the authority may determine.[49]

10.3.20 The relevant authority may decide not to proceed with the complaint if it considers that the complainant has not taken all reasonable steps to resolve the matter without complaining under Part 8, or that the complaint is frivolous or vexatious.[50] If the authority takes this course, on either basis, it must notify the 'appropriate person or persons' of the decision and the reasons for it as soon as reasonably practicable.[51] The appropriate person(s) are every complainant. It is not, however, necessary to notify the owner of the neighbouring land.

10.3.21 If the authority does not reject the complaint as described above, it must proceed to decide the following matters:

(a) whether the height of the high hedge specified in the complaint is adversely affecting the complainant's reasonable enjoyment of the domestic property (or, in the case of unoccupied land, the reasonable enjoyment of the property by a prospective occupier[52]) also specified in the complaint; and
(b) if it decides that it is, what—if any—action should be taken in relation to that hedge with a view to remedying the adverse effect or preventing its recurrence.

10.3.22 As suggested above,[53] the question of whether the hedge is adversely affecting the complainant's reasonable enjoyment of his land may well not be a straightforward issue. While the authority would presumably be entitled to take a broad common sense approach to the question in most cases, it will be obliged to consider issues such as whether it is that part of the hedge which exceeds two metres in height that is adversely affecting the domestic property,[54] whether gaps in the hedge have a significant effect on the overall effect of the hedge as a barrier to light or access at heights above two metres from ground level,[55] and whether the

[46] 2003 Act, s 68(7).
[47] 17 January 2001 (Bill 13).
[48] DETR, *High Hedges Bill: Briefing Pack*, 2 March 2001. See also House of Commons Research Paper 01/20, p 15.
[49] 2003 Act, s 68(8).
[50] ibid, s 68(2).
[51] ibid, s 68(5)(a).
[52] ibid, s 65(3).
[53] See para 10.3.17 above.
[54] The definition of 'high hedge' is such that a high hedge is only that part of a line of evergreens which rises above two metres from ground level. Accordingly, if the lower part of the line of evergreens is the part that is having the adverse effect, it will not be a 'high hedge' that is adversely affecting reasonable enjoyment and so Pt 8 will not apply to the complaint: see 2003 Act, s 66(1)(a).
[55] ibid, s 66(2).

reasonable enjoyment of the land is adversely affected to such an extent that some remedial action should be required.[56]

The potential complexity of these issues is illustrated by the powers of entry conferred by s 74(1) of the Act, which are exercisable by a person authorized by the relevant authority for the purpose of determining, inter alia, whether Part 8 applies to the complaint, and whether to issue a remedial notice. **10.3.23**

If the authority decides that the high hedge about which the complaint has been made is not adversely affecting (or would not adversely affect) the reasonable enjoyment of the land, and/or that although it is having an adverse effect, no action should be taken to remedy that effect or prevent its recurrence, it must notify the appropriate persons of that decision and the reasons for it[57] as soon as reasonably practicable. In this context, the appropriate persons are the complainant(s) and every owner or occupier of the neighbouring land.[58] **10.3.24**

If the authority decides that action should be taken to remedy an adverse effect or prevent its recurrence, it must, as soon as reasonably practicable, issue a remedial notice under s 69, send a copy of the notice to every complainant and every owner and occupier of the neighbouring land, and notify each of those people of the reasons for the decision.[59] The distinction between sending a copy of a document and notifying a person of a matter is significant in terms of the manner in which service may be given.[60] **10.3.25**

The remedial notice

A remedial notice is a notice issued by a relevant authority in respect of a complaint to which Part 8 applies and which states the following matters:[61] **10.3.26**

(a) the hedge to which the notice relates and the land on which the hedge is situated;
(b) the domestic property in respect of which the complaint was made;
(c) that a complaint about that hedge has been made under Part 8;
(d) that the authority has decided that the height of the hedge is adversely affecting the complainant's reasonable enjoyment of the domestic property (or would have such an effect on the reasonable enjoyment of that domestic property by a prospective occupier of the property)[62] specified in the notice;
(e) the 'operative date' of the notice (meaning the date on which the notice takes effect,[63] which must be at least 28 days after the date on which the notice is issued);[64]
(f) the 'initial action' (meaning remedial or preventative action or both)[65] that must be taken in relation to the hedge before the end of the period for taking that action specified in the notice (called the 'compliance period').[66] The compliance period begins on the 'operative date';[67]

[56] ibid, s 68(3)(b).
[57] ibid, s 68(5).
[58] ibid, s 68(6)(b).
[59] ibid, s 68(4).
[60] ibid, ss 79–81.
[61] ibid, s 69(1)–(2) and (5).
[62] ibid, s 65(3).
[63] ibid, s 69(4).
[64] ibid, s 69(5).
[65] ibid, s 69(9).
[66] ibid, s 69(6).
[67] ibid, s 69(5)–(6).

(g) any 'preventative action' (meaning action to prevent the recurrence of the adverse effect) which must be taken at times following the end of the compliance period while the hedge remains on the land; and

(h) the consequences under ss 75 (criminal offences) and 77 (local authority action in default at owner's expense) of failure to comply with the requirements of the notice.

10.3.27 The action specified in the remedial notice may not require or involve reducing the height of the hedge below two metres, or its removal.[68]

10.3.28 The scheme of these notice provisions is therefore clear. It gives the recipient at least 28 days grace before its 'operative date' when it comes into effect. This is the time limit for bringing an appeal against the notice.[69] It then specifies the period ('compliance period'), commencing on the operative date, by the end of which the action necessary to remedy the immediate adverse effects of the hedge ('initial action') must be taken. It may also, additionally, require further action to be taken ('preventative action'), such as periodic pruning, to keep the problem under control and remove the need for repeated complaints and remedial notices.

10.3.29 The remedial notice is a local land charge while it is in effect (which presumably will continue beyond the end of the compliance period and may last indefinitely where it specifies a requirement for 'preventative action'). The provisions of the Local Land Charges Act 1975 therefore have effect, and the charge must be registered in the authority's register of local land charges.[70] The principal advantage of this is that the remedial notice thereby becomes binding on all owners and/or occupiers for the time being of the land specified in the notice as the land on which the hedge in question is situated.[71] This is an anti-avoidance measure, preventing the effect of a remedial notice from being defeated by a change of ownership of the land on which the hedge is situated.

Withdrawal or relaxation of requirements of remedial notice

10.3.30 An authority may withdraw a remedial notice it has issued or waive or relax any of its requirements, whether before or after (or, in the case of relaxation, both) the notice has taken effect.[72] If it does so, however, it must give notice of what it has done to every complainant and every owner and every occupier of the neighbouring land.[73]

10.3.31 The withdrawal of a remedial notice does not affect the power of the authority to issue a further remedial notice in respect of the same hedge.[74]

---

[68] 2003 Act, s 69(3). [69] ibid, s 71(4)(a). [70] Local Land Charges Act 1975, s 6.
[71] 2003 Act, s 69(8), and see Local Land Charges Act 1975, s 6. [72] 2003 Act, s 70(1)–(2).
[73] ibid, s 70(3). [74] ibid, s 70(4).

Service of documents

Section 79 deals with the manner in which notifications or other documents required to be given or sent to a person under Part 8 may validly be given or sent. Service will be validly effected if it is in accordance with the provisions of that section.[75] This applies not merely to remedial notices and the relaxation, waiver or withdrawal of them, but to decisions not to issue such notices, and also to the conduct of appeals and the notification of decisions on appeal (see paras 10.3.56 et seq below). **10.3.32**

In the case of a body corporate, documents may be served on the secretary or clerk of that body; in the case of a partnership, they may be served on a partner or a person having the control or management of the partnership business. **10.3.33**

Such document may be served in any of the following ways:[76] **10.3.34**

(a) by delivering it to the person in question;
(b) by leaving it at his 'proper address'. In the case of an individual, this means his last known address[77] or any other address within the United Kingdom that he has specified as the one at which he or someone on his behalf will accept documents of a particular description.[78] In the case of a body corporate (or its secretary or clerk), the proper address is the body's registered or principal office; in the case of a partnership (or person having control or management of its business), it is the principal office of the partnership;[79] or
(c) by sending it by post to him at that address.

If a company is registered, or a partnership carries on business, outside the United Kingdom, their principal office for the purposes of service is their principal office within the United Kingdom.[80] **10.3.35**

Persons unknown

Where under Part 8 a document must be served on a person who is an owner or occupier of any land, and the name of that person cannot be ascertained after reasonable enquiries have been made, the document may be served either by leaving it in the hands of the person who is or appears to be resident or employed on the land or by leaving it conspicuously affixed to some other building or object on the land.[81] **10.3.36**

Documents in electronic form

Some documents required by Part 8 to be sent to a person may be validly sent electronically, if the person has consented to this form of service. By s 80(1), however, this does not apply to the sending of either a remedial notice to a person or the reasons for making a remedial notice. The requirements to send such **10.3.37**

[75] ibid, s 79(1). [76] ibid, s 79(2). [77] ibid, s 79(4), and Interpretation Act 1978, s 7.
[78] ibid, s 79(6). [79] ibid, s 79(4)(a)–(b). [80] ibid, s 79(5). [81] ibid, s 79(7).

documents to a person are 'not capable of being satisfied by transmitting the copy or notification electronically or by making it available on a web-site'.

Email

10.3.38 For other documents to be validly served either by transmitting them electronically or by making them available on a website, the following requirements must be satisfied.[82] A document may be transmitted electronically if the recipient has agreed that documents may be delivered to him by being transmitted to an electronic address and in an electronic form specified by him for that purpose *and* the document is a document to which that agreement applies and is transmitted to that address in that form.[83]

Website

10.3.39 A document may be served by making it available on a website if the following requirements have been complied with:

(a) the recipient has agreed that documents may be delivered to him by being made available on a website;
(b) the document is a document to which that agreement applies;
(c) the document is made available on a website; and
(d) the recipient is notified, in a manner agreed by him, of the presence of the document on the website, the address of the website, and the place on the website where the document may be accessed.[84]

10.3.40 Any document that is served electronically or by being made available on a website is deemed as having been delivered at 9 am on the working day (not a Saturday, Sunday, Christmas Day, Good Friday, or a Bank Holiday)[85] immediately following the day on which it was transmitted or on which the recipient was notified that it was available on the specified part of the specific website, unless the contrary is proved.[86]

Power to make further provision about documents in electronic form

10.3.41 The Secretary of State (in relation to complaints about hedges situated in England) and the National Assembly for Wales (in relation to complaints about hedges in Wales) have power to modify the circumstances in which and the conditions subject to which the service of a document (including a remedial notice and/or the reasons for making it) may be validly effected by electronic transmission and/or making it available on a website. The provisions concerning the time and day of deemed receipt of such documents served in this way may also be amended.[87]

---

[82] 2003 Act, s 80(2). [83] ibid, s 80(3). [84] ibid, s 80(5).
[85] ibid, s 80(7), which also defined a number of other terms used in s 80.
[86] ibid, s 80(4) and (6).
[87] ibid, s 81(1) and (2). Consequential amendments may also be made: s 81(3).

Offences

Section 75(1) creates a summary criminal offence where action required by a remedial notice is not taken within the compliance period or by any subsequent time by which it must be taken. The offence is committed by every person who is an owner or occupier of the neighbouring land at any time after the action ought to have been, but was not, taken.[88] Other criminal offences are created by other sections (s 74(7)—obstructing a power of entry; s 77(9)—obstructing a person taking action in default) and these offences are discussed in the context of the provisions to which they relate.[89] 10.3.42

Defences

So far as the s 75(1) offence is concerned, it is a defence for the defendant to show that he did everything he could be expected to do to secure compliance with the notice.[90] It is also a defence for the defendant to show: 10.3.43

(a) that he is not a person to whom a copy of the remedial notice was sent; and
(b) that it is not assumed, under s 75(5), that he had knowledge of the notice at the time of the alleged offence; and
(c) that he was not aware of the existence of the notice at that time.[91]

Section 75(5) provides that a person is assumed to have had knowledge of a remedial notice at any time if at that time he was an owner of the neighbouring land and the notice was at that time registered as a local land charge. Occupiers, therefore, are not assumed to have had knowledge of remedial notices. 10.3.44

Section 198 of the Law of Property Act 1925, which provides for constructive notice, is disregarded for the purposes of s 75. Accordingly, an occupier against whom the assumption of knowledge by the registration of the notice as a local land charge does not arise or, indeed, an owner where the notice has not in fact been registered (whether or not it should have been) will not be presumed to have been aware of the existence of the notice by reference to the doctrine of constructive notice. It is necessary that he had actual notice. 10.3.45

Punishment

The maximum punishment on summary conviction is a fine not exceeding level 3 on the standard scale (currently £1,000).[92] Where, however, it appears to the court that a failure to comply with the remedial notice is continuing and that it is within the power of the person who has been convicted of the offence to secure compliance with the notice, the court may, in addition to, or instead of, imposing a punishment, order the person to take the steps specified in the order for securing compliance with the notice within a reasonable period fixed by the order itself.[93] 10.3.46

---

[88] ibid, s 75(1)–(2).
[89] See paras 10.3.78 and 10.3.86 below.
[90] 2003 Act, s 75(3).
[91] ibid, s 75(4).
[92] ibid, s 75(1).
[93] ibid, s 75(7)–(8).

10.3.47 Failure to comply, without reasonable excuse, with an order of the court requiring the taking of steps, is itself a criminal offence, also punishable on summary conviction by a fine not exceeding level 3 on the standard scale (s 82(9)).[94] If the person, after conviction of breaching the court's order without reasonable excuse, still continues—again without reasonable excuse—to fail to take the steps that he has been ordered by the court to take, he is guilty of a further offence and is liable, on summary conviction, to a fine not exceeding one-twentieth of level 3 on the standard scale (ie £50) for each day on which the failure has continued.[95]

10.3.48 The High Hedges Bill[96] originally proposed a fine of one-twelfth of level 3, but this was reduced to one-twentieth in the High Hedges (No 2) Bill,[97] and it is this lower level of punishment that has now been enacted.

10.3.49 Accordingly a person may commit three separate offences, and be fined three times, if he fails to comply with a remedial notice: for the breach of the original order; for a breach of any order made under s 75(7) requiring him to take steps; and for continuing to fail to take steps after conviction for breach of the s 75(7) order.

Offences committed by bodies corporate

10.3.50 Where an offence under Part 8 has been committed by a body corporate, a director, manager, secretary or other similar officer of the body, or any person who was purporting to act in such a capacity, is also guilty of the offence and may be prosecuted and punished in addition to the body itself, if it can be proved that the body's offence was committed with the consent or connivance of any such person or was attributable to any neglect on the part of such a person.[98]

10.3.51 Where the affairs of a body corporate are managed by the members of the body, the members may also be prosecuted and punished for their acts and defaults in connection with their management functions as if they were directors of the body corporate.[99]

10.3.52 These provisions will be of considerable importance, not only to the directors of corporate landowners, but also to the residents of blocks of flats, where the freehold or head lease is held by a company in which each flat owner owns a share, and of which some or all of the flat owners are directors. The same will be true of flats held under the new commonhold form of ownership. In such cases, if a remedial notice is issued in respect of land forming part of that freehold, each director is likely to be criminally liable if the notice is not complied with, as is each member who assumes management functions.

10.3.53 This is of course an anti-avoidance measure, designed to give teeth to the criminal sanctions of Part 8 and prevent them being defeated by the setting up of a corporate landowner with no assets other than the land itself and so no resources

---

[94] 2003 Act, s 75(9). [95] 2003 Act, s 75(10). [96] 17 January 2001 (Bill 13).
[97] 11 December 2002 (Bill 28). [98] 2003 Act, s 78(1). [99] ibid, s 78(2).

from which to pay any fine that the court may impose. Many small resident-managed corporate freeholders or head leaseholders have no assets other than the freehold/long lease itself and the service charge contributions they raise from the individual flat owners under the terms of the long underleases for such matters as the repair, maintenance and management of the building. Such sums are generally held on trust for the leaseholders, and could not in any event, under the terms of the leases, be used by the company to pay fines incurred for failure to comply with a statutory notice. Accordingly, the imposition of such a fine could well render such companies insolvent, subject to any proceedings by the company against its directors for breach of their duties.

These offences, then, must be taken seriously, as they may well have very real consequences for all kinds of owners and occupiers of land, and not merely the stereotypical thoughtless—or deliberately selfish—(and often absentee) landowner. **10.3.54**

Appeals against decisions

A right is granted to every complainant and every owner and/or occupier of the neighbouring land[100] to appeal against the issue or withdrawal of a remedial notice, or the waiver or relaxation of any of its requirements.[101] A complainant may also appeal against a decision of the authority[102] either that the height of the high hedge is not adversely affecting his or her reasonable enjoyment of the property (or would not adversely affect the reasonable enjoyment of a prospective occupier of currently unoccupied property[103]) or that no action should be taken in relation to that hedge to remedy an adverse effect or prevent its recurrence.[104] **10.3.55**

The appeal is made not to a court, but to the 'appeal authority', ie, where the hedge is situated in England, the Secretary of State and, where the hedge is situated in Wales, the National Assembly for Wales.[105] **10.3.56**

An appeal against the issue of a remedial notice must be made within 28 days of the date of issue of the notice,[106] or such later time as the appeal authority may allow.[107] Any other appeal must be made within 28 days (or such longer time as the appeal authority may allow)[108] of the date of the notification, given by the authority, of the decision against which the appeal is brought.[109] **10.3.57**

Where an appeal is brought, the notice or the withdrawal, waiver or relaxation in question does not have effect pending the final determination or withdrawal of the appeal.[110] This provision, which appears uncontroversial, may have some odd effects. If, for example, an authority imposes a requirement in a remedial notice that the initial action of pruning the hedge back to two metres above the ground must be completed by a specific date, but then, as a result of representations by the owner of the neighbouring land, agrees to relax the requirement by **10.3.58**

[100] ibid, s 71(2). [101] ibid, s 71(1). [102] Taken under ibid, s 68(3).
[103] See ibid, s 65(3). [104] ibid, s 71(3). [105] ibid, s 71(1) and (7).
[106] ibid, s 71(4)(a) and (5)(a). [107] ibid, s 71(4)(b). [108] ibid, s 71(4)(b).
[109] ibid, s 71(5)(b). [110] ibid, s 71(6).

extending the time for compliance, that extension of time will not have effect if the complainant appeals against the decision to grant it.

10.3.59 In cases where the appeal is not determined until after the original compliance date has expired (which would seem likely to be the majority of cases where a short compliance period has been set by the authority), this will face the owner of the neighbouring land with the invidious choice of complying with the compliance period notwithstanding that he has been granted an extension that could well be upheld on appeal, or else committing a criminal offence by not complying with the original compliance period. It will not be a defence to that offence that the appeal had not been determined (because the relaxation does not have effect pending the appeal) nor even that the relaxation was upheld on appeal (for the same reason) unless the court were to conclude that the owner had done everything he could be expected to do to secure compliance with the notice.[111]

10.3.60 The effect of this is likely to be that the act of appealing assumes considerable tactical importance for complainants. It may also lead to judicial review applications against the appeal authorities, seeking to speed up the determination of appeals, and indeed abuse of process arguments in the magistrates' court should a prosecution be brought in such circumstances.

Appeals procedure

10.3.61 The procedure for appeals, and any other matters consequential on or connected with appeals will be contained in regulations made by the relevant appeal authority.[112] Such regulations may, in particular:[113]

(a) specify the grounds on which appeals may be made;
(b) prescribe the manner in which appeals are to be made;
(c) require appellants to send copies of documents, and prescribe the documents which must be sent and the persons to whom they must be sent;
(d) prescribe documents which local authorities against whom appeals are brought must send to the appeal authority, and require local authorities to send them;
(e) specify, where under (d) local authorities are required to send to the appeal authority a statement of the submissions they propose to put forward on the appeal, the matters to be included in such a statement;
(f) prescribe the period within which a requirement imposed by the regulations is to be complied with;
(g) enable the appeal authority to extend such a period;
(h) provide for a decision on an appeal to be binding on every complainant and every owner and occupier of the neighbouring land, and not merely on the person by whom the appeal is made; and
(i) provide for the awarding of costs, and for other incidental or ancillary matters.

[111] 2003 Act, s 75(2). [112] ibid, s 72(1). [113] ibid, s 72(2).

The appeal authority may appoint a person to hear and determine an appeal on its behalf,[114] require that person to exercise on its behalf any of its functions conferred on the appeal authority under s 71 or s 73 and specified in that person's appointment,[115] and pay that person such remuneration as it may determine.[116] Regulations may also make provision for any of the provisions of Sch 20 to the Environment Act 1995 (relating to the delegation of appellate functions)[117] to apply to such a person, with such modifications as the regulations may prescribe.[118] 10.3.62

This procedure is, then, highly evocative of the procedure operated in planning appeals to the Secretary of State under the Town and Country Planning Act 1990,[119] even to the extent that it seems that the Secretary of State/Welsh Assembly can make provision so that they determine some appeals personally (ie 'call in' powers) but allows their statutory appointee to determine others. 10.3.63

Determination and withdrawal of appeals

The appeal authority may allow or dismiss the appeal, either in whole or in part.[120] If the appeal is allowed to any extent, the appeal authority may also, as it considers appropriate, quash the remedial notice or decision appealed against, vary the requirements of the remedial notice, or, where the appeal relates to a decision not to issue a remedial notice, issue on behalf of the relevant authority a remedial notice which could have been issued on the complaint in question.[121] 10.3.64

On an appeal against a remedial notice, the appeal authority may correct any defect, error or misdescription in the notice if satisfied that the correction will not cause injustice to any complainant or any owner and/or occupier of the neighbouring land.[122] 10.3.65

Once the appeal authority has made its decision on the appeal it must, as soon as is reasonably practicable, give a notification of the decision, and if the decision is to issue a remedial notice or to vary or correct the requirement of a notice, send a copy of the notice as issued, varied or corrected to every complainant and every owner and/or occupier of the neighbouring land, and to the relevant authority.[123] 10.3.66

Operative date following an appeal

If the appeal authority upholds, varies, or corrects a remedial notice, the operative date of the notice (ie the date on which the notice takes effect and from which the compliance period starts to run[124]) becomes either the date of the appeal authority's decision or any later date that the appeal authority may 10.3.67

[114] ibid, s 72(3). [115] ibid, s 72(4). [116] ibid, s 72(5).

[117] eg the appointment of persons to hear appeals (para 2), the powers of an appointed person (para 3), and the holding of local enquiries (paras 4–5).

[118] ibid, s 72(6)–(7). [119] ibid, ss 78–79. [120] ibid, s 73(1). [121] ibid, s 73(2).

[122] ibid, s 73(4)(a). [123] ibid, s 73(4)(b). [124] See ibid, s 69(4)–(6).

specify in its decision.[125] Where the appellant withdraws his appeal, the operative date of the notice is the date on which the appeal is withdrawn.[126] Accordingly, in either of the above situations, the compliance period for the notice runs from the 'new' operative date, and any period that may have started to run from a date preceding the appeal is disregarded.[127]

10.3.68 These provisions do not ameliorate the issue raised above at paras 10.3.58–10.3.59: if an owner obtains the withdrawal of a remedial notice, and a complainant appeals unsuccessfully against that decision, the decision on the appeal would not appear to involve the upholding of a remedial notice, nor its variation or correction, given that, under s 70(3), a relaxation/waiver/withdrawal does not require the issue and service of an amended notice, but merely the giving of notice to the parties of what has been done.

10.3.69 If the complainant's appeal against the relaxation succeeds, so that the appeal authority, in effect, rescinds the relaxation or waiver of a requirement, or indeed the withdrawal of the notice itself, the owner of the land could well be in breach of the resurrected requirement/notice (absent any further relaxation granted by the relevant authority) and so guilty of a criminal offence, subject to persuading the court that he has done everything he could be expected to do to secure compliance with the notice.[128] Whether or not a prosecution would be brought in such a case, or would be considered not to be in the public interest (or even contrary to prosecutors' codes of guidance), is of course another matter, but it does seem unsatisfactory that a complainant's appeal can by a side wind place the recipient of a notice in breach of the criminal law.

10.3.70 It seems that these provisions have been drafted taking account only of appeals against remedial notices by the persons they require to take action, and without giving proper consideration to the position of the person to whom a notice is directed in cases where it is the complainant who appeals against the issue of the notice (in the terms it is drafted) or a decision to waive or relax the requirements of, or to withdraw, the notice. In such cases, the Act as drafted appears to give no assistance to the person to whom the notice is directed.

10.3.71 That person will not be able to ascertain the date by which he is obliged to take the action required by a notice (or whether he is obliged to do so, if the complainant's appeal is against the withdrawal of the notice) unless and until the complainant's appeal is determined, s 71(6) making it quite clear that the operation of the original notice is only suspended where the appeal is brought against that notice. Where the appeal challenges the waiver or relaxation or withdrawal of the notice, it is the waiver, relaxation or withdrawal that is suspended.

10.3.72 Once the appeal has been determined, moreover, the original operative date of the notice is only put back to the date of, or a date following, the decision on appeal, where the notice itself is upheld, varied or corrected, or the appeal is

---

[125] 2003 Act, s 73(5). [126] ibid, s 73(6). [127] 2003 Act, s 73(7).
[128] The only relevant defence under ibid, s 75(3).

withdrawn,[129] *not* where a decision to relax or waive a requirement of a notice, or to withdraw a notice altogether, is overturned. In such cases, unless the upholding of a relaxation or waiver is construed as the upholding or variation of the notice itself, and unless the rescission of a withdrawal/waiver/relaxation is construed as an upholding or variation of the notice, so that the operative date is put back,[130] it seems that the original operative date will continue to be the date from which the compliance period runs, and accordingly that the compliance period will almost inevitably have expired long before the appeal has been determined. It is hard to believe that this was the intention of Parliament.

Powers of entry

The relevant authority has power to authorize a person to enter the neighbouring land, and that person may do so, where a complaint has been made, and/or a remedial notice has been issued. The power exists only, however, to enable the obtaining of information required by the authority for the purpose of determining: **10.3.73**

(a) whether Part 8 applies to the complaint;
(b) whether to issue or withdraw a remedial notice;
(c) whether to waive or relax a requirement of a remedial notice; or
(d) whether a requirement of a remedial notice has been complied with.[131]

The appeal authority or a person appointed to determine appeals on its behalf has a like power to authorize a person to enter the neighbouring land in order to obtain information required for the purpose of determining an appeal.[132] These powers, therefore, do not authorize the taking of physical action to remedy a default in compliance. Such powers are provided by s 77. **10.3.74**

The person authorized to enter the land may take with him such other persons as may be necessary and such equipment and materials necessary to obtain the information required.[133] One of the more obvious pieces of equipment that may be necessary is some kind of measuring device to ascertain the height of the hedge alleged to be a high hedge. A ladder, and someone to hold it, may well also be necessary. **10.3.75**

At least 24 hours' notice of the intended entry, under either of these powers, must be given to every occupier of the land,[134] although there is no requirement that such notice must be in writing. Nor is it necessary to give such notice to an owner of the land, if he or she is not also an occupier. The person exercising the power of entry must produce evidence of his or her authority to enter the land, **10.3.76**

---

[129] By ibid, s 73(5) and (6).

[130] The upholding on appeal of the withdrawal of a notice does not present problems because, by definition, there are no requirements of a withdrawn notice.

[131] 2003 Act, s 74(1).

[132] ibid, s 74(2).

[133] ibid, s 74(5). See para 10.3.83 below.

[134] ibid, s 74(3).

if required to do so, before entering the land and/or at any time while he or she remains on the land.[135]

10.3.77 If the land is unoccupied, or if the persons occupying the land are temporarily absent, the person exercising the right of entry must leave the land as effectively secured against unauthorized entry as he found it.[136]

Offences

10.3.78 Wilfully obstructing a person exercising a power to enter and take action on land under s 74 is a summary offence punishable by a fine not exceeding level 3 on the standard scale.

Power to require a person to permit, and to take, action

Power to require occupier to permit action to be taken by the owner

10.3.79 Section 289 of the Public Health Act 1936, which confers power on a court to require an occupier to permit work to be done by an owner, is applied to Part 8 with the 'necessary modifications'[137] so as to give an owner of the neighbouring land the right, as against all other people with an interest in that land (including occupiers), to enter the land to comply with a remedial notice. An owner of land to which a remedial notice applies may, therefore, enter the land and carry out the works required by the notice regardless of whether another person is in occupation.

10.3.80 This will be an important provision in circumstances where an owner has not reserved a contractual right of entry in terms sufficiently broad to permit entry for the purpose of trimming back a hedge. In the absence of such a power, the owner would have no power to comply with the notice, although he would presumably have a s 75(3) defence to any prosecution if he could show that he had done everything that could be expected of him to obtain consent to enter the land.

10.3.81 The procedure under s 289 of the 1936 Act is as follows. The owner of the premises makes a complaint to the magistrates' court, which then entertains the application. The court will order the occupier to permit the execution of the work if it 'appears to' the court that the neighbour is preventing the owner from executing work required by or under the 2003 Act.

Action in default

10.3.82 Where a remedial notice requires action to be taken and such action is not taken within the time for compliance allowed by the notice, s 77 permits the relevant authority to authorize a person to enter the neighbouring land and take the required action.[138] That person may then enter the land and take such action,

---

[135] ibid, s 74(4). [136] 2003 Act, s 74(6).

[137] The Act is silent as to what are the 'necessary modifications' to s 289, but they must relate to the substitution of a reference to the 2003 Act for the reference to the 1936 Act.

[138] 2003 Act, s 77(1)–(2).

but may only enter the land if at least seven days' notice of the intended entry has been given to every occupier of the land.[139] It is noteworthy that this provision, like the s 74 power of entry to obtain information, only requires notice of entry to be given to occupiers, not to owners.[140] This is more significant in the context of the authority's default powers under this section, as the reasonable expenses incurred by the authority in taking such action may be recovered from any owner of the land as well as from an occupier.[141]

As with the powers of entry under s 74, an authorized person must produce evidence of his authority, if required to do so, before entering the land and at any time while he remains on the land.[142] He may use a vehicle to enter the land, and take with him such other persons 'as may be necessary', and equipment and materials 'needed for the purpose of taking the required action'.[143] This formulation would seem to contemplate that security personnel may enter the land on the basis that they are 'necessary' to protect the contractors taking the action, even though they are not 'needed for the purpose of' taking the action itself. **10.3.83**

If the neighbouring land is unoccupied or all occupiers are temporarily absent, the authorized person must, on departure, leave the land as effectively secured against unauthorized entry as he found it.[144] **10.3.84**

Where expenses are recoverable from two or more persons those persons are jointly and severally liable for them[145] and thus the authority may choose to pursue any owner or occupier for the full amount and leave them to seek to obtain a contribution from any other liable owner or occupier. Recoverable expenses, until paid, also constitute a local land charge binding on successive owners and occupiers of the land.[146] Such a charge is likely to rank first in priority, even outranking a first legal charge by way of mortgage.[147] **10.3.85**

Offences

Wilfully obstructing a person exercising powers under this section is a summary offence punishable by a fine not exceeding level 3 on the standard scale.[148] **10.3.86**

Application to the Crown

Part 8 and any provisions made under it bind the Crown. No criminal liability, however, is imposed on the Crown itself, though such immunity does not extend to persons in the service of the Crown.[149] **10.3.87**

Accordingly, as the explanatory notes to the original Bill suggest, a local authority will be able to investigate and determine complaints about high hedges on Crown land, such as land owned by a government department.[150] **10.3.88**

---

[139] ibid, s 77(5). [140] See ibid, s 74(3). [141] ibid, s 77(2)(b). See para 10.3.85 below.
[142] ibid, s 77(6). [143] ibid, s 77(7). [144] ibid, s 77(8). [145] ibid, s 77(4).
[146] ibid, s 77(3).
[147] See eg *Paddington BC v Finucane* [1928] Ch 567; *Bristol Corporation v Virgin* [1928] 2 KB 622.
[148] 2003 Act, s 77(9). [149] ibid, s 84.
[150] High Hedges Bill Explanatory Notes, Bill 28-EN, para 36.

11

PART 9 OF THE ACT: MISCELLANEOUS POWERS

11.1. INTRODUCTION

This Part simply contains a number of amendments to various other pieces of legislation, unconnected save in the sense that each deals with an aspect of the enforcement of substantive provisions relating to anti-social behaviour. The White Paper, *Respect and Responsibility—Taking a Stand Against Anti-Social Behaviour*[1] makes clear the aim of this Part of the Act:[2] **11.1.1**

> Effective enforcement is key. There must be a consistent message that sanctions against anti-social behaviour are extremely serious and that breach of them will lead to unwelcome consequences to the perpetrators. This is a web of rights and responsibilities that involves the whole of society; every individual and every community. Communities need to be empowered and everyone must play their part in setting and enforcing standards of behaviour.[3]

Crime and Disorder Reduction Partnerships

The White Paper refers to a number of agencies considered by the Government to be vital to tackling anti-social behaviour, specifically Crime and Disorder Reduction Partnerships (CDRPs). CDRPs were established under the Crime and Disorder Act 1998[4] to review and assess the incidence of crime and disorder in their area and develop and implement strategies to reduce them. They require local authorities, the police and other local stakeholders to co-ordinate action against such behaviour locally. **11.1.2**

---

[1] Cm 5778, 2003.
[2] Pt 9 began life as Pt 5 of the Bill, entitled 'Sanctions'.
[3] para 1.13.
[4] ss 5–6.

11.1.3 The White Paper also states[5] that the Government hopes that the local authority duty under s 17 of the Crime and Disorder Act 1998 ('the 1998 Act'), 'to exercise their functions with due regard to the likely effect of the exercise of those functions on, and do all that they reasonably can to prevent crime and disorder in their areas' coupled with the duty on CDRPs to publish strategies for dealing with anti-social behaviour, will result in those strategies becoming a mainstream factor in the delivery of local services.

11.1.4 Other essential forces in the battle against anti-social behaviour are cited as the police, special constabulary, accredited persons (see paras 11.2.63–11.2.73 below) and local authorities.[6]

11.2. PROVISIONS OF PART 9 OF THE ACT

Anti-social behaviour orders: background

11.2.1 The White Paper refers to the following methods by which anti-social behaviour may be combated:[7]

(a) warnings;
(b) acceptable behaviour contracts;
(c) injunctions; and
(d) anti-social behaviour orders (ASBOs).

11.2.2 The ASBO was introduced by s 1 of the Crime and Disorder Act 1998 and came into effect on 1 April 1999. Orders are available against anyone aged ten or over.[8] They have been used particularly against young people primarily due to the unavailability of other remedies.[9]

11.2.3 ASBOs are civil orders that seek to protect members of the public from behaviour that causes or is likely to cause harassment, alarm or distress.[10] They may be applied for by a local authority, the police, the British Transport Police (to protect persons on or in the vicinity of premises policed by them, or likely to be on or in the vicinity of such premises) or a registered social landlord (to protect persons residing in or on or in the vicinity of accommodation provided or managed by them, or likely to be on or in the vicinity of such accommodation).[11] A local authority must consult the police before making an application, and the police must consult the relevant local authority. A registered social landlord or the British Transport Police must consult both the relevant local authority and the police.[12]

11.2.4 If the court considers it necessary to make an order, the order will contain such prohibitions as are considered necessary by the court to protect the public

[5] para 4.5. [6] See generally White Paper, ch 4. [7] ibid, paras 5.10–5.24.
[8] 1998 Act, s 1(1). [9] See Chapter 4 above, especially at paras 4.1.11 and 4.3.56.
[10] 1998 Act, s 1. [11] ibid, ss 1(1A)–(1B). [12] ibid, s 1E.

from further anti-social acts by the defendant, and may include prohibitions on specific types of behaviour and/or exclusion zones.[13] An order may be made for a fixed or indefinite period, but must have effect for a minimum period of two years.[14] It is for the court to decide the duration of an order, but the applicant should make its proposals concerning the duration of the order as part of its application.[15]

Applications are made to the adult magistrates' court sitting in its civil capacity.[16] An applicant may also apply for an ASBO during proceedings which are already ongoing in the county court,[17] or an ASBO may be made by the criminal court (without the need for a formal application) as part of its sentencing of a person who has been convicted of a criminal offence.[18] Even in these circumstances, however, the order remains a civil order. **11.2.5**

The Home Office Research Study 'A Review of anti-social behaviour orders'[19] found that orders had been effective to improve the quality of life of communities around the country but that the procedures as originally enacted had created problems which resulted in some authorities using ASBOs only infrequently. **11.2.6**

Accordingly, the Police Reform Act 2002 introduced five significant amendments designed to strengthen and extend the courts' powers. These were: **11.2.7**

(a) permitting the court to make an ASBO valid throughout the country;[20]
(b) the introduction of a procedure for the making of interim ASBOs, with or without notice to the defendant;[21]
(c) extending the authorities that could apply for orders to include registered social landlords and the British Transport Police;[22]
(d) the introduction of the post-conviction ASBO;[23] and
(e) the possibility of making an application in the county court, where proceedings in that court are already on foot.[24]

'Anti-social behaviour'

Section 1(1) of the 1998 Act defines acting in an 'anti-social manner' as acting in a 'manner that caused or was likely to cause harassment, alarm or distress to one or more persons not of the same household' as the perpetrator. This definition is derived from the Public Order Act 1986,[25] and the Protection from Harassment **11.2.8**

---

[13] ibid, s 1(6).
[14] ibid, s 1(7).
[15] Relevant factors are likely to include the age of the defendant, the severity of the anti-social behaviour, the length of time it has continued and the defendant's response to previous measures.
[16] 1998 Act, s 1(3).
[17] ibid, s 1B (inserted by Police Reform Act 2002, s 63).
[18] ibid, s 1C (inserted by Police Reform Act 2002, s 64).
[19] April 2002.
[20] Police Reform Act 2002, s 61(7) inserting new s 1(6) into the 1998 Act.
[21] ibid, s 65, inserting new s 1D into the 1998 Act. See also Magistrates' Courts (Anti-Social Behaviour Orders) Rules 2002, SI 2002/2784, r 5.
[22] ibid, s 61(4) inserting new s 1(1A)–(1B) and new ss 1A and 1E into the 1998 Act.
[23] ibid, s 64, inserting s 1C into the 1998 Act.
[24] ibid, s 63, inserting s 1B into the 1998 Act.
[25] Public Order Act 1986, s 4.

Act 1997.[26] Once the claimant has satisfied the court that the conduct in question amounts to anti-social behaviour, it must also demonstrate that an order is 'necessary' for the protection of persons from further instances of anti-social behaviour by the alleged perpetrator.[27]

11.2.9 The phrase 'likely to cause' enables professional witnesses, such as police officers or enquiry agents, to give evidence of the occurrence of anti-social behaviour where the victim of the behaviour does not feel able to give evidence, perhaps due to the fear of reprisals.

11.2.10 Home Office Guidance[28] provides a non-exhaustive list of the types of behaviour that may be termed anti-social:

- graffiti—which can on its own make even the tidiest urban spaces look squalid
- abusive and intimidating language, too often directed at minorities
- excessive noise, particularly late at night
- fouling the street with litter
- drunken behaviour in the streets, and the mess it creates
- dealing drugs, with all the problems to which it gives rise.[29]

Evidence and standard of proof

11.2.11 As a civil remedy, hearsay evidence would normally be admissible,[30] and may be critical in order for the claimant to be able to demonstrate to the court the full extent of the behaviour complained of in circumstances where eye-witnesses may well be unwilling to come forward. In *R (McCann) v Manchester Crown Court*,[31] the House of Lords confirmed that ASBO proceedings were civil in nature for the purposes of domestic and Convention law, and that hearsay evidence was therefore admissible. The weight to be given to such evidence would necessarily be dependent on the facts of each case although its cumulative effect may be probative. Where a defendant has already had criminal proceedings taken against him, material from those proceedings may be used in the ASBO application.[32]

11.2.12 The House of Lords stated in *McCann*, however, that although such proceedings were civil and the standard of proof was therefore the civil standard of 'balance of probabilities', this did not mean that a bare balance of probabilities would suffice: the standard must be commensurate with the seriousness of the issues at stake which, in the case of an ASBO application, meant that when determining whether a person has been guilty of anti-social behaviour for the purposes of s 1(1) of the 1998 Act, a heightened standard of proof equivalent to the criminal standard of proof would be required.

---

[26] Protection from Harassment Act 1997, s 7(2).

[27] 1998 Act, s 1(2) as amended.

[28] 12 November 2002.

[29] Guidance, p 5.

[30] Civil Evidence Act 1995 and the Magistrates' Courts (Hearsay Evidence in Civil Proceedings) Rules 1999, SI 1999/681.

[31] [2002] UKHL 39, [2003] 1 AC 787.

[32] *S v Poole BC* [2002] EWHC 244 (Admin).

As to the issue of whether an ASBO was necessary, however, no standard of proof was required as the matter was not so much one of proof, rather it is 'an exercise of judgment or evaluation'.[33] 11.2.13

In deciding whether the alleged perpetrator has acted in an anti-social manner, the court must disregard behaviour that is shown to be reasonable in the circumstances.[34] 11.2.14

Acceptable behaviour contracts

Acceptable behaviour contracts (ABCs) were first introduced by Islington LBC in North London as a voluntary measure to deal with young people aged between ten and 17. They constitute an agreement between the local authority or the police, or even a school, and the person whose behaviour is causing concern. Unlike ASBOs, ABCs are not statutory creations and are flexible in terms of content and format. The perpetrator must be prepared voluntarily to admit his anti-social behaviour and agree to abide by a set of terms to prevent that behaviour recurring. An ABC usually lasts for a year although the period may be extended or reduced depending on the circumstances. 11.2.15

ABCs often contain very similar, or even identical, terms to ASBOs. They have no legal effect, however, and no sanctions attach to non-compliance. If a contract is breached, the only remedy available may be to apply for an ASBO. The Guidance recommends that, where an ABC is selected as the best option to pursue, it should contain a statement that the continuation of unacceptable behaviour may lead to an application for an ASBO and that where a contract is broken it should be used as evidence in the application for an ASBO. It may also be possible to use evidence of anti-social behaviour that was originally collected for the ABC in any subsequent ASBO application. 11.2.16

The ABC may come with an offer of support to assist the perpetrator in complying with the agreement. ABCs have proved effective in encouraging young people, and sometimes adults, to refrain from such activities as graffiti and verbal abuse. 11.2.17

Like ASBOs, ABCs are available in relation to anyone aged ten and over, although they are primarily aimed at young people between the ages of ten and 18. In respect of children under ten, the child's parents may be asked to sign a parental responsibility contract (see Chapter 5 above). 11.2.18

ASBO, ABC or other remedy?

An ABC, as a voluntary agreement, has greater flexibility than an ASBO which, because of its statutory status, is directly enforceable. The Guidance[35] suggests that: 11.2.19

---

33 *McCann*, n 31 above, *per* Lord Steyn at [37].

34 1998 Act, s 1(5).

35 Guidance, p 7.

It is important that all concerned should understand that ASBOs and ABCs are in no sense competing for business. Both are potentially extremely powerful tools for dealing with cases of anti-social behaviour, and it will be very much a matter for the individual practitioner to decide which of them it might be appropriate to go for in any particular case. It is particularly important to dispel any impression that anti-social behaviour orders should be regarded as measures of last resort, only to be tried when other interventions such as acceptable behaviour contracts have failed.

Individual support orders

11.2.20 The Criminal Justice Act 2003[36] makes further amendments to the 1998 Act (not in force at the date of writing) by introducing the individual support order, an order which the court must make, if the conditions are satisfied, where it makes an ASBO in respect of a child or young person. The conditions are that the court considers it desirable to make such an order to prevent the kind of behaviour in respect of which it has just made the ASBO; the child or young person is not already subject to an individual support order; and the Secretary of State has notified the court that arrangements for implementing such orders are in place.[37]

11.2.21 The individual support order may require the defendant to do all or any of the following things:

(a) to participate in activities specified in the requirements or directions at a time or times so specified;
(b) to present himself to a person or persons so specified at a place or places and at a time or times so specified;
(c) to comply with any arrangements for his education so specified.[38]

11.2.22 Such requirements, however, may not require the person to attend at a place for more than two days a week, nor may they conflict with the person's religious beliefs or attendance at school or other educational establishment.[39]

11.2.23 Breach of the terms of an individual support order is a summary offence, punishable in the case of a person aged 14 or above at the date of conviction with a fine not exceeding £1,000, and in the case of a person under 14 with a fine not exceeding £250. A referral order may not be made by way of sentence for this offence.[40] Where the ASBO expires or is varied by order of the court, the individual support order will also expire or can be varied by the court.[41] Consequential amendments to other sections in the 1998 Act are also made.[42]

---

[36] s 322, introducing new ss 1AA and 1AB into the 1998 Act.
[37] 1998 Act, s 1AA(3)—the 'Individual Support Conditions'.
[38] ibid, s 1AA(6). [39] ibid, s 1AA(7)–(8). [40] ibid, s 1AB(3)–(4).
[41] ibid, s 1AB(5)–(7). [42] Criminal Justice Act 2003, s 324.

ASBOs: the new provisions

Who can apply for an order?

Section 85 of the 2003 Act further amends s 1 of the Crime and Disorder Act 1998 by extending the list of bodies that may apply for ASBOs. The new bodies are county councils for the purpose of protecting persons in the county of the county council,[43] and housing action trusts for the purpose of protecting the same category of persons as applies to registered social landlords; namely persons residing in or who are otherwise on or likely to be on premises provided or managed by the trust or persons in the vicinity of or likely to be in the vicinity of such premises.[44] **11.2.24**

The addition of these new authorities to the list of bodies that may apply for ASBOs renders them subject to the consultation requirements in s 1E(4) of the 1998 Act to consult the police and the local authority for the area in which the person resides or appears to reside.[45] This requirement does not apply, however, to county councils for counties that have no districts (ie unitary counties).[46] **11.2.25**

County court ASBOs

The 2002 amendments to the 1998 Act conferred power on the county court to make ASBOs, on the application of any of the relevant authorities,[47] where 'principal proceedings' were ongoing in the county court and one of the parties was a person against whom the authority considered it reasonable to apply for an ASBO. A classic example of this might be where possession proceedings have been brought against a tenant and an ASBO is also sought against him. It was not necessary, however, that the authority must already be party to the proceedings—it could apply to be joined for the purpose of making the ASBO application—but the prospective ASBO defendant must already be a party.[48] **11.2.26**

Section 85(5) of the 2003 Act abolishes the requirement that the person against whom the ASBO is sought must already be a party to the principal proceedings, by inserting new subss (3A), (3B) and (3C) into s 1B of the 1998 Act. These provisions enable a relevant authority that is party to the principal proceedings to apply to join in the proceedings a person who is *not* currently a party, but whose anti-social behaviour is material to those proceedings, so that an ASBO can be sought against him.[49] A person must not be joined, however, unless his anti-social acts are material to the principal proceedings.[50] Nor can the relevant authority that is not a party to the proceedings apply to be joined under s 1B(3) of the 1998 Act in order to apply to have another non-party joined **11.2.27**

---

[43] 2003 Act, s 85(2)–(3) inserting new s 1(1A)(aa) and (e), and s 1(1B)(aa) into the 1998 Act and amending s 1(1B)(d).

[44] ibid. [45] ibid, s 85(7), inserting a new s 1E(5) into the 1998 Act. [46] ibid.

[47] ie the authorities listed in 1998 Act, s 1(1A). [48] ibid, s 1B(2)–(3).

[49] ibid, s 1(3A)–(3B), inserted by 2003 Act, s 85(5).

[50] ibid, s 1(3C), inserted by 2003 Act, s 85(5).

under these new provisions: s 1B(3) only enables an authority to apply to be joined to seek an ASBO against a person who is already a party.

11.2.28 An example of the use of the new powers is, again, where an authority is taking possession proceedings against a tenant based, wholly or in part, on the behaviour of the tenant's partner or children. In such cases the authority may join the partner or children in order to seek an ASBO against them, as their anti-social conduct will be material to the principal possession proceedings.

11.2.29 Provision is made for these provisions to be piloted for a specified period and to be commenced on different dates in relation to different age groups.[51]

11.2.30 Section 37(6) of the Act extends s 1B(5) of the 1998 Act, enabling a person who is joined to proceedings for the purpose of making an ASBO application, and against whom an ASBO is then made, to apply to the court that made the ASBO for its variation or discharge.

Post-conviction ASBOs

11.2.31 Section 1C of the 1998 Act, inserted by the Police Reform Act 2002,[52] confers power on the court to grant an ASBO on the conviction of any offender, for any offence committed after the 2002 Act came into force in December 2002, who has behaved in an anti-social manner. The order is not part of the sentence that the individual receives for the criminal offence but is in *addition* to a sentence imposed or conditional discharge for the offence.

11.2.32 Section 86 of the 2003 Act amends s 1C to make it clear that a post-conviction ASBO may be made by the court if it thinks it is appropriate to do so or at the request of the prosecutor.[53] These new provisions also spell out that for the purpose of deciding whether or not to make a post-conviction ASBO, the court may consider evidence led by the prosecution and the defence, and it is immaterial whether such evidence would have been admissible in the criminal proceedings that resulted in the conviction.[54] It is also made clear that it is only the prosecutor who can lead evidence in support of a request for the making of a post-conviction ASBO; not, for example, the local authority or a registered social landlord.

11.2.33 It is less clear whether the court would have power to hear a representative of another relevant authority[55] for the purpose of deciding whether it thinks it is appropriate to make an ASBO, ie the limb of new s 1C(3) of the 1998 Act which does not depend on a request for such an order. It is equally unclear whether the evidence led by the prosecution to support the making of an order needs to bear any relation to the criminal offence, the conviction of which is the foundation of the power to make a post-conviction ASBO. On conviction for a driving offence, for example, could the prosecution lead evidence from the residents of a housing estate to support the making of an ASBO banning the defendant from the estate?

[51] 2003 Act, s 85(9)–(11).

[52] s 64.

[53] 2003 Act, s 86(1) amending 1998 Act, s 1C(3).

[54] ibid, s 86(2), inserting new s 1C(3A)–(3B) into the 1998 Act.

[55] 1998 Act, s 1(1A).

New s 1C(3B) provides that the evidence need not have been admissible in relation to the criminal offence, but this is by no means an answer to the question just posed. It deals with the admission of hearsay evidence and evidence that demonstrates the wider picture of events than may simply be related to the criminal offence of which the defendant was convicted. For example, if a person is convicted of a public order offence outside a public house one evening, it would seem clear that, in support of an ASBO request, the prosecution would be able to adduce evidence that the person had been seen committing public order offences outside all the public houses in the locality over a period of three months. Such evidence would not have been admissible in the criminal trial but would be available to support the post-conviction ASBO application. It remains to be seen, however, whether the court will require some kind of nexus, or connection, between the basis for seeking a post-conviction ASBO and the conviction founding the jurisdiction.[56] **11.2.34**

Section 86(5) of the 2003 Act inserts identical new subss (3A) and (3B) into s 14A of the Football Spectators Act 1989[57] to provide for the adducing of evidence by the prosecution and defence in relation to whether the court should make a 'banning order' prohibiting a person from attending a football match and requiring him to attend a police station. Unlike the making of a post-conviction ASBO, a post-conviction banning order under the Football Spectators Act 1989 is mandatory where the court is satisfied that there are reasonable grounds to believe that making such an order would help to prevent violence or disorder at the types of football matches specified in the Act. **11.2.35**

Section 86(6) makes a consequential amendment, inserting a new para (fa) into s 3(2) of the Prosecution of Offences Act 1985 to allow Crown Prosecution Service (CPS) prosecutors to conduct applications for orders on conviction for anti-social behaviour and football banning orders. **11.2.36**

Reporting restrictions

There are no automatic reporting restrictions in relation to decisions of the adult magistrates' court, sitting in its civil capacity, concerning children or young persons. Section 39 of the Children and Young Persons Act 1933 confers power on the court to restrict reporting, but there is no presumption of such restrictions. In the Youth Court, however, which deals with criminal offences committed by children and young people, s 49 of the Children and Young Persons Act 1933 applies so as automatically to prevent reporting that would tend to identify the defendant. **11.2.37**

In *Chief Constable of Surrey Police v JHG*,[58] the court held that the decision whether to impose such restrictions involved a balancing exercise between the **11.2.38**

[56] See, in another context, the cases in which the court demanded a nexus for the grant of a Housing Act 1996, s 152 injunction, such as *Enfield LBC v B (A Minor)* [2000] 1 WLR 2259, CA; *Nottingham CC v Thames* [2002] EWCA Civ 1098, [2003] HLR 14; *Manchester CC v Lee* [2003] EWCA Civ 1256, [2004] 1 WLR 349.

[57] Which was inserted into that Act by Football (Disorder) Act 2000, Sch 1, para 2.

[58] [2002] EWHC 1129 (Admin).

public interest in disclosure and the welfare and right to privacy of the young person. The court must weigh the conflicting considerations carefully and set out those considerations in its decision. Where an ASBO is made the general public interest in disclosure was reinforced, because such disclosure might improve the prospects of the order being effectively enforced. The purpose of an ASBO being to protect the public from unacceptable behaviour, the public had a particular interest in knowing who was responsible for that behaviour.

11.2.39 Section 86(3) inserts new subss (9B) and (9C) into s 1C of the 1998 Act, disapplying s 49 of the Children and Young Persons Act 1933 in so far as the proceedings relate to the making of a post-conviction ASBO against a child or young person. Section 39 of that Act is applied to such proceedings instead,[59] so that the Youth Court has equivalent powers to the adult court in relation to imposing restrictions upon the reporting of ASBOs.

Mandatory parenting order

11.2.40 Parenting orders were a creation of the 1998 Act, and are dealt with in detail elsewhere.[60] Section 85(8) of the 2003 Act inserts a new subs (1B) into s 9 of the 1998 Act, requiring a court making an ASBO against a person under the age of 16 to make a parenting order against the parent of that child if it is satisfied that the 'relevant condition' is fulfilled.[61] The relevant condition, set out at s 8(6) of the 1998 Act, is that the parenting order would be desirable in the interests of preventing repetition of the behaviour that led to the ASBO. If the court is not satisfied that the relevant condition is fulfilled, the court must state that it is not so satisfied in open court and explain why it is not.[62]

Prosecution for breach

11.2.41 Breach of an ASBO (without reasonable excuse) is a criminal offence triable either way. The maximum penalty on summary conviction is six months' imprisonment and/or a fine up to the statutory maximum. On indictment, the Crown Court may impose a sentence of up to five years imprisonment and/or fine the defendant.[63] A conditional discharge is not available.[64]

11.2.42 A local authority has an express statutory power to commence legal proceedings (including prosecutions) under s 222 of the Local Government Act 1972 where it considers it expedient to do so 'for the promotion or protection of the interest of the inhabitants of their area'. In practice, this means that if the police

---

[59] 1998 Act, s 1C(9C)(b), inserted by 2003 Act, s 86(3). By s 1C(10), inserted by 2003 Act, s 86(4), 'child' and 'young person' have the same meanings in relation to s 1C as they do in the Children and Young Persons Act 1933.

[60] 1998 Act, ss 8–9. See generally, Chapter 5. [61] ibid, s 9(1B)(a). [62] ibid, s 9(1B)(b).

[63] ibid, s 1(10). The maximum sentence for breach by a 12 to 17 year old is a 24 month detention and training order (though a 12 to 14 year old must be a persistent young offender to be eligible for this sentence). A ten to 11 year old may be given a community order for breach of an ASBO.

[64] ibid, s 1(11). An absolute discharge is, however, available.

charge a person with the breach of an ASBO and the local authority wishes to conduct the proceedings, it must seek to have the charge withdrawn and begin proceedings itself. The authority, however, faces the danger of a not guilty verdict being entered on the withdrawal of the police charge and the *autrefois convict* principle rendering it impossible to bring a further charge.

The CPS can appoint someone in the local authority legal department to take over conduct of the proceedings under s 5(1) of the Prosecution of Offences Act 1985, but that person must have a legal qualification, ie a right of audience in any part of the Supreme Court and all county and magistrates' courts under s 71 of the Courts and Legal Services Act 1990. **11.2.43**

Local authorities have been reluctant to use their prosecution powers to prosecute breaches of ASBOs for a number of reasons including resources, a perceived lack of experience or independence, and the clear indication from the Guidance that breach prosecutions are a matter for the CPS. The CPS, on the other hand, have not always enjoyed the resources or an understanding of the significance of particular ASBOs to prosecute them as effectively as the authority that obtained the ASBO would wish. **11.2.44**

Sections 85(4) and 86(3) of the 2003 Act seek to remove these difficulties by inserting new subss (10A) and (10B) into s 1 of the 1998 Act, and a new subs (9A) into s 1C. Section 1(10A) grants a local authority the power to prosecute for breach of an ASBO if it is either a 'relevant authority'[65] (whether or not it is the authority that obtained the ASBO) or the council for the local government area where the person subject to the order resides or appears to reside.[66] Section 1C(9A) confers a power to prosecute a breach of a post-conviction ASBO upon the local authority for the local government area where the person subject to the order resides or appears to reside. **11.2.45**

The CPS will retain discretion to prosecute in relation to breach of an ASBO albeit with the local authority holding a concurrent power. It is to be hoped that liaison between local authorities, the police and the CPS may be improved as a result of the spelling out of the local authority's power to prosecute breaches. Local protocols ought to be able to achieve a sensible and effective division of effort and responsibility. **11.2.46**

Fixed penalty notices for disorderly behaviour by young persons

The Criminal Justice and Police Act 2001 introduced a fixed penalty notice scheme for disorderly behaviour. Twelve-month pilots commenced on 7 August 2002. The White Paper described the aim of fixed penalty notices, and the Government's intentions for them, in the following terms: **11.2.47**

---

65 1998 Act, s 1(1A).

66 By new s 1(10B), where such proceedings are brought in a Youth Court, s 47(2) of the Children and Young Persons Act 1933 has effect as if the people entitled to be present at such a hearing include one person authorized to be present by a relevant authority.

> FPNs are the first stage for most forms of low level disorder offences. They offer speedy and effective action that frees up police and court time. The offender receives an immediate punishment, which if paid, will not result in a criminal record.
>
> The Criminal Justice and Police Act 2001 provided the police with new powers to issue FPNs to those aged 18 years or older, for 11 specified offences, including being drunk and disorderly, throwing fireworks, and causing harassment, alarm or distress.
>
> Pilot schemes are progressing successfully in four areas (West Midlands, Essex, Croydon and North Wales). As of January 2003 a total of 1835 FPNs had been issued. An overall payment rate of 60% is being achieved and only 2% are ending up in court.
>
> We will build on these schemes to introduce FPNs that will bring benefits to the local community in terms of reducing anti-social behaviour. We will be consulting with police forces, including the British Transport Police, to see whether FPNs are needed for other offences.[67]

11.2.48 Section 87 amends the Criminal Justice and Police Act 2001 to extend the scheme to 16 and 17 year olds.[68] Section 87(3), moreover, confers power on the Secretary of State to amend the provisions of the 2001 Act, by statutory instrument, applying the fixed penalty notice regime to people under the age of 16, subject to a lower age limit of ten.[69] Unusually, any such statutory instrument would be subject to the affirmative resolution procedure of Parliament.[70] If extended to the under-16s, the Secretary of State also has power to make provision, in the case of a notice served on a person under 16, for a parent or guardian of that person to be notified that a penalty notice has been given and for the parent or guardian to be liable to pay the penalty under the notice.[71]

11.2.49 The Secretary of State is also given power to specify different levels of penalty for persons of different ages.[72] The explanatory notes state, however, the current position that 'it is not intended to have a different level of penalty in respect of 16 and 17 year olds'.[73]

11.2.50 The extension of the scheme to 16 and 17 year olds will be piloted and supplementary guidance will be issued to the police. The explanatory notes state that the power to extend the scheme to a younger age group at this stage will be revisited in the light of the outcome of these pilots for 16 and 17 year olds.[74]

Curfew orders and supervision orders

11.2.51 Section 88 of the 2003 Act introduces Sch 2 which amends the provisions of the Powers of Criminal Courts (Sentencing) Act 2000, so far as concerns curfew orders and supervision orders.

11.2.52 A curfew order[75] is available in respect of an offender of any age, and requires the offender to remain in a specified place for specified periods of time. Such an

---

[67] paras 5.4–5.7.
[68] In s 2(1) of that Act, '16' is substituted for '18'.
[69] 2001 Act, s 2(6)(a).
[70] ibid, s 2(8)–(9).
[71] ibid, s 2(6)(b).
[72] ibid, s 3(1A), inserted by 2003 Act, s 87(4).
[73] Explanatory notes to the 2003 Act, para 171.
[74] ibid, para 172.
[75] Powers of the Criminal Courts (Sentencing) Act 2000, s 37.

order may be monitored electronically.[76] A curfew order made in respect of a person under 16 cannot last longer than three months;[77] otherwise, the maximum period is six months.[78]

Supervision orders are available only for offenders aged under 18 and place a person under the supervision of a local authority, probation officer or member of a youth offending team.[79] They can include a range of requirements, such as to comply with the directions of the supervisor, which directions may be to live at a specified place for a specified period, and/or to present himself to a specified person at a specified place on a specified day or days, and/or to participate in a specified activity for a specified period of time,[80] although directions may not last for longer than 90 days.[81] If the order does not require compliance with directions, it can specify directly the kinds of matter that would otherwise have been included in directions, including a curfew requirement or 'night restriction' between 6 pm and 6 am.[82] In this case, the requirements of the order cannot last longer than 90 days.[83] A supervision order lasts for no longer than three years.[84] **11.2.53**

Schedule 2, para 3 to the 2003 Act inserts a new s 64A into the Powers of the Criminal Courts (Sentencing) Act 2000, which provides that nothing in Chapter V of Part IV of that Act (community orders available where the offender is aged under 18) prevents a court that makes a supervision order in respect of an offender from also making a curfew order. By Sch 2, para 2(3), moreover, the 'responsible officer' for the curfew order, ie the person who is responsible for monitoring the offender's whereabouts during the curfew periods specified in the order, will—where the offender is also subject to a supervision order—be the offender's supervisor under the supervision order.[85] **11.2.54**

Section 37 of the 2000 Act is also amended,[86] so as to remove the three month limitation on the period for which a curfew order made in respect of an offender under the age of 16 may last, and thus increasing the maximum period to that applicable for all other offenders, namely six months.[87] **11.2.55**

The length of time for which an offender may be required to comply with the supervisor's directions given under a supervision order is also increased from 90 days to 180 days.[88] Equivalent amendments are made, extending from 90 to 180 days the period of any requirements that are specified directly in the order rather than by the supervisor's direction.[89] The power of the court to impose a night restriction is also repealed, given the amendment entitling the court to combine a supervision order with a curfew order.[90] **11.2.56**

---

76 ibid, s 37.
77 ibid, s 37(4).
78 ibid, s 37(3)(a).
79 ibid, s 63.
80 ibid, Sch 6, para 2(2).
81 ibid, Sch 6, para 2(5).
82 ibid, Sch 6, para 3(2).
83 ibid, Sch 6, para 3(3).
84 ibid, s 63(7).
85 This is achieved by inserting a new subs (12) into 2000 Act, s 37.
86 2003 Act, Sch 2, para 2.
87 This is achieved simply by omitting 2000 Act, s 37(4).
88 2003 Act, Sch 2, para 4(2), amending 2000 Act, Sch 6, para 2(5).
89 ibid, Sch 2, para 4(3)(b), amending 2000 Act, Sch 6, para 3(2) and (3).
90 ibid, Sch 2, para 4(3)(a) and (4), repealing 2000 Act, Sch 6, Repeals para 3(2)(e) and para 4 ('night restrictions').

Intensive fostering

11.2.57 Schedule 2, para 4(5) inserts a new para 5A into Sch 6 to the 2000 Act, which adds a power for a court imposing a supervision order to include a foster parent residence requirement. The court may require an offender to live for a specified period of up to 12 months[91] (which may be extended to 18 months)[92] with a local authority foster parent, where certain conditions are specified.[93] The conditions are that:[94]

(a) the offence is imprisonable in the case of an offender aged 18 or over;
(b) the offence or combination of the offence and one or more offences associated with it was so serious that a custodial sentence would normally be appropriate (or, where the offender is aged ten or 11, would normally be appropriate if the offender were aged 12 or over); and
(c) the court is satisfied that the offending was due 'to a significant extent' to the home circumstances in which the offender was living, and that the imposition of a foster parent residence requirement will assist with the offender's rehabilitation.

11.2.58 The foster parent residence requirement designates the local authority in whose area the offender resides as the authority responsible for placing the offender with a local authority foster parent under s 23(2)(a) of the Children Act 1989.[95]

11.2.59 A court may not, however, impose a foster parent residence requirement unless it has consulted the designated local authority and has been notified by the Secretary of State, which notice has not been withdrawn, that arrangements for implementing the requirement are available in the local authority's area.[96]

11.2.60 Nor may such a requirement be imposed on an offender who is not legally represented when the court is considering whether or not to impose the requirement, unless either he was granted a right to representation funded by the Legal Services Commission for either the whole proceedings or that part of them related to the foster parent residence requirement, but the right was withdrawn because of his conduct, or he has been informed of his right to apply for such representation but has refused or failed to do so.[97]

11.2.61 The court may impose a combination of requirements in a supervision order with a foster parent residence requirement, ie those set out in Sch 6, paras 2 (directions by supervisor), 3 (requirements imposed directly by the court), 6 (treatment for mental condition) and 7 (education), to the 2000 Act.[98]

11.2.62 If the supervisor notifies the court that there is no suitable local authority foster parent available, and that he has applied or proposes to apply for a revo-

---

[91] 2000 Act, Sch 6, para 5A(5).
[92] ibid, Sch 7, para 5(2A), inserted by 2003 Act, Sch 2, para 6.
[93] ibid, Sch 6, para 5A(1).
[94] ibid, Sch 6, para 5A(2).
[95] ibid, Sch 6, para 5A(3).
[96] ibid, Sch 6, para 5A(4).
[97] ibid, Sch 6, para 5A(6)–(7).
[98] ibid, Sch 6, para 5A(8).

cation or variation of the supervision order, the foster parent residence requirement is treated, until that application is determined, as a requirement that the offender reside in local authority accommodation.[99]

Extension of powers of community support officers

Community support officers

The Police Reform Act 2002 allowed chief police officers to confer limited police powers on civilians so that they could perform a range of low-level duties. Two groups of civilians are covered by the 2002 Act, the first of which is 'designated' civilians, otherwise known as community support officers (CSOs), who are directly employed by, or contracted to, police authorities.[100] CSOs are uniformed and under the control of the chief officer of police. CSOs are intended to deal with low level crime and nuisance behaviour. **11.2.63**

The 2001 White Paper, *Policing A New Century: A Blueprint for Reform*,[101] explained how the Government envisaged the role of the CSO: **11.2.64**

> Other support staff ('Community Support Officers') will be empowered to carry out basic patrol functions. They will provide a visible presence in the community with powers sufficient to deal with anti-social behaviour and minor disorder.

Their functions were stated to include, among other things, monitoring compliance with ASBOs and ABCs, truancy checking, viewing CCTV footage, and dealing with off road vehicles. **11.2.65**

The powers given to an individual CSO are included in that CSO's 'designation' at the discretion of the chief police officer. Under the current provisions, CSOs may issue a range of fixed penalty notices for public nuisance. For example, a notice may be issued in relation to throwing fireworks, dog fouling and littering, cycling on footpaths and the confiscation of alcohol and tobacco.[102] **11.2.66**

Accredited persons

The second group is 'accredited persons' who are employed by other organizations with whom the chief officer of police has an arrangement in respect of the carrying out of community safety functions.[103] The 2001 White Paper explained their role as follows:[104] **11.2.67**

> This is not policing on the cheap but a realistic, hard-headed approach to deploying and co-ordinating the people who can work to rid the community of abandoned cars, graffiti, thuggish and anti-social behaviour. The extended police family gives the neighbourhood

[99] ibid, Sch 6, para 5A(9). 'Local authority accommodation' is defined in s 163 of the 2000 Act to mean accommodation provided by or on behalf of a local authority, and 'accommodation provided by or on behalf of a local authority' has the meaning given by s 105 of the Children Act 1989.

[100] Police Reform Act 2002, s 38 and Sch 4.

[101] Cm 5326, December 2001, p 11.

[102] Police Reform Act 2002, Schs 4 and 5.

[103] ibid, s 41 and Sch 5.

[104] p 11.

additional power to take responsibility for itself. The sort of functions members of the extended police family would address are broadly the same as for community support officers . . . , covering environmental matters, anti-social behaviour, stewarding, supervision of reparation scheme activities etc.

11.2.68 The 2002 Act enabled chief police officers to establish accreditation schemes so as to confer some police powers on accredited persons. Their powers, granted to them by the chief officer of police in their designation as accredited persons under Sch 5 to the 2002 Act, were more limited than those of CSOs. Accredited persons were permitted to issue fixed penalty notices in regard to cycling on the footway, dog fouling and litter, as well as having the same powers regarding the confiscation of alcohol and tobacco as CSOs.

New powers

11.2.69 Section 89(2) of the 2003 Act amends the 2002 Act as follows.

Power to stop cycles

11.2.70 Section 89(3) and (6) amends the 2002 Act to extend the powers of CSOs and accredited persons to permit them to stop a cyclist where they have reason to believe that the cyclist in question has committed an offence of cycling on a footway.[105] This amendment is designed to make it easier for CSOs and accredited persons to enforce their power to give fixed penalty notices for this offence. Failing to stop a cycle when required to do so is an offence under the Road Traffic Act 1988 and is itself liable to a fixed penalty notice of £30.

Fixed penalty notices for disorder

11.2.71 Section 89(5) permits chief officers of police to confer power on accredited persons to issue fixed penalty notices for disorder under the Criminal Justice and Police Act 2001, which power is already available to CSOs. Two offences are specifically excluded, however: being drunk on a highway, other public place or licensed premises;[106] and disorderly behaviour while drunk in a public place.[107]

11.2.72 The offences for which accredited persons will be able to issue notices are:

- use of insulting or abusive behaviour to cause harassment, alarm or distress;[108]
- throwing fireworks in a thoroughfare;[109]
- trespassing on a railway;[110]
- throwing stones etc at trains or other things on railways;[111]
- knowingly giving a false alarm to the fire brigade;[112]
- wasting police time or giving a false report;[113]

---

[105] Highway Act 1835, s 72.
[106] Licensing Act 1872, s 12.
[107] Criminal Justice Act 1967, s 91.
[108] Public Order Act 1986, s 5.
[109] Explosives Act 1975, s 80 (repealed by Fireworks Act 2003, s 15 and Sch).
[110] British Transport Commission Act 1949, s 55.
[111] ibid, s 56.
[112] Fire Services Act 1947, s 31.
[113] Criminal Law Act 1967, s 5(2).

- consumption of alcohol in a designated public place;[114]
- buying or attempting to buy alcohol for consumption on licensed premises, etc, by a child;[115] and
- using a public communications system for sending messages known to be false in order to cause annoyance.[116]

By s 1(2) of the Criminal Justice and Police Act 2001, the Secretary of State has power, by order, to add to or remove from the list of offences in s 1(1) for which fixed penalties may be given by order. Section 89(4) and (7) of the 2003 Act confers power on the Secretary of State to remove the power of CSOs and/or accredited persons to give fixed penalty notices for such offences. This is achieved by inserting new Sch 4, para 15A(2) and Sch 5, para 9A(2) into the Police Reform Act 2002. Any such order would be subject to the affirmative resolution procedure of Parliament. 11.2.73

Local authority reports where person remanded on bail

Section 23A of the Children and Young Persons Act 1969 provides that where a court does not grant bail, any remand and/or committal of a child or young person charged with or convicted of an offence must be to local authority accommodation. The court has power to impose a security requirement when remanding a child to local authority accommodation,[117] but may not impose such a requirement if the offender is not yet 12 years old.[118] 11.2.74

Section 90 of the 2003 Act inserts a new s 23B into the 1969 Act, extending the power of the courts to remand offenders aged ten or 11 into local authority accommodation. Where the offender is remanded on bail, and has either been charged with or convicted of a serious offence[119] or is in the opinion of the court a persistent offender, the court may order an oral or written report to be made by the local authority to whom the child would have been remanded if the court had remanded him to local authority accommodation within a maximum period of seven working days.[120] The report will specify where the person is likely to be placed or maintained if remanded to local authority accommodation.[121] 11.2.75

By s 90(6), the Secretary of State may, by order, extend this provision to an offender aged 12 to 16 inclusive, if a court remands him on bail, he meets the criteria for a secure remand,[122] and, where the remand is post-conviction, the court 11.2.76

---

[114] Criminal Justice and Police Act 2001, s 12.

[115] Licensing Act 2003, s 149(4). This was formerly the offence of buying or attempting to buy alcohol for consumption in a bar in licensed premises by a person under 18 under the Licensing Act 1964, s 169C(3).

[116] Telecommunications Act 1984, s 43(1)(b). Now Communications Act 2003, s 127(2): using public electronic communications network in order to cause annoyance, inconvenience or needless anxiety.

[117] Children and Young Persons Act 1969, s 23(4).

[118] ibid, s 23(5).

[119] ie if committed by an adult, punishable by a sentence of two or more years' imprisonment: Children and Young Persons Act 1969, s 23B(7).

[120] ibid, s 23B(2)–(5).

[121] ibid, s 23B(2).

[122] ibid, s 23AA(3).

is satisfied that the behaviour constituting the offence was due, to a significant extent, to the circumstances in which the offender was living.

11.2.77 The explanatory notes to the Act state that this provision is principally aimed at serious or persistent offenders aged between ten and 11, where the court might have considered a remand to secure accommodation had they been aged 12 or above. The report will give the court information about the probable placement of an offender, enabling the court to decide whether to remand the child into local authority accommodation (if the likely placement would be best for the child's welfare) or continue bail.

Power of arrest for Local Government Act, s 222 injunction

11.2.78 As stated above, at para 11.2.42, s 222(1) of the Local Government Act 1972 entitles local authorities to institute, defend and appear in both civil and criminal proceedings in their own name where they consider it to be 'expedient' to do so for the promotion or protection of the interests of the inhabitants of their area. Prior to the enactment of ss 152 and 153 of the Housing Act 1996 (injunction with power of arrest for anti-social behaviour and to enforce the nuisance conditions of tenancy agreements),[123] this was the principal provision available to local authorities to combat persistent criminal and anti-social behaviour. The disadvantage of this power, however, particularly in comparison with the Housing Act 1996 powers, was that no power of arrest was available to remove the perpetrator from the scene in the event that the injunction was breached.

11.2.79 Section 91 of the 2003 Act plugs this gap. If the court grants an injunction under s 222 which prohibits conduct that is capable of causing nuisance or annoyance to any person, and if the local authority[124] applies, the court may attach a power of arrest to any provision of the injunction if the conduct consists of or includes the use or threatened use of violence, or if there is a significant risk of harm to a person.[125]

11.2.80 This is a useful, and very wide, power, mirroring the provisions of new ss 153A–D of the Housing Act 1996.[126] In principle, for example, the court could attach a power of arrest to a mandatory as well as a prohibitive provision of the injunction.

---

[123] See Chapter 4 above.

[124] Local authority has the same meaning as in s 222 of the Local Government Act 1972: 2003 Act, s 91(5).

[125] 2003 Act, s 91(2)–(3). Harm includes serious ill-treatment or abuse whether physical or not: ibid, s 91(4).

[126] Inserted into that Act by 2003 Act, s 13.

APPENDIX 1

Anti-Social Behaviour Act 2003

CONTENTS

PART 1
PREMISES WHERE DRUGS USED UNLAWFULLY

PART 2
HOUSING

PART 3
PARENTAL RESPONSIBILITIES

Parenting orders under the 1998 Act

Truancy and exclusion from school

PART 1
PREMISES WHERE DRUGS USED UNLAWFULLY

1. Closure notice

(1) This section applies to premises if a police officer not below the rank of superintendent (the authorising officer) has reasonable grounds for believing—
  (a) that at any time during the relevant period the premises have been used in connection with the unlawful use, production or supply of a Class A controlled drug, and
  (b) that the use of the premises is associated with the occurrence of disorder or serious nuisance to members of the public.

(2) The authorising officer may authorise the issue of a closure notice in respect of premises to which this section applies if he is satisfied—
  (a) that the local authority for the area in which the premises are situated has been consulted;
  (b) that reasonable steps have been taken to establish the identity of any person who lives on the premises or who has control of or responsibility for or an interest in the premises.

(3) An authorisation under subsection (2) may be given orally or in writing, but if it is given orally the authorising officer must confirm it in writing as soon as it is practicable.

(4) A closure notice must—
  (a) give notice that an application will be made under section 2 for the closure of the premises;
  (b) state that access to the premises by any person other than a person who habitually resides in the premises or the owner of the premises is prohibited;
  (c) specify the date and time when and the place at which the application will be heard;
  (d) explain the effects of an order made in pursuance of section 2;
  (e) state that failure to comply with the notice amounts to an offence;
  (f) give information about relevant advice providers.

(5) The closure notice must be served by a constable.

(6) Service is effected by—
  (a) fixing a copy of the notice to at least one prominent place on the premises,
  (b) fixing a copy of the notice to each normal means of access to the premises,
  (c) fixing a copy of the notice to any outbuildings which appear to the constable to be used with or as part of the premises,
  (d) giving a copy of the notice to at least one person who appears to the constable to have control of or responsibility for the premises, and
  (e) giving a copy of the notice to the persons identified in pursuance of subsection (2)(b) and to any other person appearing to the constable to be a person of a description mentioned in that subsection.

(7) The closure notice must also be served on any person who occupies any other part of the building or other structure in which the premises are situated if the constable reasonably believes at the time of serving the notice under subsection (6) that the

person's access to the other part of the building or structure will be impeded if a closure order is made under section 2.

(8) It is immaterial whether any person has been convicted of an offence relating to the use, production or supply of a controlled drug.

(9) The Secretary of State may by regulations specify premises or descriptions of premises to which this section does not apply.

(10) The relevant period is the period of three months ending with the day on which the authorising officer considers whether to authorise the issue of a closure notice in respect of the premises.

(11) Information about relevant advice providers is information about the names of and means of contacting persons and organisations in the area that provide advice about housing and legal matters.

2. Closure order

(1) If a closure notice has been issued under section 1 a constable must apply under this section to a magistrates' court for the making of a closure order.

(2) The application must be heard by the magistrates' court not later than 48 hours after the notice was served in pursuance of section 1(6)(a).

(3) The magistrates' court may make a closure order if and only if it is satisfied that each of the following paragraphs applies—
  (a) the premises in respect of which the closure notice was issued have been used in connection with the unlawful use, production or supply of a Class A controlled drug;
  (b) the use of the premises is associated with the occurrence of disorder or serious nuisance to members of the public;
  (c) the making of the order is necessary to prevent the occurrence of such disorder or serious nuisance for the period specified in the order.

(4) A closure order is an order that the premises in respect of which the order is made are closed to all persons for such period (not exceeding three months) as the court decides.

(5) But the order may include such provision as the court thinks appropriate relating to access to any part of the building or structure of which the premises form part.

(6) The magistrates' court may adjourn the hearing on the application for a period of not more than 14 days to enable—
  (a) the occupier of the premises,
  (b) the person who has control of or responsibility for the premises, or
  (c) any other person with an interest in the premises,

to show why a closure order should not be made.

(7) If the magistrates' court adjourns the hearing under subsection (6) it may order that the closure notice continues in effect until the end of the period of the adjournment.

(8) A closure order may be made in respect of all or any part of the premises in respect of which the closure notice was issued.

(9) It is immaterial whether any person has been convicted of an offence relating to the use, production or supply of a controlled drug.

3. Closure order: enforcement

(1) This section applies if a magistrates' court makes an order under section 2.

(2) A constable or an authorised person may—
   (a) enter the premises in respect of which the order is made;
   (b) do anything reasonably necessary to secure the premises against entry by any person.

(3) A person acting under subsection (2) may use reasonable force.

(4) But a constable or authorised person seeking to enter the premises for the purposes of subsection (2) must, if required to do so by or on behalf of the owner, occupier or other person in charge of the premises, produce evidence of his identity and authority before entering the premises.

(5) A constable or authorised person may also enter the premises at any time while the order has effect for the purpose of carrying out essential maintenance of or repairs to the premises.

(6) In this section and in section 4 an authorised person is a person authorised by the chief officer of police for the area in which the premises are situated.

4. Closure of premises: offences

(1) A person commits an offence if he remains on or enters premises in contravention of a closure notice.

(2) A person commits an offence if—
   (a) he obstructs a constable or an authorised person acting under section 1(6) or 3(2),
   (b) he remains on premises in respect of which a closure order has been made, or
   (c) he enters the premises.

(3) A person guilty of an offence under this section is liable on summary conviction—
   (a) to imprisonment for a period not exceeding six months, or
   (b) to a fine not exceeding level 5 on the standard scale,

   or to both such imprisonment and fine.

(4) But a person does not commit an offence under subsection (1) or subsection (2)(b) or (c) if he has a reasonable excuse for entering or being on the premises (as the case may be).

(5) A constable in uniform may arrest a person he reasonably suspects of committing or having committed an offence under this section.

5. Extension and discharge of closure order

(1) At any time before the end of the period for which a closure order is made or extended a constable may make a complaint to an appropriate justice of the peace for an extension or further extension of the period for which it has effect.

(2) But a complaint must not be made unless it is authorised by a police officer not below the rank of superintendent—
   (a) who has reasonable grounds for believing that it is necessary to extend the period for which the closure order has effect for the purpose of preventing the occurrence of disorder or serious nuisance to members of the public, and

(b) who is satisfied that the local authority has been consulted about the intention to make the complaint.

(3) If a complaint is made to a justice of the peace under subsection (1) the justice may issue a summons directed to—
(a) the persons on whom the closure notice relating to the closed premises was served under subsection (6)(d) or (e) or (7) of section 1;
(b) any other person who appears to the justice to have an interest in the closed premises but on whom the closure notice was not served,
requiring such person to appear before the magistrates' court to answer to the complaint.

(4) If the court is satisfied that the order is necessary to prevent the occurrence of disorder or serious nuisance for a further period it may extend the period for which the order has effect by a period not exceeding three months.

(5) But a closure order must not have effect for more than six months.

(6) Any of the following persons may make a complaint to an appropriate justice of the peace for an order that a closure order is discharged—
(a) a constable;
(b) the local authority;
(c) a person on whom the closure notice relating to the closed premises was served under subsection (6)(d) or (e) or (7) of section 1;
(d) a person who has an interest in the closed premises but on whom the closure notice was not served.

(7) If a complaint is made under subsection (6) by a person other than a constable the justice may issue a summons directed to such constable as he thinks appropriate requiring the constable to appear before the magistrates' court to answer to the complaint.

(8) The court must not make an order discharging a closure order unless it is satisfied that the closure order is no longer necessary to prevent the occurrence of disorder or serious nuisance to members of the public.

(9) If a summons is issued in accordance with subsection (3) or (7), a notice stating the date, time and place at which the complaint will be heard must be served on—
(a) the persons to whom the summons is directed if it is issued under subsection (3);
(b) the persons mentioned in subsection (6)(c) and (d) (except the complainant) if the summons is issued under subsection (7);
(c) such constable as the justice thinks appropriate (unless he is the complainant);
(d) the local authority (unless they are the complainant).

(10) An appropriate justice of the peace is a justice of the peace acting for the petty sessions area in which the premises in respect of which a closure order is made are situated.

6. Appeals

(1) This section applies to—
(a) an order under section 2 or 5;
(b) a decision by a court not to make an order under either of those sections.

(2) An appeal against an order or decision to which this section applies must be brought to the Crown Court before the end of the period of 21 days beginning with the day on which the order or decision is made.

(3) An appeal against an order under section 2 or 5(4) may be brought by—

(a) a person on whom the closure notice relating to the closed premises was served under section 1(6)(d) or (e);

(b) a person who has an interest in the closed premises but on whom the closure notice was not served.

(4) An appeal against the decision of a court not to make such an order may be brought by—

(a) a constable;

(b) the local authority.

(5) On an appeal under this section the Crown Court may make such order as it thinks appropriate.

7. Access to other premises

(1) This section applies to any person who occupies or owns any part of a building or structure—

(a) in which closed premises are situated, and

(b) in respect of which the closure order does not have effect.

(2) A person to whom this section applies may at any time while a closure order has effect apply to—

(a) the magistrates' court in respect of an order made under section 2 or 5;

(b) the Crown Court in respect of an order made under section 6.

(3) If an application is made under this section notice of the date, time and place of the hearing to consider the application must be given to every person mentioned in section 5(6).

(4) On an application under this section the court may make such order as it thinks appropriate in relation to access to any part of a building or structure in which closed premises are situated.

(5) It is immaterial whether any provision has been made as mentioned in section 2(5).

8. Reimbursement of costs

(1) A police authority or a local authority which incurs expenditure for the purpose of clearing, securing or maintaining the premises in respect of which a closure order has effect may apply to the court which made the order for an order under this section.

(2) On an application under this section the court may make such order as it thinks appropriate in the circumstances for the reimbursement (in full or in part) by the owner of the premises of the expenditure mentioned in subsection (1).

(3) But an application for an order under this section must not be entertained unless it is made not later than the end of the period of three months starting with the day the closure order ceases to have effect.

(4) An application under this section must be served on—

(a) the police authority for the area in which the premises are situated if the application is made by the local authority;

(b) the local authority if the application is made by a police authority;

(c) the owner of the premises.

9. Exemption from liability for certain damages

(1) A constable is not liable for relevant damages in respect of anything done or omitted to be done by him in the performance or purported performance of his functions under this Part.

(2) A chief officer of police is not liable for relevant damages in respect of anything done or omitted to be done by a constable under his direction or control in the performance or purported performance of the constable's functions under this Part.

(3) Subsections (1) and (2) do not apply—
  (a) if the act or omission is shown to have been in bad faith;
  (b) so as to prevent an award of damages made in respect of an act or omission on the ground that the act or omission was unlawful by virtue of section 6(1) of the Human Rights Act 1998 (c. 42).

(4) This section does not affect any other exemption from liability for damages (whether at common law or otherwise).

(5) Relevant damages are damages in proceedings for judicial review or for the tort of negligence or misfeasance in public duty.

10. Compensation

(1) This section applies to any person who incurs financial loss in consequence of—
  (a) the issue of a closure notice, or
  (b) a closure order having effect.

(2) A person to whom this section applies may apply to—
  (a) the magistrates' court which considered the application for a closure order;
  (b) the Crown Court if the closure order was made or extended by an order made by that Court on an appeal under section 6.

(3) An application under this section must not be entertained unless it is made not later than the end of the period of three months starting with whichever is the later of—
  (a) the day the court decides not to make a closure order;
  (b) the day the Crown Court dismisses an appeal against a decision not to make a closure order;
  (c) the day a closure order ceases to have effect.

(4) On an application under this section the court may order the payment of compensation out of central funds if it is satisfied—
  (a) that the person had no connection with the use of the premises as mentioned in section 1(1),
  (b) if the person is the owner or occupier of the premises, that he took reasonable steps to prevent the use,
  (c) that the person has incurred financial loss as mentioned in subsection (1), and
  (d) having regard to all the circumstances it is appropriate to order payment of compensation in respect of that loss.

(5) Central funds has the same meaning as in enactments providing for the payment of costs.

11. Interpretation

(1) References to a controlled drug and (however expressed) to the production or supply of a controlled drug must be construed in accordance with the Misuse of Drugs Act 1971 (c. 38).

(2) A Class A controlled drug is a controlled drug which is a Class A drug within the meaning of section 2 of that Act.

(3) Premises includes—

(a) any land or other place (whether enclosed or not);

(b) any outbuildings which are or are used as part of the premises.

(4) A closure notice is a notice issued under section 1.

(5) A closure order is—

(a) an order made under section 2;

(b) an order extended under section 5;

(c) an order made or extended under section 6 which has the like effect as an order made or extended under section 2 or 5 (as the case may be).

(6) Each of the following is a local authority in relation to England—

(a) a district council;

(b) a London borough council;

(c) a county council for an area for which there is no district council;

(d) the Common Council of the City of London in its capacity as a local authority;

(e) the Council of the Isles of Scilly.

(7) Each of the following is a local authority in relation to Wales—

(a) a county council;

(b) a county borough council.

(8) References to a local authority are to the local authority for the area in which premises—

(a) to which a closure notice applies are situated;

(b) in respect of which a closure order has effect are situated.

(9) Closed premises are premises in respect of which a closure order has effect.

(10) A person is the owner of premises if either of the following paragraphs applies to him—

(a) he is a person (other than a mortgagee not in possession) who is for the time being entitled to dispose of the fee simple in the premises, whether in possession or in reversion;

(b) he is a person who holds or is entitled to the rents and profits of the premises under a lease which (when granted) was for a term of not less than three years.

(11) This section applies for the purposes of this Part.

PART 2
HOUSING

12. Anti-social behaviour: landlords' policies and procedures

(1) In Part 8 of the Housing Act 1996 (c. 52) before section 219 (power of Secretary of State to give directions as to certain charges by social landlords) there is inserted the following section—

218A. Anti-social behaviour: landlords' policies and procedures

(1) This section applies to the following landlords—

(a) a local housing authority;

(b) a housing action trust;

(c) a registered social landlord.

(2) The landlord must prepare—
   (a) a policy in relation to anti-social behaviour;
   (b) procedures for dealing with occurrences of anti-social behaviour.
(3) The landlord must not later than 6 months after the commencement of section 12 of the Anti-social Behaviour Act 2003 publish a statement of the policy and procedures prepared under subsection (2).
(4) The landlord must from time to time keep the policy and procedures under review and, when it thinks appropriate, publish a revised statement.
(5) A copy of a statement published under subsection (3) or (4)—
   (a) must be available for inspection at all reasonable hours at the landlord's principal office;
   (b) must be provided on payment of a reasonable fee to any person who requests it.
(6) The landlord must also—
   (a) prepare a summary of its current policy and procedures;
   (b) provide without charge a copy of the summary to any person who requests it.
(7) In preparing and reviewing the policy and procedures the landlord must have regard to guidance issued—
   (a) by the Secretary of State in the case of a local housing authority or a housing action trust;
   (b) by the Relevant Authority under section 36 in the case of a registered social landlord.
(8) Anti-social behaviour is any conduct to which section 153A or 153B applies.
(9) Relevant Authority has the same meaning as in Part 1.

(2) In section 36(2) of that Act (functions of the Housing Corporation relating to guidance and corresponding functions relating to Wales) after paragraph (h) there is inserted the following paragraph—

   (i) the policy and procedures a landlord is required under section 218A to prepare and from time to time revise in connection with anti-social behaviour.

13. Injunctions against anti-social behaviour on application of certain social landlords

(1) The Housing Act 1996 (c. 52) is amended as follows.
(2) Sections 152 (power to grant injunctions against anti-social behaviour) and 153 (power of arrest for breach of certain injunctions against anti-social behaviour) are omitted.
(3) Before section 154 (power of arrest in ex parte applications) there are inserted the following sections—

153A. Anti-social behaviour injunction

(1) This section applies to conduct—
   (a) which is capable of causing nuisance or annoyance to any person, and
   (b) which directly or indirectly relates to or affects the housing management functions of a relevant landlord.
(2) The court on the application of a relevant landlord may grant an injunction (an anti-social behaviour injunction) if each of the following two conditions is satisfied.
(3) The first condition is that the person against whom the injunction is sought is engaging, has engaged or threatens to engage in conduct to which this section applies.
(4) The second condition is that the conduct is capable of causing nuisance or annoyance to any of the following—
   (a) a person with a right (of whatever description) to reside in or occupy housing accommodation owned or managed by the relevant landlord;
   (b) a person with a right (of whatever description) to reside in or occupy other housing accommodation in the neighbourhood of housing accommodation mentioned in paragraph (a);

(c) a person engaged in lawful activity in or in the neighbourhood of housing accommodation mentioned in paragraph (a);
(d) a person employed (whether or not by the relevant landlord) in connection with the exercise of the relevant landlord's housing management functions.

(5) It is immaterial where conduct to which this section applies occurs.

(6) An anti-social behaviour injunction prohibits the person in respect of whom it is granted from engaging in conduct to which this section applies.

153B. Injunction against unlawful use of premises

(1) This section applies to conduct which consists of or involves using or threatening to use housing accommodation owned or managed by a relevant landlord for an unlawful purpose.

(2) The court on the application of the relevant landlord may grant an injunction prohibiting the person in respect of whom the injunction is granted from engaging in conduct to which this section applies.

153C. Injunctions: exclusion order and power of arrest

(1) This section applies if the court grants an injunction under subsection (2) of section 153A or 153B and it thinks that either of the following paragraphs applies—
(a) the conduct consists of or includes the use or threatened use of violence;
(b) there is a significant risk of harm to a person mentioned in section 153A(4).

(2) The court may include in the injunction a provision prohibiting the person in respect of whom it is granted from entering or being in—
(a) any premises specified in the injunction;
(b) any area specified in the injunction.

(3) The court may attach a power of arrest to any provision of the injunction.

153D. Injunction against breach of tenancy agreement

(1) This section applies if a relevant landlord applies for an injunction against a tenant in respect of the breach or anticipated breach of a tenancy agreement on the grounds that the tenant—
(a) is engaging or threatening to engage in conduct that is capable of causing nuisance or annoyance to any person, or
(b) is allowing, inciting or encouraging any other person to engage or threaten to engage in such conduct.

(2) The court may proceed under subsection (3) or (4) if it is satisfied—
(a) that the conduct includes the use or threatened use of violence, or
(b) that there is a significant risk of harm to any person.

(3) The court may include in the injunction a provision prohibiting the person in respect of whom it is granted from entering or being in—
(a) any premises specified in the injunction;
(b) any area specified in the injunction.

(4) The court may attach a power of arrest to any provision of the injunction.

(5) Tenancy agreement includes any agreement for the occupation of residential accommodation owned or managed by a relevant landlord.

153E. Injunctions: supplementary

(1) This section applies for the purposes of sections 153A to 153D.

(2) An injunction may—
(a) be made for a specified period or until varied or discharged;
(b) have the effect of excluding a person from his normal place of residence.

(3) An injunction may be varied or discharged by the court on an application by—
(a) the person in respect of whom it is made;
(b) the relevant landlord.

(4) If the court thinks it just and convenient it may grant or vary an injunction without the respondent having been given such notice as is otherwise required by rules of court.
(5) If the court acts under subsection (4) it must give the person against whom the injunction is made an opportunity to make representations in relation to the injunction as soon as it is practicable for him to do so.
(6) The court is the High Court or a county court.
(7) Each of the following is a relevant landlord—
 (a) a housing action trust;
 (b) a local authority (within the meaning of the Housing Act 1985);
 (c) a registered social landlord.
(8) A charitable housing trust which is not a registered social landlord is also a relevant landlord for the purposes of section 153D.
(9) Housing accommodation includes—
 (a) flats, lodging-houses and hostels;
 (b) any yard, garden, outhouses and appurtenances belonging to the accommodation or usually enjoyed with it;
 (c) in relation to a neighbourhood, the whole of the housing accommodation owned or managed by a relevant landlord in the neighbourhood and any common areas used in connection with the accommodation.
(10) A landlord owns housing accommodation if either of the following paragraphs applies to him—
 (a) he is a person (other than a mortgagee not in possession) who is for the time being entitled to dispose of the fee simple in the premises, whether in possession or in reversion;
 (b) he is a person who holds or is entitled to the rents and profits of the premises under a lease which (when granted) was for a term of not less than three years.
(11) The housing management functions of a relevant landlord include—
 (a) functions conferred by or under any enactment;
 (b) the powers and duties of the landlord as the holder of an estate or interest in housing accommodation.
(12) Harm includes serious ill-treatment or abuse (whether physical or not).

(4) In section 154—
 (a) in subsection (1) for 'section 152(6) or section 153' there is substituted 'section 153C(3) or 153D(4)';
 (b) in subsection (1)(b) for '152(1)(a) or section 153(5)(a)' there is substituted 'section 153A(4)'.
(5) In section 155—
 (a) in subsection (1) for 'section 152(6) or section 153' there is substituted 'section 153C(3) or 153D(4)';
 (b) in subsection (3) for 'section 152(6) or section 153' there is substituted 'section 153C(3) or 153D(4)'.
(6) In section 157—
 (a) in subsection (1) for 'section 152(6) or section 153' there is substituted 'section 153C(3) or 153D(4)';
 (b) in subsection (3) for 'section 152(6) or section 153' there is substituted 'section 153C(3) or 153D(4)'.
(7) In section 158—
 (a) in subsection (1) the entries relating to 'child', 'harm', 'health' and 'ill-treatment' are omitted;
 (b) subsection (2) is omitted.

14. Security of tenure: anti-social behaviour

(1) In the Housing Act 1985 (c. 68) section 82 (which makes provision in relation to security of tenure) is amended as follows—

(a) in subsection (1) for the words from 'of the court' to the end of the subsection there is substituted 'mentioned in subsection (1A)';

(b) after subsection (1) there is inserted the following subsection—

(1A) These are the orders—

(a) an order of the court for the possession of the dwelling-house;

(b) an order under subsection (3);

(c) a demotion order under section 82A.

(2) After section 82 of that Act there is inserted the following section—

82A. Demotion because of anti-social behaviour

(1) This section applies to a secure tenancy if the landlord is—

(a) a local housing authority;

(b) a housing action trust;

(c) a registered social landlord.

(2) The landlord may apply to a county court for a demotion order.

(3) A demotion order has the following effect—

(a) the secure tenancy is terminated with effect from the date specified in the order;

(b) if the tenant remains in occupation of the dwelling-house after that date a demoted tenancy is created with effect from that date;

(c) it is a term of the demoted tenancy that any arrears of rent payable at the termination of the secure tenancy become payable under the demoted tenancy;

(d) it is also a term of the demoted tenancy that any rent paid in advance or overpaid at the termination of the secure tenancy is credited to the tenant's liability to pay rent under the demoted tenancy.

(4) The court must not make a demotion order unless it is satisfied—

(a) that the tenant or a person residing in or visiting the dwelling-house has engaged or has threatened to engage in conduct to which section 153A or 153B of the Housing Act 1996 (anti-social behaviour or use of premises for unlawful purposes) applies, and

(b) that it is reasonable to make the order.

(5) Each of the following has effect in respect of a demoted tenancy at the time it is created by virtue of an order under this section as it has effect in relation to the secure tenancy at the time it is terminated by virtue of the order—

(a) the parties to the tenancy;

(b) the period of the tenancy;

(c) the amount of the rent;

(d) the dates on which the rent is payable.

(6) Subsection (5)(b) does not apply if the secure tenancy was for a fixed term and in such a case the demoted tenancy is a weekly periodic tenancy.

(7) If the landlord of the demoted tenancy serves on the tenant a statement of any other express terms of the secure tenancy which are to apply to the demoted tenancy such terms are also terms of the demoted tenancy.

(8) For the purposes of this section a demoted tenancy is—

(a) a tenancy to which section 143A of the Housing Act 1996 applies if the landlord of the secure tenancy is a local housing authority or a housing action trust;

(b) a tenancy to which section 20B of the Housing Act 1988 applies if the landlord of the secure tenancy is a registered social landlord.

(3) Section 83 of that Act is amended as follows—
   (a) in subsection (1) for the words from 'the possession' to the second 'tenancy' substitute 'an order mentioned in section 82(1A)';
   (b) in subsection (2)(b) for the words from 'an order' to 'tenancy' substitute 'the order';
   (c) after subsection (4) insert—

      (4A) If the proceedings are for a demotion order under section 82A the notice—
         (a) must specify the date after which the proceedings may be begun;
         (b) ceases to be in force twelve months after the date so specified.;

   (d) in subsection (5) for 'or (4)' substitute '(4) or (4A)'.

(4) In the Housing Act 1988 (c. 50) after section 6 (which makes provision about fixing the terms of a statutory periodic tenancy) there is inserted the following section—

6A. Demotion because of anti-social behaviour

(1) This section applies to an assured tenancy if the landlord is a registered social landlord.
(2) The landlord may apply to a county court for a demotion order.
(3) A demotion order has the following effect—
   (a) the assured tenancy is terminated with effect from the date specified in the order;
   (b) if the tenant remains in occupation of the dwelling-house after that date a demoted tenancy is created with effect from that date;
   (c) it is a term of the demoted tenancy that any arrears of rent payable at the termination of the assured tenancy become payable under the demoted tenancy;
   (d) it is also a term of the demoted tenancy that any rent paid in advance or overpaid at the termination of the assured tenancy is credited to the tenant's liability to pay rent under the demoted tenancy.
(4) The court must not make a demotion order unless it is satisfied—
   (a) that the tenant or a person residing in or visiting the dwelling-house has engaged or has threatened to engage in conduct to which section 153A or 153B of the Housing Act 1996 (anti-social behaviour or use of premises for unlawful purposes) applies, and
   (b) that it is reasonable to make the order.
(5) The court must not entertain proceedings for a demotion order unless—
   (a) the landlord has served on the tenant a notice under subsection (6), or
   (b) the court thinks it is just and equitable to dispense with the requirement of the notice.
(6) The notice must—
   (a) give particulars of the conduct in respect of which the order is sought;
   (b) state that the proceedings will not begin before the date specified in the notice;
   (c) state that the proceedings will not begin after the end of the period of twelve months beginning with the date of service of the notice.
(7) The date specified for the purposes of subsection (6)(b) must not be before the end of the period of two weeks beginning with the date of service of the notice.
(8) Each of the following has effect in respect of a demoted tenancy at the time it is created by virtue of an order under this section as it has effect in relation to the assured tenancy at the time it is terminated by virtue of the order—
   (a) the parties to the tenancy;
   (b) the period of the tenancy;
   (c) the amount of the rent;
   (d) the dates on which the rent is payable.
(9) Subsection (8)(b) does not apply if the assured tenancy was for a fixed term and in such a case the demoted tenancy is a weekly periodic tenancy.

(10) If the landlord of the demoted tenancy serves on the tenant a statement of any other express terms of the assured tenancy which are to apply to the demoted tenancy such terms are also terms of the demoted tenancy.

(11) For the purposes of this section a demoted tenancy is a tenancy to which section 20B of the Housing Act 1988 applies.

(5) Schedule 1 amends the Housing Act 1996 (c. 52) and the Housing Act 1985 (c. 68).

15. Demoted assured shorthold tenancies

(1) In the Housing Act 1988 (c. 50) after section 20A (duty of landlord to provide statement of terms for certain tenancies) there is inserted the following section—

20B. Demoted assured shorthold tenancies

(1) An assured tenancy is an assured shorthold tenancy to which this section applies (a demoted assured shorthold tenancy) if—

(a) the tenancy is created by virtue of an order of the court under section 82A of the Housing Act 1985 or section 6A of this Act (a demotion order), and

(b) the landlord is a registered social landlord.

(2) At the end of the period of one year starting with the day when the demotion order takes effect a demoted assured shorthold tenancy ceases to be an assured shorthold tenancy unless subsection (3) applies.

(3) This subsection applies if before the end of the period mentioned in subsection (2) the landlord gives notice of proceedings for possession of the dwelling house.

(4) If subsection (3) applies the tenancy continues to be a demoted assured shorthold tenancy until the end of the period mentioned in subsection (2) or (if later) until one of the following occurs—

(a) the notice of proceedings for possession is withdrawn;

(b) the proceedings are determined in favour of the tenant;

(c) the period of six months beginning with the date on which the notice is given ends and no proceedings for possession have been brought.

(5) Registered social landlord has the same meaning as in Part 1 of the Housing Act 1996.

(2) In section 21 of that Act (recovery of possession on expiry or termination of assured shorthold tenancy) after subsection (5) there is inserted the following subsection—

(5A) Subsection (5) above does not apply to an assured shorthold tenancy to which section 20B (demoted assured shorthold tenancies) applies.

(3) In Schedule 2A to that Act (assured tenancies which are not shorthold tenancies) after paragraph 5 (former secure tenancies) there is inserted the following paragraph—

5A. *Former demoted tenancies*

An assured tenancy which ceases to be an assured shorthold tenancy by virtue of section 20B(2) or (4).

16. Proceedings for possession: anti-social behaviour

(1) In the Housing Act 1985 (c. 68) after section 85 (which extends the court's discretion in certain proceedings for possession) there is inserted the following section—

85A. Proceedings for possession: anti-social behaviour

(1) This section applies if the court is considering under section 84(2)(a) whether it is reasonable to make an order for possession on ground 2 set out in Part 1 of Schedule 2 (conduct of tenant or other person).

(2) The court must consider, in particular—
(a) the effect that the nuisance or annoyance has had on persons other than the person against whom the order is sought;
(b) any continuing effect the nuisance or annoyance is likely to have on such persons;
(c) the effect that the nuisance or annoyance would be likely to have on such persons if the conduct is repeated.

(2) In the Housing Act 1988 (c. 50) after section 9 (which extends the court's discretion in certain proceedings for possession) there is inserted the following section—

9A. Proceedings for possession: anti-social behaviour

(1) This section applies if the court is considering under section 7(4) whether it is reasonable to make an order for possession on ground 14 set out in Part 2 of Schedule 2 (conduct of tenant or other person).
(2) The court must consider, in particular—
(a) the effect that the nuisance or annoyance has had on persons other than the person against whom the order is sought;
(b) any continuing effect the nuisance or annoyance is likely to have on such persons;
(c) the effect that the nuisance or annoyance would be likely to have on such persons if the conduct is repeated.

17. Devolution: Wales

In Schedule 1 to the National Assembly for Wales (Transfer of Functions) Order 1999 (S.I. 1999/672) references to the following Acts are to be treated as references to those Acts as amended by virtue of this Part—
(a) the Housing Act 1985;
(b) the Housing Act 1988;
(c) the Housing Act 1996 (c. 52).

PART 3
PARENTAL RESPONSIBILITIES

Parenting orders under the 1998 Act

18. Parenting orders under the 1998 Act

(1) Section 8 of the Crime and Disorder Act 1998 (c. 37) is amended as follows.
(2) For subsections (4) and (5) substitute—

(4) A parenting order is an order which requires the parent—
(a) to comply, for a period not exceeding twelve months, with such requirements as are specified in the order, and
(b) subject to subsection (5) below, to attend, for a concurrent period not exceeding three months, such counselling or guidance programme as may be specified in directions given by the responsible officer.
(5) A parenting order may, but need not, include such a requirement as is mentioned in subsection (4)(b) above in any case where a parenting order under this section or any other enactment has been made in respect of the parent on a previous occasion.

(3) After subsection (7) insert—

(7A) A counselling or guidance programme which a parent is required to attend by virtue of subsection (4)(b) above may be or include a residential course but only if the court is satisfied—

(a) that the attendance of the parent at a residential course is likely to be more effective than his attendance at a non-residential course in preventing any such repetition or, as the case may be, the commission of any such further offence, and
(b) that any interference with family life which is likely to result from the attendance of the parent at a residential course is proportionate in all the circumstances.

Truancy and exclusion from school

19. Parenting contracts in cases of exclusion from school or truancy

(1) This section applies where a pupil has been excluded on disciplinary grounds from a relevant school for a fixed period or permanently.
(2) This section also applies where a child of compulsory school age has failed to attend regularly at a relevant school at which he is a registered pupil.
(3) A local education authority or the governing body of a relevant school may enter into a parenting contract with a parent of the pupil or child.
(4) A parenting contract is a document which contains—
(a) a statement by the parent that he agrees to comply with such requirements as may be specified in the document for such period as may be so specified, and
(b) a statement by the local education authority or governing body that it agrees to provide support to the parent for the purpose of complying with those requirements.
(5) The requirements mentioned in subsection (4) may include (in particular) a requirement to attend a counselling or guidance programme.
(6) The purpose of the requirements mentioned in subsection (4)—
(a) in a case falling within subsection (1), is to improve the behaviour of the pupil,
(b) in a case falling within subsection (2), is to ensure that the child attends regularly at the relevant school at which he is a registered pupil.
(7) A parenting contract must be signed by the parent and signed on behalf of the local education authority or governing body.
(8) A parenting contract does not create any obligations in respect of whose breach any liability arises in contract or in tort.
(9) Local education authorities and governing bodies of relevant schools must, in carrying out their functions in relation to parenting contracts, have regard to any guidance which is issued by the appropriate person from time to time for that purpose.

20. Parenting orders in cases of exclusion from school

(1) This section applies where—
(a) a pupil has been excluded on disciplinary grounds from a relevant school for a fixed period or permanently, and
(b) such conditions as may be prescribed in regulations made by the appropriate person are satisfied.
(2) A local education authority may apply to a magistrates' court for a parenting order in respect of a parent of the pupil.
(3) If such an application is made, the court may make a parenting order in respect of a parent of the pupil if it is satisfied that making the order would be desirable in the interests of improving the behaviour of the pupil.

(4) A parenting order is an order which requires the parent—
  (a) to comply, for a period not exceeding twelve months, with such requirements as are specified in the order, and
  (b) subject to subsection (5), to attend, for a concurrent period not exceeding three months, such counselling or guidance programme as may be specified in directions given by the responsible officer.

(5) A parenting order under this section may, but need not, include a requirement mentioned in subsection (4)(b) in any case where a parenting order under this section or any other enactment has been made in respect of the parent on a previous occasion.

(6) A counselling or guidance programme which a parent is required to attend by virtue of subsection (4)(b) may be or include a residential course but only if the court is satisfied that the following two conditions are fulfilled.

(7) The first condition is that the attendance of the parent at a residential course is likely to be more effective than his attendance at a non-residential course in improving the behaviour of the pupil.

(8) The second condition is that any interference with family life which is likely to result from the attendance of the parent at a residential course is proportionate in all the circumstances.

21. Parenting orders: supplemental

(1) In deciding whether to make a parenting order under section 20, a court must take into account (amongst other things)—
  (a) any refusal by the parent to enter into a parenting contract under section 19 in respect of the pupil in a case falling within subsection (1) of that section, or
  (b) if the parent has entered into such a parenting contract, any failure by the parent to comply with the requirements specified in the contract.

(2) Before making a parenting order under section 20 in the case of a pupil under the age of 16, a court must obtain and consider information about the pupil's family circumstances and the likely effect of the order on those circumstances.

(3) Subsections (3) to (7) of section 9 of the Crime and Disorder Act 1998 (c. 37) (supplemental provisions about parenting orders) are to apply in relation to a parenting order under section 20 as they apply in relation to a parenting order under section 8 of that Act.

(4) The appropriate person may by regulations make provision as to how the costs associated with the requirements of parenting orders under section 20 (including the costs of providing counselling or guidance programmes) are to be borne.

(5) Local education authorities, head teachers and responsible officers must, in carrying out their functions in relation to parenting orders, have regard to any guidance which is issued by the appropriate person from time to time for that purpose.

22. Parenting orders: appeals

(1) An appeal lies to the Crown Court against the making of a parenting order under section 20.

(2) Subsections (2) and (3) of section 10 of the Crime and Disorder Act 1998 (appeals against parenting orders) are to apply in relation to an appeal under this section as they apply in relation to an appeal under subsection (1)(b) of that section.

23. Penalty notices for parents in cases of truancy

(1) After section 444 of the Education Act 1996 (c. 56) (failure to secure regular attendance at school of registered pupil) insert—

444A. Penalty notice in respect of failure to secure regular attendance at school of registered pupil

(1) Where an authorised officer has reason to believe—
(a) that a person has committed an offence under section 444(1), and
(b) that the school to which the offence relates is a relevant school in England,
he may give the person a penalty notice in respect of the offence.

(2) A penalty notice is a notice offering a person the opportunity of discharging any liability to conviction for the offence under section 444(1) to which the notice relates by payment of a penalty in accordance with the notice.

(3) Where a person is given a penalty notice, proceedings for the offence to which the notice relates (or an offence under section 444(1A) arising out of the same circumstances) may not be instituted before the end of such period as may be prescribed.

(4) Where a person is given a penalty notice, he cannot be convicted of the offence to which the notice relates (or an offence under section 444(1A) arising out of the same circumstances) if he pays a penalty in accordance with the notice.

(5) Penalties under this section shall be payable to local education authorities in England.

(6) Sums received by a local education authority under this section may be used by the authority for the purposes of any of its functions which may be specified in regulations.

444B. Penalty notices: supplemental

(1) Regulations may make—
(a) provision as to the form and content of penalty notices,
(b) provision as to the monetary amount of any penalty and the time by which it is to be paid,
(c) provision for determining the local education authority to which a penalty is payable,
(d) provision as to the methods by which penalties may be paid,
(e) provision as to the records which are to be kept in relation to penalty notices,
(f) provision as to the persons who may be authorised by a local education authority or a head teacher to give penalty notices,
(g) provision limiting the circumstances in which authorised officers of a prescribed description may give penalty notices,
(h) provision for or in connection with the withdrawal, in prescribed circumstances, of a penalty notice, including—
(i) repayment of any amount paid by way of penalty under a penalty notice which is withdrawn, and
(ii) prohibition of the institution or continuation of proceedings for the offence to which the withdrawn notice relates (and any offence under section 444(1A) arising out of the same circumstances),
(i) provision for a certificate—
(i) purporting to be signed by or on behalf of a prescribed person, and
(ii) stating that payment of any amount paid by way of penalty was or, as the case may be, was not received on or before a date specified in the certificate,
to be received in evidence of the matters so stated,
(j) provision as to the action to be taken if a penalty is not paid in accordance with a penalty notice,
(k) provision for or in connection with the preparation of codes of conduct in relation to the giving of penalty notices,

(l) such other provision in relation to penalties or penalty notices as the Secretary of State thinks necessary or expedient.

(2) Without prejudice to the generality of subsection (1) or section 569(4), regulations under subsection (1)(b) may make provision for penalties of different amounts to be payable in different cases or circumstances (including provision for the penalty payable under a penalty notice to differ according to the time by which it is paid).

(3) Local education authorities, head teachers and authorised officers shall, in carrying out their functions in relation to penalty notices, have regard to any guidance which is published by the Secretary of State from time to time in relation to penalty notices.

(4) In this section and section 444A—

'authorised officer' means—

(a) a constable,

(b) an officer of a local education authority in England who is authorised by the authority to give penalty notices, or

(c) an authorised staff member,

'authorised staff member' means—

(a) a head teacher of a relevant school in England, or

(b) a member of the staff of a relevant school in England who is authorised by the head teacher of the school to give penalty notices,

'penalty' means a penalty under a penalty notice,

'penalty notice' has the meaning given by section 444A(2),

'relevant school' means—

(a) a maintained school,

(b) a pupil referral unit,

(c) an Academy,

(d) a city technology college, or

(e) a city college for the technology of the arts.

(2) In section 572 of that Act (service of notices and other documents) for 'served on any person may be served' substitute 'served on, or given to, any person may be served or given'.

(3) In paragraph 1(2) of Schedule 4 to the Police Reform Act 2002 (c. 30) (powers of community support officers to issue fixed penalty notices) after paragraph (a) insert—

(aa) the power of a constable to give a penalty notice under section 444A of the Education Act 1996 (penalty notice in respect of failure to secure regular attendance at school of registered pupil);.

(4) After paragraph 1(3) of that Schedule insert—

(4) In its application to an offence which is an offence by reference to which a notice may be given to a person in exercise of the power mentioned in sub-paragraph (2)(aa), sub-paragraph (1) shall have effect as if for the words from 'who he has reason to believe' to the end there were substituted 'in the relevant police area who he has reason to believe has committed a relevant fixed penalty offence'.

(5) In paragraph 2 of that Schedule (power to detain etc) after sub-paragraph (6) insert—

(7) In its application to an offence which is an offence by reference to which a notice may be given to a person in exercise of the power mentioned in paragraph 1(2)(aa), sub-paragraph (2) of this paragraph shall have effect as if for the words 'has committed a relevant offence in the relevant police area' there were substituted 'in the relevant police area has committed a relevant offence'.

(6) In paragraph 1(2) of Schedule 5 to that Act (powers of accredited persons to issue fixed penalty notices) before paragraph (b) insert—

(ab) the power of a constable to give a penalty notice under section 444A of the Education Act 1996 (penalty notice in respect of failure to secure regular attendance at school of registered pupil);.

(7) After paragraph 1(3) of that Schedule insert—

(4) In its application to an offence which is an offence by reference to which a notice may be given to a person in exercise of the power mentioned in sub-paragraph (2)(ab), sub-paragraph (1) shall have effect as if for the words from 'who he has reason to believe' to the end there were substituted 'in the relevant police area who he has reason to believe has committed or is committing a relevant fixed penalty offence'.

(8) In paragraph 2 of that Schedule (power to require giving of name and address) after sub-paragraph (3) insert—

(4) In its application to an offence which is an offence by reference to which a notice may be given to a person in exercise of the power mentioned in paragraph 1(2)(ab), sub-paragraph (1) of this paragraph shall have effect as if for the words 'has committed a relevant offence in the relevant police area' there were substituted 'in the relevant police area has committed a relevant offence'.

(9) The National Assembly for Wales may by order amend sections 444A and 444B of the Education Act 1996 (c. 56) by removing the words 'in England' in each place where they occur.

(10) Where an order is made under subsection (9), any functions of the Secretary of State under sections 444A and 444B of the Education Act 1996 which by virtue of the order become exercisable in relation to Wales are to be treated as if they had been transferred to the National Assembly for Wales by an Order in Council under section 22 of the Government of Wales Act 1998 (c. 38).

24. Interpretation

In this section and sections 19 to 21—

'the appropriate person' means—

(a) in relation to England, the Secretary of State, and

(b) in relation to Wales, the National Assembly for Wales,

'child of compulsory school age' has the same meaning as in the 1996 Act, and 'child' is to be construed accordingly,

'head teacher' includes acting head teacher, teacher in charge and acting teacher in charge,

'local education authority' has the same meaning as in the 1996 Act,

'parent', in relation to a pupil or child, is to be construed in accordance with section 576 of the 1996 Act, but does not include a person who is not an individual,

'pupil' is to be construed in accordance with section 3(1) and (1A) of the 1996 Act,

'registered pupil' has the meaning given by section 434(5) of the 1996 Act,

'relevant school' means—

(a) a qualifying school as defined in section 1(3) of the Education Act 2002 (c. 32), or

(b) a pupil referral unit as defined in section 19(2) of the 1996 Act,

'responsible officer', in relation to a parenting order, means one of the following who is specified in the order, namely—

(a) an officer of a local education authority, and
(b) a head teacher or a person nominated by a head teacher,

but a person falling within paragraph (b) may not be specified in the order without his consent,

'the 1996 Act' means the Education Act 1996 (c. 56).

Criminal conduct and anti-social behaviour

25. Parenting contracts in respect of criminal conduct and anti-social behaviour

(1) This section applies where a child or young person has been referred to a youth offending team.

(2) The youth offending team may enter into a parenting contract with a parent of the child or young person if a member of that team has reason to believe that the child or young person has engaged, or is likely to engage, in criminal conduct or anti-social behaviour.

(3) A parenting contract is a document which contains—
(a) a statement by the parent that he agrees to comply with such requirements as may be specified in the document for such period as may be so specified, and
(b) a statement by the youth offending team that it agrees to provide support to the parent for the purpose of complying with those requirements.

(4) The requirements mentioned in subsection (3)(a) may include (in particular) a requirement to attend a counselling or guidance programme.

(5) The purpose of the requirements mentioned in subsection (3)(a) is to prevent the child or young person from engaging in criminal conduct or anti-social behaviour or further criminal conduct or further anti-social behaviour.

(6) A parenting contract must be signed by the parent and signed on behalf of the youth offending team.

(7) A parenting contract does not create any obligations in respect of whose breach any liability arises in contract or in tort.

(8) Youth offending teams must, in carrying out their functions in relation to parenting contracts, have regard to any guidance which is issued by the Secretary of State from time to time for that purpose.

26. Parenting orders in respect of criminal conduct and anti-social behaviour

(1) This section applies where a child or young person has been referred to a youth offending team.

(2) A member of the youth offending team may apply to a magistrates' court for a parenting order in respect of a parent of the child or young person.

(3) If such an application is made, the court may make a parenting order in respect of a parent of the child or young person if it is satisfied—
(a) that the child or young person has engaged in criminal conduct or anti-social behaviour, and
(b) that making the order would be desirable in the interests of preventing the child or young person from engaging in further criminal conduct or further anti-social behaviour.

(4) A parenting order is an order which requires the parent—
(a) to comply, for a period not exceeding twelve months, with such requirements as are specified in the order, and

(b) subject to subsection (5), to attend, for a concurrent period not exceeding three months, such counselling or guidance programme as may be specified in directions given by the responsible officer.

(5) A parenting order under this section may, but need not, include a requirement mentioned in subsection (4)(b) in any case where a parenting order under this section or any other enactment has been made in respect of the parent on a previous occasion.

(6) A counselling or guidance programme which a parent is required to attend by virtue of subsection (4)(b) may be or include a residential course but only if the court is satisfied that the following two conditions are fulfilled.

(7) The first condition is that the attendance of the parent at a residential course is likely to be more effective than his attendance at a non-residential course in preventing the child or young person from engaging in further criminal conduct or further anti-social behaviour.

(8) The second condition is that any interference with family life which is likely to result from the attendance of the parent at a residential course is proportionate in all the circumstances.

27. Parenting orders: supplemental

(1) In deciding whether to make a parenting order under section 26, a court must take into account (amongst other things)—

(a) any refusal by the parent to enter into a parenting contract under section 25 in respect of the child or young person, or

(b) if the parent has entered into such a parenting contract, any failure by the parent to comply with the requirements specified in the contract.

(2) Before making a parenting order under section 26 in the case of a child or a young person under the age of 16, a court must obtain and consider information about the child or young person's family circumstances and the likely effect of the order on those circumstances.

(3) Subsections (3) to (7) of section 9 of the 1998 Act (supplemental provisions about parenting orders) are to apply in relation to a parenting order under section 26 as they apply in relation to a parenting order under section 8 of that Act.

(4) Members of youth offending teams and responsible officers must, in carrying out their functions in relation to parenting orders, have regard to any guidance which is issued by the Secretary of State from time to time for that purpose.

28. Parenting orders: appeals

(1) An appeal lies to the Crown Court against the making of a parenting order under section 26.

(2) Subsections (2) and (3) of section 10 of the 1998 Act (appeals against parenting orders) are to apply in relation to an appeal under this section as they apply in relation to an appeal under subsection (1)(b) of that section.

29. Interpretation and consequential amendment

(1) In this section and sections 25 to 28—

'anti-social behaviour' means behaviour by a person which causes or is likely to cause harassment, alarm or distress to one or more other persons not of the same household as the person,

'child' has the same meaning as in the 1998 Act,
'criminal conduct' means conduct which—

(a) constitutes a criminal offence, or
(b) in the case of conduct by a person under the age of 10, would constitute a criminal offence if that person were not under that age,

'guardian' has the same meaning as in the Children and Young Persons Act 1933 (c. 12),
'parent' includes guardian,
'responsible officer', in relation to a parenting order, means a member of a youth offending team who is specified in the order,
'the 1998 Act' means the Crime and Disorder Act 1998 (c. 37),
'young person' has the same meaning as in the 1998 Act,
'youth offending team' means a team established under section 39 of the 1998 Act.

(2) In section 38(4) of the 1998 Act (meaning of 'youth justice services') after paragraph (e) insert—

(ee) the performance by youth offending teams and members of youth offending teams of functions under sections 25 to 27 of the Anti-social Behaviour Act 2003;.

PART 4
DISPERSAL OF GROUPS ETC.

30. Dispersal of groups and removal of persons under 16 to their place of residence

(1) This section applies where a relevant officer has reasonable grounds for believing—
(a) that any members of the public have been intimidated, harassed, alarmed or distressed as a result of the presence or behaviour of groups of two or more persons in public places in any locality in his police area (the 'relevant locality'), and
(b) that anti-social behaviour is a significant and persistent problem in the relevant locality.

(2) The relevant officer may give an authorisation that the powers conferred on a constable in uniform by subsections (3) to (6) are to be exercisable for a period specified in the authorisation which does not exceed 6 months.

(3) Subsection (4) applies if a constable in uniform has reasonable grounds for believing that the presence or behaviour of a group of two or more persons in any public place in the relevant locality has resulted, or is likely to result, in any members of the public being intimidated, harassed, alarmed or distressed.

(4) The constable may give one or more of the following directions, namely—
(a) a direction requiring the persons in the group to disperse (either immediately or by such time as he may specify and in such way as he may specify),
(b) a direction requiring any of those persons whose place of residence is not within the relevant locality to leave the relevant locality or any part of the relevant locality (either immediately or by such time as he may specify and in such way as he may specify), and
(c) a direction prohibiting any of those persons whose place of residence is not within the relevant locality from returning to the relevant locality or any part of the relevant locality for such period (not exceeding 24 hours) from the giving of the direction as he may specify;

but this subsection is subject to subsection (5).

(5) A direction under subsection (4) may not be given in respect of a group of persons—
 (a) who are engaged in conduct which is lawful under section 220 of the Trade Union and Labour Relations (Consolidation) Act 1992 (c. 52), or
 (b) who are taking part in a public procession of the kind mentioned in section 11(1) of the Public Order Act 1986 (c. 64) in respect of which—
  (i) written notice has been given in accordance with section 11 of that Act, or
  (ii) such notice is not required to be given as provided by subsections (1) and (2) of that section.

(6) If, between the hours of 9pm and 6am, a constable in uniform finds a person in any public place in the relevant locality who he has reasonable grounds for believing—
 (a) is under the age of 16, and
 (b) is not under the effective control of a parent or a responsible person aged 18 or over,

he may remove the person to the person's place of residence unless he has reasonable grounds for believing that the person would, if removed to that place, be likely to suffer significant harm.

(7) In this section any reference to the presence or behaviour of a group of persons is to be read as including a reference to the presence or behaviour of any one or more of the persons in the group.

31. Authorisations: supplemental

(1) An authorisation—
 (a) must be in writing,
 (b) must be signed by the relevant officer giving it, and
 (c) must specify—
  (i) the relevant locality,
  (ii) the grounds on which the authorisation is given, and
  (iii) the period during which the powers conferred by section 30(3) to (6) are exercisable.

(2) An authorisation may not be given without the consent of the local authority or each local authority whose area includes the whole or part of the relevant locality.

(3) Publicity must be given to an authorisation by either or both of the following methods—
 (a) publishing an authorisation notice in a newspaper circulating in the relevant locality,
 (b) posting an authorisation notice in some conspicuous place or places within the relevant locality.

(4) An 'authorisation notice' is a notice which—
 (a) states the authorisation has been given,
 (b) specifies the relevant locality, and
 (c) specifies the period during which the powers conferred by section 30(3) to (6) are exercisable.

(5) Subsection (3) must be complied with before the beginning of the period mentioned in subsection (4)(c).

(6) An authorisation may be withdrawn by—
 (a) the relevant officer who gave it, or

(b) any other relevant officer whose police area includes the relevant locality and whose rank is the same as or higher than that of the relevant officer mentioned in paragraph (a).

(7) Before the withdrawal of an authorisation, consultation must take place with any local authority whose area includes the whole or part of the relevant locality.

(8) The withdrawal of an authorisation does not affect the exercise of any power pursuant to that authorisation which occurred prior to its withdrawal.

(9) The giving or withdrawal of an authorisation does not prevent the giving of a further authorisation in respect of a locality which includes the whole or any part of the relevant locality to which the earlier authorisation relates.

(10) In this section 'authorisation' means an authorisation under section 30.

32. Powers under section 30: supplemental

(1) A direction under section 30(4)—

(a) may be given orally,

(b) may be given to any person individually or to two or more persons together, and

(c) may be withdrawn or varied by the person who gave it.

(2) A person who knowingly contravenes a direction given to him under section 30(4) commits an offence and is liable on summary conviction to—

(a) a fine not exceeding level 4 on the standard scale, or

(b) imprisonment for a term not exceeding 3 months,

or to both.

(3) A constable in uniform may arrest without warrant any person he reasonably suspects has committed an offence under subsection (2).

(4) Where the power under section 30(6) is exercised, any local authority whose area includes the whole or part of the relevant locality must be notified of that fact.

33. Powers of community support officers

(1) Part 1 of Schedule 4 to the Police Reform Act 2002 (c. 30) (powers of community support officers) is amended as follows.

(2) In paragraph 2 (power to detain etc) after sub-paragraph (6)(a) insert—

(aa) an offence under section 32(2) of the Anti-social Behaviour Act 2003; or.

(3) After paragraph 4 insert—

4A *Power to disperse groups and remove young persons to their place of residence*

Where a designation applies this paragraph to any person, that person shall, within the relevant police area, have the powers which, by virtue of an authorisation under section 30 of the Anti-social Behaviour Act 2003, are conferred on a constable in uniform by section 30(3) to (6) of that Act (power to disperse groups and remove persons under 16 to their place of residence).

4B (1) Where a designation applies this paragraph to any person, that person shall, within the relevant police area, have the power of a constable under section 15(3) of the Crime and Disorder Act 1998 (power to remove child to their place of residence).

(2) Section 15(1) of that Act shall have effect in relation to the exercise of that power by that person as if the reference to a constable in that section were a reference to that person.

(3) Where that person exercises that power, the duty in section 15(2) of that Act (duty to inform local authority of contravention of curfew notice) is to apply to him as it applies to a constable.

34. Code of practice

(1) The Secretary of State may issue a code of practice about—
  (a) the giving or withdrawal of authorisations under section 30, and
  (b) the exercise of the powers conferred by section 30(3) to (6).

(2) The Secretary of State may from time to time revise the whole or any part of a code of practice issued under this section.

(3) The Secretary of State must lay any code of practice issued by him under this section, and any revisions of such a code, before Parliament.

(4) In giving or withdrawing an authorisation under section 30, a relevant officer must have regard to any code of practice for the time being in force under this section.

(5) In exercising the powers conferred by section 30(3) to (6), a constable in uniform or community support officer must have regard to any code of practice for the time being in force under this section.

(6) A code of practice under this section may make different provision for different cases.

35. Authorisations by British Transport Police

(1) For the purposes of the giving of an authorisation under section 30 by a relevant officer who is an officer of the British Transport Police Force, section 30(1) is to have effect as if for 'in his police area' there were substituted 'which forms part of property in relation to which he has all the powers and privileges of a constable by virtue of section 31(1)(a) to (f) of the Railways and Transport Safety Act 2003'.

(2) Where such an authorisation is given by such an officer, section 31(6)(b) is to have effect as if for 'whose police area includes the relevant locality' there were substituted 'who is an officer of the British Transport Police Force'.

36. Interpretation

In this Part—

'anti-social behaviour' means behaviour by a person which causes or is likely to cause harassment, alarm or distress to one or more other persons not of the same household as the person,

'local authority' means—
  (a) in relation to England, a district council, a county council that is the council for a county in which there are no district councils, a London borough council, the Common Council of the City of London or the Council of the Isles of Scilly,
  (b) in relation to Wales, a county council or a county borough council,

'public place' means—
  (a) any highway, and
  (b) any place to which at the material time the public or any section of the public has access, on payment or otherwise, as of right or by virtue of express or implied permission,

'relevant locality' has the same meaning as in section 30,

'relevant officer' means a police officer of or above the rank of superintendent.

PART 5
FIREARMS

37. Possession of air weapon or imitation firearm in public place

(1) In section 19 of the Firearms Act 1968 (c. 27) (offence to carry firearm in public place) for the words from 'a loaded shot gun' to the end of the section substitute—

> (a) a loaded shot gun,
> (b) an air weapon (whether loaded or not),
> (c) any other firearm (whether loaded or not) together with ammunition suitable for use in that firearm, or
> (d) an imitation firearm.

(2) In Part I of Schedule 6 to that Act (punishment) in the entry relating to section 19—
(a) in the second column (general nature of offence) for 'loaded firearm' substitute 'firearm or imitation firearm', and
(b) in the third column (mode of prosecution) after 'not' insert 'in the case of an imitation firearm or'.

(3) The following shall be inserted after paragraph 5 of Schedule 1A to the Police and Criminal Evidence Act 1984 (c. 60) (arrestable offences)—

> 5A. *Firearms Act 1968*
>
> An offence under section 19 of the Firearms Act 1968 (carrying firearm or imitation firearm in public place) in respect of an air weapon or imitation firearm.

38. Air weapons: age limits

(1) The Firearms Act 1968 shall be amended as follows.

(2) In section 22 (acquisition and possession of firearms by minors)—
(a) in subsection (4) for 'fourteen' substitute 'seventeen', and
(b) omit subsection (5).

(3) In section 23 (the heading to which becomes 'Exceptions from s. 22(4)')—
(a) in subsection (2) omit 'or (5)', and
(b) after subsection (2) insert—

> (3) It is not an offence under section 22(4) of this Act for a person of or over the age of fourteen to have with him an air weapon or ammunition on private premises with the consent of the occupier.
> (4) But where a person has with him an air weapon on premises in circumstances where he would be prohibited from having it with him but for subsection (3), it is an offence for him to use it for firing any missile beyond those premises.

(4) In section 24(4) (offence to give air weapon or ammunition to person under fourteen)—
(a) in paragraph (a) for 'fourteen' substitute 'seventeen', and
(b) in paragraph (b) for 'that age' substitute 'the age of seventeen'.

(5) In Part I of Schedule 6 (punishment)—
(a) in the entry relating to section 22(4) in the second column (general nature of offence) for '14' substitute '17',
(b) omit the entry relating to section 22(5),
(c) in the entry relating to section 23(1) in the second column for '14' substitute '17',
(d) after that entry insert—

Section 23(4)	Person under 17 making improper use of air weapon on private premises	Summary	A fine of level 3 on the standard scale	Paragraphs 7 and 8 of Part II

and

(e) in the entry relating to section 24(4) in the second column for '14' substitute '17'.

(6) In Part II of that Schedule (supplementary)—

(a) in paragraph 7 for '22(4) or (5), 23(1)' substitute '22(4), 23(1) or (4)', and

(b) in paragraph 8 for '22(3), (4) or (5), 23(1)' substitute '22(3) or (4), 23(1) or (4)'.

39. Prohibition of certain air weapons

(1) The Firearms Act 1968 (c. 27) shall be amended as follows.

(2) In section 1(3)(b) after 'air pistol' insert 'which does not fall within section 5(1) and which is'.

(3) In section 5 (weapons subject to general prohibition) after subsection (1)(ae) insert—

(af) any air rifle, air gun or air pistol which uses, or is designed or adapted for use with, a self-contained gas cartridge system;.

(4) If at the time when subsection (3) comes into force a person has in his possession an air rifle, air gun or air pistol of the kind described in section 5(1)(af) of the Firearms Act 1968 (inserted by subsection (3) above)—

(a) section 5(1) of that Act shall not prevent the person's continued possession of the air rifle, air gun or air pistol,

(b) section 1 of that Act shall apply, and

(c) a chief officer of police may not refuse to grant or renew, and may not revoke or partially revoke, a firearm certificate under Part II of that Act on the ground that the person does not have a good reason for having the air rifle, air gun or air pistol in his possession.

(5) But subsection (4)(a) to (c) shall not apply to possession in the circumstances described in section 8 of that Act (authorised dealing).

(6) In section 1 of the Firearms (Amendment) Act 1988 (c. 45)—

(a) in subsection (4), omit the word 'or' at the end of paragraph (a) and after paragraph (b) insert— '; or

(c) any air rifle, air gun or air pistol which is not for the time being specified in that subsection but appears to him to be specially dangerous,', and

(b) after subsection (4) insert—

(4A) An order under subsection (4)—

(a) may provide for a provision of the principal Act to apply with or without modification or exception in relation to anything added to subsection (1) of section 5 by the order,

(b) may impose conditions in respect of any application, modification or exception provided for by the order (which may, in particular, include provision requiring a person to obtain a certificate in accordance with an enactment referred to or applied by the order),

(c) may make provision generally or by reference to a particular purpose or circumstance,
(d) may confer a function on the Secretary of State or another specified person, and
(e) may make transitional, consequential or incidental provision.

PART 6
THE ENVIRONMENT

Noise

40. Closure of noisy premises

(1) The chief executive officer of the relevant local authority may make a closure order in relation to premises to which this section applies if he reasonably believes that—
  (a) a public nuisance is being caused by noise coming from the premises, and
  (b) the closure of the premises is necessary to prevent that nuisance.
(2) This section applies to premises if—
  (a) a premises licence has effect in respect of them, or
  (b) a temporary event notice has effect in respect of them.
(3) In this section 'closure order' means an order which requires specified premises to be kept closed during a specified period which—
  (a) does not exceed 24 hours, and
  (b) begins when a manager of the premises receives written notice of the order.
(4) A person commits an offence if without reasonable excuse he permits premises to be open in contravention of a closure order.
(5) A person guilty of an offence under this section shall be liable on summary conviction to—
  (a) imprisonment for a term not exceeding three months,
  (b) a fine not exceeding £20,000, or
  (c) both.

41. Closure of noisy premises: supplemental

(1) Where a closure order is made in relation to premises, the chief executive officer of the relevant local authority—
  (a) may cancel the closure order by notice in writing to a manager of the premises,
  (b) shall cancel the order as soon as is reasonably practicable if he believes that it is no longer necessary in order to prevent a public nuisance being caused by noise coming from the premises, and
  (c) shall give notice of the order as soon as is reasonably practicable to the licensing authority for the area in which the premises are situated.
(2) The chief executive officer of a local authority may authorise an environmental health officer of the authority to exercise a power or duty of the chief executive officer under section 40(1) or under subsection (1) above; and—
  (a) authority under this subsection may be general or specific, and
  (b) a reference in section 40(1) or subsection (1) above to a belief of the chief executive officer includes a reference to a belief of a person authorised under this subsection.

(3) In section 40 and this section—
'chief executive officer' of an authority means the head of the paid service of the authority designated under section 4 of the Local Government and Housing Act 1989 (c. 42),
'environmental health officer' of an authority means an officer authorised by the authority for the purpose of exercising a statutory function in relation to pollution of the environment or harm to human health,
'licensing authority' has the same meaning as in the Licensing Act 2003 (c. 17),
'manager' in relation to premises means—
(a) a person who holds a premises licence in respect of the premises,
(b) a designated premises supervisor under a premises licence in respect of the premises,
(c) the premises user in relation to a temporary event notice which has effect in respect of the premises, and
(d) any other person who works at the premises in a capacity (paid or unpaid) which enables him to close them,
'premises licence' has the same meaning as in the Licensing Act 2003,
'relevant local authority' in relation to premises means an authority which has statutory functions, for the area in which the premises are situated, in relation to minimising or preventing the risk of pollution of the environment or of harm to human health, and
'temporary event notice' has the same meaning as in the Licensing Act 2003 (and is to be treated as having effect in accordance with section 170(6) of that Act).

42. Dealing with noise at night

(1) The Noise Act 1996 (c. 37) is amended as follows.
(2) For section 1 (sections 2 to 9 only apply to area of local authority if authority have so resolved or an order by Secretary of State so provides) substitute—

> **1. Application of sections 2 to 9**
>
> Sections 2 to 9 apply to the area of every local authority in England and Wales.

(3) For section 2(1) (local authority under duty to investigate complaint of noise from dwelling at night) substitute—

> (1) A local authority in England and Wales may, if they receive a complaint of the kind mentioned in subsection (2), arrange for an officer of the authority to take reasonable steps to investigate the complaint.

(4) In section 2(7) (power of local authority to act in relation to dwelling within area of other authority) omit the words from 'and accordingly' to the end.
(5) In section 9 (section 8: supplementary), for subsection (4) substitute—

> (4) A local authority may use any sums it receives under section 8 (its 'penalty receipts') only for the purposes of functions of its that are qualifying functions.
> (4A) The following are qualifying functions for the purposes of this section—
> (a) functions under this Act, and
> (b) functions of a description specified in regulations made by the Secretary of State.
> (4B) Regulations under subsection (4A)(b) may (in particular) have the effect that a local authority may use its penalty receipts for the purposes of any of its functions.
> (4C) A local authority must supply the Secretary of State with such information relating to the use of its penalty receipts as the Secretary of State may require.

(4D) The Secretary of State may by regulations—
(a) make provision for what a local authority is to do with its penalty receipts—
(i) pending their being used for the purposes of qualifying functions of the authority;
(ii) if they are not so used before such time after their receipt as may be specified by the regulations;
(b) make provision for accounting arrangements in respect of a local authority's penalty receipts.
(4E) The provision that may be made under subsection (4D)(a)(ii) includes (in particular) provision for the payment of sums to a person (including the Secretary of State) other than the local authority.
(4F) Before making regulations under this section, the Secretary of State must consult—
(a) the local authorities to which the regulations are to apply, and
(b) such other persons as the Secretary of State considers appropriate.

(6) In section 11 (interpretation and subordinate legislation), in subsection (3) after 'order', in the first place where it occurs, insert 'or regulations'.
(7) The reference to the Noise Act 1996 (c. 37) in Schedule 1 to the National Assembly for Wales (Transfer of Functions) Order 1999 (S.I. 1999/672) is to be treated as referring to that Act as amended by this section.

Penalty notices for graffiti and fly-posting

43. Penalty notices for graffiti and fly-posting

(1) Where an authorised officer of a local authority has reason to believe that a person has committed a relevant offence in the area of that authority, he may give that person a notice offering him the opportunity of discharging any liability to conviction for that offence by payment of a penalty in accordance with the notice.
(2) But an authorised officer may not give a notice under subsection (1) if he considers that the commission of the offence—
(a) in the case of a relevant offence falling within section 44(1)(c), also involves the commission of an offence under section 30 of the Crime and Disorder Act 1998 (c. 37), or
(b) in the case of any other relevant offence, was motivated (wholly or partly) by hostility—
(i) towards a person based upon his membership (or presumed membership) of a racial or religious group, or
(ii) towards members of a racial or religious group based on their membership of that group.
(3) In the case of a relevant offence falling within section 44(1)(f), an authorised officer may not give a notice to a person under subsection (1) in relation to the display of an advertisement unless he has reason to believe that that person personally affixed or placed the advertisement to, against or upon the land or object on which the advertisement is or was displayed.
(4) Where a person is given a notice under subsection (1) in respect of an offence—
(a) no proceedings may be instituted for that offence (or any other relevant offence arising out of the same circumstances) before the expiration of the period of fourteen days following the date of the notice, and

(b) he may not be convicted of that offence (or any other relevant offence arising out of the same circumstances) if before the expiration of that period he pays the penalty in accordance with the notice.

(5) A notice under subsection (1) must give such particulars of the circumstances alleged to constitute the offence as are necessary for giving reasonable information of the offence.

(6) A notice under subsection (1) must also state—
(a) the period during which, by virtue of subsection (4), proceedings will not be instituted for the offence,
(b) the amount of the penalty, and
(c) the person to whom and the address at which the penalty may be paid.

(7) Without prejudice to payment by any other method, payment of a penalty in pursuance of a notice under subsection (1) may be made by pre-paying and posting a letter containing the amount of the penalty (in cash or otherwise) to the person mentioned in subsection (6)(c) at the address so mentioned.

(8) Where a letter is sent in accordance with subsection (7) payment is to be regarded as having been made at the time at which that letter would be delivered in the ordinary course of post.

(9) A notice under subsection (1) must be in such form as the appropriate person may by order prescribe.

(10) Subject to subsection (11), the penalty payable in pursuance of a notice under subsection (1) is £50.

(11) The appropriate person may by order substitute a different amount for the amount for the time being specified in subsection (10).

44. Meaning of relevant offence

(1) 'Relevant offence' means—
(a) an offence under paragraph 10 of section 54 of the Metropolitan Police Act 1839 (c. 47) (affixing posters etc),
(b) an offence under section 20(1) of the London County Council (General Powers) Act 1954 (defacement of streets with slogans etc),
(c) an offence under section 1(1) of the Criminal Damage Act 1971 (c. 48) (damaging property etc) which involves only the painting or writing on, or the soiling, marking or other defacing of, any property by whatever means,
(d) an offence under section 131(2) of the Highways Act 1980 (c. 66) (including that provision as applied by section 27(6) of the Countryside Act 1968 (c. 41)) which involves only an act of obliteration,
(e) an offence under section 132(1) of the Highways Act 1980 (painting or affixing things on structures on the highway etc),
(f) an offence under section 224(3) of the Town and Country Planning Act 1990 (c. 8) (displaying advertisement in contravention of regulations).

(2) This section has effect for the purposes of the interpretation of section 43.

45. Penalty receipts

(1) Penalties which are payable in pursuance of notices under section 43(1) are payable to local authorities.

(2) In any proceedings a certificate which—

(a) purports to be signed by or on behalf of the person responsible for the financial affairs of a local authority, and
(b) states that payment of a penalty payable in pursuance of a notice under section 43(1) was or was not received by a date specified in the certificate,

is evidence of the facts stated.

(3) A local authority may use any sums it receives in respect of penalties payable to it in pursuance of notices under section 43(1) (its 'penalty receipts') only for the purposes of functions of its that are qualifying functions.

(4) The following are qualifying functions for the purposes of this section—
(a) functions under section 43, and
(b) functions of a description specified in regulations made by the appropriate person.

(5) Regulations under subsection (4)(b) may (in particular) have the effect that a local authority may use its penalty receipts for the purposes of any of its functions.

(6) A local authority must supply the appropriate person with such information relating to its use of its penalty receipts as the appropriate person may require.

(7) The appropriate person may by regulations—
(a) make provision for what a local authority is to do with its penalty receipts—
(i) pending their being used for the purposes of qualifying functions of the authority;
(ii) if they are not so used before such time after their receipt as may be specified by the regulations;
(b) make provision for accounting arrangements in respect of a local authority's penalty receipts.

(8) The provision that may be made under subsection (7)(a)(ii) includes (in particular) provision for the payment of sums to a person (including the appropriate person) other than the local authority.

(9) Before making regulations under this section, the appropriate person must consult—
(a) the local authorities to which the regulations are to apply, and
(b) such other persons as the appropriate person considers appropriate.

46. Powers of police civilians

(1) In paragraph 1 of Schedule 4 to the Police Reform Act 2002 (c. 30) (powers of community support officers to issue fixed penalty notices)—
(a) at the end of sub-paragraph (2)(c) omit 'and', and
(b) after sub-paragraph (2)(c) insert—

> (ca) the power of an authorised officer of a local authority to give a notice under section 43(1) of the Anti-social Behaviour Act 2003 (penalty notices in respect of graffiti or fly-posting); and.

(2) In paragraph 1 of Schedule 5 to that Act (powers of accredited persons to issue fixed penalty notices)—
(a) at the end of sub-paragraph (2)(b) omit 'and', and
(b) after sub-paragraph (2)(b) insert—

> (ba) the power of an authorised officer of a local authority to give a notice under section 43(1) of the Anti-social Behaviour Act 2003 (penalty notices in respect of graffiti or fly-posting); and.

47. Interpretation etc

(1) In this section and sections 43 and 45—
'advertisement' and 'land' have the meanings given by section 336(1) of the Town and Country Planning Act 1990 (c. 8),
'appropriate person' means—
(a) in relation to England, the Secretary of State, and
(b) in relation to Wales, the National Assembly for Wales,
'authorised officer' means an officer of a local authority who is authorised in writing by the authority for the purpose of giving notices under section 43(1),
'local authority' means an authority in England and Wales which is a litter authority for the purposes of section 88 of the Environmental Protection Act 1990 (c. 43),
'racial group' and 'religious group' have the meanings given by section 28(4) and (5) of the Crime and Disorder Act 1998 (c. 37).

(2) Section 28(2) of the Crime and Disorder Act 1998 is to apply for the purposes of section 43(2)(b)(i) as it applies for the purposes of section 28(1)(a) of that Act.

(3) The appropriate person may issue guidance—
(a) about the exercise of the discretion to give notices under section 43(1), and
(b) about the giving of such notices.

Removal of graffiti

48. Graffiti removal notices

(1) This section applies where a local authority is satisfied—
(a) that a relevant surface in an area has been defaced by graffiti, and
(b) that the defacement is detrimental to the amenity of the area or is offensive.

(2) The authority may serve a notice (a 'graffiti removal notice') upon any person who is responsible for the surface imposing the requirement mentioned in subsection (3).

(3) That requirement is a requirement that the defacement be removed, cleared or otherwise remedied within a period specified in the notice being not less than 28 days beginning with the day on which the notice is served.

(4) If the requirement mentioned in subsection (3) is not complied with, the authority or any person authorised by the authority may remove, clear or otherwise remedy the defacement.

(5) In exercising the power under subsection (4) the authority or any person authorised by the authority may enter any land to the extent reasonably necessary for that purpose.

(6) A graffiti removal notice must explain the effect of subsections (4) and (5) and sections 49 and 51.

(7) Subject to subsection (8), section 160 of the Environmental Protection Act 1990 (c. 43) has effect in relation to graffiti removal notices as if they were notices within subsection (2) of that section.

(8) Where after reasonable enquiry a local authority is unable to ascertain the name or proper address of any person who is responsible for a relevant surface, the authority may—
(a) affix a graffiti removal notice to the surface, and
(b) enter any land to the extent reasonably necessary for that purpose;
and that notice shall be treated as having been served upon a person responsible for the surface.

(9) In this section a 'relevant surface' is any of the following surfaces, whether internal or external or open to the air or not—
   (a) the surface of any street or of any building, structure, apparatus, plant or other object in or on any street;
   (b) the surface of any land owned, occupied or controlled by a statutory undertaker or of any building, structure, apparatus, plant or other object in or on any such land;
   (c) the surface of any land owned, occupied or controlled by an educational institution (including its governing body) or of any building, structure, apparatus, plant or other object in or on any such land.

(10) But a surface is not a relevant surface unless—
   (a) in the case of a surface within subsection (9)(a), the street is public land;
   (b) in the case of a surface within subsection (9)(b) or (c)—
      (i) the land is public land,
      (ii) the surface is visible from public land, or
      (iii) the surface is otherwise visible to members of the public using the services or facilities of the statutory undertaker or educational institution in question or any other statutory undertaker or educational institution.

(11) A person is responsible for a relevant surface if—
   (a) where it is the surface of any land (including a street), he owns, leases, occupies, controls, operates or maintains the land, and
   (b) where it is the surface of any other thing mentioned in subsection (9), he owns, leases, occupies, controls, operates or maintains the thing.

(12) In this section and in sections 49 to 52—

'educational institution' has the meaning given by section 98(2) of the Environmental Protection Act 1990,

'graffiti' includes painting, writing, soiling, marking or other defacing by whatever means,

'graffiti removal notice' has the meaning given by subsection (2),

'local authority' means an authority in England and Wales which is a litter authority for the purposes of section 88 of the Environmental Protection Act 1990 (c. 43),

'proper address' is to be read in accordance with section 160(4) and (5) of the Environmental Protection Act 1990,

'public land' means land to which the public are entitled or permitted to have access with or without payment (including any street to which the public are so entitled or permitted),

'statutory undertaker' has the meaning given by section 98(6) of the Environmental Protection Act 1990,

'street' has the meaning given by section 48(1) of the New Roads and Street Works Act 1991 (c. 22).

49. Recovery of expenditure

(1) A local authority may recover from the person on whom a graffiti removal notice was served expenditure reasonably incurred in exercise of the power under section 48(4).

(2) A local authority may not recover expenditure from a person under subsection (1) unless it has served on that person a notice which sets out the amount of, and details of, the expenditure which it proposes to recover.

(3) Section 160 of the Environmental Protection Act 1990 has effect in relation to notices under subsection (2) as if they were notices within subsection (2) of that section.

50. Guidance

(1) The Secretary of State must issue guidance to local authorities in England for the purposes of sections 48 and 49.
(2) The National Assembly for Wales must issue guidance to local authorities in Wales for the purposes of sections 48 and 49.
(3) A local authority must have regard to any guidance issued to it under this section.

51. Appeals

(1) A person on whom a graffiti removal notice is served may, within the period of 21 days beginning with the day on which it is served, appeal against the notice to a magistrates' court on any of the following grounds.
(2) They are—
  (a) that the defacement is neither detrimental to the amenity of the area nor offensive,
  (b) that there is a material defect or error in, or in connection with, the notice,
  (c) that the notice should be served on another person.
(3) Where an appeal under subsection (1) is brought, the graffiti removal notice shall be of no effect pending the final determination or withdrawal of the appeal.
(4) On the determination of such an appeal, the magistrates' court must do one of the following—
  (a) quash the notice,
  (b) modify the notice,
  (c) dismiss the appeal.
(5) Where the court modifies the notice or dismisses the appeal, it may extend the period specified in the notice.
(6) A person on whom a notice under section 49(2) is served may, within the period of 21 days beginning with the day on which it is served, appeal to a magistrates' court on the grounds that the expenditure which the authority is proposing to recover is excessive.
(7) On the determination of an appeal under subsection (6), the magistrates' court must do either of the following—
  (a) confirm that the amount which the authority is proposing to recover is reasonable, or
  (b) substitute a lower amount as the amount which the authority is entitled to recover.

52. Exemption from liability in relation to graffiti removal notices

(1) None of the persons mentioned in subsection (2) is to have any liability to any person responsible for the relevant surface for damages or otherwise (whether at common law or otherwise) arising out of anything done or omitted to be done in the exercise or purported exercise of—
  (a) the power under subsection (4) of section 48 (including as provided for in subsection (5) of that section), or

(b) the power under subsection (8) of that section.

(2) Those persons are—

(a) in the case of the power mentioned in subsection (1)(a)—

(i) the local authority and any employee of the authority, and

(ii) any person authorised by the authority under section 48(4) and the employer or any employee of that person, and

(b) in the case of the power mentioned in subsection (1)(b), the local authority and any employee of the authority.

(3) Subsection (1) does not apply—

(a) if the act or omission is shown to have been in bad faith;

(b) to liability arising out of a failure to exercise due care and attention;

(c) so as to prevent an award of damages made in respect of an act or omission on the ground that the act or omission was unlawful by virtue of section 6(1) of the Human Rights Act 1998 (c. 42).

(4) This section does not affect any other exemption from liability (whether at common law or otherwise).

(5) Section 48(11) is to apply for the purposes of this section as it applies for the purposes of that section.

Advertisements

53. Display of advertisements in contravention of regulations

In section 224(3) of the Town and Country Planning Act 1990 (c. 8) (offence of displaying advertisement in contravention of regulations) for 'level 3', in both places where it occurs, substitute 'level 4'.

Aerosol paints

54. Sale of aerosol paint to children

(1) A person commits an offence if he sells an aerosol paint container to a person under the age of sixteen.

(2) In subsection (1) 'aerosol paint container' means a device which—

(a) contains paint stored under pressure, and

(b) is designed to permit the release of the paint as a spray.

(3) A person guilty of an offence under this section shall be liable on summary conviction to a fine not exceeding level 4 on the standard scale.

(4) It is a defence for a person charged with an offence under this section in respect of a sale to prove that—

(a) he took all reasonable steps to determine the purchaser's age, and

(b) he reasonably believed that the purchaser was not under the age of sixteen.

(5) It is a defence for a person charged with an offence under this section in respect of a sale effected by another person to prove that he (the defendant) took all reasonable steps to avoid the commission of an offence under this section.

Waste and litter

55. Unlawfully deposited waste etc

(1) The Control of Pollution (Amendment) Act 1989 (c. 14) is amended in accordance with subsections (2) and (3).

(2) In subsection (1) of section 7 (further enforcement provisions) for 'relevant authority' substitute 'waste regulation authority'.

(3) After subsection (1) of section 9 (interpretation) insert—

(1A) In sections 5 to 7 above 'regulation authority' also means a waste collection authority falling within section 30(3)(a), (b) or (bb) of the Environmental Protection Act 1990.

(4) After section 59 of the Environmental Protection Act 1990 (c. 43) insert—

59A. Directions in relation to exercise of powers under section 59

(1) The Secretary of State may issue directions setting out categories of waste to which a waste regulation authority or waste collection authority in England and Wales should give priority for the purposes of exercising its powers under section 59 above.

(2) Priorities set out in directions under subsection (1) above may be different for different authorities or areas.

(3) But nothing in this section or in any directions issued under it affects any power of an authority under section 59 above.

(5) In section 71 of the Environmental Protection Act 1990 (c. 43) (obtaining information from persons and authorities), after subsection (3) insert—

(4) The Secretary of State may, by notice in writing, require a waste regulation authority or waste collection authority in England and Wales to supply to him, or to such other person as may be specified in the notice, such information as may be so specified in respect of—

(a) cases where the authority has exercised any powers under section 59 above, and

(b) cases where the authority has taken action under any other enactment in respect of any deposit or other disposal of controlled waste in contravention of section 33(1) above.

(6) Subsection (15) of section 108 of the Environment Act 1995 (c. 25) (powers of enforcing authorities and persons authorised by them) is amended in accordance with subsections (7) to (9).

(7) In the definition of 'enforcing authority' after paragraph (b) insert—

(ba) a waste collection authority;.

(8) After the definition of 'pollution control functions' in relation to the Agency or SEPA insert—

'pollution control functions', in relation to a waste collection authority, means the functions conferred on it by section 59 of the Environmental Protection Act 1990;.

(9) After the definition of 'premises' insert—

'waste collection authority' shall be construed in accordance with section 30(3)(a), (b) and (bb) of the Environmental Protection Act 1990.

(10) The reference to the Environmental Protection Act 1990 in Schedule 1 to the National Assembly for Wales (Transfer of Functions) Order 1999 (S.I. 1999/ 672) is to be treated as referring to that Act as amended by this section.

56. Extension of litter authority powers to take remedial action

(1) For section 92(10) of the Environmental Protection Act 1990 (restriction on remedial action by litter authorities) substitute—

(10) Subsection (9) above does not apply in relation to any land to which subsections (11) or (12) below applies.
(11) This subsection applies to any relevant Crown land which is occupied for naval, military or air force purposes.
(12) This subsection applies to any relevant land of a statutory undertaker in relation to which the Secretary of State has specified, by order, that it is requisite or expedient that, in the national interest, subsection (9) above should not apply.

(2) The reference to the Environmental Protection Act 1990 (c. 43) in Schedule 1 to the National Assembly for Wales (Transfer of Functions) Order 1999 (S.I. 1999/ 672) is to be treated as referring to that Act as amended by this section.

PART 7
PUBLIC ORDER AND TRESPASS

57. Public assemblies

In section 16 of the Public Order Act 1986 (c. 64) (which defines 'public assembly' for the purposes of the power in section 14 of that Act to impose conditions on public assemblies), in the definition of 'public assembly' for '20' substitute '2'.

58. Raves

(1) Section 63 of the Criminal Justice and Public Order Act 1994 (c. 33) (powers in relation to raves) is amended as follows.
(2) In subsection (1) for '100' substitute '20'.
(3) After subsection (1) insert—

(1A) This section also applies to a gathering if—
  (a) it is a gathering on land of 20 or more persons who are trespassing on the land; and
  (b) it would be a gathering of a kind mentioned in subsection (1) above if it took place on land in the open air.

(4) In subsection (2) omit 'in the open air'.
(5) In subsection (7) for 'this section' substitute 'subsection (6) above'.
(6) After subsection (7) insert—

(7A) A person commits an offence if—
  (a) he knows that a direction under subsection (2) above has been given which applies to him, and
  (b) he makes preparations for or attends a gathering to which this section applies within the period of 24 hours starting when the direction was given.
(7B) A person guilty of an offence under subsection (7A) above is liable on summary conviction to imprisonment for a term not exceeding three months or a fine not exceeding level 4 on the standard scale, or both.

59. Aggravated trespass

(1) The Criminal Justice and Public Order Act 1994 is amended as follows.

(2) In section 68 (offence of aggravated trespass), in subsection (1) (which defines the offence by reference to trespass on land in the open air and lawful activity on land in the open air) omit 'in the open air' in both places where those words appear.

(3) In section 69 (powers to remove persons committing or participating in aggravated trespass), in subsection (1) (which confers the power by reference to trespass on land in the open air) omit 'in the open air' in both places where those words appear.

60. Power to remove trespassers: alternative site available

After section 62 of the Criminal Justice and Public Order Act 1994 (c. 33) insert—

62A. Power to remove trespassers: alternative site available

(1) If the senior police officer present at a scene reasonably believes that the conditions in subsection (2) are satisfied in relation to a person and land, he may direct the person—
   (a) to leave the land;
   (b) to remove any vehicle and other property he has with him on the land.

(2) The conditions are—
   (a) that the person and one or more others ('the trespassers') are trespassing on the land;
   (b) that the trespassers have between them at least one vehicle on the land;
   (c) that the trespassers are present on the land with the common purpose of residing there for any period;
   (d) if it appears to the officer that the person has one or more caravans in his possession or under his control on the land, that there is a suitable pitch on a relevant caravan site for that caravan or each of those caravans;
   (e) that the occupier of the land or a person acting on his behalf has asked the police to remove the trespassers from the land.

(3) A direction under subsection (1) may be communicated to the person to whom it applies by any constable at the scene.

(4) Subsection (5) applies if—
   (a) a police officer proposes to give a direction under subsection (1) in relation to a person and land, and
   (b) it appears to him that the person has one or more caravans in his possession or under his control on the land.

(5) The officer must consult every local authority within whose area the land is situated as to whether there is a suitable pitch for the caravan or each of the caravans on a relevant caravan site which is situated in the local authority's area.

(6) In this section—
   'caravan' and 'caravan site' have the same meanings as in Part 1 of the Caravan Sites and Control of Development Act 1960;
   'relevant caravan site' means a caravan site which is—
   (a) situated in the area of a local authority within whose area the land is situated, and
   (b) managed by a relevant site manager;
   'relevant site manager' means—
   (a) a local authority within whose area the land is situated;
   (b) a registered social landlord;
   'registered social landlord' means a body registered as a social landlord under Chapter 1 of Part 1 of the Housing Act 1996.

(7) The Secretary of State may by order amend the definition of 'relevant site manager' in subsection (6) by adding a person or description of person.

(8) An order under subsection (7) must be made by statutory instrument and is subject to annulment in pursuance of a resolution of either House of Parliament.

61. Failure to comply with direction: offences

After section 62A of the Criminal Justice and Public Order Act 1994 (c. 33) (inserted by section 60) insert—

62B. Failure to comply with direction under section 62A: offences

(1) A person commits an offence if he knows that a direction under section 62A(1) has been given which applies to him and—
   (a) he fails to leave the relevant land as soon as reasonably practicable, or
   (b) he enters any land in the area of the relevant local authority as a trespasser before the end of the relevant period with the intention of residing there.

(2) The relevant period is the period of 3 months starting with the day on which the direction is given.

(3) A person guilty of an offence under this section is liable on summary conviction to imprisonment for a term not exceeding 3 months or a fine not exceeding level 4 on the standard scale or both.

(4) A constable in uniform who reasonably suspects that a person is committing an offence under this section may arrest him without a warrant.

(5) In proceedings for an offence under this section it is a defence for the accused to show—
   (a) that he was not trespassing on the land in respect of which he is alleged to have committed the offence, or
   (b) that he had a reasonable excuse—
      (i) for failing to leave the relevant land as soon as reasonably practicable, or
      (ii) for entering land in the area of the relevant local authority as a trespasser with the intention of residing there, or
   (c) that, at the time the direction was given, he was under the age of 18 years and was residing with his parent or guardian.

62. Failure to comply with direction: seizure

(1) After section 62B of the Criminal Justice and Public Order Act 1994 (inserted by section 61) insert—

62C. Failure to comply with direction under section 62A: seizure

(1) This section applies if a direction has been given under section 62A(1) and a constable reasonably suspects that a person to whom the direction applies has, without reasonable excuse—
   (a) failed to remove any vehicle on the relevant land which appears to the constable to belong to him or to be in his possession or under his control; or
   (b) entered any land in the area of the relevant local authority as a trespasser with a vehicle before the end of the relevant period with the intention of residing there.

(2) The relevant period is the period of 3 months starting with the day on which the direction is given.

(3) The constable may seize and remove the vehicle.

(2) In section 67(1) (retention and charges for seized vehicles) after 'section 62(1)' insert ', 62C(3)'.

63. Common land: modifications

After section 62C of the Criminal Justice and Public Order Act 1994 (c. 33) (inserted by section 62) insert—

62D. Common land: modifications

(1) In their application to common land sections 62A to 62C have effect with these modifications.

(2) References to trespassing and trespassers have effect as if they were references to acts, and persons doing acts, which constitute—

(a) a trespass as against the occupier, or

(b) an infringement of the commoners' rights.

(3) References to the occupier—

(a) in the case of land to which the public has access, include the local authority and any commoner;

(b) in any other case, include the commoners or any of them.

(4) Subsection (1) does not—

(a) require action by more than one occupier, or

(b) constitute persons trespassers as against any commoner or the local authority if they are permitted to be there by the other occupier.

(5) In this section 'common land', 'commoner' and 'the local authority' have the meanings given by section 61.

64. Interpretation

After section 62D of the Criminal Justice and Public Order Act 1994 (inserted by section 63) insert—

62E. Sections 62A to 62D: interpretation

(1) Subsections (2) to (8) apply for the interpretation of sections 62A to 62D and this section.

(2) 'Land' does not include buildings other than—

(a) agricultural buildings within the meaning of paragraphs 3 to 8 of Schedule 5 to the Local Government Finance Act 1988, or

(b) scheduled monuments within the meaning of the Ancient Monuments and Archaeological Areas Act 1979.

(3) 'Local authority' means—

(a) in Greater London, a London borough or the Common Council of the City of London;

(b) in England outside Greater London, a county council, a district council or the Council of the Isles of Scilly;

(c) in Wales, a county council or a county borough council.

(4) 'Occupier', 'trespass', 'trespassing' and 'trespasser' have the meanings given by section 61 in relation to England and Wales.

(5) 'The relevant land' means the land in respect of which a direction under section 62A(1) is given.

(6) 'The relevant local authority' means—

(a) if the relevant land is situated in the area of more than one local authority (but is not in the Isles of Scilly), the district council or county borough council within whose area the relevant land is situated;

(b) if the relevant land is situated in the Isles of Scilly, the Council of the Isles of Scilly;

(c) in any other case, the local authority within whose area the relevant land is situated.

(7) 'Vehicle' has the meaning given by section 61.

(8) A person may be regarded as having a purpose of residing in a place even if he has a home elsewhere.

PART 8
HIGH HEDGES

Introductory

65. Complaints to which this Part applies

(1) This Part applies to a complaint which—
   (a) is made for the purposes of this Part by an owner or occupier of a domestic property; and
   (b) alleges that his reasonable enjoyment of that property is being adversely affected by the height of a high hedge situated on land owned or occupied by another person.

(2) This Part also applies to a complaint which—
   (a) is made for the purposes of this Part by an owner of a domestic property that is for the time being unoccupied, and
   (b) alleges that the reasonable enjoyment of that property by a prospective occupier of that property would be adversely affected by the height of a high hedge situated on land owned or occupied by another person,

   as it applies to a complaint falling within subsection (1).

(3) In relation to a complaint falling within subsection (2), references in sections 68 and 69 to the effect of the height of a high hedge on the complainant's reasonable enjoyment of a domestic property shall be read as references to the effect that it would have on the reasonable enjoyment of that property by a prospective occupier of the property.

(4) This Part does not apply to complaints about the effect of the roots of a high hedge.

(5) In this Part, in relation to a complaint—

   'complainant' means—
   (a) a person by whom the complaint is made; or
   (b) if every person who made the complaint ceases to be an owner or occupier of the domestic property specified in the complaint, any other person who is for the time being an owner or occupier of that property;

   and references to the complainant include references to one or more of the complainants;

   'the neighbouring land' means the land on which the high hedge is situated; and

   'the relevant authority' means the local authority in whose area that land is situated.

66. High hedges

(1) In this Part 'high hedge' means so much of a barrier to light or access as—
   (a) is formed wholly or predominantly by a line of two or more evergreens; and
   (b) rises to a height of more than two metres above ground level.

(2) For the purposes of subsection (1) a line of evergreens is not to be regarded as forming a barrier to light or access if the existence of gaps significantly affects its overall effect as such a barrier at heights of more than two metres above ground level.

(3) In this section 'evergreen' means an evergreen tree or shrub or a semi-evergreen tree or shrub.

67. Domestic property

(1) In this Part 'domestic property' means—
  (a) a dwelling; or
  (b) a garden or yard which is used and enjoyed wholly or mainly in connection with a dwelling.

(2) In subsection (1) 'dwelling' means any building or part of a building occupied, or intended to be occupied, as a separate dwelling.

(3) A reference in this Part to a person's reasonable enjoyment of domestic property includes a reference to his reasonable enjoyment of a part of the property.

Complaints procedure

68. Procedure for dealing with complaints

(1) This section has effect where a complaint to which this Part applies—
  (a) is made to the relevant authority; and
  (b) is accompanied by such fee (if any) as the authority may determine.

(2) If the authority consider—
  (a) that the complainant has not taken all reasonable steps to resolve the matters complained of without proceeding by way of such a complaint to the authority, or
  (b) that the complaint is frivolous or vexatious,

  the authority may decide that the complaint should not be proceeded with.

(3) If the authority do not so decide, they must decide—
  (a) whether the height of the high hedge specified in the complaint is adversely affecting the complainant's reasonable enjoyment of the domestic property so specified; and
  (b) if so, what action (if any) should be taken in relation to that hedge, in pursuance of a remedial notice under section 69, with a view to remedying the adverse effect or preventing its recurrence.

(4) If the authority decide under subsection (3) that action should be taken as mentioned in paragraph (b) of that subsection, they must as soon as is reasonably practicable—
  (a) issue a remedial notice under section 69 implementing their decision;
  (b) send a copy of that notice to the following persons, namely—
    (i) every complainant; and
    (ii) every owner and every occupier of the neighbouring land; and
  (c) notify each of those persons of the reasons for their decision.

(5) If the authority—
  (a) decide that the complaint should not be proceeded with, or
  (b) decide either or both of the issues specified in subsection (3) otherwise than in the complainant's favour,

  they must as soon as is reasonably practicable notify the appropriate person or persons of any such decision and of their reasons for it.

(6) For the purposes of subsection (5)—
  (a) every complainant is an appropriate person in relation to a decision falling within paragraph (a) or (b) of that subsection; and
  (b) every owner and every occupier of the neighbouring land is an appropriate person in relation to a decision falling within paragraph (b) of that subsection.

(7) A fee determined under subsection (1)(b) must not exceed the amount prescribed in regulations made—
   (a) in relation to complaints relating to hedges situated in England, by the Secretary of State; and
   (b) in relation to complaints relating to hedges situated in Wales, by the National Assembly for Wales.

(8) A fee received by a local authority by virtue of subsection (1)(b) may be refunded by them in such circumstances and to such extent as they may determine.

69. Remedial notices

(1) For the purposes of this Part a remedial notice is a notice—
   (a) issued by the relevant authority in respect of a complaint to which this Part applies; and
   (b) stating the matters mentioned in subsection (2).

(2) Those matters are—
   (a) that a complaint has been made to the authority under this Part about a high hedge specified in the notice which is situated on land so specified;
   (b) that the authority have decided that the height of that hedge is adversely affecting the complainant's reasonable enjoyment of the domestic property specified in the notice;
   (c) the initial action that must be taken in relation to that hedge before the end of the compliance period;
   (d) any preventative action that they consider must be taken in relation to that hedge at times following the end of that period while the hedge remains on the land; and
   (e) the consequences under sections 75 and 77 of a failure to comply with the notice.

(3) The action specified in a remedial notice is not to require or involve—
   (a) a reduction in the height of the hedge to less than two metres above ground level; or
   (b) the removal of the hedge.

(4) A remedial notice shall take effect on its operative date.

(5) 'The operative date' of a remedial notice is such date (falling at least 28 days after that on which the notice is issued) as is specified in the notice as the date on which it is to take effect.

(6) 'The compliance period' in the case of a remedial notice is such reasonable period as is specified in the notice for the purposes of subsection (2)(c) as the period within which the action so specified is to be taken; and that period shall begin with the operative date of the notice.

(7) Subsections (4) to (6) have effect in relation to a remedial notice subject to—
   (a) the exercise of any power of the relevant authority under section 70; and
   (b) the operation of sections 71 to 73 in relation to the notice.

(8) While a remedial notice has effect, the notice—
   (a) shall be a local land charge; and
   (b) shall be binding on every person who is for the time being an owner or occupier of the land specified in the notice as the land where the hedge in question is situated.

(9) In this Part—

'initial action' means remedial action or preventative action, or both;
'remedial action' means action to remedy the adverse effect of the height of the hedge on the complainant's reasonable enjoyment of the domestic property in respect of which the complaint was made; and
'preventative action' means action to prevent the recurrence of the adverse effect.

70. Withdrawal or relaxation of requirements of remedial notices

(1) The relevant authority may—
(a) withdraw a remedial notice issued by them; or
(b) waive or relax a requirement of a remedial notice so issued.

(2) The powers conferred by this section are exercisable both before and after a remedial notice has taken effect.

(3) Where the relevant authority exercise the powers conferred by this section, they must give notice of what they have done to—
(a) every complainant; and
(b) every owner and every occupier of the neighbouring land.

(4) The withdrawal of a remedial notice does not affect the power of the relevant authority to issue a further remedial notice in respect of the same hedge.

Appeals

71. Appeals against remedial notices and other decisions of relevant authorities

(1) Where the relevant authority—
(a) issue a remedial notice,
(b) withdraw such a notice, or
(c) waive or relax the requirements of such a notice,
each of the persons falling within subsection (2) may appeal to the appeal authority against the issue or withdrawal of the notice or (as the case may be) the waiver or relaxation of its requirements.

(2) Those persons are—
(a) every person who is a complainant in relation to the complaint by reference to which the notice was given; and
(b) every person who is an owner or occupier of the neighbouring land.

(3) Where the relevant authority decide either or both of the issues specified in section 68(3) otherwise than in the complainant's favour, the complainant may appeal to the appeal authority against the decision.

(4) An appeal under this section must be made before—
(a) the end of the period of 28 days beginning with the relevant date; or
(b) such later time as the appeal authority may allow.

(5) In subsection (4) 'the relevant date'—
(a) in the case of an appeal against the issue of a remedial notice, means the date on which the notice was issued; and
(b) in the case of any other appeal under this section, means the date of the notification given by the relevant authority under section 68 or 70 of the decision in question.

(6) Where an appeal is duly made under subsection (1), the notice or (as the case may be) withdrawal, waiver or relaxation in question shall not have effect pending the final determination or withdrawal of the appeal.

(7) In this Part 'the appeal authority' means—
   (a) in relation to appeals relating to hedges situated in England, the Secretary of State; and
   (b) in relation to appeals relating to hedges situated in Wales, the National Assembly for Wales.

72. Appeals procedure

(1) The appeal authority may by regulations make provision with respect to—
   (a) the procedure which is to be followed in connection with appeals to that authority under section 71; and
   (b) other matters consequential on or connected with such appeals.

(2) Regulations under this section may, in particular, make provision—
   (a) specifying the grounds on which appeals may be made;
   (b) prescribing the manner in which appeals are to be made;
   (c) requiring persons making appeals to send copies of such documents as may be prescribed to such persons as may be prescribed;
   (d) requiring local authorities against whose decisions appeals are made to send to the appeal authority such documents as may be prescribed;
   (e) specifying, where a local authority are required by virtue of paragraph (d) to send the appeal authority a statement indicating the submissions which they propose to put forward on the appeal, the matters to be included in such a statement;
   (f) prescribing the period within which a requirement imposed by the regulations is to be complied with;
   (g) enabling such a period to be extended by the appeal authority;
   (h) for a decision on an appeal to be binding on persons falling within section 71(2) in addition to the person by whom the appeal was made;
   (i) for incidental or ancillary matters, including the awarding of costs.

(3) Where an appeal is made to the appeal authority under section 71 the appeal authority may appoint a person to hear and determine the appeal on its behalf.

(4) The appeal authority may require such a person to exercise on its behalf any functions which—
   (a) are conferred on the appeal authority in connection with such an appeal by section 71 or 73 or by regulations under this section; and
   (b) are specified in that person's appointment;

   and references to the appeal authority in section 71 or 73 or in any regulations under this section shall be construed accordingly.

(5) The appeal authority may pay a person appointed under subsection (3) such remuneration as it may determine.

(6) Regulations under this section may provide for any provision of Schedule 20 to the Environment Act 1995 (c. 25) (delegation of appellate functions) to apply in relation to a person appointed under subsection (3) with such modifications (if any) as may be prescribed.

(7) In this section, 'prescribed' means prescribed by regulations made by the appeal authority.

73. Determination or withdrawal of appeals

(1) On an appeal under section 71 the appeal authority may allow or dismiss the appeal, either in whole or in part.

(2) Where the appeal authority decides to allow such an appeal to any extent, it may do such of the following as it considers appropriate—

(a) quash a remedial notice or decision to which the appeal relates;

(b) vary the requirements of such a notice; or

(c) in a case where no remedial notice has been issued, issue on behalf of the relevant authority a remedial notice that could have been issued by the relevant authority on the complaint in question.

(3) On an appeal under section 71 relating to a remedial notice, the appeal authority may also correct any defect, error or misdescription in the notice if it is satisfied that the correction will not cause injustice to any person falling within section 71(2).

(4) Once the appeal authority has made its decision on an appeal under section 71, it must, as soon as is reasonably practicable—

(a) give a notification of the decision, and

(b) if the decision is to issue a remedial notice or to vary or correct the requirements of such a notice, send copies of the notice as issued, varied or corrected,

to every person falling within section 71(2) and to the relevant authority.

(5) Where, in consequence of the appeal authority's decision on an appeal, a remedial notice is upheld or varied or corrected, the operative date of the notice shall be—

(a) the date of the appeal authority's decision; or

(b) such later date as may be specified in its decision.

(6) Where the person making an appeal under section 71 against a remedial notice withdraws his appeal, the operative date of the notice shall be the date on which the appeal is withdrawn.

(7) In any case falling within subsection (5) or (6), the compliance period for the notice shall accordingly run from the date which is its operative date by virtue of that subsection (and any period which may have started to run from a date preceding that on which the appeal was made shall accordingly be disregarded).

Powers of entry

74. Powers of entry for the purposes of complaints and appeals

(1) Where, under this Part, a complaint has been made or a remedial notice has been issued, a person authorised by the relevant authority may enter the neighbouring land in order to obtain information required by the relevant authority for the purpose of determining—

(a) whether this Part applies to the complaint;

(b) whether to issue or withdraw a remedial notice;

(c) whether to waive or relax a requirement of a remedial notice;

(d) whether a requirement of a remedial notice has been complied with.

(2) Where an appeal has been made under section 71, a person authorised—

(a) by the appeal authority, or

(b) by a person appointed to determine appeals on its behalf,

may enter the neighbouring land in order to obtain information required by the appeal authority, or by the person so appointed, for the purpose of determining an appeal under this Part.

(3) A person shall not enter land in the exercise of a power conferred by this section unless at least 24 hours' notice of the intended entry has been given to every occupier of the land.

(4) A person authorised under this section to enter land—
 (a) shall, if so required, produce evidence of his authority before entering; and
 (b) shall produce such evidence if required to do so at any time while he remains on the land.

(5) A person who enters land in the exercise of a power conferred by this section may—
 (a) take with him such other persons as may be necessary;
 (b) take with him equipment and materials needed in order to obtain the information required;
 (c) take samples of any trees or shrubs that appear to him to form part of a high hedge.

(6) If, in the exercise of a power conferred by this section, a person enters land which is unoccupied or from which all of the persons occupying the land are temporarily absent, he must on his departure leave it as effectively secured against unauthorised entry as he found it.

(7) A person who intentionally obstructs a person acting in the exercise of the powers under this section is guilty of an offence and shall be liable, on summary conviction, to a fine not exceeding level 3 on the standard scale.

Enforcement powers etc.

75. Offences

(1) Where—
 (a) a remedial notice requires the taking of any action, and
 (b) that action is not taken in accordance with that notice within the compliance period or (as the case may be) by the subsequent time by which it is required to be taken,

every person who, at a relevant time, is an owner or occupier of the neighbouring land is guilty of an offence and shall be liable, on summary conviction, to a fine not exceeding level 3 on the standard scale.

(2) In subsection (1) 'relevant time'—
 (a) in relation to action required to be taken before the end of the compliance period, means a time after the end of that period and before the action is taken; and
 (b) in relation to any preventative action which is required to be taken after the end of that period, means a time after that at which the action is required to be taken but before it is taken.

(3) In proceedings against a person for an offence under subsection (1) it shall be a defence for him to show that he did everything he could be expected to do to secure compliance with the notice.

(4) In any such proceedings against a person, it shall also be a defence for him to show, in a case in which he—
 (a) is not a person to whom a copy of the remedial notice was sent in accordance with a provision of this Part, and
 (b) is not assumed under subsection (5) to have had knowledge of the notice at the time of the alleged offence,

that he was not aware of the existence of the notice at that time.

(5) A person shall be assumed to have had knowledge of a remedial notice at any time if at that time—
  (a) he was an owner of the neighbouring land; and
  (b) the notice was at that time registered as a local land charge.

(6) Section 198 of the Law of Property Act 1925 (c. 20) (constructive notice) shall be disregarded for the purposes of this section.

(7) Where a person is convicted of an offence under subsection (1) and it appears to the court—
  (a) that a failure to comply with the remedial notice is continuing, and
  (b) that it is within that person's power to secure compliance with the notice,

  the court may, in addition to or instead of imposing a punishment, order him to take the steps specified in the order for securing compliance with the notice.

(8) An order under subsection (7) must require those steps to be taken within such reasonable period as may be fixed by the order.

(9) Where a person fails without reasonable excuse to comply with an order under subsection (7) he is guilty of an offence and shall be liable, on summary conviction, to a fine not exceeding level 3 on the standard scale.

(10) Where a person continues after conviction of an offence under subsection (9) (or of an offence under this subsection) to fail, without reasonable excuse, to take steps which he has been ordered to take under subsection (7), he is guilty of a further offence and shall be liable, on summary conviction, to a fine not exceeding one-twentieth of that level for each day on which the failure has so continued.

76. Power to require occupier to permit action to be taken by owner

Section 289 of the Public Health Act 1936 (c. 49) (power of court to require occupier to permit work to be done by owner) shall apply with any necessary modifications for the purpose of giving an owner of land to which a remedial notice relates the right, as against all other persons interested in the land, to comply with the notice.

77. Action by relevant authority

(1) This section applies where—
  (a) a remedial notice requires the taking of any action; and
  (b) that action is not taken in accordance with that notice within the compliance period or (as the case may be) after the end of that period when it is required to be taken by the notice.

(2) Where this section applies—
  (a) a person authorised by the relevant authority may enter the neighbouring land and take the required action; and
  (b) the relevant authority may recover any expenses reasonably incurred by that person in doing so from any person who is an owner or occupier of the land.

(3) Expenses recoverable under this section shall be a local land charge and binding on successive owners of the land and on successive occupiers of it.

(4) Where expenses are recoverable under this section from two or more persons, those persons shall be jointly and severally liable for the expenses.

(5) A person shall not enter land in the exercise of a power conferred by this section unless at least 7 days' notice of the intended entry has been given to every occupier of the land.

(6) A person authorised under this section to enter land—
  (a) shall, if so required, produce evidence of his authority before entering; and
  (b) shall produce such evidence if required to do so at any time while he remains on the land.

(7) A person who enters land in the exercise of a power conferred by this section may—
  (a) use a vehicle to enter the land;
  (b) take with him such other persons as may be necessary;
  (c) take with him equipment and materials needed for the purpose of taking the required action.

(8) If, in the exercise of a power conferred by this section, a person enters land which is unoccupied or from which all of the persons occupying the land are temporarily absent, he must on his departure leave it as effectively secured against unauthorised entry as he found it.

(9) A person who wilfully obstructs a person acting in the exercise of powers under this section to enter land and take action on that land is guilty of an offence and shall be liable, on summary conviction, to a fine not exceeding level 3 on the standard scale.

78. Offences committed by bodies corporate

(1) Where an offence under this Part committed by a body corporate is proved to have been committed with the consent or connivance of, or to be attributable to any neglect on the part of—
  (a) a director, manager, secretary or other similar officer of the body corporate, or
  (b) any person who was purporting to act in any such capacity,

he, as well as the body corporate, shall be guilty of that offence and be liable to be proceeded against and punished accordingly.

(2) Where the affairs of a body corporate are managed by its members, subsection (1) applies in relation to the acts and defaults of a member in connection with his functions of management as if he were a director of the body corporate.

Supplementary

79. Service of documents

(1) A notification or other document required to be given or sent to a person by virtue of this Part shall be taken to be duly given or sent to him if served in accordance with the following provisions of this section.

(2) Such a document may be served—
  (a) by delivering it to the person in question;
  (b) by leaving it at his proper address; or
  (c) by sending it by post to him at that address.

(3) Such a document may—
  (a) in the case of a body corporate, be served on the secretary or clerk of that body;
  (b) in the case of a partnership, be served on a partner or a person having the control or management of the partnership business.

(4) For the purposes of this section and of section 7 of the Interpretation Act 1978 (c. 30) (service of documents by post) in its application to this section, a person's proper address shall be his last known address, except that—

(a) in the case of a body corporate or their secretary or clerk, it shall be the address of the registered or principal office of that body; and
(b) in the case of a partnership or person having the control or the management of the partnership business, it shall be the principal office of the partnership.

(5) For the purposes of subsection (4) the principal office of—
(a) a company registered outside the United Kingdom, or
(b) a partnership carrying on business outside the United Kingdom,
shall be their principal office within the United Kingdom.

(6) If a person has specified an address in the United Kingdom other than his proper address within the meaning of subsection (4) as the one at which he or someone on his behalf will accept documents of a particular description, that address shall also be treated for the purposes of this section and section 7 of the Interpretation Act 1978 as his proper address in connection with the service on him of a document of that description.

(7) Where—
(a) by virtue of this Part a document is required to be given or sent to a person who is an owner or occupier of any land, and
(b) the name or address of that person cannot be ascertained after reasonable inquiry,
the document may be served either by leaving it in the hands of a person who is or appears to be resident or employed on the land or by leaving it conspicuously affixed to some building or object on the land.

80. Documents in electronic form

(1) A requirement of this Part—
(a) to send a copy of a remedial notice to a person, or
(b) to notify a person under section 68(4) of the reasons for the issue of a remedial notice,
is not capable of being satisfied by transmitting the copy or notification electronically or by making it available on a web-site.

(2) The delivery of any other document to a person (the 'recipient') may be effected for the purposes of section 79(2)(a)—
(a) by transmitting it electronically, or
(b) by making it available on a web-site,
but only if it is transmitted or made available in accordance with subsection (3) or (5).

(3) A document is transmitted electronically in accordance with this subsection if—
(a) the recipient has agreed that documents may be delivered to him by being transmitted to an electronic address and in an electronic form specified by him for that purpose; and
(b) the document is a document to which that agreement applies and is transmitted to that address in that form.

(4) A document which is transmitted in accordance with subsection (3) by means of an electronic communications network shall, unless the contrary is proved, be treated as having been delivered at 9 a.m. on the working day immediately following the day on which it is transmitted.

(5) A document is made available on a web-site in accordance with this subsection if—

(a) the recipient has agreed that documents may be delivered to him by being made available on a web-site;
(b) the document is a document to which that agreement applies and is made available on a web-site;
(c) the recipient is notified, in a manner agreed by him, of—
(i) the presence of the document on the web-site;
(ii) the address of the web-site; and
(iii) the place on the web-site where the document may be accessed.

(6) A document made available on a web-site in accordance with subsection (5) shall, unless the contrary is proved, be treated as having been delivered at 9 a.m. on the working day immediately following the day on which the recipient is notified in accordance with subsection (5)(c).

(7) In this section—
'electronic address' includes any number or address used for the purposes of receiving electronic communications;
'electronic communication' means an electronic communication within the meaning of the Electronic Communications Act 2000 (c. 7) the processing of which on receipt is intended to produce writing;
'electronic communications network' means an electronic communications network within the meaning of the Communications Act 2003 (c. 21);
'electronically' means in the form of an electronic communication;
'working day' means a day which is not a Saturday or a Sunday, Christmas Day, Good Friday or a bank holiday in England and Wales under the Banking and Financial Dealings Act 1971 (c. 80).

81. Power to make further provision about documents in electronic form

(1) Regulations may amend section 80 by modifying the circumstances in which, and the conditions subject to which, the delivery of a document for the purposes of section 79(2)(a) may be effected by—
(a) transmitting the document electronically; or
(b) making the document available on a web-site.

(2) Regulations may also amend section 80 by modifying the day on which and the time at which documents which are transmitted electronically or made available on a web-site in accordance with that section are to be treated as having been delivered.

(3) Regulations under this section may make such consequential amendments of this Part as the person making the regulations considers appropriate.

(4) The power to make such regulations shall be exercisable—
(a) in relation to documents relating to complaints about hedges situated in England, by the Secretary of State; and
(b) in relation to documents relating to complaints about hedges situated in Wales, by the National Assembly for Wales.

(5) In this section 'electronically' has the meaning given in section 80.

82. Interpretation

In this Part—
'the appeal authority' has the meaning given by section 71(7);
'complaint' shall be construed in accordance with section 65;

'complainant' has the meaning given by section 65(5);
'the compliance period' has the meaning given by section 69(6);
'domestic property' has the meaning given by section 67;
'high hedge' has the meaning given by section 66;
'local authority', in relation to England, means—

(a) a district council;
(b) a county council for a county in which there are no districts;
(c) a London borough council; or
(d) the Common Council of the City of London;

and, in relation to Wales, means a county council or a county borough council;
'the neighbouring land' has the meaning given by section 65(5);
'occupier', in relation to any land, means a person entitled to possession of the land by virtue of an estate or interest in it;
'the operative date' shall be construed in accordance with sections 69(5) and 73(5) and (6);
'owner', in relation to any land, means a person (other than a mortgagee not in possession) who, whether in his own right or as trustee for any person—

(a) is entitled to receive the rack rent of the land, or
(b) where the land is not let at a rack rent, would be so entitled if it were so let;

'preventative action' has the meaning given by section 69(9);
'the relevant authority' has the meaning given by section 65(5);
'remedial notice' shall be construed in accordance with section 69(1);
'remedial action' has the meaning given by section 69(9).

83. Power to amend sections 65 and 66

(1) Regulations may do one or both of the following—
  (a) amend section 65 for the purpose of extending the scope of complaints relating to high hedges to which this Part applies; and
  (b) amend section 66 (definition of 'high hedge').

(2) The power to make such regulations shall be exercisable—
  (a) in relation to complaints about hedges situated in England, by the Secretary of State; and
  (b) in relation to complaints about hedges situated in Wales, by the National Assembly for Wales.

(3) Regulations under this section may make such consequential amendments of this Part as the person making the regulations considers appropriate.

84. Crown application

(1) This Part and any provision made under it bind the Crown.
(2) This section does not impose criminal liability on the Crown.
(3) Subsection (2) does not affect the criminal liability of persons in the service of the Crown.

PART 9
MISCELLANEOUS POWERS

85. Anti-social behaviour orders

(1) The Crime and Disorder Act 1998 (c. 37) is amended as follows.

(2) In section 1(1A) (authorities who may apply for anti-social behaviour orders)—
   (a) after paragraph (a) there is inserted—
      '(aa) in relation to England, a county council;';
   (b) after paragraph (c) 'or' is omitted;
   (c) after paragraph (d) there is inserted 'or
      (e) a housing action trust established by order in pursuance of section 62 of the Housing Act 1988.'.

(3) In section 1(1B) (persons requiring protection from anti-social acts)—
   (a) after paragraph (a) there is inserted—
      '(aa) in relation to a relevant authority falling within paragraph (aa) of subsection (1A), persons within the county of the county council;';
   (b) in paragraph (d) after 'paragraph (d)' there is inserted 'or (e)'.

(4) In section 1 after subsection (10) (penalty for breach of anti-social behaviour order) there are inserted the following subsections—

   (10A) The following may bring proceedings for an offence under subsection (10)—
      (a) a council which is a relevant authority;
      (b) the council for the local government area in which a person in respect of whom an anti-social behaviour order has been made resides or appears to reside.

   (10B) If proceedings for an offence under subsection (10) are brought in a youth court section 47(2) of the Children and Young Persons Act 1933 (c. 12) has effect as if the persons entitled to be present at a sitting for the purposes of those proceedings include one person authorised to be present by a relevant authority.

(5) In section 1B (anti-social behaviour orders in county court proceedings) after subsection (3) there are inserted the following subsections—

   (3A) Subsection (3B) applies if a relevant authority is a party to the principal proceedings and considers—
      (a) that a person who is not a party to the proceedings has acted in an anti-social manner, and
      (b) that the person's anti-social acts are material in relation to the principal proceedings.

   (3B) The relevant authority may—
      (a) make an application for the person mentioned in subsection (3A)(a) to be joined to the principal proceedings to enable an order under subsection (4) to be made in relation to that person;
      (b) if that person is so joined, apply for an order under subsection (4).

   (3C) But a person must not be joined to proceedings in pursuance of subsection (3B) unless his anti-social acts are material in relation to the principal proceedings.

(6) In section 1B(5) for 'party to the principal proceedings' there is substituted 'person'.

(7) In section 1E (consultation requirements) after subsection (4) there is inserted—

   (5) Subsection (4)(a) does not apply if the relevant authority is a county council for a county in which there are no districts.

(8) In section 9 (which makes supplemental provision about parenting orders) after subsection (1A) there is inserted the following subsection—

(1B) If an anti-social behaviour order is made in respect of a person under the age of 16 the court which makes the order—
(a) must make a parenting order if it is satisfied that the relevant condition is fulfilled;
(b) if it is not so satisfied, must state in open court that it is not and why it is not.

(9) An order under section 93 below made in relation to subsection (5) above may make provision for that subsection to come into force—
(a) for such period as is specified in the order;
(b) on different days in respect of persons of different ages.

(10) Subsection (9) does not affect section 94(2) below.

(11) The making of an order as mentioned in subsection (9)(a) does not prevent the making of a further order under section 93 below—
(a) whether for the same or a different purpose, or
(b) in relation to the same area.

86. Certain orders made on conviction of offences

(1) In section 1C of the Crime and Disorder Act 1998 (c. 37) (orders on conviction of an offence to prevent anti-social acts) in subsection (3) for the words from 'whether or not' to the end there is substituted '—
(a) if the prosecutor asks it to do so, or
(b) if the court thinks it is appropriate to do so.'.

(2) After subsection (3) of that section there are inserted the following subsections—

(3A) For the purpose of deciding whether to make an order under this section the court may consider evidence led by the prosecution and the defence.

(3B) It is immaterial whether evidence led in pursuance of subsection (3A) would have been admissible in the proceedings in which the offender was convicted.

(3) After subsection (9) of that section there are inserted the following subsections—

(9A) The council for the local government area in which a person in respect of whom an anti-social behaviour order has been made resides or appears to reside may bring proceedings under section 1(10) (as applied by subsection (9) above) for breach of an order under subsection (2) above.

(9B) Subsection (9C) applies in relation to proceedings in which an order under subsection (2) is made against a child or young person who is convicted of an offence.

(9C) In so far as the proceedings relate to the making of the order—
(a) section 49 of the Children and Young Persons Act 1933 (c. 12) (restrictions on reports of proceedings in which children and young persons are concerned) does not apply in respect of the child or young person against whom the order is made;
(b) section 39 of that Act (power to prohibit publication of certain matter) does so apply.

(4) In subsection (10) of that section before the entry relating to 'the commencement date' there is inserted—

'child' and 'young person' have the same meaning as in the Children and Young Persons Act 1933 (c. 12);.

(5) In section 14A of the Football Spectators Act 1989 (c. 37) after subsection (3) there are inserted the following subsections—

(3A) For the purpose of deciding whether to make an order under this section the court may consider evidence led by the prosecution and the defence.

(3B) It is immaterial whether evidence led in pursuance of subsection (3A) would have been admissible in the proceedings in which the offender was convicted.

(6) In section 3(2) of the Prosecution of Offences Act 1985 (c. 23) (functions of the Director of Public Prosecutions) after paragraph (f) the word 'and' is omitted and there is inserted the following paragraph—

(fa) to have the conduct of applications for orders under section 1C of the Crime and Disorder Act 1998 (orders made on conviction of certain offences) and section 14A of the Football Spectators Act 1989 (banning orders made on conviction of certain offences);.

87. Penalty notices for disorderly behaviour by young persons

(1) The Criminal Justice and Police Act 2001 (c. 16) is amended as follows.

(2) In section 2(1) (penalty notices for disorderly behaviour by persons aged 18 or over) for '18' substitute '16'.

(3) After section 2(5) insert—

(6) The Secretary of State may by order—

(a) amend subsection (1) by substituting for the age for the time being specified in that subsection a different age which is not lower than 10, and

(b) if that different age is lower than 16, make provision as follows—

(i) where a person whose age is lower than 16 is given a penalty notice, for a parent or guardian of that person to be notified of the giving of the notice, and

(ii) for that parent or guardian to be liable to pay the penalty under the notice.

(7) The provision which may be made by virtue of subsection (6)(b) includes provision amending, or applying (with or without modifications), this Chapter or any other enactment (whenever passed or made).

(8) The power conferred by subsection (6) is exercisable by statutory instrument.

(9) No order shall be made under subsection (6) unless a draft of the order has been laid before and approved by a resolution of each House of Parliament.

(4) After section 3(1) (amount of penalty) insert—

(1A) The Secretary of State may specify different amounts for persons of different ages.

88. Curfew orders and supervision orders

Schedule 2 (which relates to curfew orders and supervision orders under the Powers of Criminal Courts (Sentencing) Act 2000 (c. 6)) shall have effect.

89. Extension of powers of community support officers etc.

(1) The Police Reform Act 2002 (c. 30) is amended as follows.

(2) In section 105 (powers of Secretary of State to make orders and regulations) in subsection (3)(b) after '99(6)' insert 'or paragraph 15A(2) of Schedule 4 or paragraph 9A(2) of Schedule 5'.

(3) In Part 1 of Schedule 4 (powers exercisable by community support officers) after paragraph 11 insert—

11A. *Power to stop cycles*

(1) Subject to sub-paragraph (2), where a designation applies this paragraph to any person, that person shall, within the relevant police area, have the power of a constable in uniform under section 163(2) of the Road Traffic Act 1988 to stop a cycle.

(2) The power mentioned in sub-paragraph (1) may only be exercised by that person in relation to a person who he has reason to believe has committed an offence under section 72 of the Highway Act 1835 (riding on a footway) by cycling.

(4) In Part 1 of that Schedule, after paragraph 15 insert—

15A. *Power to modify paragraph 1(2)(a)*

(1) The Secretary of State may by order provide that paragraph 1(2)(a) is to have effect as if the reference to the powers there mentioned did not include those powers so far as they relate to an offence under any provision for the time being mentioned in the first column of the Table in section 1(1) of the Criminal Justice and Police Act 2001 which is specified in the order.

(2) The Secretary of State shall not make an order containing (with or without any other provision) any provision authorised by this paragraph unless a draft of that order has been laid before Parliament and approved by a resolution of each House.

(5) In paragraph 1(2) of Schedule 5 (powers of accredited persons to issue fixed penalty notices) after paragraph (a) insert—

(aa) the powers of a constable in uniform to give a penalty notice under Chapter 1 of Part 1 of the Criminal Justice and Police Act 2001 (fixed penalty notices in respect of offences of disorder) except in respect of an offence under section 12 of the Licensing Act 1872 or section 91 of the Criminal Justice Act 1967;.

(6) After paragraph 8 of that Schedule insert—

8A. *Power to stop cycles*

(1) Subject to sub-paragraph (2), a person whose accreditation specifies that this paragraph applies to him shall, within the relevant police area, have the power of a constable in uniform under section 163(2) of the Road Traffic Act 1988 to stop a cycle.

(2) The power mentioned in sub-paragraph (1) may only be exercised by that person in relation to a person who he has reason to believe has committed an offence under section 72 of the Highway Act 1835 (riding on a footway) by cycling.

(7) After paragraph 9 of that Schedule insert—

9A. *Power to modify paragraph 1(2)(aa)*

(1) The Secretary of State may by order provide that paragraph 1(2)(aa) is to have effect as if the reference to the powers there mentioned did not include those powers so far as they relate to an offence under any provision for the time being mentioned in the first column of the Table in section 1(1) of the Criminal Justice and Police Act 2001 which is specified in the order.

(2) The Secretary of State shall not make an order containing (with or without any other provision) any provision authorised by this paragraph unless a draft of that order has been laid before Parliament and approved by a resolution of each House.

90. Report by local authority in certain cases where person remanded on bail

After section 23A of the Children and Young Persons Act 1969 (c. 54) there is inserted—

23B. Report by local authority in certain cases where person remanded on bail

(1) Subsection (2) below applies where a court remands a person aged 10 or 11 on bail and either—

(a) the person is charged with or has been convicted of a serious offence, or

(b) in the opinion of the court the person is a persistent offender.

(2) The court may order a local authority to make an oral or written report specifying where the person is likely to be placed or maintained if he is further remanded to local authority accommodation.

(3) An order under subsection (2) above must designate the local authority which is to make the report; and that authority must be the local authority which the court would have designated under section 23(2) of this Act if the person had been remanded to local authority accommodation.

(4) An order under subsection (2) above must specify the period within which the local authority must comply with the order.

(5) The maximum period that may be so specified is seven working days.

(6) If the Secretary of State by order so provides, subsection (2) above also applies where—

(a) a court remands on bail any person who has attained the age of 12 and is under the age of 17,

(b) the requirement in section 23AA(3) of this Act is fulfilled, and

(c) in a case where he is remanded after conviction, the court is satisfied that the behaviour which constituted the offence was due, to a significant extent, to the circumstances in which the offender was living.

(7) In this section—

'serious offence' means an offence punishable in the case of an adult with imprisonment for a term of two years or more;

'working day' means any day other than—

(a) a Saturday or a Sunday,

(b) Christmas Day or Good Friday, or

(c) a bank holiday in England and Wales under the Banking and Financial Dealings Act 1971.

91. Proceedings under section 222 of the Local Government Act 1972: power of arrest attached to injunction

(1) This section applies to proceedings in which a local authority is a party by virtue of section 222 of the Local Government Act 1972 (c. 70) (power of local authority to bring, defend or appear in proceedings for the promotion or protection of the interests of inhabitants of their area).

(2) If the court grants an injunction which prohibits conduct which is capable of causing nuisance or annoyance to a person it may, if subsection (3) below applies, attach a power of arrest to any provision of the injunction.

(3) This subsection applies if the local authority applies to the court to attach the power of arrest and the court thinks that either—

(a) the conduct mentioned in subsection (2) consists of or includes the use or threatened use of violence, or

(b) there is a significant risk of harm to the person mentioned in that subsection.

(4) Harm includes serious ill-treatment or abuse (whether physical or not).

(5) Local authority has the same meaning as in section 222 of the Local Government Act 1972.

PART 10
GENERAL

92. Repeals

Schedule 3 contains repeals.

93. Commencement

(1) Except as provided in subsections (2) and (3), the preceding provisions of this Act (other than subsections (9) to (11) of section 85) come into force in accordance with provision made by the Secretary of State by order.

(2) Part 2 and sections 19 to 22, 24, 40 to 45, 47 to 52, 55, 56 and 91—
   (a) so far as relating to England, come into force in accordance with provision made by the Secretary of State by order;
   (b) so far as relating to Wales, come into force in accordance with provision made by the National Assembly for Wales by order.

(3) Part 8 comes into force—
   (a) in relation to complaints about hedges situated in England, in accordance with provision made by the Secretary of State by order;
   (b) in relation to complaints about hedges situated in Wales, in accordance with provision made by the National Assembly for Wales by order.

94. Orders and regulations

(1) References in this section to subordinate legislation are to—
   (a) an order of the Secretary of State or the National Assembly for Wales under this Act;
   (b) regulations under this Act.

(2) Subordinate legislation—
   (a) may make different provision for different purposes, different cases and different areas;
   (b) may include incidental, supplemental, consequential, saving or transitional provisions (including provisions applying, with or without modification, provision contained in an enactment).

(3) A power to make subordinate legislation is exercisable by statutory instrument.

(4) A statutory instrument is subject to annulment in pursuance of a resolution of either House of Parliament if it contains subordinate legislation made by the Secretary of State other than—
   (a) regulations under section 81 or 83; or
   (b) an order under section 93.

(5) No regulations shall be made by the Secretary of State under section 81 or 83 (whether alone or with other provisions) unless a draft of the statutory instrument containing the regulations has been laid before, and approved by a resolution of, each House of Parliament.

95. Money

There shall be paid out of money provided by Parliament any increase attributable to this Act in the sums payable out of money so provided under any other enactment.

96. Extent

(1) Parts 1 to 4 and 6 to 9 extend to England and Wales only.
(2) Part 5 and this Part do not extend to Northern Ireland.

97. Short title

This Act may be cited as the Anti-social Behaviour Act 2003.

SCHEDULES

SCHEDULE 1

Section 14

DEMOTED TENANCIES

1 In the Housing Act 1996 (c. 52) after section 143 the following sections are inserted as Chapter 1A of Part 5—

CHAPTER 1A
DEMOTED TENANCIES

General provisions

143A. Demoted tenancies

(1) This section applies to a periodic tenancy of a dwelling-house if each of the following conditions is satisfied.
(2) The first condition is that the landlord is either a local housing authority or a housing action trust.
(3) The second condition is that the tenant condition in section 81 of the Housing Act 1985 is satisfied.
(4) The third condition is that the tenancy is created by virtue of a demotion order under section 82A of that Act.
(5) In this Chapter—
  (a) a tenancy to which this section applies is referred to as a demoted tenancy;
  (b) references to demoted tenants must be construed accordingly.

143B. Duration of demoted tenancy

(1) A demoted tenancy becomes a secure tenancy at the end of the period of one year (the demotion period) starting with the day the demotion order takes effect; but this is subject to subsections (2) to (5).
(2) A tenancy ceases to be a demoted tenancy if any of the following paragraphs applies—
  (a) either of the first or second conditions in section 143A ceases to be satisfied;
  (b) the demotion order is quashed;
  (c) the tenant dies and no one is entitled to succeed to the tenancy.
(3) If at any time before the end of the demotion period the landlord serves a notice of proceedings for possession of the dwelling-house subsection (4) applies.
(4) The tenancy continues as a demoted tenancy until the end of the demotion period or (if later) until any of the following occurs—
  (a) the notice of proceedings is withdrawn by the landlord;
  (b) the proceedings are determined in favour of the tenant;
  (c) the period of 6 months beginning with the date on which the notice is served ends and no proceedings for possession have been brought.
(5) A tenancy does not come to an end merely because it ceases to be a demoted tenancy.

143C. Change of landlord

(1) A tenancy continues to be a demoted tenancy for the duration of the demotion period if—
  (a) at the time the demoted tenancy is created the interest of the landlord belongs to a local housing authority or a housing action trust, and
  (b) during the demotion period the interest of the landlord transfers to another person who is a local housing authority or a housing action trust.

(2) Subsections (3) and (4) apply if—
  (a) at the time the demoted tenancy is created the interest of the landlord belongs to a local housing authority or a housing action trust, and
  (b) during the demotion period the interest of the landlord transfers to a person who is not such a body.

(3) If the new landlord is a registered social landlord or a person who does not satisfy the landlord condition the tenancy becomes an assured shorthold tenancy.

(4) If the new landlord is not a registered social landlord and does satisfy the landlord condition the tenancy becomes a secure tenancy.

(5) The landlord condition must be construed in accordance with section 80 of the Housing Act 1985.

Proceedings for possession

143D. Proceedings for possession

(1) The landlord may only bring a demoted tenancy to an end by obtaining an order of the court for possession of the dwelling-house.

(2) The court must make an order for possession unless it thinks that the procedure under sections 143E and 143F has not been followed.

(3) If the court makes such an order the tenancy comes to an end on the date on which the tenant is to give up possession in pursuance of the order.

143E. Notice of proceedings for possession

(1) Proceedings for possession of a dwelling-house let under a demoted tenancy must not be brought unless the landlord has served on the tenant a notice of proceedings under this section.

(2) The notice must—
  (a) state that the court will be asked to make an order for the possession of the dwelling-house;
  (b) set out the reasons for the landlord's decision to apply for the order;
  (c) specify the date after which proceedings for the possession of the dwelling-house may be begun;
  (d) inform the tenant of his right to request a review of the landlord's decision and of the time within which the request must be made.

(3) The date specified under subsection (2)(c) must not be earlier than the date on which the tenancy could (apart from this Chapter) be brought to an end by notice to quit given by the landlord on the same date as the notice of proceedings.

(4) The court must not entertain proceedings begun on or before the date specified under subsection (2)(c).

(5) The notice must also inform the tenant that if he needs help or advice—
  (a) about the notice, or
  (b) about what to do about the notice,

he must take the notice immediately to a Citizen's Advice Bureau, a housing aid centre, a law centre or a solicitor.

143F. Review of decision to seek possession

(1) Before the end of the period of 14 days beginning with the date of service of a notice for possession of a dwelling-house let under a demoted tenancy the tenant may request the landlord to review its decision to seek an order for possession.
(2) If a request is made in accordance with subsection (1) the landlord must review the decision.
(3) The Secretary of State may by regulations make provision as to the procedure to be followed in connection with a review under this section.
(4) The regulations may include provision—
  (a) requiring the decision on review to be made by a person of appropriate seniority who was not involved in the original decision;
  (b) as to the circumstances in which the tenant is entitled to an oral hearing, and whether and by whom he may be represented at the hearing.
(5) The landlord must notify the tenant—
  (a) of the decision on the review;
  (b) of the reasons for the decision.
(6) The review must be carried out and notice given under subsection (5) before the date specified in the notice of proceedings as the date after which proceedings for possession of the dwelling-house may be begun.

143G. Effect of proceedings for possession

(1) This section applies if the landlord has begun proceedings for the possession of a dwelling-house let under a demoted tenancy and—
  (a) the demotion period ends, or
  (b) any of paragraphs (a) to (c) of section 143B(2) applies (circumstances in which a tenancy ceases to be a demoted tenancy).
(2) If any of paragraphs (a) to (c) of section 143B(2) applies the tenancy ceases to be a demoted tenancy but the landlord (or the new landlord as the case may be) may continue the proceedings.
(3) Subsection (4) applies if in accordance with subsection (2) a tenancy ceases to be a demoted tenancy and becomes a secure tenancy.
(4) The tenant is not entitled to exercise the right to buy unless—
  (a) the proceedings are finally determined, and
  (b) he is not required to give up possession of the dwelling-house.
(5) The proceedings must be treated as finally determined if—
  (a) they are withdrawn;
  (b) any appeal is abandoned;
  (c) the time for appealing expires without an appeal being brought.

Succession

143H. Succession to demoted tenancy

(1) This section applies if the tenant under a demoted tenancy dies.
(2) If the tenant was a successor, the tenancy—
  (a) ceases to be a demoted tenancy, but
  (b) does not become a secure tenancy.
(3) In any other case a person is qualified to succeed the tenant if—
  (a) he occupies the dwelling-house as his only or principal home at the time of the tenant's death,
  (b) he is a member of the tenant's family, and
  (c) he has resided with the tenant throughout the period of 12 months ending with the tenant's death.
(4) If only one person is qualified to succeed under subsection (3) the tenancy vests in him by virtue of this section.

(5) If there is more than one such person the tenancy vests by virtue of this section in the person preferred in accordance with the following rules—
 (a) the tenant's spouse or (if the tenant has no spouse) the person mentioned in section 143P(1)(b) is to be preferred to another member of the tenant's family;
 (b) if there are two or more other members of the tenant's family the person preferred may be agreed between them or (if there is no such agreement) selected by the landlord.

143I. No successor tenant: termination

(1) This section applies if the demoted tenant dies and no person is qualified to succeed to the tenancy as mentioned in section 143H(3).
(2) The tenancy ceases to be a demoted tenancy if either subsection (3) or (4) applies.
(3) This subsection applies if the tenancy is vested or otherwise disposed of in the course of the administration of the tenant's estate unless the vesting or other disposal is in pursuance of an order under—
 (a) section 23A or 24 of the Matrimonial Causes Act 1973 (property adjustment orders in connection with matrimonial proceedings);
 (b) section 17(1) of the Matrimonial and Family Proceedings Act 1984 (property adjustment orders after overseas divorce, etc);
 (c) paragraph 1 of Schedule 1 to the Children Act 1989 (orders for financial relief against parents).
(4) This subsection applies if it is known that when the tenancy is vested or otherwise disposed of in the course of the administration of the tenant's estate it will not be in pursuance of an order mentioned in subsection (3).
(5) A tenancy which ceases to be a demoted tenancy by virtue of this section cannot subsequently become a secure tenancy.

143J. Successor tenants

(1) This section applies for the purpose of sections 143H and 143I.
(2) A person is a successor to a secure tenancy which is terminated by a demotion order if any of subsections (3) to (6) applies to him.
(3) The tenancy vested in him—
 (a) by virtue of section 89 of the Housing Act 1985 or section 133 of this Act;
 (b) under the will or intestacy of the preceding tenant.
(4) The tenancy arose by virtue of section 86 of the Housing Act 1985 and the original fixed term was granted—
 (a) to another person, or
 (b) to him jointly with another person.
(5) He became the tenant on the tenancy being assigned to him unless—
 (a) the tenancy was assigned in proceedings under section 23A or 24 of the Matrimonial Causes Act 1973 (property adjustment orders in connection with matrimonial proceedings) or section 17(1) of the Matrimonial and Family Proceedings Act 1984 (property adjustment orders after overseas divorce, etc), and
 (b) neither he nor the other party to the marriage was a successor.
(6) He became the tenant on assignment under section 92 of the Housing Act 1985 if he himself was a successor to the tenancy which he assigned in exchange.
(7) A person is the successor to a demoted tenancy if the tenancy vested in him by virtue of section 143H(4) or (5).
(8) A person is the successor to a joint tenancy if he has become the sole tenant.

Assignment

143K. Restriction on assignment

(1) A demoted tenancy is not capable of being assigned except as mentioned in subsection (2).

(2) The exceptions are assignment in pursuance of an order made under—
   (a) section 24 of the Matrimonial Causes Act 1973 (property adjustment orders in connection with matrimonial proceedings);
   (b) section 17(1) of the Matrimonial and Family Proceedings Act 1984 (property adjustment orders after overseas divorce, etc);
   (c) paragraph 1 of Schedule 1 to the Children Act 1989 (orders for financial relief against parents).

Repairs

143L. Right to carry out repairs

The Secretary of State may by regulations under section 96 of the Housing Act 1985 (secure tenants: right to carry out repairs) apply to demoted tenants any provision made under that section in relation to secure tenants.

Provision of information

143M. Provision of information

(1) This section applies to a local housing authority or a housing action trust if it is the landlord of a demoted tenancy.
(2) The landlord must from time to time publish information about the demoted tenancy in such form as it thinks best suited to explain in simple terms and so far as it considers appropriate the effect of—
   (a) the express terms of the demoted tenancy;
   (b) the provisions of this Chapter;
   (c) the provisions of sections 11 to 16 of the Landlord and Tenant Act 1985 (landlord's repairing obligations).
(3) The landlord must ensure that information published under subsection (2) is, so far as is reasonably practicable, kept up to date.
(4) The landlord must supply the tenant with—
   (a) a copy of the information published under subsection (2);
   (b) a written statement of the terms of the tenancy, so far as they are neither expressed in the lease or written tenancy agreement (if any) nor implied by law.
(5) The statement required by subsection (4)(b) must be supplied on the grant of the tenancy or as soon as practicable afterwards.

Supplementary

143N. Jurisdiction of county court

(1) A county court has jurisdiction—
   (a) to determine questions arising under this Chapter;
   (b) to entertain proceedings brought under this Chapter;
   (c) to determine claims (for whatever amount) in connection with a demoted tenancy.
(2) The jurisdiction includes jurisdiction to entertain proceedings as to whether a statement supplied in pursuance of section 143M(4)(b) (written statement of certain terms of tenancy) is accurate.
(3) For the purposes of subsection (2) it is immaterial that no relief other than a declaration is sought.
(4) If a person takes proceedings in the High Court which, by virtue of this section, he could have taken in the county court he is not entitled to recover any costs.
(5) The Lord Chancellor may make such rules and give such directions as he thinks fit for the purposes of giving effect to this section.
(6) The rules and directions may provide—
   (a) for the exercise by a district judge of a county court of any jurisdiction exercisable under this section;

(b) for the conduct of proceedings in private.

(7) The power to make rules must be exercised by statutory instrument subject to annulment in pursuance of a resolution of either House of Parliament.

143O. Meaning of dwelling-house

(1) For the purposes of this Chapter a dwelling-house may be a house or a part of a house.

(2) Land let together with a dwelling-house must be treated for the purposes of this Chapter as part of the dwelling-house unless the land is agricultural land which would not be treated as part of a dwelling-house for the purposes of Part 4 of the Housing Act 1985.

143P. Members of a person's family

(1) For the purposes of this Chapter a person is a member of another's family if—

(a) he is the spouse of that person;

(b) he and that person live together as a couple in an enduring family relationship, but he does not fall within paragraph (c);

(c) he is that person's parent, grandparent, child, grandchild, brother, sister, uncle, aunt, nephew or niece.

(2) For the purposes of subsection (1)(b) it is immaterial that two persons living together in an enduring family relationship are of the same sex.

(3) For the purposes of subsection (1)(c)—

(a) a relationship by marriage must be treated as a relationship by blood;

(b) a relationship of the half-blood must be treated as a relationship of the whole blood;

(c) a stepchild of a person must be treated as his child.

2 (1) The Housing Act 1985 (c. 68) is amended as follows.

(2) In section 105 (requirement to consult secure tenants on certain housing management matters) after subsection (6) there is inserted the following subsection—

(7) For the purposes of this section—

(a) secure tenants include demoted tenants within the meaning of section 143A of the Housing Act 1996;

(b) secure tenancies include demoted tenancies within the meaning of that section.

(3) In section 171B (extent of preserved right to buy) after subsection (1) there is inserted the following subsection—

(1A) A person to whom this section applies ceases to have the preserved right to buy if the tenancy of a relevant dwelling-house becomes a demoted tenancy by virtue of a demotion order under section 6A of the Housing Act 1988.

(4) In Schedule 1 (tenancies which are not secure tenancies) after paragraph 1A (introductory tenancies) there is inserted the following paragraph—

1B A tenancy is not a secure tenancy if it is a demoted tenancy within the meaning of section 143A of the Housing Act 1996.

(5) In Schedule 4 (qualifying period for right to buy and discount) after paragraph 9 (the tenant condition) there is inserted the following paragraph—

9A The tenant condition is not met during any period when a tenancy is a demoted tenancy by virtue of section 20B of the Housing Act 1988 or section 143A of the Housing Act 1996.

SCHEDULE 2

Section 88

CURFEW ORDERS AND SUPERVISION ORDERS

Interpretation

1 In this Schedule 'the 2000 Act' means the Powers of Criminal Courts (Sentencing) Act 2000 (c. 6).

Curfew orders

2 (1) Section 37 of the 2000 Act (curfew orders) is amended as follows.

(2) Subsection (4) (which limits to three months the duration of a curfew order made in respect of a person aged under 16 on conviction) is omitted.

(3) For subsection (12) there is substituted—

(12) In this Act, 'responsible officer', in relation to an offender subject to a curfew order, means—

(a) where the offender is also subject to a supervision order, the person who is the supervisor in relation to the supervision order, and

(b) in any other case, the person who is responsible for monitoring the offender's whereabouts during the curfew periods specified in the order.

Supervision orders

3 After section 64 of the 2000 Act there is inserted—

64A. Supervision orders and curfew orders

Nothing in this Chapter prevents a court which makes a supervision order in respect of an offender from also making a curfew order in respect of him.

4 (1) Schedule 6 to the 2000 Act (requirements which may be included in supervision orders) is amended as follows.

(2) In paragraph 2(5) (total number of days during which offender may be required to comply with directions of supervisor not to exceed 90), for '90' there is substituted '180'.

(3) In paragraph 3 (requirements as to activities, reparation, night restrictions etc)—

(a) sub-paragraph (2)(e) (night restriction) is omitted, and

(b) in sub-paragraph (3) (total number of days in respect of which an offender may be subject to requirements imposed by virtue of any of sub-paragraphs (2)(a) to (e) not to exceed 90)—

(i) for the words ', (d) or (e)' there is substituted 'or (d)', and

(ii) for '90' there is substituted '180'.

(4) Paragraph 4 (night restrictions) is omitted.

(5) After paragraph 5 there is inserted—

Requirement to live for specified period with local authority foster parent

5A (1) Where the conditions mentioned in sub-paragraph (2) below are satisfied, a supervision order may impose a requirement ('a foster parent residence requirement') that the offender shall live for a specified period with a local authority foster parent.

(2) The conditions are that—
(a) the offence is punishable with imprisonment in the case of an offender aged 18 or over;
(b) the offence, or the combination of the offence and one or more offences associated with it, was so serious that a custodial sentence would normally be appropriate (or, where the offender is aged 10 or 11, would normally be appropriate if the offender were aged 12 or over); and
(c) the court is satisfied that—
(i) the behaviour which constituted the offence was due to a significant extent to the circumstances in which the offender was living, and
(ii) the imposition of a foster parent residence requirement will assist in his rehabilitation.

(3) A foster parent residence requirement shall designate the local authority who are to place the offender with a local authority foster parent under section 23(2)(a) of the Children Act 1989, and that authority shall be the authority in whose area the offender resides.

(4) A court shall not impose a foster parent residence requirement unless—
(a) the court has been notified by the Secretary of State that arrangements for implementing such a requirement are available in the area of the designated authority;
(b) the notice has not been withdrawn; and
(c) the court has consulted the designated authority.

(5) Subject to paragraph 5(2A) of Schedule 7 to this Act, the maximum period which may be specified in a foster parent residence requirement is twelve months.

(6) A court shall not impose a foster parent residence requirement in respect of an offender who is not legally represented at the relevant time in that court unless—
(a) he was granted a right to representation funded by the Legal Services Commission as part of the Criminal Defence Service for the purposes of the proceedings but the right was withdrawn because of his conduct; or
(b) he has been informed of his right to apply for such representation for the purposes of the proceedings and has had opportunity to do so, but nevertheless refused or failed to apply.

(7) In sub-paragraph (6) above—
(a) 'the relevant time' means the time when the court is considering whether or not to impose the requirement, and
(b) 'the proceedings' means—
(i) the whole proceedings, or
(ii) the part of the proceedings relating to the imposition of the requirement.

(8) A supervision order imposing a foster parent residence requirement may also impose any of the requirements mentioned in paragraphs 2, 3, 6 and 7 of this Schedule.

(9) If at any time while a supervision order imposing a foster parent residence requirement is in force, the supervisor notifies the offender—
(a) that no suitable local authority foster parent is available, and
(b) that the supervisor has applied or proposes to apply under paragraph 5 of Schedule 7 for the variation or revocation of the order,

the foster parent residence requirement shall, until the determination of the application, be taken to require the offender to live in local authority accommodation (as defined by section 163 of this Act).

(10) This paragraph does not affect the power of a local authority to place with a local authority foster parent an offender to whom a local authority residence requirement under paragraph 5 above relates.

(11) In this paragraph 'local authority foster parent' has the same meaning as in the Children Act 1989.

Consequential amendments

5 In section 21 of the Children Act 1989 (c. 41) (provision of accommodation for children in police protection or detention or on remand, etc) in subsection (2)(c)(ii) after '2000' there is inserted 'or a foster parent residence requirement under paragraph 5A of that Schedule'.

6 (1) Schedule 7 to the 2000 Act (breach, revocation and amendment of supervision orders) is amended as follows.

(2) In paragraph 2 (breach of requirement of supervision order)—

(a) in sub-paragraph (1), after '5' there is inserted ', 5A',

(b) in sub-paragraph (2)(a)(ii) after 'subject to' there is inserted 'sub-paragraph (2A) below and', and

(c) after sub-paragraph (2) there is inserted—

(2A) The court may not make a curfew order under sub-paragraph (2)(a)(ii) above in respect of an offender who is already subject to a curfew order.

(3) In paragraph 5 (revocation and amendment of supervision order)—

(a) after sub-paragraph (2) there is inserted—

(2A) In relation to a supervision order imposing a foster parent residence requirement under paragraph 5A of Schedule 6 to this Act, the power conferred by sub-paragraph (1)(b)(ii) above includes power to extend the period specified in the requirement to a period of not more than 18 months beginning with the day on which the requirement first had effect.,

and

(b) sub-paragraph (3)(b) and the word 'or' immediately preceding it are omitted.

SCHEDULE 3

Section 92

REPEALS

Short title and chapter	Extent of repeal
Firearms Act 1968 (c. 27)	Section 22(5). In section 23(2) the words 'or (5)'. In Part 1 of Schedule 6, the entry relating to section 22(5).
Prosecution of Offences Act 1985 (c. 23)	In section 3(2), the word 'and' after paragraph (f).
Firearms (Amendment) Act 1988 (c. 45)	In section 1(4), the word 'or' at the end of paragraph (a).
Criminal Justice and Public Order Act 1994 (c. 33)	In section 63(2), 'in the open air'. In section 68(1), 'in the open air' in both places. In section 69(1), 'in the open air' in both places.
Noise Act 1996 (c. 37)	In section 2(7) the words from 'and accordingly' to the end.
Housing Act 1996 (c. 52)	Sections 152 and 153.

	In section 158— (a) in subsection (1), the entries relating to 'child', 'harm', 'health' and 'ill-treatment'; (b) subsection (2).
Crime and Disorder Act 1998 (c. 37)	In section 1(1A), the word 'or' after paragraph (c).
Powers of Criminal Courts (Sentencing) Act 2000 (c. 6)	Section 37(4). In Schedule 6— (a) in paragraph 3(2), the words 'and paragraph 4 below' and paragraph (e), and (b) paragraph 4. In Schedule 7, paragraph 5(3)(b) and the word 'or' immediately preceding it.
Police Reform Act 2002 (c. 30)	In Schedule 4, the word 'and' at the end of paragraph 1(2)(c). In Schedule 5, the word 'and' at the end of paragraph 1(2)(b).

APPENDIX 2

Regulations

THE ANTI-SOCIAL BEHAVIOUR ACT 2003 (COMMENCEMENT NO 1 AND TRANSITIONAL PROVISIONS) ORDER 2003, SI 2003/3300

In exercise of the powers conferred upon him by section 93(1) of the Anti-social Behaviour Act 2003, the Secretary of State hereby makes the following Order:

1. This Order may be cited as the Anti-social Behaviour Act 2003 (Commencement No 1 and Transitional Provisions) Order 2003.

2. The following provisions of the Anti-social Behaviour Act 2003 shall come into force on 20th January 2004—

(a) Part 1 (sections 1 to 11) (premises where drugs used unlawfully);

(b) Part 4 (sections 30 to 36) (dispersal of groups etc.);

(c) in Part 5 (firearms)—

(i) section 37 (possession of air weapon or imitation firearm in a public place);

(ii) section 38 (air weapons: age limits); and

(iii) section 39(1), (2), (3) in so far as it relates to the purchase, acquisition, manufacture, sale or transfer of the prohibited weapon, (4), (5) and (6) (prohibition of certain air weapons);

(d) in Part 6 (the environment), section 53 (display of advertisements in contravention of regulations);

(e) in Part 7 (public order and trespass)—

(i) section 57 (public assemblies);

(ii) section 58 (raves); and

(iii) section 59 (aggravated trespass);

(f) in Part 9 (miscellaneous powers)—

(i) section 85(1), (2), (3), (4) in so far as it relates to section 1(10B) of the Crime and Disorder Act 1998 and (7) (anti-social behaviour orders);

(ii) section 86(3) in so far as it relates to section 1C(9B) and (9C) of the Crime and Disorder Act 1998, (4), (5) and (6) (certain orders made on conviction of offences);

(iii) section 87 (penalty notices for disorderly behaviour by young persons); and
(iv) section 89(1), (2), (3), (4), (6) and (7) (extension of powers of community support officers etc.);

(g) in Part 10 (general)—
(i) section 92 (repeals) in so far as it relates to the entries in Schedule 3 in paragraph (ii) below; and
(ii) in Schedule 3 (repeals), the entries relating to—
(a) the Firearms Act 1968;
(b) the Prosecution of Offences Act 1985;
(c) the Firearms (Amendment) Act 1988;
(d) the Criminal Justice and Public Order Act 1994;
(e) the Crime and Disorder Act 1998;
(f) the Police Reform Act 2002.

3. The following provisions of the Anti-social Behaviour Act 2003 shall come into force on 27th February 2004—
(a) in Part 3 (parental responsibilities)—
(i) section 18 (parenting orders under the 1998 Act);
(ii) section 23 (penalty notices for parents in cases of truancy); and
(iii) sections 25 to 29 (criminal conduct and anti-social behaviour);
(b) in Part 7 (public order and trespass), sections 60 to 64 (powers to remove trespassers: alternative site available etc.);
(c) in Part 9 (miscellaneous powers), section 85(8) (anti-social behaviour orders).

4. The following provisions of Part 3 of the Anti-social Behaviour Act 2003 shall come into force on 27th February 2004 in England only—
(a) section 19 (parenting contracts in cases of exclusion from school or truancy);
(b) section 20 (parenting orders in cases of exclusion from school);
(c) section 21 (parenting orders: supplemental);
(d) section 22 (parenting orders: appeals); and
(e) section 24 (interpretation).

5.—(1) Section 39(3) (prohibition of certain air weapons) of the Anti-social Behaviour Act 2003 shall, subject to paragraph (2), to the extent not already in force come into force on 30th April 2004.

(2) Section 1(1)(a) of the Firearms Act 1968 shall not apply to a person who has in his possession any air rifle, air gun or air pistol which uses, or is designed or adapted for use with, a self-contained gas cartridge system where he has applied before 30th April 2004 for a firearm certificate under Part 2 of that Act and either that application is still being processed or any appeal in respect of it has not been determined.

THE MAGISTRATES' COURTS (PARENTING ORDERS) RULES 2004, SI 2004/247

The Lord Chancellor, in exercise of the powers conferred upon him by section 144 of the Magistrates' Courts Act 1980, and after consultation with the rule committee appointed by him under that section, hereby makes the following Rules:

Citation, interpretation and commencement

1. These Rules may be cited as the Magistrates' Courts (Parenting Orders) Rules 2004 and shall come into force on 27th February 2004.
2. In these Rules the '2003 Act' means the Anti-social Behaviour Act 2003.

Parenting Orders under the Anti-social Behaviour Act 2003

3. An application for a parenting order made under section 20 of the 2003 Act shall be made by complaint and in the form set out at Schedule 1 or a form to like effect.
4. A parenting order made under section 20 of the 2003 Act shall be in the form set out at Schedule 2 or a form to like effect.
5. An application for a parenting order made under section 26 of the 2003 Act shall be made by complaint and in the form set out at Schedule 3 or a form to like effect.
6. A parenting order made under section 26 of the 2003 Act shall be in the form set out at Schedule 4 or a form to like effect.

Parenting Orders under the Crime and Disorder Act 1998

7. A parenting order made under section 8 of the Crime and Disorder Act 1998 shall be in the form set out at Schedule 5 or a form to like effect.

Parenting Orders under the Powers of Criminal Courts (Sentencing) Act 2000

8. A parenting order made under paragraph 9D of Schedule 1 to the Powers of Criminal Courts (Sentencing) Act 2000 shall be in the form set out at Schedule 6 or a form to like effect.

Application for variation or discharge

9. An application for the variation or discharge of an order made under section 20(3) or section 26(3) of the 2003 Act, or under paragraph 9D of Schedule 1 to the Powers of Criminal Courts (Sentencing) Act 2000 shall be made by complaint to the magistrates' court which made the order, and shall specify the reason why the applicant for variation or discharge believes the court should vary or discharge the order, as the case may be.

SCHEDULE 1

Rule 3

Application for Parenting Order (Anti-social Behaviour Act 2003, section 20)

.... Magistrates' Court
(Code)

Date:

Child or young person:

Child or young person's address:

Child or young person's age:

Parent:

Parent's address:

which is in the area of [ ] Local Education Authority

Parent:

Parent's address:

which is in the area of [ ] Local Education Authority

Applicant Local Education Authority:

It is alleged that:
(a) the child or young person has been excluded from school on disciplinary grounds; and
(b) the prescribed conditions are satisfied in that [*insert details*].

[The parent(s) entered into a parenting contract on [*date*].] [It is alleged that the parent(s) have failed to comply with the parenting contract, a copy of which is attached to this application form.

Short description of alleged failure to comply with parenting contract:

Evidence of this alleged failure to comply is attached.]

[It is alleged that the parent(s) have refused to enter into a parenting contract.]

[The child or young person is under 16. Information as to the family circumstances of the child or young person is attached.]

[It is alleged that:
(a) the attendance of the parent at a residential course is likely to be more effective than their attendance at a non-residential course in improving the child's or young person's behaviour; and
(b) any interference with family life which is likely to result from the attendance of the parent at a residential course is proportionate in all the circumstances.

The court is requested to order that the counselling or guidance programme may include a residential element.]

Short description of the counselling/guidance programme to be attended by the parent(s):

Further requirements to be included in the order:

SCHEDULE 2

Rule 4

Parenting Order (Anti-social Behaviour Act 2003, section 20)

Magistrates' Court
(Code)

Date: . . . .

Person(s) named in order: . . . .

Age(s): . . . . years (if under 18)

. . . . years (if under 18)

Address(es): . . . .

Applicant Local Education Authority: . . . .

Responsible officer: . . . .

[*insert child's/young person's name*] of [*insert address*], who is believed to have been born on [*insert date of birth*], has been excluded from [*details of school at which the child or young person is registered*] and that the prescribed conditions are met in that [*insert details*].

Decision: In exercise of its powers under section 20(3) of the Anti-social Behaviour Act 2003 (the '2003 Act') and having complied with its duties under that section[, and having complied with its duty under section 21(1) of the 2003 Act in considering the failure of the persons named above to [enter into] [comply with] a parenting contract], the court has decided to impose a parenting order on the person(s) named above being parent(s) of the pupil because the court considers that the order would be desirable in the interests of improving the behaviour of the pupil.

The requirements of the order are as follows:

[*insert person's name*] shall for a period of [*insert length of requirement*] beginning with the date of the order comply with such requirements as are listed in the Schedule to the order.

[*insert person's name*] shall for a concurrent period of [*insert length of requirement*] not exceeding three months attend a counselling or guidance programme as directed by the responsible officer.

[The court is satisfied that the requirements of section 20(7) and (8) of the 2003 Act have been met and the counselling or guidance programme may be or include a residential course.]

[(*In the event that the child/young person is under 16.*) The court has complied with its duties under section 21(2) of the 2003 Act and has obtained and considered information about the child's/young person's family circumstances, and the likely effect of the order on those circumstances.]

The court has complied with its duties under section 21(3) of the 2003 Act, and has explained to the person(s) named above the effect of the order and its requirements, what may happen if he/she/they fail(s) to comply with these requirements (as set out in section 9(7) of the Crime and Disorder Act 1998), and that the court has power (under section 9(5) of the Crime and Disorder Act 1998) to review the order on the application of the person(s) named above or the responsible officer.

Justice of the Peace
[or By order of the Court,
Clerk of the Court]

SCHEDULE

Any requirement(s) imposed by the court under section 20(4)(a) and (b) of the 2003 Act should be listed here.

SCHEDULE 3

Rule 5

Application for Parenting Order (Anti-social Behaviour Act 2003, section 26)

Magistrates' Court
(Code)

Date:

Child or young person:

Child or young person's address:

Child or young person's age:

Parent/Guardian:

Parent/Guardian's address:

Parent/Guardian:

Parent/Guardian's address:

Applicant:

Responsible officer:

It is alleged that:
(a) the child or young person has acted on [*insert date(s)*] at [*insert place(s)*] in an anti-social manner, that is to say, in a manner that caused or was likely to cause harassment, alarm or distress to one or more persons not of the same household as himself; or
(b) the child or young person has on [*insert date(s)*] at [*insert place(s)*] engaged in criminal conduct.

Short description of acts:

[Evidence of these acts is attached.]

[The parent(s)/guardian(s) entered into a parenting contract on [*insert date*].] [It is alleged that the parent(s)/guardian(s) have failed to comply with the parenting contract, a copy of which is attached to this application form.

Short description of alleged failure to comply with parenting contract:

Evidence of this alleged failure to comply is attached.]

[It is alleged that the parent(s)/guardian(s) have refused to enter into a parenting contract.]

[The child or young person is under 16. Information as to the family circumstances of the child or young person is attached.]

[It is alleged that:
(a) the attendance of the parent(s)/guardian(s) at a residential course is likely to be more effective than their attendance at a non-residential course in preventing the child or young person from engaging in further criminal conduct or anti-social behaviour; and

(b) any interference with family life which is likely to result from the attendance of the parent(s)/guardian(s) at a residential course is proportionate in all the circumstances.

The court is requested to order that the counselling or guidance programme may [include] [consist of] a residential course.

Evidence to support the request for a residential requirement is attached.]

Short description of the counselling/guidance programme to be attended by the parent(s)/guardian(s):

Further requirements to be included in the order:

SCHEDULE 4

Rule 6

Parenting Order (Anti-social Behaviour Act 2003, section 26)

Magistrates' Court
(Code)

Date: . . . .

Person(s) named in order: . . . .

Age(s): . . . . years (if under 18)

. . . . years (if under 18)

Address(es): . . . .

Applicant Youth Offending Team: . . . .

Responsible officer: . . . .

[*insert child's/young person's name*] of [*insert address*], who is believed to have been born on [*insert date of birth*], has [behaved in a manner which is anti-social, that is to say, in a manner that caused or was likely to cause harassment, alarm or distress to one or more persons not of the same household as himself] [engaged in criminal conduct] [*delete as applicable*].

Decision: In exercise of its powers under section 26(3) of the Anti-social Behaviour Act 2003 (the '2003 Act') and having complied with its duties under that section[, and having complied with its duty under section 27(1) of the 2003 Act in considering the failure of the persons named above to [enter into] [comply with] a parenting contract], the court has decided to impose a parenting order on the person(s) named above because the court considers that the order would be desirable in the interests of preventing the child or young person from engaging in further [anti-social behaviour] [criminal conduct] [*delete as applicable*].

The requirements of the order are as follows:

[*insert person's name*] shall for a period of [*insert length of requirement*] beginning with the date of the order comply with such requirements as are listed in the Schedule to the order.

[*insert person's name*] shall for a concurrent period of [*insert length of requirement*] not exceeding three months attend a counselling or guidance programme as directed by the responsible officer.

[[*insert person's name*] shall on [*insert dates*] attend a residential course at [*insert address*] as directed by the responsible officer. The court is satisfied that the requirements of section 26(7) and (8) of the 2003 Act have been met.]

[(*In the event that the child/young person is under 16.*) The court has complied with its duties under section 27(2) of the 2003 Act and has obtained and considered information about the child's/young person's family circumstances, and the likely effect of the order on those circumstances.]

The court has complied with its duties under section 27(3) of the 2003 Act, and has explained to the person(s) named above the effect of the order and its requirements, what may happen if he/she/they fail(s) to comply with these requirements (as set out in section 9(7) of the Crime and Disorder Act 1998), and that the court has power (under section 9(5) of the Crime and Disorder Act 1998) to review the order on the application of the person(s) named above or the responsible officer.

Justice of the Peace
[or By order of the Court,
Clerk of the Court]

SCHEDULE

Any requirement(s) imposed by the court under section 26(4)(a) and (b) of the 2003 Act should be listed here.

SCHEDULE 5

Rule 7

Parenting Order (Crime and Disorder Act 1998, section 8)

[Family Proceedings] [[Youth] [Magistrates']
Court (Code)

Date: . . . .

Person(s) named in order: . . . .

Age(s): . . . . years (if under 18)

. . . . years (if under 18)

Address(es): . . . .

Responsible officer: . . . .

[[*insert child's/young person's name*] of [*insert address*] who is believed to have born on [*insert date of birth*], has been [made subject to a [child safety order] [anti-social behaviour order] [sex offender order] [referral order]] [found guilty of an offence, namely, [brief details of offence and statute]].; [The above named has been convicted of an offence under [section 443] [section 444] of the Education Act 1996] [*delete as applicable*].

Decision: In exercise of its powers under section 8 of the Crime and Disorder Act 1998 (the '1998 Act') and having complied with its duties under [section 9(1) and (2)] [section 9(2) and (2A) *(in the case of a referral order)*] of the 1998 Act, the court has decided to impose a parenting order on the person(s) named above because the court considers that the order would be desirable in the interests of preventing [a repetition of the kind of

behaviour which led to the imposition of a [child safety order] [anti-social behaviour order] [sex offender order]] [the commission of further offences by the child or young person] [the commission of further offences under [section 443] [section 444] of the Education Act 1996] [*delete as applicable*].
The requirements of the order are as follows:

[*insert person's name*] shall for a period of [*insert length of requirement*] beginning with the date of the order comply with such requirements as are listed in the Schedule to the order.

[*insert person's name*] shall for a concurrent period of [*insert length of requirement*] not exceeding three months attend a counselling or guidance programme as directed by the responsible officer.

[[*insert person's name*] shall on [*insert dates*] attend a residential course at [*insert address*] as directed by the responsible officer. The court is satisfied that the requirements of section 8(7A) of the 1998 Act have been met.]

[(*In the event that the child/young person is under 16.*) The court has complied with its duties under section 9(2) of the 1998 Act and has obtained and considered information about the child's/young person's family circumstances, and the likely effect of the order on those circumstances.]

The court has complied with its duties under section 9(3) to 9(7) of the 1998 Act, and has explained to the person(s) named above the effect of the order and its requirements, what may happen if he/she/they fail(s) to comply with these requirements, and that the court has power to review the order on the application of the person(s) named above or the responsible officer.

Justice of the Peace
[or By order of the Court,
Clerk of the Court]

SCHEDULE

Any requirement(s) imposed by the court under section 8(4)(a) and (b) of the 1998 Act should be listed here.

SCHEDULE 6

Rule 8

Parenting Order (Powers of Criminal Courts (Sentencing) Act 2000, Schedule 1, paragraph 9D)

Magistrates' Court
(Code)

Date: . . . .

Person(s) named in order: . . . .

Age(s): . . . . years (if under 18)

. . . . years (if under 18)

Address(es): . . . .

Child or young person: . . . .

Applicant Youth Offender Panel: . . . .

Responsible officer: . . . .

[*insert parent's name*] of [*insert address*], the parent of [*insert name of child or young person*], has failed without reasonable excuse to comply with the order made under section 20 of the Powers of Criminal Courts (Sentencing) Act 2000 (the '2000 Act') to attend meetings of the youth offender panel dated [*insert date(s)*], a copy of which is attached to this order.

Decision: Having complied with its duties under paragraph 9D of Schedule 1 to the 2000 Act, the court has decided to impose a parenting order on the person(s) named above because the court is satisfied that the order would be desirable in the interests of preventing the commission of any further offence by the child or young person.

The requirements of the order are as follows:

[*insert person's name*] shall for a period of [*insert length of requirement*] not exceeding twelve months beginning with the date of the order comply with such requirements as are listed in the Schedule to the order.

[*insert person's name*] shall for a concurrent period of [*insert length of requirement*] not exceeding three months attend a counselling or guidance programme as directed by the responsible officer.

[[*insert person's name*] shall on [*insert dates*] attend a residential course at [*insert address*] as directed by the responsible officer. The court is satisfied that the requirements of paragraph 9D(5) of Schedule 1 to the 2000 Act have been met.]

[(*In the event that the child/young person is under 16.*) The court has complied with its duties under paragraph 9D(6) of Schedule 1 to the 2000 Act and has obtained and considered information about the child's/young person's family circumstances, and the likely effect of the order on those circumstances.]

The court has complied with its duties under paragraph 9D(7) of Schedule 1 to the 2000 Act, and has explained to the person(s) named above the effect of the order and its requirements, what may happen if he/she/they fail(s) to comply with these requirements (as set out in section 9(7) of the Crime and Disorder Act 1998), and that the court has power (under section 9(5) of the Crime and Disorder Act 1998) to review the order on the application of the person(s) named above or the responsible officer.

Justice of the Peace
[or By order of the Court,
Clerk of the Court]

SCHEDULE

Any requirement(s) imposed by the court under paragraph 9D(2) of Schedule 1 to the 2000 Act should be listed here.

THE ANTI-SOCIAL BEHAVIOUR ACT 2003 (COMMENCEMENT NO 2) ORDER 2004, SI 2004/690

In exercise of the powers conferred upon him by section 93 of the Anti-social Behaviour Act 2003, the Secretary of State hereby makes the following Order:

1. This Order may be cited as the Anti-social Behaviour Act 2003 (Commencement No 2) Order 2004.

2. The following provisions of the Anti-social Behaviour Act 2003 shall come into force on 31st March 2004—

(a) in Part 6 (the environment)—

(i) section 46 (powers of police civilians); and

(ii) section 54 (sale of aerosol paint to children);

(b) in Part 9 (miscellaneous powers)—

(i) section 85(4) to the extent not already in force, (9), (10) and (11) (anti-social behaviour orders);

(ii) section 85(5) and (6) in so far as they relate to persons aged 18 or over (anti-social behaviour orders);

(iii) section 86(1), (2) and (3) to the extent not already in force (certain orders made on conviction of offences); and

(iv) section 89(5) (extension of powers of community support officers etc);

(c) in Part 10 (general)—

(i) section 92 (repeals) in so far as it relates to the entry in Schedule 3 in paragraph (ii) below; and

(ii) the entry in Schedule 3 relating to the Noise Act 1996.

3. The following provisions of Part 6 (the environment) of the Anti-social Behaviour Act 2003 shall come into force on 31st March 2004 in England only—

(a) section 40 (closure of noisy premises);

(b) section 41 (closure of noisy premises: supplemental);

(c) section 42 (dealing with noise at night);

(d) section 43 (penalty notices for graffiti and fly-posting);

(e) section 44 (meaning of relevant offence);

(f) section 45 (penalty receipts);

(g) section 47 (interpretation etc);

(h) section 55 (unlawfully deposited waste etc); and

(i) section 56 (extension of litter authority powers to take remedial action).

4.—(1) The following provisions of Part 6 (the environment) of the Anti-social Behaviour Act 2003 shall come into force in the areas of the local authorities in England specified in paragraph (2) below on 31st March 2004—

(a) section 48 (graffiti removal notices);

(b) section 49 (recovery of expenditure);

(c) section 50 (guidance);

(d) section 51 (appeals); and

(e) section 52 (exemption from liability in relation to graffiti removal notices).

(2) The following local authorities are specified for the purposes of paragraph (1) above—

(a) Barnsley Metropolitan Borough Council;
(b) Bristol City Council;
(c) Cambridge City Council;
(d) Dartford Borough Council;
(e) Doncaster Metropolitan Borough Council;
(f) Epping Forest District Council;
(g) Kirklees Metropolitan Borough Council;
(h) London Borough of Merton;
(i) London Borough of Westminster;
(j) Northampton Borough Council;
(k) Southampton City Council; and
(l) Wansbeck District Council.

APPENDIX 3

Guidance

ANTI-SOCIAL BEHAVIOUR ACT 2003
PART ONE, SECTION 1–11[1]

Closure of Premises used in connection with the production, supply or use of Class A drugs and associated with the occurrence of disorder or serious nuisance

Notes of Guidance: Premises where drugs used unlawfully

1. Introduction

This guidance is designed principally for:

- The courts
- The police

Whilst these are essentially police powers, they should be used in consultation with the local authority; and in the context of the problem as set out in paragraph 1.1 below, as part of the discharge of their responsibilities as members of Crime and Disorder Reduction Partnerships under the Crime and Disorder Act 1998. This guidance is thus also directly relevant to the local authority as statutory partners in tackling community safety, and as such working with the police in tackling drug crime problems. It also addresses the requirement placed on the police to consult them in the use of the powers. It is also directly relevant to local housing authorities, Registered Social Landlords, housing advice providers, drug services and legal advice providers, each of whom are affected by their application.

This guidance relates to the provisions contained in Part 1 of the Anti-Social Behaviour Act 2003 (Premises where drugs used unlawfully) and is designed to help those who are responsible for the exercise of those powers to:

[1] Available at *www.drugs.gov.uk/ReportsandPublications/Communities/1074606449*.

—Use the powers effectively and efficiently
—See the use of the powers in the broader context of tackling drug problems
—Understand the implications of the powers as they relate to affected persons and the communities in which they occur

These powers are available for England and Wales only and the guidance here is designed for use in those two countries. It may however be of interest in the management of similar situations in Scotland and Northern Ireland.

The powers set out here should be used in the context of much wider action to tackle the problem of drugs, and in the context of other powers, closely related, which are available under civil or criminal law.

These powers are designed to enable the police to close premises from which Class A drugs are produced, used or supplied and which are associated with disorder or serious nuisance. The powers have been designed to allow police forces to take rapid and effective action against a specific form of drug activity which causes great harm to communities.

1.1. The intention of the new powers

This power has been created in order to allow police forces, working in consultation with Local Authorities, to tackle 'crack houses' and other locations which cause disorder or serious nuisance to the local community through association with Class A drugs. The supply and use of drugs from residential properties has emerged as a major cause of harm to communities and has a negative impact on community life, regeneration and social capital. The powers created offer a real opportunity to act swiftly and decisively to control these problems. Whilst premises from which crack is sold and used have been the greatest single example of such harm, the intention is that these powers are used wherever Class A drugs are accompanied by problems of disorder or serious nuisance.

This guidance is issued by the Home Office to assist with the use of this power and has been written by the Drug Strategy Directorate. For further information or advice on certain aspects of the power please contact:

Jacob Hawkins
Policy Advisor
Drug Strategy Directorate
Home Office
jacob.hawkins@homeoffice.gsi.gov.uk

For specific advice on Crack Cocaine Policy please contact:

Michael Murray
Crack Cocaine Policy Advisor
Drug Strategy Directorate
Home Office
michael.murray3@homeoffice.gsi.gov.uk

2. Definition of Terms

2.1. The drugs covered

This power covers Class A drugs as defined by the Misuse of Drugs Act 1971. A complete list of Class A controlled drugs as prescribed by the Misuse of Drugs Act (MDA) can be found at Annex A. For the purposes of this power some examples and how it could be used against them are listed here:

Principal Drugs involved	Classification under the MDA	How the power could be applied
Cocaine Crack Cocaine Heroin Ecstasy	Class A	Against Production, Supply or Use
The following drugs may be found but are not subject to the power to close premises		
Amphetamines	Class B	No power under this Act where these drugs only are involved but MDA powers may be used to act against production, supply or possession
Cannabis	Class C	No power where only cannabis is involved—Cannabis is however specifically included in Section 8 of the Misuse of Drugs Act; and other MDA action for production, supply or possession offences may be applied

It should be noted that whilst simultaneous charges against persons for the production, supply or possession of Class A drugs may be brought at the same time as the application of this power they are not a precondition for the use of this power. It is not required to demonstrate that a specific individual is producing, supplying or in the possession of drugs, just that there are reasonable grounds for believing that such activities are occurring from the premises. This power is significantly different from the MDA powers as it applies to a place, not a person.

Similarly, it is not required to demonstrate by a forensic test that the drugs involved are Class A drugs, simply that there is reasonable grounds for believing that they are. However, where tests are available, they should be used to confirm the status of the drugs involved.

2.2. Production

The closure power will potentially be available where premises are used for the production of any Class A controlled drug. This will be particularly relevant in using the power against Crack Cocaine, and synthetic drugs such as Ecstasy, both of which are commonly produced in the UK in residential or other property. The intention is to enable rapid closure of premises used for commercial production of Class A drugs which may not otherwise be closed for the supply or use of the drug. For example, crack is often produced or 'cooked' in a separate venue from where it is sold. Where there is no evidence of the use or sale of crack but clear evidence of the production and disorder or serious nuisance arising from persons using the property, then the power can be used.

2.3. Supply

The closure power will potentially be available where premises are used for the supply of any Class A controlled drug. Gathering sufficient evidence to prosecute individuals for supply in closed settings such as 'crack houses' can be very difficult to achieve. Thus this power can be used to close the premises on the basis of reasonable grounds for believing there is supply, confirmed by the presence of drugs and drug paraphernalia amongst other evidence. These powers are intended to be used against a place, not a specific person. It is not necessary to the success of the closure procedure to bring charges against any specific person for the supply of a controlled drug.

2.4. Use

The closure power will potentially be available where any Class A controlled drug is used. The inclusion of use is not an attempt to further criminalise a person's *use* of drugs in the sense of their consumption or ingestion. The power is suitable for those circumstances where *use*, rather than production or supply, is related to disorder or serious nuisance, and those circumstances where proving production, supply or possession is difficult. It is the *use* of drugs which is required to be identified, rather than their *possession*, as is covered by the MDA. The premises cannot be closed simply because drugs are used without disorder or serious nuisance. The court will have to decide whether the evidence points to there being production, supply or use of drugs on the premises. It is not required to charge any person with possession of Class A drugs to confirm the use of such drugs in the premises but all evidence will assist in gaining a Closure Order.

2.5. Disorder or Serious Nuisance

2.5.1. These terms are not currently defined in law. It will be up to the courts to define these terms. In all cases of the use of this power it is required to demonstrate disorder or serious nuisance is associated with the use of the premises. When a Superintendent assesses the need for the issue of a Closure Notice he or she has to have reasonable grounds for believing there is disorder or serious nuisance associated with the premises. It does not need to be demonstrated that the disorder or serious nuisance is associated or resultant from the drug use, production or supply, simply that both are present at the same premises.

2.5.2. Problems which may constitute disorder or serious nuisance related to the premises are outlined below. The following suggestions should act as a guideline as to the level of nuisance to be considered serious in this context:

- Intimidating and threatening behaviour towards residents
- A significant increase in crime in the immediate area surrounding the accommodation
- The presence or discharge of a firearm in or adjacent to the premises
- Significant problems with prostitution
- Sexual acts being committed in public
- Consistent need to collect and dispose of drugs paraphernalia and other dangerous items
- Violent offences and crime being committed on or in the vicinity of the premises
- High numbers of people entering and leaving the premises over a 24 hour period and the resultant disruption they cause to residents
- Noise—constant/intrusive noise—excessive noise at all hours associated with visitors to the property

2.5.3. Serious nuisance is often demonstrated by accounts from neighbours and/or professional witnesses of the distress caused to the community by the activities of the premises. The accounts should provide an objective basis for an assessment of the gravity of the problem. The accurate recording of events, over time, will also be very important to prove the sustained and intrusive nature of the disorder and serious nuisance.

2.5.4. Evidence of disorder or serious nuisance will often be available in the testimony of residents who feel terrorised, threatened and may fear to leave their houses. Professional witnesses may be appropriate.

2.5.5. In many cases disorder or serious nuisance will be similar to that defined by the Tort for public nuisance or common nuisance, which is proved to be of such degree or volume to disrupt people's lives to the extent that this can be considered to be 'disorder or serious nuisance'. Statutory nuisances such as noise from persons or machinery should be considered as they can impact upon neighbours' lives preventing sleep and the quiet enjoyment of the home.

2.6. The meaning of consultation for the purposes of the Act

(Clause 1, sub-section 2(a))

2.6.1. The purpose of consultation

The purpose of consultation is to seek the views of the local authority. Consideration should be given to those views when received, although there is no obligation as such on the police to accept them or act upon them. The requirement to consult the local authority, nor to an RSL if informed, does not give the authority any right to veto the service of a Notice.

2.6.2. Who should be consulted

The Act places an obligation on the police to consult with the local authority for the area in which the premises are situated before serving a notice. The local authority in England will be either a district council, a London borough council, a county council for an area for which there is no district council, the Common Council for the City of London or the Council of the Isles of Scilly. In Wales the local authority will be either a county council or a county borough council. The police may also wish to inform the relevant Registered Social Landlord (RSL) where they own or manage the premises concerned if this will not compromise the operation.

2.6.3. The appropriate point of notification is the office of the Chief Executive or Director of Housing in the local authority, and the same in the RSL, should they be informed. Local arrangements should dictate a reasonable time period in which this consultation should take place. This period would, however, be expected to be brief considering that the intention of the power is that it can be utilised quickly.

2.6.4. Though not strictly speaking consultation, the police may also benefit from working with the local authority in their housing or landlord role, or with the RSL where they are the landlord. It is important also to contact social services departments. In some instances the local authority will be responsible for housing but have no responsibility for social services. In such instances the police should consult the relevant social services authority separately and in single tier authorities they are advised to consult the social services department as well as housing departments.

2.6.5. It is important that local authorities are consulted at as early a stage as is practicable. The advantage of this sort of approach (both the statutory and informal consultation) is that it enables the police to involve the local authority or RSL in the following ways as appropriate to their function:

- By gaining their support for the operation, where possible
- By notifying them of the impending action in an attempt to ensure that the timing is appropriate
- By obtaining from them valuable information relating to the disorder or serious nuisance—particularly complaints from residents and information on collection of drugs paraphernalia
- By ensuring that the information about relevant advice providers for the closure notice is correct. Relevant advice providers are persons and organisations in the area that provide advice about housing and legal matters
- By enabling them to alert the housing department to the likely demands that may be made upon them if the magistrates' court makes the closure order

2.6.6. Through the consultation, notification can be given to the relevant RSL, and alerting other local authority services, such as childcare and social services, that may need to be given advance warning of potential demands to be made on their services. Additionally, the local authority or Registered Social Landlord, where they own the premises, may have a dedicated service or contractors essential to the process of securing and sealing the premises subject to the Closure Order who may need to be prepared. Such services may not usually be available out of hours for example.

2.6.7. There may also be others who could usefully be informed on a case by case basis, for example Private Sector landlords, but this is an operational issue dependent on the judgement of the authorising officer on the requirements of the individual case. They could, however, be many varying organisations or persons including local treatment and other housing services. Ascertaining if they have had contact with the premises or drug users frequenting it will assist in the use of the power and provision for persons from the premises.

2.6.8. The context for consultation

There should be arrangements in place for the overall strategic management of such premises and other problems of this type between the local authority and the police. These will form the context for any specific incident or location for which a closure order is required. Joint working such as this should be encouraged at all stages and close work with local authorities, and Registered Social Landlords as appropriate, in targeting areas where 'crack houses' have proved a problem, should result in dramatic falls in crime and considerable resident satisfaction. Such collaborative working in handling disorder of this type should be linked to an overall strategy including work on treatment, regeneration, and environmental work. The should be especially integrated with effective housing management of drug issues generally, as set out in the Home Office/DETR publication, 'Tackling Drugs in Rented Housing, a good practice guide' (2002). This should be organised through the Drug Action Team/Crime and Disorder Reduction Partnership and Local Strategic Partnership. In doing so, police action will be viewed as increasingly successful and civic renewal and community engagement encouraged. A sample protocol for the management of such behaviours is contained at Annex B.

2.7. The definition of premises

2.7.1. The Act defines 'premises' as including (a) any land or other place (whether enclosed or not); and (b) any outbuildings which are or are used as part of the premises. Any of the following are therefore included:

- Houses
- Flats
- Apartments
- Sheds
- Common areas adjacent to houses or flats
- Garages
- Factories
- Shops
- Pubs
- Clubs
- Public buildings
- Community centres or halls

2.7.2. In practice therefore, any type of structure or place where drugs are used, supplied or produced and where disorder or serious nuisance is occurring is covered. This includes such buildings as schools and hospitals. It would rarely be appropriate that the power be used against such premises although the senior officer in line with operational priorities has this discretion unless the specific premises or type of premises has been exempted by order of the Secretary of State. Upon commencement of the power no types or individual properties were currently exempted.

2.7.3. In theory the power could be used in relation to definable areas of a street or field or other land. However, the difficulty of securing such premises or areas means that the power is unlikely to be appropriate for these locations.

2.7.4. The premises can be a sub-section of a larger building, such as a single flat within a block, or a room within a hostel or bed and breakfast hotel, where the room or flat could be closed while access maintained to the rest of the building. The power can be used flexibly to the need of the individual case. The majority of problems of this type occur in rented residential accommodation.

2.8. The definition of an interested party

2.8.1. An interested party is an identifiable person with an interest in the premises on whom the police should attempt to serve a Closure Notice, if they can be identified. The police must take reasonable steps to identify those with an interest in the premises.

2.8.2. It is not possible to offer a precise definition of the term 'interested party'. The intention is to include as many people as possible who will be affected by the Closure Notice and subsequent Order.

2.8.3. Failure to serve a Notice, Order or Summons on an interested person cannot in any way invalidate the proceedings of the court if reasonable steps have been taken to identify them. Such a person could however raise the matter on appeal to the Crown Court.

3. The Closure Notice explained

3.1. The purpose of the Closure Notice

The Closure Notice alerts those using the property, those resident, the owner and any others with an interest who can be identified, of the intention to apply to the court for a Closure Order. It sends a clear message to the community that action is being taken against the premises, and informing drug dealers that their activities will no longer be tolerated. It gives notice that impending closure of the premises is being sought and details of what this entails. In many cases persons in these premises involved in drug related offending will have been previously warned of impending action, in an attempt to reform their behaviour, or may have been the subject of other law enforcement activity before any notice is served. It is, however, still essential that when the Closure Notice is served persons in or associated with the premises understand its meaning and that even at this point they have a chance to reform the behaviour associated with the premises. The notice is intended to encourage those who are not habitually resident to find alternative accommodation.

3.2. Requirements for the serving of the Notice

3.2.1. There is a requirement in the Act for the police to take reasonable steps to identify those with an interest, control or responsibility or who live in the premises before the Notice can be authorised. Where possible consultation with Local Authorities should have involved discussions and exchange of information relating to the identification of these persons.

3.2.2. The police are not required to *ensure* that all such persons, who may have an interest in the premises and who may suffer financial loss as a result of the closure, are notified prior to the Notice being issued. The Act requires 'reasonable steps' to have been taken. It may be the case that all such persons are difficult to trace and the delay required to identify them would remove the benefits of the Power. However, the Closure Notice must be served on any such person who is identifiable at the property or who appears to have an interest or to be affected by potential closure, who can be easily identified by immediate enquiries to the tenant or those resident, or neighbours; or through Local Authority records. The fixing of the Notice to the building is also intended to ensure the closure is publicised to anyone with an interest.

3.3. The effect of the Notice

3.3.1. It should be remembered that the Closure Notice in itself may on its own achieve the intended outcome of stopping the premises being used for the production, supply or use of Class A drugs and related disorder or serious nuisance. For this reason Closure Notices should be considered as part of strategic and tactical action against drug supply overseen at a senior level. For the initial 48-hour period before the Court considers the application it may provide immediate relief to the community.

3.3.2. It also creates offences, backed with the power of arrest, for any persons who do not habitually reside in the property, who enter or remain in the premises. The intention is to encourage all those not properly resident to leave at this point and relief to be obtained during the notice period. However, it allows for the tenant to stay whilst they arrange alternative accommodation.

3.3.3. Some persons occupying the property may need alternative accommodation and may seek housing advice. However, the direction as to how and where such advice may be obtained should be determined at a local level.

4. The Decision to Issue a Closure Notice

4.1. How a decision to issue a notice should be authorised

4.1.1. The decision to use the power must be taken by a senior police officer of Superintendent rank or above. He or she holds the appropriate overview of police action as a whole, enabling the decision to issue a Closure Notice to be made without compromising existing enforcement and intelligence operations. It is essential that this officer ensures that the correct consultation with the relevant local authority has occurred. The relevant local authority will be the authority for the area in which the premises are situated. The senior police officer may also decide that it is appropriate to inform the Registered Social Landlord where they own or manage the property concerned. In certain cases this may require that out of hours contact details are maintained.

4.1.2. The officer should authorise a Closure Notice in writing. But where this written consent is not immediately possible, oral authorisation is sufficient as long as it is confirmed in writing at the earliest possible opportunity, and in any case, before the court hearing. In order to authorise the service of the Closure Notice the authorising officer must be satisfied of the following:

- That there is reasonable suspicion of Class A drug production, supply or use occurring at the premises within the last 3 months

And

- That there is reasonable grounds for believing that the use of the premises was associated with disorder or serious nuisance

And

- That the relevant local authority has been consulted and where possible been given enough notice to put in place effective housing management solutions and prevent homelessness

And

- That reasonable steps have been taken to identify interested persons

4.1.3. In making this decision the officer should take into account:

- Whether the proposed actions will have the intended impact on the problem at hand
- The suitability of the powers, with all their implications
- The evidence about the level of disorder and nuisance and anti-social behaviour associated with the premises
- How this action is to be followed up ensuring the premises does not become re-occupied for similar purposes and how the Closure can be followed up as part of a Neighbourhood Policing plan
- The views of the relevant local authority
- Any other powers that may be more suitable or achieve the same result, without the need for the implications the closure power contains
- The availability of other powers which can be used alongside the power to support the overall aim of reduction of nuisance

4.1.4. The impact on the local community will need to be a crucial factor in deciding whether to seek closure. The police must ensure they have taken into account the views of local residents in planning any action against supply, but it is particularly important in these circumstances. The availability and willingness of persons to give evidence is likely to be a factor and the police should take into account what facilities and services are available to protect and support witnesses who may be subject to intimidation. Given this risk, the role of professional witnesses should be considered in gathering evidence against such a property. This work should be conducted in line with the Government's strategy to improve witness experience and confidence in the Criminal Justice System, '*A new deal for victims and witnesses*'.

4.1.5. The police are not required to have forensic proof of the types of drugs being used, produced or sold in the property prior to serving notice; simply that there is reasonable grounds for believing that these are Class A drugs. However, where such tests are available they should be used.

4.2. Other potential powers

There are a variety of other powers that may be suitable for dealing with situations of this type. The officer is not required to demonstrate that he or she has considered all these options before authorising the issue of a Closure Notice, but it is a matter of good practice to consider them. If other powers can be used as an alternative to the displacement that might result from the use of these powers, but achieve the same result, then these should be seriously considered. These options are attached as Annex E as guidance to what can be done. The implications of serving the order on vulnerable persons, and thus what alternative solutions might be better applied in some circumstances, is relevant here.

5. Serving and Enforcing a Closure Notice

5.1. The contents of the Notice

The Closure Notice must contain the following information:

- A Closure Order is being sought.
- Only the owner or persons who are habitually resident at the premises may now enter the building.
- The date, time and place at which an application for a Closure Order will be considered.
- An explanation of what will happen should a Closure Order be granted—in particular that there will be no further entry to the premises and it will be totally sealed. If the premises are residential then the occupier will be forced to find alternative accommodation.
- An explanation that any person who does enter the premises who is not the owner or habitually resident there commits an offence and can be arrested.
- Information on relevant advice providers who will be able to assist in relation to housing and legal matters. This will depend on the particular arrangements in place for the area, and should be agreed with the relevant local authority as part of the consultation. Advice providers are likely to be the Housing Advice Centre or point of contact for applications for homeless persons, the Citizens Advice Bureaux and the Local Law Centre. Information on help with drugs and leaving sex work is also desirable.

5.2. Whom the Notice should be served on

5.2.1. The notice must, where reasonably identified, be served on all those with an interest in the property, including residents (who may not be tenants but who live there nonetheless), the tenant and their dependants at the property; the owner or their representative; and persons affected through access to their property.

5.2.2. Identifying these persons need not delay the service of the Notice. Normal police information resources and information requests from the local authority in the area in which the premises are situated should identify the owner or occupier. As in all such circumstances partnership working and identification of routes of co-operation make for the best exchange of information. If this information simply identifies a letting agent, serving notice on them is acceptable. Service of the Closure Notice can be effected by the affixing of the Notice to the premises, but effort should also be made to give a copy of the Notice to any interested persons. Posting a notice is not desirable, due to the speed and effects of the Notice. However, if the owner or letting agent identified is not local, posting the Notice may be considered sufficient as the only practicable means.

5.3. The service of the Notice

5.3.1. It may be that the police may apply for a warrant to search the property and seek to bring charges against persons involved in the manufacture, supply or possession of drugs, at the same time as serving the Closure Notice. This may be entirely appropriate. However, it is not a requirement. The Closure Notice may be served by a police officer of any rank.

5.3.2. Entry to the property is not required to serve the Notice; it can be affixed outside or handed to the residents at the door with clear explanation of its nature and effect.

5.3.3. It will be for the police and the relevant local authority to decide the level of joint working on the service of the Closure Notice. In some areas, where it is considered safe to do so, it may be appropriate for the police to be accompanied by the relevant local authority or RSL officer.

5.4. Dealing with those in the premises

5.4.1. Once served, those at a premises affected by the Closure Notice may well choose to leave voluntarily. Those who habitually reside there should be advised to seek alternative accommodation. If they have failed to do so themselves, they should be referred to the Closure Notice or the advice providers referred to in the Closure Notice, regarding help with accommodation, drug problems, leaving the sex trade, and obtaining legal assistance. It may still be possible for those resident to change the way the premises are used. However, it is an arrestable offence for a person who does not normally live at the premises or is not the owner to continue to reside at or enter the property during the Closure Notice period.

5.4.2. The extent to which this power of arrest is used is the decision of the officer in charge based on an assessment of the likelihood of continued disorder or serious nuisance. The application of this power is useful if by it, drug users, where their gathering together has caused nuisance, are removed from the house. If arrest serves this purpose it should be used. Use of the power may be appropriate as a tool in acting against persons identified through service of notice where intelligence suggests they have engagement in supply or other criminal matters.

5.4.3. It is also an offence to obstruct a police officer serving the Closure Notice. This is also an arrestable offence.

5.5. The welfare of those to be removed from a premises

There will be heightened concerns and hence partnership action needed when the closure of a premises which may be home to a family, and especially children, is sought. In these cases it is essential that early contact is made with social services as well as the local authority, education and housing authorities in order that the effects of closure are mitigated for such vulnerable persons. Where women are removed from premises during closure childcare issues may not be immediately apparent due to these children being in the temporary care of members of the family. In this case contact with these families where identified by social services, would be appropriate.

6. The Magistrates' Court

6.1. The Hearing

6.1.1. The key issue that will need to be demonstrated is that both disorder or serious nuisance and the use, production or supply of Class A drugs are both present. Most care should be undertaken to ensure that convincing evidence of this arising or being directly associated with the premises is presented.

6.1.2. The court is asked to decide whether the making of the order is necessary to prevent the occurrence of disorder or serious nuisance. The court may also wish to consider whether alternative methods would be more appropriate, and what other action might have been attempted, which is why the history of action and considered action against the premises and its occupants may be important. It is not a requirement for the court to have evidence that these other methods have been tried first, or exhausted, nor need they have been tried, but the court may feel that other powers have more likelihood of achieving control and prevent occurrence of serious nuisance or disorder more effectively, and as a result the order need not be made.

6.1.3. Police must agree with court staff a date, time and place for a hearing, prior to the service of the Closure Notice. The date, time and place of the hearing must be on the face of the Closure Notice when it is served no more than 48 hours prior to that date. There are no requirements for specific magistrates to hear the case.

6.1.4. Prior to the hearing the police should ensure that the evidence to be presented is in good order. Support for community witnesses at the court will be essential to enable them to give evidence.

6.1.5. The court is asked in the Act to decide whether there is a civil standard of proof that at the premises subject to the Closure Notice there is

a) the unlawful production, supply or use of Class A controlled drugs
b) serious nuisance or disorder
c) that closure is necessary to prevent the recurrence of such disorder or serious nuisance for the length of the order.

6.1.6. At the court hearing the evidence should be presented by the police and supported, if appropriate, by evidence from the local authority, to establish the grounds for believing that the house is associated with disorder or serious nuisance related to Class A drugs. As indicated, this need be no more than reasonable grounds for believing that these drugs and behaviours are involved. It is not required that there are charges relating to drugs offences; however, witness testimonies that drugs are being sold in the house, or that they have heard strong report of the same, or that the house is frequented actively by drug users are appropriate. Evidence of use of drugs is more likely to be available even if there is difficulty demonstrating supply or production. As said, the simple presence of controlled Class A drugs, rather than the proven possession by any named individual, is all that is required to demonstrate that this criterion is met.

6.1.7. As stated above, the court is not required to have forensic proof that the drugs being sold, used or produced are Class A drugs. A forensic test that would be required for determining criminal responsibility for such drugs under the MDA may take longer than 48 hours to complete. Given that this criminal level of proof is not required it is undesirable that the court adjourns proceedings until forensic tests are completed. Simpler tests are available which will give an indication of the drug involved. Whilst such tests are not considered sufficient proof of the drug involved for the purposes of conviction under the MDA, they have been considered suitable by courts for the purposes of assessing bail under that legislation. Accordingly, whilst such tests are not required by the court in handling these cases, Police may feel that they add some weight in preparing evidence for the court, and so could be considered.

6.1.8. The court is not asked to decide on the relative merits of applying the power to certain types of premises rather than others. The court is simply asked to decide whether the use of the power in the specific circumstances involved is necessary to prevent the occurrence of the behaviour (Clause 2, subsection 3). The court must make its decision upon the balance of probabilities and no property is exempt unless it has been made exempt by order of the Secretary of State. Therefore, the status of the property in itself is not a necessary consideration of the court, unless the police have taken action against exempted premises.

6.2. Dealing with the arguments presented against closure

6.2.1. The owner of the premises, or any person who has an interest or is affected, may contest the making of an Order.

6.2.2. The court will wish to hear why the order should not be made. The Act does not specify what reasons there should be for not making the order. This will be for the court to decide in each case. Possible reasons include:

- The landlord, owner or tenant has just been appraised of the situation, and can demonstrate that effective action is being taken to deal with it; or
- There is evidence that disputes the evidence presented by the police, or evidence that cannot be presented at this time but which will be presented subsequently, thus presenting a case for adjournment.

The court operates on a civil rather than a criminal standard of proof (i.e. balance of probabilities). It is not required to have demonstrated the same burden of proof required under the Misuse of Drugs Act to enable conviction of persons for relevant drugs offences.

6.2.3. The court can of course decide that notwithstanding the owner or landlord's contention that they will address the problem, that a closure order should still be made, whilst they attempt to do so. If they believe they can subsequently demonstrate, sooner than the specified order period, that the problem has been successfully addressed, then an application can be made to the court for the order to be revoked. The court must then make an assessment of the capability or willingness of the landlord to be able to do so.

6.2.4. Hence whilst the court nominally has three options, denial of the application, adjournment or closure, in practice the ability to vary the length of the order gives the court flexibility to deal with different circumstances where a shorter order may be appropriate, bring immediate relief whilst the landlord and police deal with the problem, but not leading to extended and costly closure.

6.2.5. The maximum length of an order is 3 months with possibility of further extension to total not more than 6. The length of the order should reflect the circumstances above and the desire to bring the property back into management as quickly as possible—see also Appeals, Section 10.3.

6.3. Dealing with arguments for adjournment

6.3.1. The court can defer hearing of the application for the order by adjournment for 14 days to allow those persons to prepare their case.

6.3.2. It is not the intention that all cases should be routinely adjourned. This would defeat the object of the power, which is speed. The court must decide whether an adjournment is needed. Anyone seeking an adjournment must demonstrate reasonable grounds why it is needed.

6.3.3. The arguments for an adjournment will be similar to those above for a closure order not to be made. However, in certain circumstances the court may believe that an adjournment, during which the powers of the Closure Notice continue, is the best way to ensure that the activities of the premises are controlled and other action to resolve the problems with the premises given the correct impetus.

7. The Closure Order explained

Part 1 Clauses 3–5 define the Closure Order and how it is used.

7.1. The effect of the Closure Order

7.1.1. The closure order gives a power to close a property completely and remove access by any persons, even those with rights of abode or ownership, except where they are allowed to enter the property under the supervision or direction or permission of the police or the court. The order allows for a property to be sealed, closed, and removed from public use for the period of the order. The Closure Order comes into force immediately the court makes the order.

7.1.2. Breach of the Closure Order is an offence and persons can be arrested if they enter the building.

7.2. Enforcing a Closure Order

7.2.1. As soon as a Closure Order is granted by the courts it should be enforced. This means the premises in question can be cleared of all persons present including residents and those with an interest in the property who may have remained after the service of the Closure Notice.

The police can use reasonable force to enter and seal a property. This is to allow removal of defences that are often built into such premises and to seal the premises with the required temporary building work or shutters.

7.2.2. It may be that the service of the Notice did not involve entering the premises. The process of entering to enforce the Order should be treated with extreme caution. Whilst in many cases the occupants will already have left, in others they may be resistant to leaving. They may also be armed. Therefore the operation should be undertaken following a risk assessment reflecting the strong linkage between Class A drugs, guns and violence. On occasion, firearms support may be required. If this is the case, and bearing in mind that obtaining evidence for charges related to supply could be possible, the serving of the Order could require a substantial operational support. Authorised persons such as local authority workers, maintenance staff, utility persons or Housing Officers should not be present until any safety issues have been addressed and the property cleared.

7.2.3. Large quantities of drugs or money may be securely hidden in the premises and in some cases dealers may return to gather these possessions or to recommence their business. Both a thorough search should be undertaken and subsequently, strong means of property sealing applied.

7.3. Dealing with those still occupying the premises

7.3.1. Those found contravening the Closure Order can be arrested, as officers on the scene feel is appropriate on the basis of the evidence available. Those inside or residing are likely to fall into these groups:

- The tenant/owner. They may be involved in supply of drugs, but they are as likely to be a vulnerable person, who may have social care and housing needs, related to mental health, age or some other cause, and whilst not involved in supply, may be involved in the use of drugs
- Dependants of the dealer/tenant, including children, all of whom will have a housing need, and some of whom may need to be taken into care
- Drug users who happen to be there, some of whom may have nowhere to go, and have profound drug needs
- Sex workers, who could have problems of vulnerability, dependency and lack of shelter
- Other criminal associates of those involved in the production, supply or use of Class A drugs

These are only examples of persons likely to be found. The only persons who are able to enter the premises following the Closure Order are police officers or persons authorised by the chief police officer or those persons granted access by the court. (See Section 9.)

7.3.2. Some of these persons may be able to be charged with offences under the MDA. However, it is quite probable that the only obvious charge is possession of small personal quantities of crack, heroin or Class B or C drugs, which of course may also be found at the property. In some cases such charges will be appropriate; in other cases the bringing of such charges could be counter-productive. Such evidence as is obtained is irrelevant to the continuation of the Order but may be relevant to any subsequent appeal or extension or any other action which could also be applied to control the behaviour of individuals, such as under section 222 of the Local Government Act 1972. All of the users should have access to an arrest referral worker whether formally arrested or not. In practice this may also be a valuable opportunity to provide exit strategies for sex workers or others who are identified through the process. The provision of such services is very valuable in response to closure of this type. The availability of treatment when a house is closed is quite crucial and if possible residential based programmes should be available to displaced users.

7.3.3. There are real advantages in developing systems and protocols between the police, drug services and local authorities and social landlords before the issue of a Closure Notice to cope with the possible displacement from the closure, particularly in cases of 'crack houses' (an example of such a protocol is contained as annex B below). These should cover issues determining what would go in the Closure Notice, advice to those affected by the Notice, practical arrangements for managing situations of this type, affected vulnerable persons, handling any homelessness and any housing, drugs and legal advice that might be needed.

7.3.4. Good liaison, protocols and systems can also help to take advantage of the likelihood that users will experience a drought in the supply of their drugs and hence be more ready to enter treatment. Similarly for others who are arrested, they can provide an opportunity for assessment and appropriate service allocation by an Arrest Referral Worker.

7.3.5. The local authority will have been informed of the service of the order. This enables the local authority to develop appropriate mechanisms for those who may need alternative accommodation.

The following are matters in which the local authority may be concerned:

- Housing advice services
- Cleaning services to remove paraphernalia
- Building maintenance to assess the condition of the premises
- Securing the premises, where they are part of their own housing stock, through the imposition of metal window blinds, secure doors and any other measures necessary to prevent further access to the premises
- Local Authority Supporting People Programmes
- Tenancy management
- Removal of possessions to future addresses

7.3.6. The police may also wish to ensure that the drug services and sex work projects are informed of the closure as well as ensuring the availability of arrest referral services.

7.3.7. The landlord will also need to decide what to do in relation to any tenancy or other rights of abode any person residing at the property may have. When an order is made it has no impact on ownership or tenancy or other rights to the property. If a landlord wishes to obtain possession of the premises or otherwise recover it to be re-allocated to another occupant they will need to follow the appropriate circumstances in each case.

7.3.8. It is possible that the tenant or similar will simply give up their rights to the property. If they have been exploited and had their house taken over by the dealer, then they may choose to surrender their rights and seek alternative accommodation. They may choose to retain their tenancy. In these circumstances the local authority or other landlord shall have to decide how it intends to handle this situation. Where the local authority does re-house any person displaced by such orders, which will be decided on a case by case basis, then they may have to consider paying rent on two properties. How this can be achieved is covered in separate advice provided directly to local authorities from ODPM. The protocol contained at annex B also covers this issue.

8. Management of a Closure Order

8.1. Issues during closure

8.1.1. It is important that following the closure, the empty premises do not cause greater problems than before the Closure Order was made, such as through vandalism or being taken over illegally—including by the very persons who have been displaced. They should continue to be monitored and the sealing maintained in good order. It will not be required to obtain another order to re-close the building as the original one still applies until the court decides.

8.1.2. The power to close premises can be a genuine quick win with communities who can see the direct consequences of information they may have supplied. It is essential that this trust is built on, creating suitable channels for the provision of intelligence on individuals involved in drug supply, and its associated crime and violence, from the community. The Police and the local authority, where it is the landlord, and Registered Social Landlords if appropriate, should work to build on the momentum created by closure to build further trust through good community liaison. The use of this time for good work on drugs to be kick-started is not to be under-estimated.

8.2. Special considerations for non-residential premises

8.2.1. As this power is available for use against any premises where there is the production, supply or use of Class A drugs and serious nuisance or disorder all premises which fall into this category can be considered. Warehouses or business premises for example can be closed if subject to a Closure Order. Closure would have a dramatic effect on the viability of a business, especially a small one and hence can be used as a very effective incentive to reform where this is necessary.

8.2.2. Licensed premises are the main group other than residential premises where it is likely that this power could be used. As with any use of this power, especially against businesses, it is likely that other powers and the threat of the use of this power will be exhausted first. They fall into two groups: pubs and bars, and nightclubs or dance venues, which have been associated at times with Class A drug use such as ecstasy and cocaine. In the case of licensed premises such as clubs where there are Class A drug problems this power could be used as part of recommended policing action to control such premises, especially where the threat of closure by withdrawal of a licence to sell alcohol has been tried. The use of these powers against clubs of this type should be considered within the context of published guidance on their management contained in 'Safer Clubbing' (Home Office 2002). Other powers are also available to close licensed premises such as pubs where the police can demonstrate that disorder is occurring and which provide an alternative route using powers under the Licensing Act 2003.

9. Access during a Closure Order

9.1. This is covered by two Clauses: 3 and 7. The intention of section 7 is to allow persons access to areas such as common parts or stairwells. This section permits the variation of the closure order to allow them access to those common areas.

9.2. Clause 3 allows for the police or persons nominated by the police to conduct building work via access to the building. It enables the police to authorise any non-police persons to enter the premises. This should not be the occupier or other persons unless there are very good grounds for doing so, and such persons should be accompanied if they are permitted, as they may be complicit in the criminal behaviour involved; unless the owner is the local authority or other responsible authority.

10. Extension, Appeals and Discharge of Orders

10.1. The effect of these clauses

The Act entitles any persons on whom a Closure Notice was served, as well as any person who has an interest in the closed premises, to appeal against the making or extension of a Closure Order. An appeal may also be brought either by a police constable or by a local authority against the refusal to make or extend an order. Such appeals must be made to the Crown Court within 21 days of the initial decision. The Act also allows for any of the persons referred to here to seek to have the closure order discharged by a justice of the peace.

10.2. Extension

10.2.1. It is undesirable that the extension of a Closure Order after three months will be a routine occurrence. There are many disadvantages in leaving properties empty for an extended period, and few advantages. Only where there are real concerns that the property will return to its former use should an extension be made.

10.2.2. The police are the only body or person who may seek the extension of the closure order. As with Closure Notices, this must be first authorised by a senior officer, after consultation with the relevant local authority and tests are the same as those for the issue of a Closure Notice. Where this route is taken it should only be used where more time is needed to change the nature of the premises or to allow proceedings for its compulsory purchase, for example, to be completed. Where the police had involved the relevant social landlord in the issue of the Closure Notice, they may wish to involve them again at this stage.

10.2.3. In the case of buildings not occupied, which have been taken over illegally, then closed by order and which otherwise stand empty, there may be a risk that once they are unsealed, the dealers will return. This is a decision for the court to make, but continuing emptiness through extension on the basis that there is a risk they may return to their former use is not productive. Good housing management rather than this action will help them return to productive use. The owners should be asked to show what would happen once the property is unsealed. It may be necessary to commence compulsory purchase proceedings as soon as possible if these premises continue to pose risks of criminal activity.

10.2.4. Non-residential properties or owner occupied property will need separate handling. In some of these cases the owner might have been charged with a supply offence, and may later be sent to prison, or any other sentence. In these cases it is difficult to predict what may happen if the owner returns. However, the closure period cannot be decided with a regard to the possible length of sentence as this case will be heard far later than the closure hearing. An appeal may come from a person awaiting trial for supply; or as is more likely, a landlord who wishes to see the property returned to them sooner, who has no proven connection to the behaviour. In such cases the police may apply for an extension.

10.3. Appeal

The Crown Court, in hearing an appeal, shall judge each case on its merits. The Act does not define the grounds on which an appeal shall be granted; simply that the court must make an appropriate order. It may be the case that the appeal case rests on the basis that the problem is now under control rather than that the Order should never have been made. The Court shall have to decide on the basis of such factors as:

- The case made by the police for the Closure Order to continue and the evidence presented that continuance of the order is required to prevent re-occurrence of disorder or serious nuisance
- The evidence that the problem is now under control, and
- The arguments presented that the original decision was wrong

10.4. Discharge of a Closure Order

10.4.1. The police or local authority may wish to have the Order discharged before 3 months expires. This is completely desirable where the problem has been satisfactorily addressed. In relation to discharge, the court must decide that the order is no longer necessary to prevent the occurrence of disorder or serious nuisance. Wherever early discharge is possible it should be encouraged. No property should stay empty longer than is necessary. Where the tenant is prepared to surrender the tenancy immediately and those involved with drugs have disappeared, the property can be brought back into management almost straightaway and the order can be discharged more quickly. Other occupants with other housing status (such as licensees) may have their rights to occupation of the property taken away where this is felt appropriate, and again the property brought back into management more quickly and the order revoked. Other tenants may not give up their tenancy and the landlord may choose to act against them to recover it by obtaining a possession order, which may take some time, and which therefore may be a ground for continuing the closure. However, many local authorities have considerably speeded up eviction procedures through improved systems and procedures and these should be applied to recover properties of this type. Where this occurs the property can be safely discharged from an order and re-opened for letting more quickly.

10.4.2. The court may wish to be reassured that the owner or landlord is prepared and able to provide the required level of support needed to ensure the same pattern does not re-occur, before discharging the order. Certain properties are more prone to be taken over in this way due to their location, or the pattern of allocation of tenancies to vulnerable persons. The court must be reassured that if vulnerable persons are to be accommodated in this property—including perhaps the original vulnerable tenant whose house was taken over—then the right level of support should be available before this is considered to prevent events re-occurring. Such re-letting will require strong co-operation between the police and landlord depending on the circumstances. It may be that the original tenant wishes to return to the premises, but this will have to be thought through very carefully and the person offered considerable support. This is a matter for the court to consider as well as the housing body as discharge in these circumstances may be ill-advised without necessary support and good housing management practice.

10.4.3. However, where those with a legal right to occupy or those connected with the premises seek the discharge of the Order themselves, careful consideration must be given to the likelihood of the previous behaviour returning and what other solutions are being pursued by the police or local authority to control the behaviour.

10.4.4. In the case of private landlords or owners, the court will need to have many of the same reassurances, and in particular evidence that the private landlord will try to manage the situation more firmly. Only if the court is satisfied with their capability and willingness to get the problem under control should the order be discharged. Where the court has grounds for believing the landlord was culpably involved in the original behaviour, discharge of the order should rarely be granted.

11. Costs and Financial Compensation

11.1. Costs

The court may approve an order of costs against the owner for any expenses incurred by the police or local authority in enforcing the Closure Order. In order to gain these, the police or local authority must apply to the courts detailing their expenses. If the court decides that the owner of the premises is liable for these costs, for example for the mismanagement of the premises, then appropriate costs can be awarded.

11.2. Compensation

11.2.1. Persons who incur loss as a result of either a Closure Notice or Order can apply for recompense to the court. However, this ability to claim compensation has been tightly drawn so that whilst we do not wish to impose an extra burden upon the private rented sector it is also impossible for those persons involved in the behaviour in any way to gain compensation. It is in particular necessary for the owner of the premises to demonstrate that they took reasonable steps to prevent the unacceptable use of the premises.

Reasonable steps might include:

- Taking action to evict or otherwise control the behaviour of any such persons involved in such behaviour where those persons are their tenant or associates of their tenant
- Securing the property if such persons have been removed
- Co-operating with the police, and
- Demonstrating good standards of tenant management, such as understanding the needs of tenants, securing references where possible or visiting the property regularly

11.2.2. The court has discretion in deciding whether it is appropriate to make an order for compensation. It is not required to have demonstrable proof of the engagement of the applicant for compensation in the behaviour before refusing to grant them compensation. The court is simply asked to be satisfied that any person applying for compensation is not connected and took reasonable steps.

12. How This Action Must be Seen in the Wider Context

12.1. Whilst at the simplest level this guidance is about the specific way these powers should be used, in practice their use needs to be set in the context of the wider need to address drug problems in such settings.

Police action against houses given through these powers is designed to 'complete the loop' in action against serious criminality and drug supply. Thus it must be considered as part of a programme of action to attack criminal activities. It is a fact that the majority of times this power is used it will be in the context of a poor, low demand for housing area with high crime and drug misuse. Thus, to use it effectively and tackle the issues of displacement, action must be taken against Class A drug supply and related crime in a broader context.

12.2. One method of doing this is by designing a 'Management protocol' codifying joint police and local authority systems for managing this type of property (see annex B for a crack specific example). Even this systematic approach to the specific problem of 'crack houses' must be placed within wider initiatives to tackle the problems of social housing, which can create environments where such criminality and drug misuse is rife. Full co-operation between local authority and police is essential, not just on a case by case basis but strategically to tackle the relationship between drug problems and housing, especially in those areas of decline and disadvantage. As indicated, this is covered in detail in 'Tackling drugs and rented housing: a good practice guide' (Home Office/DETR 2002), but also in 'Tackling drugs as part of neighbourhood renewal' (Home Office 2003), from which useful guidance can be obtained. The use of this power should always be seen in that broader context of responsibilities placed upon local authorities in the Crime and Disorder Act 1998. This requires local authorities to work with partners to address crime issues of this type, and as a consequence engagement in planning and using this power is desirable in the context of these responsibilities.

12.3. Police action should where possible be co-ordinated with action against more than one 'crack house'—or a systematic campaign against the venues. Such action is outlined in the Home Office publication 'Disrupting Crack Markets'(HO, 2003) and takes the form of high visibility policing, designing out crime through neighbourhood renewal and environmental management, and the use of intelligence to challenge the security of dealers. Test purchase operations are indeed one of the most valuable tools in gathering evidence to secure the successful prosecution of Class A drug dealers.

12.4. The use of this power may have the effect of displacement of dealers from one house to another, to the street, or to mobile phone arrangements. Action to cover all of these is covered in the above publication. Any use of the powers contained in this Act must be seen in this larger context and planned accordingly.

12.5. Arresting a network of dealers has another effect and it is important to pick up on this. Services will be needed to respond to the addicts with reduced access to supplies, quickly. This will need to happen quickly, for otherwise other dealers will move into the area often increasing the problem of supply locally. Services should not be seen as simply treatment in its narrowest sense of medical or clinical interventions and any treatment service should be backed by housing arrangements and efforts to reintegrate users into society through work, counselling and support.

12.6. The help provided to the displaced tenant or vulnerable person, if they are not involved in supply of drugs, is crucial. It is all too easy for them to be intimidated by aggressive dealers again. Within the statutory framework the local authority may be unwilling to provide alternative accommodation to such persons due to arrears or debts as well as the history of neighbour problems. How they are accommodated, and with what support, is crucial. Support services may be available through the Supporting People programme or other appropriate schemes.

12.7. It is strongly recommended that a sub-group of the DAT or Crime and Disorder Reduction Partnership work with the police to plan strategic use of a wide range of powers, including these powers, to manage drug dealing of this sort. This may be best achieved through already existing Supply or Communities sub-groups. It should work as part of the network of groups set up under the National Intelligence Model. This should examine a wide range of policing responses, including under the MDA, alongside other powers that may be available, as detailed above, to control the behaviour of problematic residents. For example, intercepting illegally obtained utility supplies may be one way of tackling such behaviours. Housing management policies can ensure that vulnerable tenants receive the right kind of support from supporting people funded workers or treatment from drug agencies, or are housed using letting arrangements and forms of tenure which permit quick recovery of the premises in cases of difficulty. Appropriate strategic planning and management of public services can prevent the need for the use of powers of this sort, and place the use of these powers in a context which ensures that help is provided for the individuals involved and punishment for offending that occurs. It cannot be stressed enough how important it is for the police to work closely and strategically in planning action against supply with civil colleagues in the local authority and beyond. It is equally important for the local authority to look strategically at its allocation and housing management policies in relation to drugs. The guidance supplied by the Home Office and the then DTLR, 'Tackling Drugs in rented housing, a good practice guide' (HO/DTLR, 2002), is essential here.

Annex A: Class A Controlled Drugs Under the Misuse of Drugs Act

MISUSE OF DRUGS ACT 1971 (as amended—August 2003)

Schedule 2

Part I—Class A Drugs

1. The following substances and products, namely:—
   (a) Acetorphine.
   Alfentanil.
   Allylprodine.
   Alphacetylmethadol.
   Alphameprodine.
   Alphamethadol.
   Alphaprodine.
   Anileridine.
   Benzethidine.
   Benzylmorphine (3-benzylmorphine).

Betacetylmethadol.
Betameprodine.
Betamethadol.
Betaprodine.
Bezitramide.
Bufotenine.
Cannabinol, except where contained in cannabis or cannabis resin.
Cannabinol derivatives.
Carfentanil.
Clonitazene.
Coca leaf.
Cocaine.
Desomorphine.
Dextromoramide.
Diamorphine.
Diampromide.
Diethylthiambutene.
Difenoxin (1-(3-cyano-3,3-diphenylpropyl) -4-phenylpiperidine-4-carboxylic acid).
Dihydrocodeinone O-carboxymethyloxime.
Dihydroetorphine.
Dihydromorphine.
Dimenoxadole.
Dimepheptanol.
Dimethylthiambutene.
Dioxaphetyl butyrate.
Diphenoxylate.
Dipipanone.
Drotebanol (3,4-dimethoxy-17-methylmorphinan-6 beta, 14-diol).
Ecgonine, and any derivative of ecgonine which is convertible to ecgonine or to cocaine.
Ethylmethylthiambutene.
Eticyclidine.
Etonitazene.
Etorphine.
Etoxeridine.
Etryptamine.
Fentanyl.
Furethidine.
Hydrocodone.
Hydromorphinol.
Hydromorphone.
Hydroxypethidine.
Isomethadone.
Ketobemidone.
Levomethorphan.
Levomoramide.
Levophenacylmorphan.

Levorphanol.
Lofentanil.
Lysergamide.
Lysergide and other N-alkyl derivatives of lysergamide.
Mescaline.
Metazocine.
Methadone.
Methadyl acetate.
Methyldesorphine.
Methyldihydromorphine (6-methyldihydromorphine).
Metopon.
Morpheridine.
Morphine.
Morphine methobromide, morphine N-oxide and other pentavalent nitrogen morphine derivatives.
Myrophine.
Nicomorphine (3,6-dinicotinoyl-morphine).
Noracymethadol.
Norlevorphanol.
Normethadone.
Normorphine.
Norpipanone.
Opium—whether raw, prepared or medicinal.
Oxycodone.
Oxymorphone.
Pethidine.
Phenadoxone.
Phenampromide.
Phenazocine.
Phencyclidine.
Phenomorphan.
Phenoperidine.
Piminodine.
Piritramide.
Poppy-straw and concentrate of poppy-straw.
Proheptazine.
Properidine (1-methyl-4-phenyl-piperidine-4-carboxylic acid isopropyl ester).
Psilocin.
Racemethorphan.
Racemoramide.
Racemorphan.
Remifentanil.
Rolicyclidine.
Sufentanil.
Tenocylidine.
Thebacon.
Thebaine.
Tilidate.

Trimeperidine.
4-Bromo-2,5-dimethoxy-alpha-methylphenethylamine.
4-Cyano-2-dimethylamino-4, 4-diphenylbutane.
4-Cyano-1-methyl-4-phenyl-piperidine.
N,N-Diethyltryptamine.
N,N-Dimethyltryptamine.
2,5-Dimethoxy-alpha,4-dimethylphenethylamine.
N-Hydroxy-tenamphetamine.
1-Methyl-4-phenylpiperidine-4-carboxylic acid.
2-Methyl-3-morpholino-1, 1-diphenylpropanecarboxylic acid.
4-Methyl-aminorex.
4-Phenylpiperidine-4-carboxylic acid ethyl ester.

(b) any compound (not being a compound for the time being specified in sub-paragraph (a) above) structurally derived from tryptamine or from a ring-hydroxy tryptamine by substitution at the nitrogen atom of the sidechain with one or more alkyl substituents but no other substituent;

(ba) the following phenethylamine derivatives, namely:—
Allyl(a-methyl-3,4-methylenedioxyphenethyl)amine
2-Amino-1-(2,5-dimethoxy-4-methylphenyl)ethanol
2-Amino-1-(3,4-dimethoxyphenyl)ethanol
Benzyl(a-methyl-3,4-methylenedioxyphenethyl)amine
4-Bromo-b,2,5-trimethoxyphenethylamine
N-(4-sec-Butylthio-2,5-dimethoxyphenethyl)hydroxylamine
Cyclopropylmethyl(a-methyl-3,4-methylenedioxyphenethyl)amine
2-(4,7-Dimethoxy-2,3-dihydro-1H-indan-5-yl)ethylamine
2-(4,7-Dimethoxy-2,3-dihydro-1H-indan-5-yl)-1-methylethylamine
2-(2,5-Dimethoxy-4-methylphenyl)cyclopropylamine
2-(1,4-Dimethoxy-2-naphthyl)ethylamine
2-(1,4-Dimethoxy-2-naphthyl)-1-methylethylamine
N-(2,5-Dimethoxy-4-propylthiophenethyl)hydroxylamine
2-(1,4-Dimethoxy-5,6,7,8-tetrahydro-2-naphthyl)ethylamine
2-(1,4-Dimethoxy-5,6,7,8-tetrahydro-2-naphthyl)-1-methylethylamine
a,,a -Dimethyl-3,4-methylenedioxyphenethylamine
a,,a -Dimethyl-3,4-methylenedioxyphenethyl(methyl)amine
Dimethyl(a-methyl-3,4-methylenedioxyphenethyl)amine
N-(4-Ethylthio-2,5-dimethoxyphenethyl)hydroxylamine
4-Iodo-2,5-dimethoxy-a-methylphenethyl(dimethyl)amine
2-(1,4-Methano-5,8-dimethoxy-1,2,3,4-tetrahydro-6-naphthyl)ethylamine
2-(1,4-Methano-5,8-dimethoxy-1,2,3,4-tetrahydro-6-naphthyl)-1-methylethylamine
2-(5-Methoxy-2,2-dimethyl-2,3-dihydrobenzo[b]furan-6-yl)-1-methylethylamine
2-Methoxyethyl(a-methyl-3, 4-methylenedioxyphenethyl)amine
2-(5-Methoxy-2-methyl-2, 3-dihydrobenzo[b]furan-6-yl)-1-methylethylamine
b;-Methoxy-3,4-methylenedioxyphenethylamine
1-(3,4-Methylenedioxybenzyl)butyl(ethyl)amine
1-(3,4-Methylenedioxybenzyl)butyl(methyl)amine

2-(a-Methyl-3,4-methylenedioxyphenethylamino)ethanol
a-Methyl-3,4-methylenedioxyphenethyl(prop-2-ynyl)amine
N-Methyl-N-(a-methyl-3,4-methylenedioxyphenethyl)hydroxylamine
O-Methyl-N-(a-methyl-3,4-methylenedioxyphenethyl)hydroxylamine
a-Methyl-4-(methylthio)phenethylamine
b,3,4,5-Tetramethoxyphenethylamine
b,2,5-Trimethoxy-4-methylphenethylamine;]

(c) any compound (not being methoxyphenamine or a compound for the time being specified in sub-paragraph (a) above) structurally derived from phenethylamine, an N-alkylphenethylamine, alpha-methylphenethylamine, an N-alkyl-alpha-methylphenethylamine, alpha-ethylphenethylamine, or an N-alkyl-alpha-ethyl-phenethylamine by substitution in the ring to any extent with alkyl, alkoxy, alkylene-dioxy or halide substituents, whether or not further substituted in the ring by one or more other univalent substituents.]

(d) any compound (not being a compound for the time being specified in sub-paragraph (a) above) structurally derived from fentanyl by modification in any of the following ways, that is to say,—
   (i) by replacement of the phenyl portion of the phenethyl group by any heteromonocycle whether or not further substituted in the heterocycle;
   (ii) by substitution in the phenethyl group with alkyl, alkenyl, alkoxy, hydroxy, halogeno, haloalkyl, amino or nitro groups;
   (iii) by substitution in the piperidine ring with alkyl or alkenyl groups;
   (iv) by substitution in the aniline ring with alkyl, alkoxy, alkylenedioxy, halogeno or haloalkyl groups;
   (v) by substitution at the 4-position of the piperidine ring with any alkoxycarbonyl or alkoxyalkyl or acyloxy group;
   (vi) by replacement of the N-propionyl group by another acyl group;

(e) any compound (not being a compound for the time being specified in sub-paragraph (a) above) structurally derived from pethidine by modification in any of the following ways, that is to say,
   (i) by replacement of the 1-methyl group by an acyl, alkyl whether or not unsaturated, benzyl or phenethyl group, whether or not further substituted;
   (ii) by substitution in the piperidine ring with alkyl or alkenyl groups or with a propano bridge, whether or not further substituted;
   (iii) by substitution in the 4-phenyl ring with alkyl, alkoxy, aryloxy, halogeno or haloalkyl groups;
   (iv) by replacement of the 4-ethoxycarbonyl by any other alkoxycarbonyl or any alkoxyalkyl or acyloxy group;
   (v) by formation of an N-oxide or of a quaternary base.

2. Any stereoisomeric form of a substance for the time being specified in paragraph 1 above not being dextromethorphan or dextrorphan.
3. Any ester or ether of a substance for the time being specified in paragraph 1 or 2 above not being a substance for the time being specified in Part II of this Schedule.
4. Any salt of a substance for the time being specified in any of paragraphs 1 to 3 above.
5. Any preparation or other product containing a substance or product for the time being specified in any of paragraphs 1 to 4 above.
6. Any preparation designed for administration by injection which includes a substance or product for the time being specified in any of paragraphs 1 to 3 of Part II of this Schedule.

Annex B: The development of a local co-operation protocol for the closure of premises where there is the unlawful use of Class A drugs

When considering the use of this power it is recommended that appropriate local agreements and funding be first put in place for the co-ordinated and sustained action against all premises of this type in an area. Funding can possibly be secured from, for example, existing police funds, Building Safer Communities Funding, Anti Social Behaviour Funds or Neighbourhood Renewal Funds. It is recommended that each police force area agree its own protocols with partners most likely to be involved in their area.

Partners are then advised to establish a multi-agency working group which can perhaps be best co-ordinated through the local Drug Action Team or otherwise directly by the police force. It is essential that the police and local authority at the very least be represented on this body. It is also advisable that various arms of the local authority, such as Housing Management, Social Services, Education and others with an interest, be represented as broadly as possible in the planning phases at this group. Another important member of this group are drug services and homeless or drug charities or agencies who may provide much assistance in providing outcomes to those persons removed from a premises. Housing agencies and Registered Social Landlords should also be considered for inclusion in this group.

This group is best placed to agree a standard protocol and co-ordination of action against problem premises using the new power or those already in existence and described in the 'Notes of Guidance for Part One of the ASB Act 2004' (Home Office, 2004).

The objectives of this group should be to establish a Protocol:

- To utilise community and police intelligence to identify 'crack houses' and other premises requiring action at the earliest opportunity.
- To ensure a rapid response from all partner agencies to deal with a premises once identified.
- To minimise the risks of a premises being re-established after closure causing further nuisance to the community.
- To share best practice between partnership agencies in countering the supply and communal consumption of Class A drugs in a premises.
- To share information and establish procedures to best deal with vulnerable or displaced persons from a closed premises.
- To protect the most vulnerable communities and residents from drug related crime.

The Protocol should ensure that the police and the local authority have access to best practice examples and expert advice from those most experienced in dealing with 'crack houses' and other premises where there is the production, supply or use of a Class A drug.

The intention should be that within a limited period from a premises being identified, action can be agreed which may eventually lead to its closure by a multi-agency co-ordinated response.

Agencies should work to develop an information sharing protocol to reduce the possibility of vulnerable tenants being housed inappropriately in areas that may put them at greater risk of being targeted by drug dealers. Such a database will facilitate the action under the protocol.

The group should agree an optimum number of premises which can be realistically targeted in any one period.

The Protocol

1. Protocol 'Triggers' and Initial Action

1.1. Preliminary Factors

On a daily basis Police Officers, Housing Officers and Social Workers meet tenants with a drug dependency.

A Protocol should not be intended to replace the problem solving and enforcement activity characterised by these interactions.

Protocols should consider how to remove vulnerable or non-vulnerable tenants, occupiers or owners (henceforth called habitual residents; see paragraphs 2.3 and 2.4), both when other interventions have been unsuccessful or are unlikely to prove successful and the power to close premises is to be used.

1.2. Protocol 'Triggers'

The Protocol should be triggered on the basis of a build up of information provided by a wide range of sources.

A possible list of members of statutory organisations who could provide the supporting intelligence is given below:

- Permanent Beat Officer
- Tenancy Management Officer or RSL Housing Officer
- Social Worker
- Sector Inspector
- Neighbourhood Watch Co-ordinator
- Environmental Health
- Neighbourhood Wardens
- Community Safety Officers

Their information should be passed either to the group or to the police directly to develop the intelligence and to instigate initial action. Where possible and necessary a police officer could be assigned to lead on these types of investigations and co-ordinate supporting material and development of a multi-agency response.

1.3. Initial Action

The group or handling officer should then prompt the following action:

i) Identification of the relevant social landlord, landlord or owner.

ii) Where there is a social tenant request the Housing Officer to check the tenant's file for any history of substance misuse or other anti-social behaviour; and identify any support currently being offered to the tenant. Where the tenant is not a social tenant or is the owner of the premises police, local authority and agency records may be checked for incidents.

iii) Course of action decided based upon assessment of the premises and any residents. The resident will generally fall into the following categories:

  - Vulnerable habitual resident
  - Non-vulnerable habitual resident
  - Class A drug user
  - Person involved in the supply of Class A drugs
  - Spouse or family of drug user/supplier
  - Person manufacturing Class A drugs

An 'Assessment Meeting' should then be called and appropriate action decided by the wider group and facilities put in place for this action. The situation should continue to be monitored if there is insufficient intelligence to take action at this point.

2. Assessment Meeting

2.1. Assessment Meeting Objectives

The Assessment Meeting is an inter-agency meeting called to review whether premises should be targeted for intervention. The meeting will then decide whether the habitual resident will be considered as 'Vulnerable' or 'Non-Vulnerable' for the purpose of action under a Protocol. The assessment will be based upon the information available to the partnership agencies. Normally, each agency should be prepared at the meeting to disclose the information which would be necessary to take an informed decision. The assessment is not a fixed decision and a Protocol should allow this decision to be changed as the process develops.

2.2. Inter-Agency Participation

The Assessment Meeting should be an inter-agency meeting chaired by the Police Sector Inspector or other relevant person.

The lead Managers present will be:

- TMO or RSL Housing Manager
- Police Sector Inspector
- Substance Use Resettlement Officer
- Substance Use Team Manager

Any assigned police officer should attend the meeting in an advisory capacity to provide an assessment of intelligence.

2.3. A 'Vulnerable' habitual resident

A habitual resident should be considered 'vulnerable' where it is considered that he/she would accept re-housing and where that person would benefit from a drug/alcohol treatment programme. Factors to be considered include:

- Does the habitual resident have any effective control over the use of his/her residence?
- Is the habitual resident a drug user but not a drug supplier?
- Has the habitual resident a proven record of compliance with a tenancy agreement?
- Is the habitual resident receiving Social Services support and making a positive response to this intervention?
- Would the immediate removal of the habitual resident substantially interfere with the activity of the premises?
- Should removal, therefore, be considered before closure or would it be best instigated alongside the closure of the premises?
- Has the habitual resident previously complied with the requirements of a drug/alcohol treatment programme?
- If resettled, is the habitual resident likely to continue meeting with drug suppliers, communal drug consumers or sex workers?

2.4. A 'Non-Vulnerable' habitual resident

A habitual resident should be considered 'non-vulnerable' where that person is clearly not vulnerable and making an informed life-style choice. He/she could be considered 'non-vulnerable' when an offer to be considered under the 'Vulnerable' option of the Protocol is either declined, or not responded to. Factors to be considered include:

- Does the habitual resident have a history of Class A drug supply or is the habitual resident believed to be involved in or assisting the supply of Class A drugs?
- Is the habitual resident voluntarily allowing the premises to be used for the supply or communal consumption of Class A drugs?
- Is there a high level of violence, intimidation or acquisitive crime linked to the premises?
- Has the habitual resident a long history of allowing anti-social behaviour or obscene conduct to be linked to the residence?
- Has the habitual resident used threats or violence towards neighbours, housing staff or other people visiting the neighbourhood?

In instances requiring immediate action, where evidence points to it being the case, action may need to be taken before an accurate assessment of a person as vulnerable can be made against a premises for the benefit of residents.

2.5. Information to the habitual resident

The group will need to decide whether or not it is advisable to inform the habitual resident of a premises of their decision to take action.

Where the Assessment Meeting considers the habitual resident to be 'Vulnerable', it will be necessary to establish whether the habitual resident will agree to participate in a drug/alcohol treatment and housing support programme. Where possible this should be included as part of the Protocol based upon local agreements.

The development of viable resettlement programmes will be a key part of a successful Protocol. The care and provision of appropriate services for vulnerable persons moved from their housing to prevent the production, supply or use of Class A drugs and serious nuisance or disorder should ensure they do not become problematic tenants or occupiers in the future.

3. Key items to be included in a Protocol

Rapid action

It will be necessary for strategies to be developed which give precise deadlines and an action-plan to be taken forward in each incidence where a premises is in need of closure.

3.1. Care for a 'Vulnerable Tenant'

A meeting could be called to instigate and allocate specific housing and drug/alcohol treatment resources.

A Programme of Care could then be drawn up for those whose premises is to be controlled and the recovery of the premises planned.

The Inter-Agency Meeting will be chaired by the relevant TMO or RSL Housing Manager.

The meeting will involve:

- TMO or RSL Housing Manager
- Substance Use Resettlement Officer
- Substance Use Team Manager
- Relevant health support workers

The support of the Drug Action Team (DAT) would be extremely helpful in this process, identifying best practice and providing administrative support to the actions agreed in order to support police and local authority action.

3.2. Initial Programme for 'Vulnerable Tenant'

Below is a possible course of action, which could be taken with a vulnerable tenant.

A vulnerable tenant could initially be offered the following programme:

i) Up to six months in Temporary Accommodation
ii) A Drug/Alcohol Treatment Programme

The Temporary Accommodation placement will be agreed by the multi-agency working group. The vulnerable tenant could make a Statutory Homeless application under the Housing Act (1996), on the grounds that it is unreasonable for the Tenant to live in their current accommodation. Funds could be made available in the 'Crack House' Protocol will pay for the Temporary Accommodation costs. This may enable the tenancy to be maintained subject to the 'Crack House' being closed down.

3.3. Substance Use Team—Treatment Programme

Once a programme of action for an individual has been agreed as a 'Vulnerable Tenant' the substance use team is notified and agrees a course of action with partners.

- Where an individual does not require a drug or alcohol treatment programme or dual diagnosis intervention the role of the Substance Use Team will be advisory only.
- Where the individual is not currently known to the team and requires treatment intervention the substance use team will fully assess the needs of the individual. The individual will be allocated a care manager who will facilitate access to treatment services. The Substance Use Team in partnership with health will meet the costs of 'detox' and rehabilitation programmes. If an individual does not require formal treatment interventions the care manager would access tier 1/2 services provided by voluntary sector partners.
- The Care Manager will review regularly the case in accordance with team standards and the appropriate steering group members will be kept informed of progress. If appropriate they will be referred on to the resettlement stage on completion of their treatment package.
- Care Managers may remain involved during the initial stages of resettlement and work together with housing in relation to ongoing support in the community.

3.4. Resettlement

A decision must be taken as to whether the protocol intends to resettle persons removed from their habitual residence or tenancy. This may be considered the most appropriate course of action if it is believed that persons may otherwise enter into unmanaged tenancies or become homeless.

For example subject to satisfactory completion of the Drug/Alcohol Treatment Programme, a Tenant could be re-settled by the tenant's landlord or Housing Needs Service. If a tenant has been persuaded to voluntarily terminate his/her tenancy in order to resolve the problem without recourse to closure and in co-operation with the protocol, re-settlement will be most appropriate. The Steering Group should maintain oversight of the process of allocation of a suitable property, to the Tenant.

Any resettlement programme must be built into the entirety of a person's rehabilitation programme. It may be appropriate that upon successful completion of the Drug/Alcohol Treatment Programme, the Tenant will sign an Acceptable Behaviour Contract (ABC), which could be enforceable in both Temporary and Permanent Accommodation. The ABC will be agreed and signed by the Tenant, Landlord and the Police.

A programme of continuing support should be developed for the Tenant, dependent upon the particular needs of the individual. Where appropriate, this could involve floating support and/or referrals to community drug/alcohol support programmes.

4. Rapid Reaction Protocol—The 'Non-Vulnerable Tenant'

Below is a copy of the Royal Borough of Kensington and Chelsea's programme for rapid action against non-vulnerable persons. This could be adapted to local conditions and would need updating to include the new power.

4.1. Action within Seven Days

An Inter-Agency Meeting will be held to consider developments since the Assessment meeting.

The meeting will consider the resourcing of an appropriate short-term enforcement based response.

The inter-agency partnership will make tactical decisions to instigate civil legal proceedings and expedite the recovery of the property on behalf of the Landlord. This will include a consideration of whether a 'litigation friend' would be appropriate.

The Inter-Agency Meeting will be chaired by the relevant TMO or RSL Housing Manager. The meeting will involve:

- Sector Inspector
- RBKC or RSL Legal Advisor
- Drug Focus Officer
- Probation Officer (if appropriate)

The Inter-Agency Meeting will be supported by the Drug Action Team (DAT) Information and Support Officer. The DAT Information and Support Officer will provide a comparative view with other referrals. The DAT Information and Support Officer will also record the factors that led to the action decided upon. The DAT Information and Support Officer will maintain a financial record of actions arising out of the Inter-Agency Meeting.

4.2. Initial Protocol Response to 'Non-Vulnerable Tenant'

An Initial Court Application will be made to the County Court for the recovery of premises from the Tenant. Where it is thought appropriate, the Initial Application will be accompanied by application for an immediate Injunction, which will attempt to restrain the Tenant's anti-social behaviour.

Prior to the Possession Hearing, high profile police enforcement activity will target the Tenant's residence and its environs. The three-fold purpose of this activity will be: to reduce the impact of the 'crack house' for neighbours and housing workers; to gain evidence to support the Landlord at the Possession Hearing; and to gain a criminal conviction of the Tenant for drug related offences.

4.3. Possession Hearing

The Police will support civil proceedings by providing professional evidence in the form of witness statements. The Drug Focus Officer will collate police evidence at an early stage. When required, Police Officers will attend the Possession Hearing to provide evidence.

The above was designed before the power to close premises was devised. It would be expected that now the following paragraph could be included:

4.4. Closure Notice and subsequent Order to be sought

Police in continuation of the work outlined above may decide that the appropriate form of action, in consultation with the local authority, is for a Closure Notice to be issued and Closure Order sought. This action may take place in the interim of a possession hearing where delays at that hearing may be expected and there is a need to provide relief to the community by the use of the power.

The above established protocols for the welfare of vulnerable tenants and management of the closure of 'crack houses' should continue to be followed and action agreed in consultation with the partners in the protocol. This will ensure that appropriate provision can be made for both the occupants and the premises itself, before, during and after the closure.

Annex C: Characteristics of 'crack houses'

C.1.1. This power is designed to be principally used against 'crack houses' and it is envisioned that initially this is the only type of premises which will be targeted. The characteristics below are not a statutory or even prescribed definition of a 'crack house'. They are simply guidance on characteristics which are often found at such premises. The presence of any of these factors does not ensure a successful Closure Order, as the Order is dependent on the Court's interpretation of the individual merits of the case. However, 'crack houses' which cause distress to the community through disorder or serious nuisance and which therefore are liable to be issued with a Closure Notice through this power may have certain characteristics:

- Crack Cocaine is supplied and used there
- Cocaine may be 'baked' on the premises to produce crack
- Other Class A drugs such as Heroin may be supplied and used there
- Class B or C drugs may also be available
- There is often a trade in stolen goods—particularly Credit Cards and Mobile Phones
- Users will often take drugs on the premises so chances of arrests for possession are lower
- Activity in the house will peak once a delivery has been made—this can involve hundreds of people visiting
- Dealers will sometimes use prostitutes or runners to deliver the drugs or will take drugs there themselves if they do not have a trusted proxy
- Internal transportation is a favoured method of delivering the drugs
- Sex may be sold or sexual acts obvious in public around the premises
- Houses will often be sparsely furnished and will in most cases contain much drug paraphernalia

- The occupant of the house may or may not be present
- The occupier will usually be a drug user but if not will be a vulnerable person
- It is rare for owner occupiers or private sector rented accommodation to be involved but this will depend upon the effectiveness of action which may already have caused displacement from Social Housing
- Crime in the area surrounding the premises will be high—particularly acquisitive crime
- There may be a measurable increase in crime in the 500m^2 around the location following the establishment of a 'crack house'
- Drugs paraphernalia will often be found in the vicinity
- There will often be a defensible space within the premises from where dealing can take place away from public view
- There will be separate spaces where people can use the drugs for what are often long periods of time

Annex D: The Anti-Social Behaviour Act 2003

[This material is a statutory extract and is available in Appendix 1.]

Annex E: Other potential powers or procedures available to close premises and deal with drugs or nuisance

E.1. Powers to control landlords who tolerate drug use and dealing

E.1.1. It is possible that any landlord or owner with responsibility for the property may be complicit in the dealing occurring. It may be that the landlord has been warned already by the police that the premises have been used for this purpose and has not taken action to redress the offending behaviour. There are other powers, the threat or actual use of which can be used to encourage a landlord or owner to act in these circumstances—Section 8b of the Misuse of Drugs Act 1971, which makes it a criminal offence to knowingly allow the use of cannabis or opium on premises or Section 8d knowingly allowing the supply of any controlled drug on a premises. If the cessation of the behaviour can be achieved by threat of action using this power rather than closure, then this is an alternative course of action that could be used. This could also be used additionally to the closure powers to act against landlords or owners of this type.

E.2. Powers to charge those selling or producing drugs for offences under various drug legislation

E.2.1. The Powers contained in this Act are not designed to replace the powers available to act against individuals for drug manufacture, supply or possession offences. However, they are designed to add to those powers to close places where such behaviour occurs. Where possible, it is still desirable to proceed against individuals using criminal charges of drugs offences. However, it is recognised that there are circumstances where the evidence is not available to proceed to use these powers and yet the nuisance and harm associated with drugs continues. Therefore it is not a requirement on the senior officer to bring charges under the criminal law for production, supply or possession before the Powers of Closure are applied for. It is simply sufficient for them to have reasonable suspicion that the premises are being used for these purposes and that there is evidence of disorder or serious nuisance being involved. Ideally charges will be brought against specific individuals operating from the premises which are involved; but it is not a requirement.

E.2.2. The Police should consider whether there is more appropriateness to those powers contained in the Misuse of Drugs Act first and whether the use of the powers in this Act would compromise the use of the alternative powers. Both may have an impact on the closure of the property.

E.3. Circumstances of simple use of drugs

E.3.1. As covered above, under definition of use, this power is intended to allow for closure related to the simple use of drugs only where there is disorder or serious nuisance associated with that use. The Misuse of Drugs Act is the primary legal machinery for control and regulation of simple possession of drugs. This power is concerned to address various forms of Anti-Social behaviour associated with such use. Therefore use of this power should be predicated firstly by the scale of nuisance involved rather than use of Class A drugs alone. It is not the intention of this power to allow for further criminalisation of personal drug use, but to create powers appropriate to disorder or serious nuisance that occur in connection with the use of drugs.

E.3.2. In considering action against premises where the principal concern is serious nuisance alongside the use of Class A drugs, police should ensure appropriate liaison and discussion, of the best way to handle the premises and any persons likely to be displaced from it with treatment and housing agencies. This may be best facilitated through the local Drug Action Team or Crime Reduction Partnership which will have appropriate membership on its sub-groups.

E.4. Other powers to control nuisance

E.4.1. It is similarly not a requirement to apply other powers to control behaviour before using the Powers of Closure, such as ASBOs. Such powers may be suitable and may be adequate to control certain types of anti-social behaviour but it is not a requirement for such other methods to have been used previously. Where there is disorder or serious nuisance on its own, not associated with drugs, or minor nuisance, perhaps associated with the simple use of drugs, then other means of controlling the behaviour may be more appropriate. However, where disorder or serious nuisance is clearly and demonstrably involved alongside Class A drug misuse it may be appropriate to use this Power to provide immediate relief to the community. It is a requirement that there is disorder or serious nuisance present before proceeding to use these powers. There is a three month set time limit on when such behaviour must be shown to have occurred within to enable a Closure Notice to be served.

E.5. Powers to exclude persons from an area

E.5.1. Section 222 of the Local Government Act 1972 grants the power to a Local Authority to bring an order excluding persons from an area entirely. This injunction has been used successfully against suspected operators of 'crack houses'. An ASBO has a similar function but this power may be more flexible and easier to obtain. The court is likely to require a similar set of evidence as would be required for a Closure Order. Both sets of orders can be applied together to give closure of the property and exclusion of the perpetrators, and could be added to with prosecution for supply or intent to supply under the Misuse of Drugs Act. Action in this manner would be seen as part of a concerted effort to control the supply and use of Class A drugs in a community. Where the premises are owned by a Registered Social Landlord, or by a local authority (and other relevant landlords, see legislation for definition), the new injunctions in Part 2 of the Anti-social Behaviour Act amend s.153 of the 1996 Housing Act to also allow for a power of exclusion to be attached to injunctions.

E.6. Certain sensitive types of premises on which it may not be suitable to issue a Closure Notice

E.6.1. The senior authorising officer must take into account the potential harm that may result in the closure of some types of properties and consider the overall social good in doing so. Whilst no specific types of premises are exempt from these powers, the appropriateness of their use in some circumstances should be considered. Ultimately it is for the court to decide whether the closure of any specific premises on a specific occasion is justified, but the authorising officer should also be mindful of the implications and whether other methods of control may be more appropriate. These circumstances may include:

- Properties where closure cannot be effected without removing access to large numbers of persons who would be made homeless, have no right of re-housing, or would otherwise be caused harm through closure. Examples might include hostels with many residents (although not smaller units) and bed and breakfast hotels
- Hospitals
- Schools
- Children's homes
- Drug treatment services

E.6.2. The court is not asked to decide whether it is in the public good whether such premises are closed; simply whether the criteria for closure are met and the making of the order will prevent the occurrence. Hence the Police officer making the decision must be mindful of the implications of closure when he seeks to apply the power to premises where many persons, many vulnerable, will be displaced, and which provide valuable services to many others. This risk must be balanced against the risk arising from allowing the behaviour to continue, and the other powers that may be available. It is likely however that in the vast majority of cases such behaviour will not occur in places of this type.

E.6.3. The consultation requirement is crucial here. Whilst the opposition of the Local Authority is not a bar to closure, it should be crucial in the process of making a decision. The Secretary of State also has the ability to exempt by Statutory Instrument certain types of premises from the scope of the power. Any such exemption will prevent the issue of a Closure Notice or Order against any such defined premises.

Annex F: Closure Notice Approval Check List for Senior Officer

[This material is a statutory extract and is available in Appendix 1.]

Annex G: Flowchart showing the use of the power

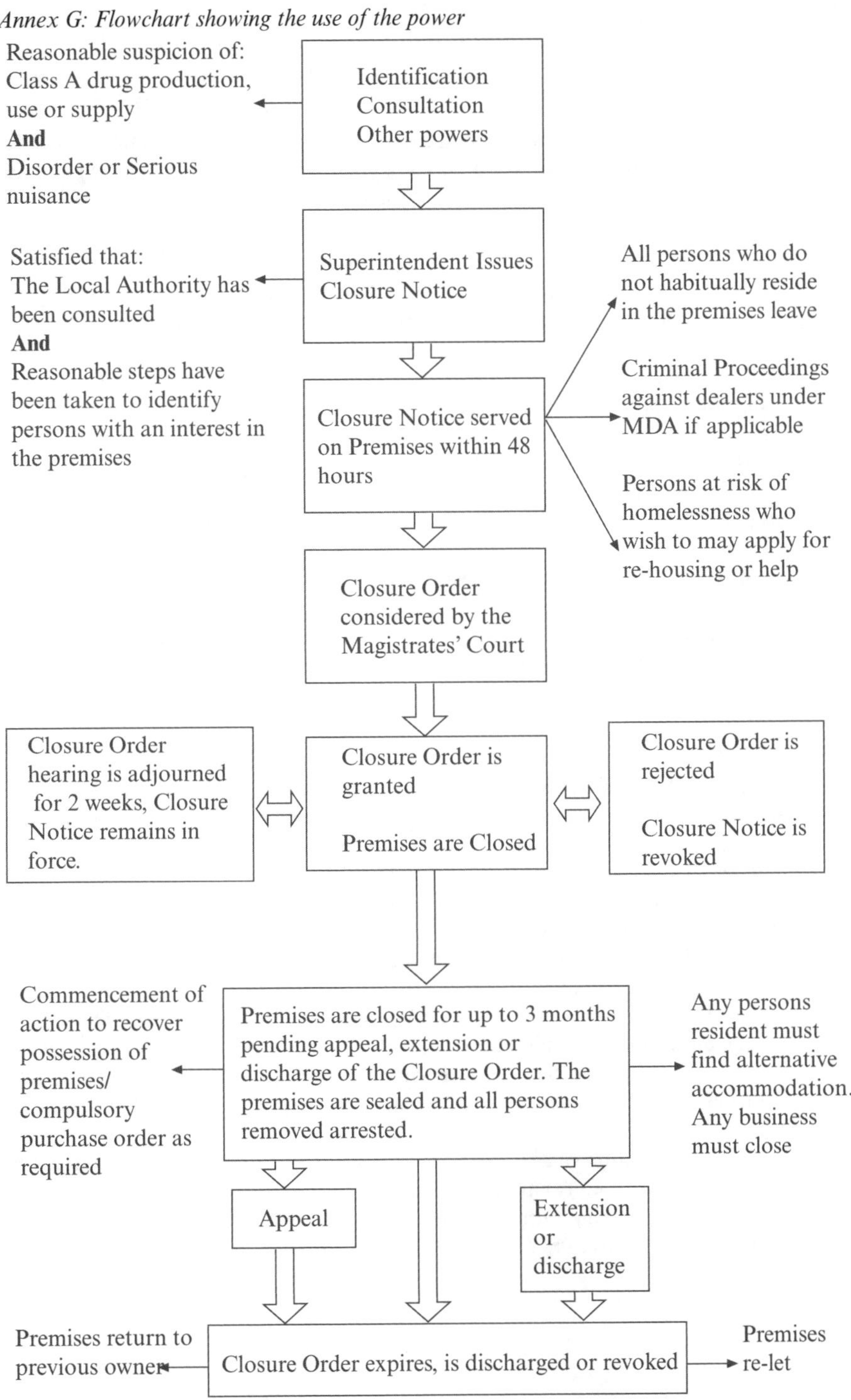

HOME OFFICE CIRCULAR 04/2004

Summary

This circular describes the provisions contained in Part 4 of the Anti-social Behaviour Act 2003, which received Royal Assent on 20 November 2003. It gives details of guidance which will be produced. This Part comes into force on 20 January 2004.

Overview

2. Part 4 of the Anti-social Behaviour Act 2003 provides the police with powers to disperse groups of 2 or more and return young people under 16 who are unsupervised in public places after 9pm to their homes. The powers can only be used in areas where members of the public have suffered intimidation, harassment, alarm or distress due to the presence of groups *and* where anti-social behaviour is a significant and persistent problem.
3. The aim of these powers is to prevent people from feeling frightened and discouraged from using public spaces because they feel threatened by groups of people hanging around. It also aims to protect children and young people from the risks of being unaccompanied on the streets late at night—risks of older peers encouraging them into criminal activities.
4. These new powers will enable police and local authorities to work together to identify particular problem areas that need targeted action to help local communities to remove intimidation and anti-social behaviour from their streets. These powers are not intended to be used in isolation, but should form part of an integrated response to tackling crime and disorder in local areas.

The authorisation

5. An officer of at least the rank of superintendent can make an authorisation where he or she has reasonable grounds for believing that members of the public have been intimidated, harassed, alarmed or distressed; as a result of the presence or behaviour of groups of two or more people in public places in any locality in his police area *and* that anti-social behaviour is a significant and persistent problem in that relevant area.
6. 'Anti-social behaviour' is defined in section 36 as 'behaviour by a person which causes or is likely to cause harassment, alarm or distress to one or more other persons not of the same household as the person'.
7. An authorisation may be made for a period not exceeding six months. The area to which the authorisation applies must fall within the officer's police area. It must be in writing, signed by the officer giving it and must specify the area it covers (the 'relevant locality'), the grounds on which the authorisation is given and the period for which it is valid.
8. Before an authorisation can be given the relevant officer must obtain the agreement of the local authority. Local authority for these purposes is defined for England as a district council, a unitary authority, the Common Council of the City of London or the Council of the Isles of Scilly and for Wales as a county council or a county borough council.

Publicity for the authorisation

9. Once agreement on an authorisation has been obtained, an authorisation notice must be produced and publicised. The authorisation notice must specify the relevant locality to which it applies, the grounds on which the authorisation has been given and the period when the power to disperse is exercisable. Before the authorisation comes into force, the authorisation notice must be published in a newspaper which is circulated in the relevant locality and/or posted in a conspicuous place or places within the relevant locality.

Withdrawal of the authorisation

10. If at any time it is deemed appropriate to withdraw the authorisation notice then the relevant local authorities must be consulted. The authorisation must be withdrawn by the relevant officer who gave it, or any relevant officer whose police area includes the relevant locality and whose rank is the same or higher than the relevant issuing officer. The giving or withdrawal of an authorisation does not prevent a further authorisation for part or the whole of the same area being given.

The direction

11. Once an authorisation has been given for a relevant locality then these new measures will allow a constable or a community support officer (CSO) to give one or more directions. Before giving a direction the officer must have reasonable grounds for believing that the presence or behaviour of a group of two or more persons in any public place in the relevant locality has resulted, or is likely to result, in any members of the public being intimidated, harassed, alarmed or distressed.
12. The directions which may be given are:
    § a direction requiring the persons in the group to disperse (either immediately or at a specified time)
    § a direction requiring those persons who do not live within the relevant locality to leave the relevant locality or any part of the relevant locality (either immediately or at a specified time)
    § a direction prohibiting the return of those persons who do live within the relevant locality from returning to the relevant area for a period as stated when giving the direction, but not exceeding 24 hours.
13. When making a decision to disperse conditions can be attached to which persons must adhere. Officers can specify the time and area to which persons directed to disperse cannot return. If those persons to whom the direction applies do not live in that relevant locality, the officer issuing the direction can order them not to return to the relevant area for a specific period as long as it does not exceed 24 hours.
14. A direction to disperse may be given orally, to any person individually or to two or more persons together and may be withdrawn or varied by the person issuing the direction.
15. A group cannot be given a direction if they are engaged in conduct which is lawful under section 220 of the Trade Union and Labour Relations (Consolidation) Act 1992, or if they are taking part in a public procession as defined in section 11 of the Public Order Act 1986.

Sanction for refusing to obey a direction

16. An individual who knowingly refuses to comply with a direction issued is liable on summary conviction to a fine and/or a term of imprisonment not exceeding 3 months or both. A constable in uniform may arrest without warrant an individual who fails to comply with a direction to disperse.

Taking a child home

17. If an authorisation is in force, a further power to return a person under the age of 16 to their place of residence will be available to constables and Community Support Officers.
18. If between 9pm and 6am, an officer finds a person in any public place in the relevant locality who he has reasonable grounds for believing is under the age of 16 and is not under the effective control of a parent or a responsible person aged 18 or over then they may return that person to their place of residence.
19. Before exercising this power, the officer must be satisfied by returning the person to their place of residence they are not likely to suffer significant harm.
20. If the decision is made to return that person to their place of residence, any local authority whose area includes the whole or part of the relevant area must be informed.

Powers of Community Support Officers

21. Section 33(2) amends Part 1 of Schedule 4 to the Police Reform Act 2002. It adds an offence under section 32(2) of the Anti-social Behaviour Act 2003 to which the power to detain applies to a designated person.
22. Section 33(3) inserts paragraphs (4A) and (4B) into Part 1 of Schedule 4 to the Police Reform Act 2002, so that Community Support Officers, if designated, can use the powers in section 30(3) to (6) of the Anti-social Behaviour Act (power to disperse groups and remove persons under 16 to their place of residence).
23. Section 33(3) also gives Community Support Officers the powers of a constable to return children under 10 to their place of residence where a Local Child Curfew Scheme authorised by a Local Authority is contravened (Crime and Disorder Act 1998 section 14). Community Support Officers have the powers and duties of a constable under section 15(1), 15(2) and 15(3) of the Crime and Disorder Act 1998.

Further Guidance

24. Under section 34, the Secretary of State may issue a code of practice. The National Centre for Policing Excellence (NCPE) has been asked to produce further guidance on these powers, and will consult widely, particularly with stakeholders and practitioners.

HOME OFFICE CIRCULAR 01/2004

Anti-social Behaviour Act 2003: Firearms

Summary

This circular, which has been prepared in consultation with ACPO and ACPO(S), describes the purpose and effect of the firearms provisions contained in the Anti-social

Behaviour Act 2003, which received Royal Assent on 20 November 2003. It gives details of the arrangements for bringing the provisions into force and offers advice and guidance on some of the issues they raise.

The Anti-social Behaviour Act 2003

2. For a number of years there has been a steady rise in the misuse of air weapons and imitation firearms. Much of this is criminal damage and nuisance, often involving young people, but it also includes people who carry imitation firearms in order to intimidate others. The firearms provisions in the Anti-social Behaviour Act are intended to tackle these problems. They also deal with a specific problem concerning air weapons that use a self-contained gas cartridge system, which are particularly vulnerable to conversion to fire live ammunition and have become popular with criminals.

Section 37: Possession of air weapon or imitation firearm in public place

3. This section will come into force *on 20 January 2004*. It adds to the list of firearms covered by the offence in section 19 of the Firearms Act 1968 of carrying a firearm in a public place without lawful authority or reasonable excuse. That offence currently applies to loaded shotguns, loaded air weapons or any other firearm (whether loaded or not) together with its ammunition. Subsection 1 of section 37 adds to this unloaded air weapons and imitation firearms. Subsection 3 adds the offence to the list of arrestable offences in England and Wales set out in Schedule 1A to the Police and Criminal Evidence Act 1984.
4. An imitation firearm is already defined in section 57(4) of the 1968 Act and covers anything which has the appearance of being a firearm whether or not it is capable of discharging a shot, bullet or other missile.
5. A public place is also defined in section 57(4) of the 1968 Act. It includes any highway and any other premises or place to which at the material time the public have or are permitted to have access, whether on payment or otherwise.
6. There is no statutory definition of a reasonable excuse. This will depend on the facts and circumstances prevailing at the time and police officers will need to exercise discretion when deciding what action, if any, is appropriate in each individual case. It should be borne in mind that the intention of the offence is to protect the public from the misuse of firearms and there is no intention of preventing legitimate activities such as actors using imitations for film or theatrical work or historical re-enactment.

Section 38: Air weapons—age limits

7. This section also comes into force *on 20 January 2004*. It makes a number of amendments to sections 22, 23 and 24 of the 1968 Act in order to change the age at which a young person may have an air weapon and to strengthen the supervision requirements.
8. Subsection 2 raises from 14 to 17 the age limit under section 22(4) of the 1968 Act for a young person to have with him an air weapon or ammunition for an air weapon. This means that no-one under 17 will be able to have with them an air weapon at any time unless supervised by someone who is aged at least 21 or as part of an approved target shooting club or shooting gallery. The redundant section 22(5) is omitted.

9. Subsection 3 adds to section 23 of the 1968 Act a new exception to the section 22(4) offence. No offence will be committed under that section if a young person aged 14 to 16 is on private premises and has the consent of the occupier to have an air weapon with him. However, it has been made an offence for anyone benefiting from this exception to fire any missile beyond the premises. Subsection 5 sets the maximum penalty for this offence at a level 3 fine (currently £1,000).
10. Subsection 4 raises from 14 to 17 the age limit in section 24(4) of the 1968 Act. It therefore becomes an offence to make a gift of an air weapon, or ammunition for it, to a person under 17 or to part with possession of an air weapon or ammunition to a person under 17, unless the young person benefits from an exception under section 23 of the 1968 Act (for example, the exception for private premises explained in paragraph 9 above).

Section 39: Prohibition of certain air weapons

11. This section contains a ban on air weapons that use a self-contained gas cartridge system. Subsection 3 adds to section 5(1) of the 1968 Act 'any air rifle, air gun or air pistol that uses, or is designed or adapted for use with, a self-contained gas cartridge system'. SCGC weapons are often known as 'Brococks' after the main UK importer of the weapons (however, not all weapons manufactured or sold by Brocock Limited are SCGC weapons, and there are also other models of SCGC weapon in circulation which were manufactured or sold by other companies). Weapons that use a CO2 bulb system are *not* affected because CO2 bulbs do not contain a projectile and are not therefore self-contained. The effect of adding SCGC weapons to section 5(1) is to make them prohibited weapons which cannot be possessed, purchased, acquired, manufactured, sold or transferred without the authority of the Secretary of State. With the exception of the offence of *possessing* an SCGC weapon, section 39 will come into force *on 20 January 2004*.
12. The offence of possession is being brought into force separately in order to cater for subsection 4, which makes provision for existing owners to keep and continue to use their weapons, provided they have them entered onto a firearm certificate. Existing owners are those people who possess a SCGC weapon on 20 January 2004. They will not require the Secretary of State's authority to continue to possess their weapon and by virtue of subsection 4 will not need to show good reason when applying to the police for a firearm certificate. However, chief officers will still need to satisfy themselves that applicants are fit to be entrusted with the gun, are not a prohibited person, and will not represent a danger to public safety or to the peace. Subsection 4 also removes good reason considerations when renewing, revoking or partially revoking a certificate for a SCGC weapon.
13. Applicants will be required to put in place appropriate security measures to prevent unauthorised access to their weapon. The level of security required will be the same as for section 1 weapons held on a firearm certificate, as set out in Chapter 19 of *Firearms Law: Guidance to the Police*. The precise arrangements are for the police to determine based on the level of risk involved in each case, taking account of factors such as local crime rates and location of the property.
14. Given that applicants will not need to show good reason, only the standard certificate conditions are likely to apply.
15. The possession offence will come into force *on 30 April 2004*. Existing owners have until that date to apply for a firearm certificate. The commencement order for section

39 provides that no offence will be committed where someone has applied for a firearm certificate before 30 April 2004 and their application remains outstanding or is the subject of an outstanding appeal. It has been agreed that existing owners who do not wish to apply for a certificate can hand their weapon in to the police for disposal (no compensation is payable for weapons handed in). Again, this must be done before 30 April 2004.

16. Subsection 5 makes clear that the arrangements for existing owners do not apply to registered firearms dealers. This is to avoid dealers retaining stocks of SCGC weapons that they are unable to sell. However, a dealer could apply in an individual capacity to retain SCGC weapons on a firearm certificate for personal use.
17. Retailers will not be able to trade in SCGC weapons from 20 January 2004 although they may continue to possess their existing stock until 30 April 2004. If they wish to sell the weapons abroad or to provide a repair service, they must apply to the Home Office for the Secretary of State's authority and, where necessary, to register with the police as a firearms dealer. Applications must be submitted before 30 April 2004.
18. To help the Home Office monitor implementation of these provisions, police forces are requested to keep records of:
    a) the number of SCGC weapons handed in;
    b) the number of SCGC weapons which are the subject of applications for firearm certificates (both new applications and variations); and
    c) the number of SCGC weapons in (b) where the application is refused,

    up to 30 April 2004.
19. Subsection 6 amends the order-making power under section 1 of the Firearms (Amendment) Act 1988 to enable the Secretary of State to prohibit or introduce other controls in respect of any air weapon which appears to him to be especially dangerous.

GUIDANCE ON EDUCATION-RELATED PARENTING CONTRACTS, PARENTING ORDERS AND PENALTY NOTICES

(DFFS Guidance)

Overview of the Guidance

This guidance applies to England only.

The guidance in relation to parenting contracts and orders only covers those arising from truancy and exclusion from school. Separate guidance on parenting orders and contracts arising from criminal conduct and/or anti-social behaviour has been published by the Home Office.

Local Education Authorities (LEAs), school governing bodies (GBs), school staff, and the police, including community support officers and accredited persons, will be required by law to have regard to the relevant parts of the following guidance when making decisions on:

- entering into a parenting contract following a pupil's exclusion from school or truancy under section 19 of the Anti-social Behaviour Act 2003 (GBs and LEAs);
- applying for or monitoring a parenting order following a pupil's exclusion from school or truancy under section 20 of the Anti-social Behaviour Act 2003 (LEAs and schools);
- issuing a penalty notice under section 23 of the Anti-social Behaviour Act 2003 (LEAs, head teachers and deputy and assistant heads authorised by them,[1] the police, including community support officers and accredited persons) and, in the case of LEAs, when making local protocols and administering the penalty notice scheme.

This means that while the guidance does not have the force of statute, there is an expectation that it will be followed unless there is good reason to depart from it. The guidance is not exhaustive and judgements will need to take account of the circumstances of individual cases.

Part 1 of the guidance highlights overarching considerations which practitioners should take into account when using any of the provisions covered in the guidance.

Part 2 outlines the law relating to school attendance and where parenting contracts and penalty notices for parents of truants will fit in relation to other school attendance measures. Parenting contracts and penalty notices are by no means intended to replace any other existing measures but to provide alternative options for tackling truancy.

Part 3 of the guidance includes a good practice section entitled 'Resolving School Attendance Problems'. This is issued in order to be helpful to LEAs and schools, but they are not under a statutory duty to have regard to it.

Part 4 explains how the provisions available in cases of exclusion from school, namely parenting contracts and orders, fit in with other measures for tackling poor behaviour in school. Again parenting contracts and parenting orders are not intended to replace existing practice but to provide additional options for improving the pupil's behaviour.

Part 5 explains the method for entering into parenting contracts and common considerations which should be taken into account in respect of parenting contracts in cases of exclusion from school or truancy.

---

[1] Regulations limit those who may be authorised by head teachers to issue penalty notices to deputy head teachers and assistant head teachers.

Part 1: Considerations to Take into Account in Applying the Measures

Purpose of the Measures

1. Parenting contracts, parenting orders and penalty notices are important additions to the interventions available to promote better school attendance and behaviour. Improving behaviour and attendance is essential to improve children's educational prospects and to avoid putting them at risk of criminal or anti-social behaviour.
2. These measures are intended to help ensure that parents take seriously their responsibilities to ensure their children regularly attend school and behave well when they get there. As such, it is important that professionals involved in applying the measures are aware of the different types of strategies and support that will be appropriate in engaging different parents.
3. The measures themselves are described in detail later in this guidance. But in order to be helpful to those implementing the measures some reminders about other relevant legislation and good practice are set out in the paragraphs below.

Human Rights Act (HRA) 1998

4. LEAs, schools and the police must apply their powers fairly and consistently, having regard to this guidance and, in the case of penalty notices, the local code of conduct issued by the relevant LEA. Inconsistency or unfairness may lead to challenges under the HRA. Further information on the HRA can be found at *http://www.humanrights.gov.uk/*

Race Equality

5. In addition to the duty not to discriminate on racial grounds, the Race Relations Amendment Act 2000 places a general duty on all public authorities, including LEAs, schools and the police, to have due regard to the need to eliminate unlawful racial discrimination and promote equality of opportunity and good relations between people of different racial groups. The Race Relations (Statutory Duties) Order 2001 also places a number of specific duties on LEAs, schools and the police, including duties to assess the impact of their policies on minority groups and to monitor the operation of those policies by ethnicity and make that information publicly available.
6. LEAs, schools and the police should therefore monitor the application of their powers to ensure that there is no underlying bias which would lead to disproportionate, unequal or unfair treatment on account of ethnicity. For example, schools and LEAs should consider the reasons behind any disproportionate number of black or ethnic minority pupils excluded when using their powers in respect of parenting contracts and orders in cases of exclusion from school.
7. The law also recognises the special position of Traveller families in relation to prosecution for irregular attendance. Penalty notices should not be issued in circumstances where a parent would have a defence to prosecution under section 444(1) Education Act 1996 (see paragraph 30).
8. See the Commission for Race Equality's web-site for further information: *www.cre.gov.uk*.

Disability

9. The amended Disability Discrimination Act 1995 applies to education and LEAs and school governing bodies will have to be mindful of their responsibilities under that legislation as they exercise their powers.
10. The definition of disability under the Disability Discrimination Act covers pupils with physical, sensory, intellectual or mental impairments. It is unlawful for schools or LEAs, without justification, to discriminate against disabled pupils and prospective pupils for a reason related to their disability in the provision of education and associated services. Discrimination means treating disabled pupils less favourably than other pupils without justification. It also means failing to take reasonable steps to ensure that disabled pupils are not placed at a substantial disadvantage compared to their non-disabled peers. What constitutes a reasonable step will depend on the circumstances of each case. The Disability Discrimination Act makes specific provision in respect of exclusions and provides mechanisms for claims of discrimination to be made in relation to allegations of discrimination.
11. Parenting contracts, parenting orders and penalty notices are not, and should not be used as, alternatives to complying with the duties under the Disability Discrimination Act.
12. For more information see the Disability Rights Commission's 'Code of Practice for Schools—Disability Discrimination Act 1995: Part 4' or go to the Disability Rights Commission website at *www.drc-gb.org*.

Special Educational Needs

13. Behaviour and attendance problems could, in some instances, relate to a child's special educational needs. School governing bodies have a statutory duty to do their best to ensure that the necessary provision is made for any pupil who has SEN. LEAs have specific duties in relation to identifying, assessing and making provision for pupils with SEN, including those with behavioural, social and emotional needs. Statutory guidance in carrying out those duties is given in the Special Educational Needs Code of Practice. Schools and LEAs must have regard to this guidance.
14. Before proceeding to making a parenting contract, applying for a parenting order or issuing a penalty notice schools and LEAs should consider whether behaviour and/or attendance problems may be related to a pupil's special educational needs. Maintained schools should be able to demonstrate that they have done their best, in conjunction with the LEA where appropriate, to make appropriate provision for the pupil's needs. This may include action to support the pupil at School Action and School Action Plus of the SEN Code of Practice or asking the LEA to carry out a statutory assessment of the pupil's needs.
15. Parenting contracts, parenting orders and penalty notices are not, and should not be used as, alternatives to taking appropriate action to meet a pupil's special educational needs.

Information for Parents

16. LEAs, schools and other professionals involved in applying the new measures will need to ensure that parents in the area have access to clear, accurate information about the new measures and their rights and responsibilities. Parent guides to the

new measures are available on *www.parentcentre.gov.uk*. Depending on the local authority area, practitioners may need to make such documentation available in several different languages.

Involvement of Children and Young People

17. LEAs, schools and the police should seek to involve the pupil as much as possible in any discussions around the pupil's behaviour and attendance. Schools and LEAs should also seek, subject to the pupil's age, maturity and understanding, to involve the pupil in the discussions leading to a parenting contract and in the drawing up of the contract itself.
18. For further information and guidance on involving pupils, please refer to the DfES guidance 'Working Together: Giving children and young people a say', available from DfES publications under reference DfES/0492/2003.

Multi-agency Working

19. Truancy and poor behaviour in school are often symptoms of deeper underlying causes. Steps should be taken to investigate these underlying causes and to provide the most appropriate form of support to the pupil and their family. This will often require LEAs, schools and the police to work closely with other agencies (e.g. social services, the voluntary sector, behaviour support teams) which may already be involved or may need to be involved in working with the pupil or family.
20. In working with other agencies, practitioners may need to share information about parents and pupils. Practitioners should ensure that such information-sharing is compliant with the Data Protection Act 1998 and should refer to their Local Authority Data Protection policy. The Local Authority Data Protection Officer will also be able to assist in case of queries. Further guidance including a toolkit for data sharing in the public sector is available at *www.dca.gov.uk/foi/sharing/* and at *www.informationcommissioner.gov.uk.*

Child Protection Issues

21. From time to time, the processes outlined in this guidance may lead practitioners to identify actual or potential child protection issues. At the time of writing, DfES guidance on child protection arrangements is contained in circular 10/95 available from DfES at *www.dfes.gov.uk/publications/guidanceonthelaw/*. Updated guidance will be issued in June 2004.

The Definition of Parent

22. The education-related provisions of the Anti-social Behaviour Act apply to all parents who fall within the definition set out in section 576 of the Education Act 1996. This defines 'parent' as: all natural parents, whether they are married or not; any person who, although not a natural parent, has parental responsibility (as defined in the Children Act 1989) for a child or young person; and any person who, although not a natural parent, has care of a child or young person. Having care of a child or young person means that a person with whom the child lives and who looks after the child, irrespective of what their relationship is with the child, is considered to be a parent in education law.

23. Throughout this document, references to 'parent' mean each and every parent coming within the definition (whether acting jointly or separately) and should not be taken to mean that provisions only apply to 'parent' in the singular.

Part 2: Truancy Provisions

Parental Responsibility for Regular School Attendance

Outline of school attendance legislation

24. Under Section 7 of the Education Act 1996, the parent is responsible for making sure that their child of compulsory school age[2] receives efficient full-time education that is suitable to the child's age, ability and aptitude and to any special educational needs the child may have. This can be by regular attendance at school or by education otherwise (the parent can choose to educate their child at home).
25. If it appears to the LEA that a child of compulsory school age is not receiving a suitable education, either by regular attendance at school or otherwise, they must begin procedures for issuing a School Attendance Order under Section 437 of the Education Act 1996.
26. If a child of compulsory school age who is registered at a school fails to attend regularly at the school then the parent is guilty of an offence under Section 444(1) of the Education Act 1996.
27. Since March 2001 there has been a further offence where a parent, knowing that their child is failing to attend regularly at school, fails without reasonable justification to cause him to attend (Education Act 1996, section 444(1A) as amended by the Criminal Justice and Court Service Act 2000). This offence requires proof that the parent knew of their child's non-attendance and failed to act. Under this aggravated offence a warrant can be issued compelling a parent to attend court and conviction can lead to a custodial sentence.
28. An LEA must consider applying for an Education Supervision Order (ESO) before prosecuting a parent (Children Act 1989, section 36). An LEA may apply for an ESO instead of or as well as prosecuting the parent.
29. For further details, please see the following documents:

    Education Act 1996
    Children Act 1989
    Crime and Disorder Act 1998
    Ensuring Regular School Attendance: Guidance on the Legal Measures to Secure Regular School Attendance
    All are available on the Department for Education and Skills website: *www.dfes.gov.uk/schoolattendance.*

Parenting contracts and penalty notices and how these fit with school attendance legislation and with each other

30. As outlined at paragraph 26, section 444(1) of the Education Act 1996 provides that a parent commits an offence if his or her compulsory school age child who is a

[2] Compulsory school age is defined as beginning from the start of the term commencing on or after the child's fifth birthday. A child continues to be of compulsory school age until the last Friday of June in the school year that they reach sixteen.

registered pupil fails to attend school regularly. It is the commission of that offence that can trigger the use of a parenting contract or a penalty notice for truancy. The proof required that the offence has been committed is the same as that which would be required for a prosecution for the strict liability offence under section 444(1) of the Education Act 1996 i.e. that the child has failed to attend regularly unless the parent can show one of the following defences:

- the pupil's absence was authorised by the school;[3]
- the pupil was ill or prevented from attending by any unavoidable cause;
- the absence was on a day exclusively set aside for religious observance by the religious body to which the parent belongs;
- the school is not within walking distance[4] of the child's home and the LEA has made no suitable arrangements for:
  - the child's transport to and from school;
  - boarding accommodation at or near the school; or
  - enabling the child to attend a school nearer their home
- the parent can show that their trade or business requires them to travel, and the child has attended school as regularly as the nature of the trade or business allows, and the child has attended school for at least 200 sessions during the preceding twelve months.

31. If it appears that the offence under section 444(1) of the Education Act 1996 has been committed and none of the defences outlined above applies, consideration can be given to making a parenting contract or issuing a penalty notice.

Parenting Contracts for Truancy

Overview

32. If a pupil fails to attend school regularly, the LEA or governing body of the school may consider whether it would be appropriate to offer a parenting contract to the parent.
33. A parenting contract is a formal written agreement between a parent and either the LEA or the governing body of a school and should contain:
    a) a statement by the parent that they agree to comply for a specified period with whatever requirements are specified in the contract; and
    b) a statement by the LEA or governing body agreeing to provide support to the parent for the purpose of complying with the contract.
34. Entry into a parenting contract is voluntary. The parent cannot be compelled to enter into a parenting contract if they do not wish to do so. Equally, there is no

[3] Schools are required to take an attendance register twice a day: at the start of the morning session and once during the afternoon session. The register shows whether the pupil is present, engaged in an approved educational activity off-site, or absent.

The register must show whether any absence is authorised or unauthorised. Authorised absence is where the school has either given approval in advance for a pupil of compulsory school age to be away, or has accepted an explanation offered afterwards as satisfactory justification for absence. All other absences must be treated as unauthorised. Schools, not parents, authorise absence. Schools must adhere to DfES Guidelines in authorising absence. Schools should be consistent in applying the same rules in authorising absence.

[4] Defined in section 444(5) of the Education Act 1996.

obligation on the LEA or governing body to offer a parenting contract in cases of non-attendance.

35. Parenting contracts will, however, often be a useful tool in identifying and focusing on the issues behind the non-attendance and in developing a productive relationship with parents to address these issues.
36. The LEA or governing body should be responsive to the needs of the parent in deciding what type of support they will provide. The issues behind truancy can be complex and the type of support required will depend on each individual case.
37. The LEA or governing body may agree to provide support in the form of a parenting programme. The contract may specify that the parent is required to attend the sessions of any such programme. There is a wide range of providers of parenting programmes including voluntary organisations, Youth Offending Teams and LEAs. In assessing the nature of the counselling or guidance programme in which the parent should take part, the LEA or governing body should consider who will administer the sessions, the training and experience of the facilitators including their ability to engage with parents, the curriculum used, whether classes will be group or individually-based and whether there are particular cultural and social factors to be considered.
38. Failure to comply with the parenting contract cannot lead to action for breach of contract or for civil damages. There is no direct sanction for a parent's failure to comply with or refusal to sign a parenting contract. However, if the pupil's irregular attendance continues or escalates to such a level where a prosecution is deemed appropriate, this should be presented as evidence in the case.
39. All those defined as a parent under section 576 of the Education Act (see paragraphs 22 and 23) are parents for the purposes of these provisions with the exception of local authorities who have parental responsibility as a result of being named in a care order ('corporate parents') who are not included here. Parenting contracts can apply to each and any parent coming within the definition.
40. A parenting contract can be used in conjunction with a Pastoral Support Plan and is not intended to replace the excellent practice that already exists in this area, but instead provides an additional mechanism which is more focused on the potential of the parent to improve their child's attendance. There is nothing to prevent an LEA or school entering into an agreement (either formal or informal) with a parent in relation to their child's attendance at any time. Parenting contracts simply provide an additional option which has the backing of statute.

Circumstances in which a parenting contract might be pursued

41. In considering whether the necessary conditions for a parenting contract are fulfilled, LEAs and school governing bodies should have regard to all their statutory duties and in particular to the points set out in paragraphs 1–23 of this guidance.
42. A parenting contract may be used in cases of truancy where a pupil has failed to attend regularly at the school at which he is registered.
43. The purpose of a parenting contract is to improve the pupil's attendance at school and to address any underlying issues. It is not to be seen or used as a punitive measure against the parent. Nor will it be appropriate in all cases. A parenting contract will be an appropriate course of action where the parent is willing to address their child's truanting behaviour, but needs support to do so effectively.

44. Parenting contracts can apply to parents of pupils of:
    a) a community, foundation or voluntary school or a community or foundation special school;
    b) a maintained nursery school;
    c) a city technology college;
    d) a city college for the technology of the arts;
    e) an Academy; or
    f) a pupil referral unit.

Assessing the appropriateness of a parenting contract

45. In deciding whether a parenting contract might be appropriate, the LEA or governing body should consider all the issues behind the non-attendance, in particular whether attendance may be improved through working with the parent and providing support to them and, if so, what form this support should take.

At what point should the contract be arranged

46. In cases of truancy, attendance should be assessed over a period of not less than 4 weeks during term-time before a parenting contract is arranged.

Liaison between the head teacher, governing body, LEA and other agencies involved

47. Parenting contracts require the party entering into the contract to fund any cost of the supportive element of the contract. In the context of a school, this will be the governing body (which has control of the school budget under the School Standards Framework Act 1998). Therefore it is the governing body's name that must appear on the contract and the governing body that will have ultimate responsibility for the parenting contract.
48. The governing body may delegate responsibility for parenting contracts to the head teacher and the head teacher may commit funds on behalf of the governing body where the governing body has chosen to delegate this power. However, the overall policy decision of whether parenting contracts should form part of the school's attendance policy must remain with the governing body.
49. Regardless of whether the school or LEA enters into a parenting contract, it is important that both the LEA and the school are aware of the fact that a parenting contract has been entered into with the parent. The LEA and the school should liaise prior to entering into any parenting contract in order to share information about the pupil and family and any other agencies that might be involved with the pupil and family. If other agencies are identified, the school and LEA should consult them to discuss any underlying issues and to consider the types of requirements and support that might usefully be included in the contract itself.
50. Part 5 contains further details of considerations which are relevant to parenting contracts both for truancy and in cases of exclusion and gives suggestions of the types of support that may be helpful.

Penalty Notices for Parents of Truants

Overview

51. Subsection (1) of section 23 of the Anti-social Behaviour Act 2003 adds two new sections (444A and 444B) after section 444 of the Education Act 1996. These new

sections introduce penalty notices as an alternative to prosecution under section 444 and enable parents to discharge potential liability for conviction for that offence by paying a penalty. The offence of irregular attendance has not changed.

52. The parent cannot be prosecuted for the particular offence for which the notice was issued until after the final deadline for payment has passed (42 days after receipt of the notice) and cannot be convicted of that offence if they pay a penalty in accordance with the notice. Penalties are to be paid to LEA.

53. The penalty is £50 if paid within 28 days of receipt of the notice, rising to £100 if paid after 28 days but within 42 days of receipt of the notice (a notice served by post is deemed to have been received on the second day after posting it by first class post). If the penalty is not paid in full by the end of the 42 day period the LEA must either prosecute for the offence to which the notice applies or withdraw the notice (which they can only do in limited circumstances, see below). Unlike other penalty notice schemes the prosecution is not for non-payment of the notice. If there is a prosecution it will follow the usual procedures of a prosecution for irregular attendance. Prosecutions will be brought by the LEA under section 444 Education Act 1996.

54. LEAs may only withdraw a penalty notice in the following circumstances:

- Where it ought not to have been issued i.e. where it has been issued outside the terms of the local code of conduct or where no offence has been committed;
- Where it has been issued to the wrong person.

55. The new provisions enable the following to issue penalty notices, although there is no requirement for them to do so:

- authorised LEA staff;
- head teachers and school staff authorised by them (limited by regulations to deputy and assistant heads); and
- the police, community support officers and accredited persons.

56. These procedures apply to the parents of children of compulsory school age who are registered at a maintained school, a pupil referral unit, an Academy, a city technology college, or a city college for the technology of the arts.

57. All those defined as a parent under section 576 of the Education Act (see paragraphs 22 and 23) are parents for the purposes of these provisions. As with prosecutions under section 444 Education Act 1996, a penalty notice may be issued to each parent liable for the offence or offences.

58. The Education (Penalty Notices) (England) Regulations 2004 set out the framework for the operation of the penalty notice scheme (see Annex A).

Circumstances in which a penalty notice might be issued

59. In considering whether the necessary conditions for a penalty notice are fulfilled, LEAs and school governing bodies should have regard to all their statutory duties and in particular to the points set out in paragraphs 1–23 of this guidance.

60. The key consideration in deciding whether to issue a penalty notice will be whether it can be effective in helping to get the pupil who is truanting back into school.

61. A penalty notice is a suitable intervention in circumstances of parentally condoned truancy, where the parent is judged capable of securing their child's regular attendance but is not willing to take responsibility for doing so, for example where the

parent has failed to engage with any voluntary or supportive measures proposed. It will be particularly useful as a sanction at an early stage before attendance problems become entrenched and where the LEA consider that a prosecution would be too heavy-handed.

62. The normal response to a first offence should be a warning rather than a penalty. However, authorised officers have the discretion to issue a penalty notice for a first offence in exceptional circumstances. This could be where the unauthorised absence was for an extended period and condoned by the parent, for example where the parent has chosen to take their child on holiday during term time without authorisation.

63. It is for LEAs to set out in their local code of conduct the levels of unauthorised absence above which a penalty notice may be issued and in doing so, they should take into account the level of unauthorised absence at which they will be willing and able to prosecute for the offence of irregular attendance. The Education (Penalty Notices) (England) Regulations 2004 limit the circumstances in which an LEA can withdraw a penalty notice and the normal response to non-payment of a penalty notice will be prosecution for the offence to which the notice relates.

Circumstances in which prosecution may be appropriate

64. If casework, other intervention strategies (including a parenting contract) and/or a penalty notice have been unsuccessful in securing regular school attendance and/or the Education Welfare Service considers that prosecution may bring about an improvement in the pupil's school attendance, the LEA may choose to prosecute the parent under section 444(1) or 444(1A) of the Education Act 1996.

65. LEAs must judge whether and when to prosecute on a case by case basis. In some cases, prosecution may be used as the last resort when other strategies have failed to bring about an improvement in school attendance. In other cases prosecution may be the only appropriate response where acting early will prevent problems from worsening.

66. Before prosecuting a parent for poor attendance an LEA must consider whether to apply for an Education Supervision Order (ESO) instead of, or as well as, prosecuting. However, it is not necessary for there to have been a parenting contract or penalty notice before proceeding to prosecution.

Formally Notifying the Parent

67. At the outset of casework by the school or LEA the parent should be given a formal written notification explaining the actions that may be taken. It is good practice to make sure the parent understands the consequences of failing to ensure their child's regular attendance, in particular that the case could result in a penalty and/or prosecution. However, in exceptional circumstances such as those outlined in paragraph 62 above, a penalty notice may be issued without formal written notification.

68. There is no statutory right of appeal against the issuing of a penalty notice (although the regulations make provisions for the LEA to withdraw them in certain limited circumstances). Therefore it is important, where feasible, to warn the parent or parents of the possibility of a notice being issued to allow them to make whatever representations they wish.

69. It is good practice to allow 15 school days for the parent to improve the situation before issuing a notice or commencing proceedings.

70. Sometimes the prospect of a penalty or prosecution may lead to a significant improvement in a pupil's attendance and a penalty notice or court proceedings may not be necessary if it is believed that the improvement will be sustained.

Roles and Responsibilities of the LEA

71. Primary responsibility for issuing penalty notices rests with the LEA and they must not seek to delegate this responsibility to schools or the police. Nor should they seek to prevent schools or the police from issuing notices if they are willing to do so.
72. However, LEAs are responsible for the administration of the scheme and for bringing prosecutions for truancy and must therefore issue a local code of conduct (see paragraphs 82–86) to ensure the smooth administration and operation of the scheme and that it operates consistently across the LEA area.

Roles and Responsibilities of Schools

73. Head teachers are empowered to issue penalty notices and to authorise their deputy and assistant head to do the same.
74. Head teachers wishing to issue, or authorise their staff to issue, penalty notices must first gain the agreement of their governing body. The school's attendance policy (where applicable) must be revised accordingly.
75. Head teachers and deputy and assistant heads must comply with the local code of conduct issued by their LEA when issuing penalty notices and provide to the LEA a copy of any notice issued.

Roles and Responsibilities of the Police

76. The police, including community support officers and accredited persons, are empowered to issue penalty notices.
77. The police must comply with the local code of conduct issued by the relevant LEA when issuing penalty notices and provide to the LEA a copy of any notice issued.

Holidays in Term Time

78. Under the Education (Pupil Registration) Regulations 1995 head teachers are able to grant up to ten school days authorised absence for the purpose of family holidays during term time. Save in exceptional circumstances a parent shall not be granted more than ten school days leave of absence in any school year. It is for head teachers to determine if the request is reasonable. Each request can only be judged on a case by case basis and we expect that head teachers will use their discretion sparingly. Head teachers should not fetter their discretion by applying policies (for example, blanket bans) which might suggest that each application has not been considered on its individual merits.

Truancy Sweeps

79. LEAs should consider making use of penalty notices during (this will only be possible where the facts are already known), or as a follow up to, truancy sweeps during which instances of parentally condoned truancy are identified.

Administration of the Penalty Notice Scheme

80. The detail of how the penalty notice scheme must operate is set out in The Education (Penalty Notices) (England) Regulations 2004, attached at Annex A.

A specimen notice is set out at Annex C. LEAs are responsible for drawing up a penalty notice pro forma and distributing this to those issuing them.

81. The LEA is responsible for the overall administration of the scheme and it is for them to make such arrangements for the operation of the scheme, not provided for in this guidance or in the associated regulations, as they see fit.

Local Codes of Conduct

82. The purpose of the local code of conduct is to ensure that the powers are applied consistently and fairly across the local authority area and that suitable arrangements are in place for the administration of the scheme. Local codes should contain a statement to this effect and highlight that penalty notices offer a swift intervention which may be used to combat truancy problems before they become entrenched.
83. Anyone issuing a penalty notice must do so within the terms of the local code. It is the responsibility of each LEA to draw up a code of conduct after consulting as set out in the regulations.
84. The local code of conduct is key to the successful use of penalty notices. It ensures consistency, fairness and transparency in the way penalty notices are applied and allows LEAs to manage the system and tailor it to local needs and resources. The regulations specify that the following must be included in the local code:

- Means of avoiding the issuing of duplicate notices and of ensuring that notices are not issued when a prosecution is being planned or commenced for the offence. *A simple way of achieving this would be to include a requirement to check with the Education Welfare Service before issuing.*
- When it will be appropriate to issue a penalty notice for an offence. *This must include the level of unauthorised absence which is necessary to trigger a penalty notice. In considering this trigger, LEAs should take into account the level of unauthorised absence at which they will be willing and able to prosecute for the offence of irregular attendance as the LEA will normally be following this course of action where a penalty notice is not paid. Other criteria may be included.*
- The maximum number of penalty notices that can be issued to one parent in any twelve month period.
- Arrangements for co-ordination between the LEA and its local partners.

85. Although not specifically provided for in the regulations, the code could include locally agreed criteria for authorising or not authorising absence provided that this can be agreed between head teachers and the LEA.
86. It is good practice to publicise the contents of local codes, for example by including them in any local authority or school attendance policies.
87. For examples of local codes go to *www.dfes.gov.uk/behaviourandattendance.*

Retention of Receipts & Revenue Collection

88. Regulations provide that the LEA can retain revenue from their penalty notice scheme to cover the costs of issuing or enforcing notices, or the cost of prosecuting recipients who do not pay.
89. The LEA are required to produce an auditor's statement as part of the usual audit procedure showing that income received from fines does not exceed enforcement as defined. The surplus, if any, must be surrendered to the consolidated fund.

90. LEAs should consider the possibility of making arrangements with another part of the local authority already involved in revenue collection to administer the collection of receipts from penalty notices. This will avoid having to establish new systems and procedures and allow for some economies of scale.

Penalty Notices as Evidence in Legal Proceedings

91. Payment of a penalty notice discharges liability for prosecution for the offence to which the notice relates (ss 444A(2) & (4) of the Education Act 1996 as inserted by s 23 of the Anti-social Behaviour Act 2003).
92. This means that neither the fact that a penalty notice was issued and paid nor the pattern of unauthorised absence to which a paid notice relates can be submitted as evidence in a prosecution for any subsequent offence.
93. However, when sections 98 to 101 of the Criminal Justice Act 2003 come into force, these will bring penalty notices within the definition of 'bad character' in that legislation. Evidence of the issue of a paid penalty notice may therefore be introduced under the conditions in sections 101 to 106, which include for example:
    - if agreed by all parties; or
    - if it is necessary to contradict a false impression given by the defendant; or
    - if the defendant attacks the character of another person.
94. If a penalty is not paid, LEAs may use the fact that a notice was issued and unpaid as evidence in a subsequent prosecution. The unauthorised absence for which the notice was issued can be used as evidence in the usual way.

Part 3: Further Guidance on Resolving School Attendance Problems

95. While the parent is primarily responsible for ensuring their child attends school regularly, where school attendance problems occur the key to successfully resolving these problems is engaging the child through collaborative working between the parent, the school and the LEA.

School-level Action

96. Outside of the home, it is often at the school level that the biggest direct influence can be brought to bear on raising levels of attendance. Absence from school undoubtedly has a detrimental effect on a pupil's progress and attainment. Therefore schools need to monitor and support pupils to maintain regular school attendance. Senior management and all teaching staff should work to raise the level of enjoyment and commitment to learning among pupils.
97. Schools are required to take an attendance register twice a day: at the start of the morning session and once during the afternoon session. The register shows whether the pupil is present, engaged in an approved educational activity off-site, or absent. The register must show whether any absence is authorised or unauthorised. Schools must adhere to DfES guidelines in authorising absence and be consistent in their application of them. Schools must keep registers up-to-date and must ensure that they are accurately completed.
98. Where possible schools should use ICT or radio communication systems (i.e. Electronic Registration) to record attendance. Electronic Registration enables more effective and efficient monitoring of attendance on a daily basis as well as allowing

the identification of longer-term trends in absence which can be used to inform school policy and practice.

99. All schools should have effective systems and procedures for encouraging regular school attendance and investigating the underlying causes of poor attendance which should be set out in an attendance policy. The attendance policy should also set out the circumstances in which the school will consider entering into a parenting contract and issuing a penalty notice. These systems should be reviewed regularly and modified where necessary to reflect the circumstances of the school.

100. Schools should make parents aware of any school attendance policy and should be encouraged to cooperate with the systems and procedures that the policy describes.

101. Schools should have systems and procedures for:

- Registering pupils;
- Categorising absence;
- Collating and analysing attendance data to identify trends and enable action to be taken;
- Determining in which exceptional circumstances leave of absence will be granted for holidays during term-time;
- Monitoring attendance and punctuality for all lessons;
- Dealing with late arrivals;
- Dealing with unauthorised absence (i.e. when contact will be made with parents, how and when standard letter systems will be used, what measures will be taken to reengage disaffected pupils, what rewards/incentives will be used to encourage attendance, what sanctions will be taken including the circumstances in which the school will consider entering into a parenting contract and issuing a penalty notice);
- Referring cases to the LEA (i.e. when, how and by whom);
- Reintegrating pupils who have been absent (e.g. providing pastoral support, the role of the Learning Support Unit, using learning/peer mentoring).

102. If the school has an attendance policy it should clearly set out staff roles and responsibilities for dealing with attendance and should link to the school's behaviour and bullying policies. It should reflect the LEA's attendance strategy and its code of conduct for issuing penalty notices and should be endorsed by the School Governors. Parents and pupils should be consulted on the policy. The Head teacher is responsible for the operational management of the attendance policy.

103. School administrative staff or support staff should contact parents on any day a registered pupil of compulsory school age is absent without explanation (i.e. First Day Contact), including in cases where the pupil skips lessons after registration. This makes it clear to pupils and parents that unauthorised absence is taken seriously. By contacting the parent the school also ensures that the parent is aware that their child is not in school enabling the parent to take steps, where necessary, to establish that their child is safe.

104. Pastoral or support staff should follow up individual pupils and analyse attendance data to identify trends for individual pupils, classes or year groups which can then enable the school to target its efforts.

105. Attendance problems are often a symptom of some underlying cause. The school should investigate whether there are any school or home factors (or both) which are affecting the pupil's school attendance.

106. Wherever practicable, action should be taken by the school to improve a pupil's attendance and investigate and address any underlying cause of problems[5] before considering whether to issue a penalty notice or making a referral to the LEA. Schools can undertake a range of actions to overcome attendance problems. These will depend on the pupil and their circumstances and will involve working closely with the parent. For example:

- early discussion of unauthorised absence between the pupil and the teacher responsible for their registration;
- meetings between the school, parents and the pupil to establish the reasons for unauthorised absence;
- consideration of whether attendance problems could be related to an unidentified SEN and, as appropriate, provision of extra support at School Action, School Action Plus or request for a statutory assessment;
- meetings with parents to discuss strategies in school and at home which encourage regular school attendance;
- engaging the parent in a parenting contract;
- consideration of timetable and subject choice with regard to engaging the pupil;
- use of Learning Mentors to build positive relationships with pupils and parents;
- use of Peer Mentors to provide a social support network;
- use of methods of encouraging/rewarding good or improving attendance. This can be extremely effective—see *www.dfes.gov.uk/schoolattendance* for examples of successful reward schemes and other good practice;
- use of methods for discouraging absence (i.e. placing the pupil on report, letters home);
- extra help with work missed;
- in-school counselling;
- where a pupil is at risk of failure at school through long-term disaffection the Head teacher should establish a pastoral support programme for the pupil.

107. Schools should work closely with the LEA to determine the course of action that should be taken in cases of non-attendance. Other agencies such as Social Services, Connexions, the Police or Youth Offending Teams should be engaged where appropriate.

108. Where intervention at school level fails to bring about an improvement in school attendance, a referral to the LEA must be made. The types of actions to be taken at school level and the trigger for referral to the LEA should be set through negotiation between the school and the LEA. Schools should work closely with the Education Welfare Service to establish a clear protocol for referral.

LEA-level Action

109. LEAs are under a duty to ensure that a child for whom they are responsible is receiving a suitable education either by regular attendance at school or otherwise (section 437 Education Act 1996). The service responsible for carrying out the LEA's duty is often known as the Education Welfare Service (EWS) and staffed by Education

---

[5] These can include bullying, ill health, unmet special educational needs (SEN), or unidentified SEN or disability. The list is not exhaustive.

Welfare Officers (EWOs). References to the EWS or EWOs should be taken to mean any service or individual carrying out the LEA's duty under section 437.

110. Education Welfare Officers should build an effective working relationship with schools to resolve attendance problems by:

- Working closely with schools to define their role and responsibilities surrounding school attendance;
- Defining the Education Welfare Service's roles and responsibilities;
- Ensuring that policies and operational practices are shared between the EWS and schools;
- Agreeing arrangements for referral, regular review, monitoring and evaluation;
- Agreeing procedures for resolving enquiries.

111. The LEA must work with schools to ensure that school registers are kept up-to-date and are accurately completed. Where legal action is taken against the parent only unauthorised absence can be considered by the court because, by definition, any authorised absence has been approved by the school.

112. The LEA should set out the amount of support that schools can expect from the Education Welfare Service. The support should be based on clear and straightforward criteria. Any formula for EWS resource allocation should take into account the extent of absence from school and the number of pupils on the school roll.

113. Each school maintained by the LEA should have a named EWO who is responsible for liaison with the school. LEAs should monitor carefully the use of all different types of intervention strategies to assess whether they are effective and appropriate.

114. When a case is referred to the LEA, the Education Welfare Officer should make an assessment of the case and work closely with the pupil and their family as well as the school to resolve issues surrounding their poor school attendance. This may involve making home visits and securing a problem-solving dialogue between home and school.

115. The Education Welfare Service should consider and attempt to resolve any possible factors that may be contributing to school attendance problems. Documentary evidence should be kept to prove that the Education Welfare Officer has undertaken casework to address possible reasons for non-attendance. This should also include evidence of action taken by the school.

Multi-agency and Cross Border Working

116. Where the pupil lives in a different LEA, the LEA where the pupil attends school should take the lead in any LEA-level action necessary to improve the pupil's attendance e.g. in offering a parenting contract, issuing a penalty notice or bringing a prosecution. In such cases, the LEA where the pupil lives and the LEA where he or she attends school will need to work closely together. This will particularly be the case if a parenting order is made following prosecution as the most appropriate and convenient parenting programme may be located in the LEA where the pupil lives.

117. LEAs are advised to draw up protocols setting out the basis under which cross border working will take place.

118. The Education Welfare Service should engage other agencies where appropriate. It may be that the pupil is a child in need (section 17 of the Children Act) and with parental agreement a child and family meeting with relevant professionals may

assist the family and the pupil. There are legal (e.g. data protection requirements), professional and gate-keeping restrictions on obtaining help and/or information from other agencies such as the Benefits Agency, Health Trusts and Social Services Departments. Under section 27 of the Children Act 1989, an authority whose help is requested will comply with the request if it is compatible with their own statutory or other duties and obligations and does not unduly prejudice the discharge of any of their functions.

119. There are a number of individuals and organisations that may be able to assist in various ways with resolving poor attendance problems. These include: educational psychologists, health workers, social services departments, child and adolescent mental health services (CAMHS), Connexions, SEN Coordinators (SENCOs), youth offending teams (YOTs), Behaviour and Education Support Teams (BESTs) and the police. This list is not exhaustive and schools and LEAs should endeavour to make links with all relevant organisations in their area.

Part 4: Behaviour Provisions

Encouraging Acceptable Behaviour in School

School-level Action

120. All schools are required by law to have a written behaviour policy.[6] The governing body of a school is responsible for making sure that the behaviour policy is in place and the head teacher is responsible for ensuring the behaviour policy is implemented on a day-to-day basis.

121. Department for Education and Skills advice for schools on Behaviour, Attendance and Anti-Bullying Policies is available on the Improving Behaviour in Schools website (*www.dfes.gov.uk/ibis*), the behaviour and attendance website (*www.dfes.gov.uk/behaviourandattendance*) and the anti-bullying website (*www.dfes.gov.uk/bullying*). Schools will need to draw upon a range of effective practice in dealing with poor behaviour in school.

122. Schools should only decide to exclude in cases where serious breaches of the school's behaviour policy have occurred and allowing the pupil to remain in school would seriously harm the education or welfare of the pupil or others in the school (in accordance with the current DfES guidance on exclusions).

LEA-level Action

123. An effective LEA works with schools to encourage review of their behaviour policies and support practice across the whole school. It does this in a number of ways including through the work of Behaviour Support Services (BSS), which support both individual pupils and wider school practice. In a number of areas, LEAs also manage school-based multi-disciplinary teams who support schools with high numbers of pupils with complex emotional and behavioural needs.

124. Most LEAs are also required to have a Behaviour Support Plan (BSP). The BSP details arrangements available, or proposed, for the education of children with behavioural difficulties. The emphasis of these local plans is on building good

[6] Section 61 School Standards and Framework Act 1998.

practice, early intervention, working with parents, and collaborating with specialist support services.

125. LEAs also have statutory duties in the exclusion process. All exclusions should be reported to the LEA as set out in DfES guidance on exclusions. The LEA is often involved in the exclusion review process and has responsibility for the appeal process.

126. In cases where a pupil has been permanently excluded from school, the LEA is responsible for making arrangements for the pupil to continue receiving a suitable full-time education.

Cross Border Working

127. If a pupil who lives in a different LEA to the school is permanently excluded, they become the responsibility of the LEA in which they live and the LEA in which they live should take the lead in any action necessary to improve their behaviour. In the case of a fixed term exclusion, where the pupil lives in a different LEA, the LEA where the pupil attends school should take the lead in any LEA-level action necessary to improve the pupil's behaviour e.g. in offering a parenting contract or applying for a parenting order. In such cases, the LEA where the pupil lives and the LEA where they attend school will need to work closely together. This will particularly be the case if a parenting order is made as the most appropriate and convenient parenting programme may be located in the LEA where the pupil lives.

128. LEAs are advised to draw up protocols setting out the basis under which cross border working will take place.

The New Provisions

129. Parenting contracts and parenting orders are intended to add to the range of strategies available for tackling poor behaviour in school and to enable schools and LEAs to engage with parents effectively, whether on a voluntary or compulsory basis.

130. The provisions are only available in cases where an exclusion has taken place. The provisions are not intended to replace any existing practice but to provide additional options for working with the parent and pupil to bring about an improvement in the pupil's behaviour. Parenting contracts and parenting orders could form part of the school's behaviour policy.

Parenting Contracts in Cases of Exclusion

Overview

131. If a pupil is excluded from school whether for a fixed term or permanently, the LEA or governing body of the school may consider whether it would be appropriate to offer a parenting contract to the parent.

132. A parenting contract is a formal written agreement between a parent and either the LEA or the governing body of a school and should contain:
    a) a statement by the parent that they agree to comply for a specified period with whatever requirements are specified in the contract; and
    b) a statement by the LEA or governing body agreeing to provide support to the parent for the purpose of complying with the contract.

133. Entry into a parenting contract is voluntary. The parent cannot be compelled to enter into a parenting contract if they do not wish to do so. Equally, there is no

obligation on the LEA or governing body to offer a parenting contract following an exclusion.

134. Parenting contracts will, however, often be a useful tool in identifying and focusing on the issues behind the behaviour which gave rise to the exclusion and in developing a productive relationship with parents to address these issues.

135. The LEA or governing body should be responsive to the needs of the parent in deciding what type of support they will provide. The issues behind the behaviour may be complex and the type of support required will depend on each individual case.

136. The LEA or governing body may agree to provide support in the form of a parenting programme. The contract may specify that the parent is required to attend the sessions of any such programme. There is a wide range of parenting programme providers including voluntary organisations, youth offending teams and LEAs. In assessing the nature of the counselling or guidance programme in which the parent should take part, the LEA or governing body should consider who will administer the sessions, the training and experience of the facilitators including their ability to engage with parents, the curriculum used, whether classes will be group or individually-based and whether there are particular cultural and social factors to be considered.

137. Failure to keep to the terms of the parenting contract cannot lead to action for breach of contract or for civil damages.

138. There is no direct sanction for a parent's failure to comply with or refusal to sign a parenting contract. However, if the pupil's misbehaviour continues or escalates to such a level that the school or LEA considers an application for a parenting order is appropriate, the court will be required to take this failure or refusal into account in deciding whether to make the order.

139. All those defined as a parent under section 576 of the Education Act (see paragraphs 22 and 23) are parents for the purposes of these provisions with the exception of local authorities who have parental responsibility as a result of being named in a care order ('corporate parents') who are not included here. Parenting contracts can apply to each and any parent coming within the definition.

140. A parenting contract can be used in conjunction with a Pastoral Support Plan and is not intended to replace the excellent practice that already exists in this area, but instead provides an additional mechanism which is more focused on the potential of the parent to improve their child's attendance. There is nothing to prevent an LEA or school entering into an agreement (either formal or informal) with parents in relation to their child's behaviour at any time. Parenting contracts are not intended to replace existing practice but simply to provide an additional option which has the backing of statute.

Circumstances in which a parenting contract might be pursued

141. In considering whether the necessary conditions for a parenting contract are fulfilled, LEAs and school governing bodies should have regard to all their statutory duties and in particular to the points set out in paragraphs 1–23 of this guidance.

142. A parenting contract may be offered to a parent where a child is excluded from school, whether for a fixed term or permanently.

143. The purpose of a parenting contract is to improve the pupil's behaviour at school and to address any underlying causes. It is not to be seen or used as a punitive measure against the parent. Nor will it be appropriate in all cases. A parenting contract

will be an appropriate course of action where the parent wishes to address their child's poor behaviour in school but needs support to do so effectively.

144. Parenting contracts can apply to pupils of:
   a) a community, foundation or voluntary school or a community or foundation special school;
   b) a maintained nursery school;
   c) a city technology college;
   d) a city college for the technology of the arts;
   e) an Academy; or
   f) a pupil referral unit.

Assessing when a parenting contract is appropriate

145. In deciding whether a parenting contract might be appropriate, the LEA or governing body should consider all the issues behind the exclusion, in particular whether the pupil's behaviour may be improved through working with the parent and providing support to them and, if so, what form this support should take.

At what point should the contract be arranged

146. The parenting contract should be arranged as soon as possible after the exclusion and completion of any exclusions review and appeal process.

147. In the case of permanent exclusions this would be:

   - the date by which it is known that the parent does not wish to lodge an appeal against the head teacher's decision to exclude, which has subsequently been upheld by the governing body. This would be the date set out in the letter sent to the parent by the governing body (covered in existing guidance), informing the parent of their decision to uphold the permanent exclusion, as the date by which time the parent must have notified the LEA that they wish to lodge an appeal; or
   - the date upon which the Independent Appeal Panel endorses the decision to exclude.

148. In the case of fixed-term exclusions the date on which the review process is complete would be:

   - the date upon which the governing body endorses the head teacher's decision to exclude; or
   - if the exclusion is not considered by the governing body, the date on which the exclusion began.

149. For a pupil referral unit, the review process is complete when the LEA endorses the decision of the teacher in charge to exclude; or if the LEA does not consider it, the date on which the exclusion began.

Liaison between the head teacher, governing body, LEA and other agencies involved

150. Parenting contracts require the party entering into the contract to fund any cost of the supportive element of the contract. In the context of the school, this will be the governing body (which controls the school budget under the School Standards Framework Act 1998). Therefore it is the governing body's name that must appear on the contract and the governing body that will have ultimate responsibility for the parenting contract.

151. The governing body may delegate responsibility for parenting contracts to the head teacher and the head teacher may commit funds on behalf of the governing body where the governing body has chosen to delegate this power. However, the overall policy decision of whether parenting contracts should form part of the school's behaviour policy must remain with the governing body.

152. Regardless of whether the school or the LEA enters into a parenting contract, it is important that both parties are aware of the fact that a parenting contract has been entered into with the parent. The LEA and the school should liaise prior to entering into any parenting contract in order to share information about the pupil and family and any other agencies that might be involved with the pupil and family. If other agencies are identified, the school and LEA should consult them to discuss any underlying issues and to consider the types of requirements and support that might usefully be included in the contract itself.

Parenting Contracts following Permanent Exclusion

153. In cases of permanent exclusion from school, it will usually be the LEA that will consider arranging a parenting contract in relation to the pupil. In most cases, the excluded pupil will be the responsibility of the LEA until arrangements can be made for the pupil to continue their education elsewhere.

154. The governing body of any school which takes in an excluded pupil may also consider arranging a parenting contract if it wishes, but is under no obligation to do so. However, in accordance with the law on admissions, a school may not require a parent to sign a parenting contract as a condition of their child being accepted by the school.

Drawing up the Contract

155. Part 5 contains further details of considerations which are relevant to parenting contracts both for truancy and in cases of exclusion and gives suggestions of the types of support that may be helpful.

Parenting Orders in Cases of Exclusion from School

Overview

156. Where a pupil is permanently excluded from school or receives more than one fixed term exclusion within 12 months, the LEA may apply to the court for a parenting order.

157. Parenting orders compel parents who have been unwilling or unable to engage on a voluntary basis to address their child's poor behaviour in school by providing support including parenting classes.

158. The parenting order consists of 2 elements:

- A requirement for the parent to attend counselling or guidance sessions (e.g. parenting education or parenting support classes) where they will receive help and support to enable them to improve their child's behaviour. This is the core of the parenting order and can last for up to 3 months;
- A requirement for the parent to comply with such requirements as are specified in the order. This element can last up to 12 months.

159. Parenting orders available in cases of exclusion from school are civil orders available on application to the court. Unlike the parenting orders imposed in attendance

cases, they do not follow prosecution for a criminal offence. A pro forma application for a parenting order is attached at Annex D.

160. The LEA is responsible for making an application for a parenting order and for all costs associated with it including the costs of the parenting programme.
161. The court can impose a parenting order on any or all parents coming within the definition (see paragraphs 22 and 23) and their consent is not required.
162. All parenting orders must be supervised by a 'responsible officer'. This could be an officer of the LEA, a head teacher or a person nominated by the head teacher.
163. If the parent fails to comply with an Order, then breach proceedings must be considered. If proven guilty of breaching a parenting order, the parent is liable for a fine not exceeding level 3 (currently up to £1000). In considering the level of fine, the magistrates must take into account the means of the parent to pay. The court may also consider any other sentence available for a non-imprisonable offence.

Circumstances in which a parenting order might be pursued

164. In considering whether the necessary conditions for a parenting order are fulfilled, LEAs and school governing bodies should have regard to all their statutory duties and in particular to the points set out in paragraphs 1–23 of this guidance.
165. An LEA may apply to a magistrates' court for a free-standing parenting order when:
    a) a pupil has been excluded from school for a second fixed term within a period of 12 months; or
    b) a pupil has been permanently excluded from school.
166. Parenting orders can apply to parents of pupils of:
    a) a community, foundation or voluntary school or a community or foundation special school;
    b) a maintained nursery school;
    c) a city technology college;
    d) a city college for the technology of the arts;
    e) an Academy; or
    f) a pupil referral unit.

Assessing when a parenting order is appropriate

167. A parenting order is only appropriate where the exclusion has been made in response to serious misbehaviour.
168. Serious misbehaviour would include, for example: continual disruptive behaviour in the classroom, threatening behaviour, verbal abuse, assault (including sexual assault), damage to school property, theft from an individual or from the school, supplying an illegal drug and carrying an offensive weapon or replica. Bullying (including homophobic and racist abuse) could also constitute serious misbehaviour. This list is not exhaustive.
169. In deciding whether a parenting order might be appropriate, the LEA must make a judgement about whether parenting is a significant factor in the pupil's misbehaviour, whether a parenting programme could remedy this and what other requirements might be useful in an order to address the pupil's behaviour.
170. An application for a parenting order can be made in respect of one or more persons who come within the definition of parent (see paragraphs 22 and 23).

Parenting orders in different circumstances

171. Section 26 of the Anti-social Behaviour Act 2003 enables youth offending teams to apply for parenting orders in respect of criminal conduct and anti-social behaviour. LEAs should consider in each case whether the order for exclusion should also cover criminal conduct and anti-social behaviour. If the youth offending team agrees that the order should cover these areas, they would usually, depending on the circumstances of the case and local arrangements, be the lead agency in bringing the application and supervising the order. Local protocols will need to be agreed about cooperating and supplying resources for such cases.

Timing of an application for a parenting order

172. An application for a parenting order must be made after the date upon which the exclusion review and appeal process ends.

173. In the case of a permanent exclusion, the date on which the appeal process is complete would be:

- the date by which it is known that the parent does not wish to lodge an appeal against the head teacher's decision to exclude, which has subsequently been upheld by the governing body. This would be the date set out in the letter sent to the parent by the governing body (covered in current exclusions guidance), informing the parent of their decision to uphold the permanent exclusion, as the date by which time the parent must have notified the LEA that they wish to lodge an appeal; or
- the date upon which the Independent Appeal Panel endorses the decision to exclude.

174. In the case of a fixed term exclusion, the date on which the review process is complete would be:

- the date upon which the governing body endorses the Head teacher's decision to exclude (or the LEA in the case of a PRU); or
- if there is no consideration by the governing body (or the LEA in the case of a PRU), the date on which the exclusion began.

175. If there is no parenting contract in place, the LEA has 40 school days to carry out any necessary assessment, prepare their evidence and make the application to the court. Applications should be made as soon as possible within this time limit to allow for quick and effective intervention.

176. If the parent has already entered into a parenting contract (or is offered and accepts a parenting contract in respect of the exclusion in question which subsequently proves to be ineffective), the LEA may make an application for a parenting order within 6 months of the date on which the contract was signed.

Liaison between the head teacher, governing body, LEA and other agencies involved

177. Although only the LEA can apply for the parenting order and the final decision as to whether the application is appropriate will rest with the LEA, the head teacher may in the case of fixed term exclusions, where the child remains a registered pupil at the school, ask the LEA to apply for a parenting order where he or she considers that this may have a positive impact on the pupil's behaviour, preventing further fixed term exclusions or permanent exclusion.

178. Making any application for a parenting order in cases of exclusion from school will require close collaborative working between the school and the LEA. LEAs should also make checks to find out what other agencies are involved with the family and should consult them to ascertain existing interventions, discuss any underlying issues and consider the types of requirements that might usefully be included in the parenting order.

Costs

179. LEAs are under no obligation to apply for a parenting order in cases of exclusion from school. Nor will it be appropriate in all circumstances.
180. Where an application for a parenting order is made, the LEA will have to cover the costs of making the application and the costs associated with any order made including the costs of any counselling or guidance programme.

Making the Application

181. Applications must be made in accordance with the Magistrates' Courts (Parenting Order) Rules 2004[7] which specify the form of application that should be used. A copy of the specimen application form for a parenting order is included at the back of this guidance at Annex D.

Evidence that the pupil has been excluded and that the exclusion was made in response to serious misbehaviour at school

182. In addition, the LEA will need to prepare evidence in support of their application. Evidence that the pupil has been excluded from school should take the form of a statement by the head teacher of the school, the minutes of the governing body (where applicable) and, in the case of permanent exclusions where the parent lodges an appeal, the minutes or decision letter of the independent appeal panel hearing.
183. Supporting evidence might include witness statements from witnesses who saw the incident or physical evidence where appropriate.

Evidence that making the order would be desirable in the interests of preventing any further poor behaviour in school which may lead to exclusion

184. The court has discretion to consider all the circumstances of the case in deciding whether it is desirable to make a parenting order including the evidence of parents and other witnesses in court. The assessments of the pupil and their parent by the LEA and details of the LEA's ability to deliver the parenting programme should be presented to support the application.
185. The LEA should also provide evidence of any experience of trying to engage the parent through a parenting contract. Magistrates are obliged to take into account any parental refusal to enter into, or failure to comply with, a parenting contract. This evidence is relevant to the consideration of whether the order is desirable in the interests of preventing further poor behaviour in school which may trigger an exclusion. If the parent will fully engage with support offered on a voluntary basis, a parenting order would not usually be desirable.

---

[7] SI 2004/247.

Procedural Points

Providing information about family circumstances

186. Before making a parenting order where the pupil is under the age of 16, the court must obtain and consider information about the parent's family circumstances and the likely effect of the order on those circumstances.
187. The LEA should be prepared to provide information about the parent's family circumstances. The LEA could submit a report along with the application for the parenting order. Alternatively, the court could rely on an oral report in court (e.g. where the family circumstances are known to the LEA), or ask questions of the parent or of the pupil if they are present in court. The format in which this information should be presented will be for the court to determine and will depend on the circumstances of the case.

Children in the care of the local authority or living in local authority accommodation

188. Parenting orders in cases of exclusion from school apply only to parents as individuals and not to corporate bodies. Therefore this type of parenting order cannot be made against local authorities in respect of looked after children (i.e. children in the local authority's direct care). They will however apply to foster parents.

Parental attendance at court

189. Magistrates' courts, including youth courts, have power to enforce parental attendance at court, where appropriate, by issuing a summons. It is desirable to ensure all parents falling within the definition (see paragraphs 22 and 23) attend court and that all parents are involved in any parenting intervention.

Requirements of parenting orders

190. The requirements specified in the parenting order or in directions given under the order should, as far as practicable, avoid any conflict with the parent's religious beliefs and any interference with the times at which the parent normally works or attends an educational establishment. A balance will need to be struck between imposing requirements that address the problems which led to the imposition of the parenting order and these other issues.

Counselling or guidance programme

191. The core requirement of a parenting order is that the parent attends a counselling or guidance programme (e.g. a parenting support or parenting education programme) as specified in directions given by the responsible officer. This requirement must be imposed in all cases when an order is made (except where the parent has previously received a parenting order) and the programme can last for up to three months. The arrangements for meeting this requirement should be as flexible as possible, not least to take account of the availability and timing of such a programme.
192. The counselling or guidance programme may be provided by the responsible officer or by another provider, such as the local authority social services department or a local voluntary sector organisation working with parents. There is a wide range of parenting programme providers. The LEA should be aware of what provision exists in its area and in neighbouring authorities (for cross-border cases).

193. The court will decide the length of this requirement. It should be such as to allow for a sufficient number of weekly sessions. Experience suggests that this should be no less than 6 or 7 two-hour sessions. The period of up to three months for this requirement must run concurrently with the overall length of the order and any specific requirements but, taking account of the availability of an appropriate counselling and guidance programme, does not have to run from the date the order is made.

194. If the only requirement to be included in the order is to attend a counselling or guidance programme then the court can still make the order last for twelve months if it considers it reasonable to do so to allow for the possibility of the order being breached and varied to require the parent to attend a new counselling or guidance programme. See also paragraphs 208 to 218.

195. The responsible officer will need, in consultation with the provider of any parenting course or group where appropriate, to make an assessment about the nature of the counselling or guidance programme in which the parent should take part. In assessing the nature of the counselling or guidance programme in which the parent should take part, the responsible officer should consider who will administer the sessions, the training and experience of the facilitators including their ability to engage with parents, the curriculum used, whether classes will be group or individually-based and whether there are particular cultural and social factors to be considered.

196. During the course of the parent's attendance at the counselling or guidance programme the parent, the responsible officer and the programme provider (if different) will need to consider the progress which is being made—the frequency of this will depend on the extent to which the responsible officer is directly involved in the delivery of the programme. The parent might also find it helpful to be involved in some voluntary follow-up work when the order has been completed; this might involve attending a parent support group or similar activity.

Residential requirement

197. A parenting order can include a residential course but only if two conditions are met:
    a) that the attendance of the parent at a residential course is likely to be more effective than their attendance at a non-residential course in preventing their child from engaging in a repetition of the behaviour which led to the making of the order; and
    b) that any likely interference with family life is proportionate in all the circumstances.

198. This is designed to ensure that any residential component to a parenting order would be proportionate under Article 8 of the European Convention on Human Rights—right to respect for private and family life. LEAs should therefore consider whether there would be a breach of Article 8 and, if so, whether that is justifiable.

199. If an LEA wishes to recommend or apply for a parenting order with a residential component they should provide evidence that these conditions are met. An example would be where the parent's home life is so chaotic that they need a structured setting where sustained counselling and guidance can be undertaken.

200. In order for the court to decide whether any likely interference with family life is proportionate LEAs will need to inform the court what the programme will be. It need not be continuous. A small number of residential weekends structured within a wider non-residential programme may be suitable. Arrangements for the care of

the child (and any siblings and dependants) will be a crucial consideration. Voluntary attendance by the child and siblings may be desirable as intensive family work can be particularly effective.

Specific requirements

201. The court may also include in a parenting order a requirement for the parent to comply for a period of not more than 12 months with such requirements as are specified in the order.
202. The LEA should make a recommendation to the court as to how long the parenting order should be imposed for. This will depend on the circumstances of the case. In many cases it will be desirable to recommend to the court that the parenting order should last for the full 12 month period. The imposition of a parenting order for this time period is more likely to bring about a sustained improvement as a consequence of the ongoing support and monitoring delivered through the order.
203. The requirements specified in the order may be such as the court considers desirable in the interests of preventing any repetition of the behaviour which led to the pupil being excluded from school in the first place. Although discretionary, it is likely to be appropriate to include requirements relating to the supervision of the pupil in order to address their behaviour. The LEA should recommend to the court what these requirements should consist of. Possible requirements might include: setting and reinforcing agreed boundaries at home; ensuring the pupil's regular attendance at alternative provision; signing regular behaviour reports or updates; attending regular meetings with the pupil's education provider.
204. The requirements imposed under this element of the order will need to be tailored to address the problems which caused the court to make the parenting order and should, if possible, be linked to any work being undertaken by the LEA or school with the pupil.
205. When deciding on specific requirements it is important to consider that breach of the order is a criminal offence. It is therefore vital to ensure that the requirements are specific, measurable and clear enough for a parent to know when they are breaching them and for the responsible officer to be able to monitor the parent's compliance.

Managing parenting orders and further court involvement

Role of the responsible officer

206. A parenting order must specify a responsible officer who, in the case of an order made following exclusion from school, will usually be an officer of the LEA, a head teacher or a member of staff nominated by the head teacher.
207. The responsible officer will provide or arrange for the provision of the counselling or guidance programme, and will supervise any other requirements included in the order. The responsible officer will also need to identify and liaise with other agencies involved with the pupil or family (e.g. social services, the youth offending team, any voluntary organisations) to ensure that all interventions fit together well and are complementary.
208. In deciding who is best placed to act as the responsible officer for a parenting order, the LEA should take into account the skills that will be required to supervise the order properly and the time commitment required. The responsible officer will need

to be sensitive to the needs of the pupil and the parent. Ideally they should have training, experience or a qualification in social work issues, a knowledge of education law, policy and practice and some familiarity with court procedures. In most circumstances the responsible officer will be an officer of the LEA.

209. Head teachers may only accept responsibility for acting as a responsible officer (either themselves or through a member of the school staff) where they have consulted and received the backing of the school's governing body. In considering whether it would be appropriate for a member of school staff to act as the responsible officer, head teachers should have regard to the time commitment, skills and experience necessary to supervise the order effectively (as set out in paragraph 208 above). LEAs may only designate a head teacher or a person nominated by the head teacher to be the responsible officer if they are satisfied that the school's governing body is supportive of this arrangement.

210. It is good practice for the initial contact between the responsible officer and the parent to take place before the end of the next working day after the order is made. The initial meeting should be an opportunity for the responsible officer to explain further to the parent the nature of the parenting order, its purpose and how it will work in practice (and provide them with a copy of the order). The practical details of the requirements will need to be set out, the monitoring arrangements described and the consequences of failure to comply with any requirements explained. If the counselling or guidance programme under the order are to be provided by someone other than the responsible officer, a pre-meeting between the parent and that person should take place no more than two weeks before the sessions are due to start.

211. The success of the relationship between the parent and the responsible officer will be a key feature of the successful completion of the order. Whilst the requirements of the parenting order are in force, the responsible officer should maintain regular contact with the parent. This should enable the responsible officer to determine the extent to which the parent is complying with the requirements set by the court. If the requirements are proving difficult to comply with through no fault of the parent, the responsible officer may consider the need to apply to the court for the order to be varied.

Variation and discharge

212. While a parenting order is in force the court which made the order may, on the application of the responsible officer or the parent, vary or discharge it. Under Rule 114 of the Magistrates' Courts Rules 1981 ((inserted by Rule 4(4) of the Magistrates' Courts (Miscellaneous Amendments) Rules 1998), application is by complaint. These are civil procedures and are governed by sections 51–57 of the Magistrates' Courts Act 1980 and Rules 4 and 98 of the 1981 Rules. These sections and Rules deal with, amongst other things, the issuing of summonses and the non-appearance of the parties.

213. The order can be varied either by inserting in the order (in addition to or in substitution for any of its provisions) any provision that could have been included in the order if the court had then had the power to make the order and were exercising that power, or by cancelling any provision included in the order. Parenting orders may be varied for a number of reasons, for example, where the family moves to another area or where the requirements are not proving effective.

214. Where an application for the discharge of a parenting order has been dismissed, no further application may be made without the court's consent. This is largely to prevent spurious or repeat applications.

Dealing with Appeals and Breach of an Order

Appeals

215. Where a parenting order in a case of exclusion from school has been made, any appeal against the order should be made to the Crown Court.

Breach

216. The parenting order is primarily designed to help and support the parent in addressing their child's behaviour. The responsible officer should be seeking to secure and maintain the parent's co-operation and compliance with the requirements of the order to ensure that it is successfully completed, and will need to make a judgement about what is reasonable in all the circumstances of the case.

217. If a parent fails to comply with a requirement of the order, it is good practice for the responsible officer to make contact with the parent within one working day by visit, telephone or letter. If there is no acceptable reason for the non-compliance, the responsible officer should give the parent a written warning and if possible a warning in person.

218. If the parent has good reason for the failure to comply with the requirements of the parenting order, it may be appropriate for the responsible officer to consider whether to apply to the court for the terms of the order to be varied.

219. In the event of more than one unacceptable failure to comply within a period of three months, the responsible officer should meet the parent to review the order and how it can be made to work. In the light of this discussion the responsible officer should consider whether the failure to comply should form the basis of a prosecution.

220. If a prosecution is brought, there will be a hearing to determine whether the parent is guilty of failing without reasonable excuse to comply with a requirement of a parenting order. In all cases this will be heard in the adult magistrates' court, except when the parent is under 18 where it would be more appropriate for the case to be heard in a youth court. The hearing will provide an opportunity for the parent to explain why a failure to comply with a requirement of the order has occurred.

221. If the parent is convicted, they will be liable to a fine not exceeding level 3 on the standard scale (currently up to £1,000). The court will also have available to it an absolute or conditional discharge, probation order or curfew order. The imposition of a community sentence would be subject to the restrictions set out in sections 6 and 7 of the Criminal Justice Act 1991. Courts cannot re-issue parenting orders in breach proceedings but the original order will continue to be valid.

222. Under section 127 of the Magistrates' Court Act 1980 there is a six-month time limit for bringing breach proceedings. Proceedings can be brought after an order has expired. They will however be most effective when brought as soon as possible after the breach is discovered and completed within the life of the order. This will allow the Court more options, for instance to vary the order to require the parent to attend a new parenting programme and fulfil specific requirements to exercise

control over their child. The penalty for breach could be a fine or community sentence dependent on the parent attending a new programme and meeting other requirements.

Part 5: Common considerations for Parenting Contracts

Making the Decision to Offer a Parenting Contract

223. In considering whether it would be appropriate to offer a parenting contract, LEAs and school governing bodies should have regard to all their statutory duties and in particular to the points set out in paragraphs 1–23 of this guidance.

224. The LEA or governing body of a school should take into account a number of issues before deciding to enter into a parenting contract. These include whether other agencies are already involved in working with the pupil and family, whether a parenting contract would complement or join up this work, the type of support that might be helpful to the parent and how a parenting contract arranged by the LEA or governing body will be funded.

Making Contact with Other Agencies Involved with the Pupil and Family

225. The pupil and family may already be in contact with or receiving support from other agencies—for example, social services, the youth offending team or a voluntary organisation. Before the LEA or the governing body of a school decides to enter into a parenting contract, they should identify and consult other agencies involved with the pupil and their parent to ascertain any underlying issues that should be taken into account when deciding whether a parenting contract would be appropriate and the types of support that could usefully be included if it is.

226. A multi-agency approach is necessary to ensure that all work being carried out with the pupil and their parent fits well together and avoids duplication.

Parenting Contracts in Different Circumstances

227. Section 19 of the Anti-social Behaviour Act 2003 sets out provisions for governing bodies and LEAs to enter into parenting contracts in cases of exclusion from school or truancy. Section 25 of the Anti-social Behaviour Act 2003 enables youth offending teams to enter into parenting contracts in respect of criminal conduct and anti-social behaviour.

228. Governing bodies and LEAs should consider in each case whether the contract should cover both exclusion and truancy and/or criminal conduct and anti-social behaviour. If the youth offending team agrees that the order should cover these areas, they would usually, depending on the circumstances of the case and local arrangements, be the lead agency in bringing the application and supervising the order. Local protocols will need to be agreed about cooperating and supplying resources for such cases.

Types of Support that Might be Included in a Parenting Contract

229. Parents will often be unaware of the different types of support available and the LEA or governing body should provide information about this and give contact details of appropriate national and local agencies and helplines. Other useful support might include family group conferencing, peer mentoring, parenting classes,

literacy classes, benefits and drugs/alcohol advice, provision of a key link worker for the parent and help with transport to and from school. This list is not exhaustive.

Funding a Parenting Contract

230. The party entering into the parenting contract with the parent (namely the LEA or the governing body of a school) is responsible for bearing the costs of any support provided under a parenting contract.
231. The cost of a parenting contract will be largely dependent on the type of support provided. LEAs and schools are encouraged to use parenting contracts innovatively, making use of existing resources where appropriate. This might include, for example, the facilities of the local extended school, the local Citizens Advice Bureau, on-site learning mentors, Educational psychologists, BESTs, an existing parenting peer group, or asking another parent to act as a mentor.

Contacting Parents and Drawing up a Parenting Contract with Them

232. Once all agencies involved with the family have been consulted, the governing body or LEA should arrange a meeting with the parent to discuss the pupil's non-attendance and any related issues. In contacting the parent, the governing body or LEA should give consideration to the best way to approach the parent, bearing in mind that some parents may find it harder to engage than others. Ideally all parents falling within the definition (see paragraphs 22 and 23) should be invited to attend, whether resident with the child or not. However, it will be a matter of judgement for the governing body or LEA to consider which parents should attend and whether it would be appropriate for parents to attend separate meetings.
233. Depending on the pupil's age and understanding, the pupil should also be invited to attend the meeting.
234. The LEA or governing body should write to the parent before the meeting outlining what a parenting contract is and making clear that it is not a punitive or compulsory measure, but intended to support the parent and improve the pupil's attendance or behaviour. Parent guides to parenting contracts are available on *www.parentcentre.gov.uk* and the LEA or governing body may wish to send a copy to the parent.
235. At the meeting, the LEA or governing body should explain the purpose of the meeting and the parenting contract and why they feel it may be helpful. The parent should be asked to outline their views on the pupil's behaviour and/or attendance at school, any underlying issues, how they believe these should be tackled and what they think of the idea of a parenting contract. They should also be given an opportunity to specify the type of support which they would find helpful. Parents will often be unaware of different types of support and the LEA and governing body may need to list or summarise the different types of support available in the area to stimulate this discussion. Once again, depending on the pupil's age and understanding, the pupil should be encouraged to contribute to this discussion. A similar discussion should take place in respect of the requirements with which the parent will be expected to comply to ensure that any requirements specified in the contract are realistic and address the issues behind the non-attendance or behaviour. The aim should be to work in partnership in order to improve the behaviour or attendance of the child.

236. Once the requirements and support elements of the contract have been agreed, the governing body or LEA and the parent should write up the contract together and sign it. The contract should be written in language that the parent can easily understand (including a translation where necessary). One parenting contract may be arranged with all parents, or in circumstances where it is desirable to have different requirements for each parent, a separate parenting contract could be arranged for each parent.
237. If the parent fails to attend the meeting without good reason or notification, further attempts should be made to contact them and arrange a meeting. A letter would be appropriate in these circumstances. All such attempts should be recorded.
238. The specified requirements for the parent under s19(4)(a) of the ASB Act should be devised to prevent further truancy or poor behaviour in school which might lead to a further exclusion. Examples of specified requirements will depend on the particular circumstances of the case but may include: ensuring that the pupil attends school or alternative provision punctually and regularly, attending meetings with the school or LEA, signing weekly behaviour reports and ensuring that the pupil does not contact certain pupils. This list is not exhaustive.
239. Where there is separate work being carried out with the pupil (for example, through a pastoral support plan) it may be desirable for the contract to support this or include work involving the parent and pupil together.
240. A further requirement will normally be that the parent attends some form of guidance or counselling programme based on an assessment of the parent's needs. This might typically consist of a parenting support or parenting education programme but could be any form of support that might help the parent improve their child's behaviour or attendance at school. In assessing the nature of any counselling or guidance programme, the LEA or governing body should consider who will administer the sessions, the training and experience of the facilitators including their ability to engage with parents, the curriculum used, whether classes will be group or individually-based and whether there are particular cultural and social factors to be considered.
241. The contract will need to be written in language the parent can understand and should strike an effective balance between specific and general requirements. General requirements are normally clearer about aims whereas specific requirements should be clear about exactly what the parent must do.
242. The governing body or LEA's side of the contract is a statement that it agrees to provide the parent with support for the purpose of complying with the requirements and should specify the types of support that will be provided under the contract.
243. The parent and a representative of the governing body or LEA (preferably the person who will deliver the governing body or LEA's part of the contract) must sign the contract and all parties should be given a copy. It may also be appropriate to give a copy to other agencies working with the family.

Duration of Contracts

244. There is no specified time limit for contracts in the Anti-social Behaviour Act so this is a question of what is reasonable and effective. The 12-month limit for parenting orders can be taken as the limit normally applying to contracts as a matter of good practice. There will normally be requirements relating to the pupil's behaviour or

attendance in addition to the provision of some sort of support, which would normally last for under 3 months. It will often be desirable, however, to maintain some level of support after the contract has come to an end and schools and LEAs will need to consider how to ensure that such support is sustainable after the end of the contract.

Delivering the Contract

245. Responsibility for delivering the LEA's or school's part of the contract and for helping to manage its overall outcome must be allocated to an officer of the LEA or a member of the school's governing body. Alternatively the governing body may choose to delegate the responsibility to the head teacher who may delegate to a senior member of staff.

246. Delivering the contract will involve regular contact with the parent to discuss progress and any problems in meeting the contract's requirements. It will also involve contact with other interested agencies such as the provider of a parenting programme.

Dealing with Breaches

247. The LEA or governing body (or head teacher on behalf of the governing body) should be working with the parent to gain their co-operation and compliance with the contract but will have to judge whether any breaches are reasonable and whether the contract remains useful and should continue.

248. There is no liability in tort or contract for breaching a parenting contract.

249. However, in cases of exclusion from school, failure by the parent to comply with the contract would be a relevant consideration for the LEA in deciding whether to apply for a parenting order (see paras 152–166) and, in deciding whether to make a parenting order, the court must take into account any failure by the parent to comply with the requirements specified in a parenting contract (see para 181).

250. Similarly, in cases of truancy, failure to comply with a contract may lead the LEA or school to consider issuing a penalty notice to the parent or may lead the LEA to consider prosecuting the parent for failing to ensure their child attends school regularly in which case evidence that the parent failed to comply with the contract could be presented to the court.

251. It is therefore important that any breach of the contract is recorded so that it can be presented to the court if necessary.

252. Every breach discovered should have a response. Upon learning of a breach the LEA officer or member of the governing body/senior school staff responsible for overseeing the contract should contact the parent within one working day to seek an explanation for the breach. If the explanation is reasonable and the contract is still proving useful then this should all be recorded and the contract should continue as normal. If the explanation shows that the contract is proving difficult to comply with through no fault of the parent, then a meeting should be arranged with the parent to review the contract and amend it, if appropriate.

253. If no explanation is given or the LEA officer or member of the governing body/senior school staff responsible for overseeing the contract is not satisfied with the explanation, they should serve the parent with a warning, which may be in the form of a letter, and keep a record of this. If there are further breaches, the LEA

officer or member of the governing body/senior school staff responsible for overseeing the contract should arrange a meeting with the parent to review the contract and how it can be made to work. The parent should be reminded that if a contract fails the LEA may seek to apply for a parenting order in cases of exclusion either immediately or if a further exclusion occurs or in cases of truancy the LEA may issue a penalty notice or seek to prosecute the parent under section 444 of the Education Act if the parent continues to fail in their duty to ensure their child attends school regularly. They should also be informed that a court would consider the parent's level of compliance with a contract when deciding whether to make an order and would be likely to take this into account in any truancy prosecution.

254. In the light of this meeting, it should be decided whether the non-compliance is undermining the contract to the extent that it is no longer useful in which case an alternative course of action would need to be decided upon. The decision and reasons for that decision should be recorded. This can be used in any future application for a parenting order in cases of exclusion or in any truancy prosecution.

Parents who Refuse to Enter into a Parenting Contract or with whom it is Impossible to Agree a Contract

255. Parenting contracts are voluntary, but the LEA or governing body should make all efforts to engage with the parent to negotiate a parenting contract if it considers that it would be appropriate and helpful to the parent to do so. If a parent refuses to enter into a contract then the LEA officer or member of the governing body/senior school staff responsible for overseeing the contract should seek constructively to meet all legitimate concerns and ensure that a written record is kept of all efforts to negotiate a contract. This would include whether the parent was at least willing to meet to discuss the possibility and, if so, what was said.

256. If a parent refuses to enter into a contract or fails to agree to an appropriate contract, the LEA or governing body may consider the alternative courses of action available. For example, in cases of exclusion, an application for a parenting order may be made immediately if the child has been excluded permanently or in the future should the child's poor behaviour continue to the point where a second fixed term exclusion occurs and, in cases of truancy, a penalty notice may be issued or the LEA may consider prosecution. The LEA officer or member of staff responsible for liaising with the parent should inform the parent that this action may be taken. They should also make clear that, on an application for a parenting order, the court is required to take into account the refusal to enter into a parenting contract under section 21(a) of the Anti-social Behaviour Act and that the refusal may be presented in evidence in the event of a prosecution for irregular attendance.

Annex A: Penalty Notice Regulations

STATUTORY INSTRUMENTS
2004 No. 181
EDUCATION, ENGLAND

The Education (Penalty Notices) (England) Regulations 2004

Made 29th January 2004
Laid before Parliament 4th February 2004
Coming into force 27th February 2004

The Secretary of State for Education and Skills, in exercise of the powers conferred upon him by sections 444A, 444B and 569 of the Education Act 1996(**a**), hereby makes the following Regulations:

Citation, commencement, interpretation and application

1.—(1) These Regulations may be cited as the Education (Penalty Notices) (England) Regulations 2004 and shall come into force on 27th February 2004.

(2) In these Regulations—
'the Act' means the Education Act 1996;
'recipient' means a person to whom a penalty notice is given in accordance with section 444A(1) of the Act.

(3) These Regulations apply only in relation to England.

Form and content of penalty notices

2. A penalty notice shall give such particulars of the circumstances alleged to constitute the offence to which the notice relates as are necessary to give reasonable information as to the offence and shall contain—

(a) the name and address of the recipient;
(b) the name and address of the child who is failing to attend school regularly, and the name of the school where he is a registered pupil;
(c) the name and official particulars of the authorised officer issuing the notice;
(d) the date of the offence and of the issue of the notice;
(e) the amount of the penalty which is to be paid, and any variation in the amount under regulation 3;
(f) the name and the address of the local education authority to which the penalty is to be paid and to which any correspondence relating to the penalty notice may be sent, being the local education authority in whose area is the school at which the recipient's child is a registered pupil;
(g) the method or methods by which payment of the penalty may be made;
(h) the period for paying the penalty, in accordance with regulation 3;
(i) a statement that payment will discharge any liability for the offence;
(j) the consequences of the penalty not being paid before the expiration of the period for paying it; and
(k) the grounds on which the notice may be withdrawn.

(a) 1996 c. 56 Sections 444A and 444B were inserted by s. 23 of the Anti-Social Behaviour Act (2003) c. 38.

Amount and payment of penalty

3. The amount of the penalty to be paid shall be —

(a) £50 where the amount is paid within 28 days of receipt of the notice;

(b) £100 where the amount is paid within 42 days of receipt of the notice.

4.—(1) The penalty shall be payable to the local education authority named in the penalty notice.

(2) A certificate purporting to be signed by the proper officer or the chief education officer of a local education authority to the effect that the recipient of a penalty notice has or has not paid the amount due on or before a date stated in the certificate shall be received in evidence in any legal proceedings and shall be evidence of the matters stated in it.

Effect of issue of penalty notice

5. The period prescribed for the purposes of section 444A(3) of the Act shall be 42 days.

6. If the penalty is not paid in full before the expiry of the period for paying it the local education authority named in the notice shall either institute proceedings against the recipient for the offence to which the notice relates or shall withdraw the notice in accordance with regulation 7.

Withdrawal of penalty notice

7.—(1) A penalty notice may be withdrawn by the local education authority in any case in which that authority determines that—

(a) it ought not to have been issued, or

(b) it ought not to have been issued to the person named as the recipient.

(2) Where a penalty notice has been withdrawn in accordance with paragraph (1)—

(a) notice of the withdrawal shall be given to the recipient;

(b) any amount paid by way of penalty in pursuance of that notice shall be repaid to the person who paid it; and

(c) no proceedings shall be continued or instituted against the recipient for the offence in connection with which the withdrawn notice was issued or for an offence under section 444(1A) of the Act arising out of the same circumstances.

Authority to issue penalty notices

8. A head teacher may authorise a deputy or assistant head teacher to issue penalty notices.

9. An authorised staff member may only issue a penalty notice in respect of a child who is a registered pupil at his school.

10. An officer of a local education authority may only issue a penalty notice in respect of a child who is a registered pupil at a school in the area of—

(a) that local education authority; or

(b) another local education authority which has an agreement to that effect with his local education authority.

11. Where there is more than one person liable for the offence a separate notice may be issued to each person.

Codes of conduct

12. Each local education authority shall draw up a code of conduct which sets out measures to ensure consistency in the issuing of penalty notices, including—

(a) means of avoiding the issue of duplicate notices;

(b) measures to ensure that a notice is not issued when proceedings for an offence under section 444 of the Act are contemplated or have been commenced by the local education authority;

(c) the occasions when it will be appropriate to issue a penalty notice for an offence;

(d) a maximum number of penalty notices that may be issued to one parent in any twelve month period; and

(e) arrangements for co-ordination between the local education authority, neighbouring local education authorities where appropriate, the police and authorised officers.

13. In preparing the code of conduct the local education authority shall consult governing bodies, head teachers and the chief officer of police for a police area which includes all or part of the area of the local education authority, and shall have regard to any guidance issued by the Secretary of State.

14. Any person issuing a penalty notice shall do so in accordance with the code of conduct drawn up by the local education authority.

15. The Secretary of State may at any time direct a local education authority—

(a) (if it has not already drawn up a code of conduct under regulation 12) to prepare a draft code for his approval by the date specified in the direction; or

(b) (if it has already drawn up such a code but the code appears to the Secretary of State to make inappropriate provisions) to prepare a draft of revisions to the code for his approval by the date specified in the direction.

16. The Secretary of State may approve a draft code or draft revisions to the code submitted under regulation 15 with or without modifications and—

(a) where a draft code has been approved (pursuant to regulation 15(a) and this regulation) it shall have effect as approved; and

(b) where draft revisions to the code have been approved (pursuant to regulation 15(b) and this regulation) the code shall have effect with the approved revisions.

Information

17. A person issuing a penalty notice shall forthwith provide a copy to the local education authority which is named in the notice.

18. A local education authority shall keep records of penalty notices which shall include—

(a) a copy of each notice issued;

(b) a record of all payments made and on what dates;

(c) whether the notice was withdrawn and on what grounds;

(d) and whether the recipient was prosecuted for the offence for which the notice was issued.

19. A local education authority shall supply to the Secretary of State such information as he may require in respect of penalty notices.

Service of notices

20.—(1) A penalty notice may be served by—
(a) giving it to the recipient; or
(b) leaving it at the recipient's usual or last-known address; or
(c) sending it to the recipient at that address by first class post.
(2) Service by post shall be deemed to have been effected on the second day after posting the notice by first class post.

Use of monies received

21. Any sums received by local education authorities by way of penalties must be applied in meeting the costs of issuing and enforcing notices, or the cost of prosecuting recipients who do not pay.

Ivan Lewis
Parliamentary Under Secretary of State
Department for Education and Skills

29th January 2004

EXPLANATORY NOTE

(This note is not part of the Regulations)

These regulations prescribe the necessary details for the operation of the penalty notice scheme under section 444A of the Education Act 1996 (inserted by the Anti-Social Behaviour Act 2003). They only apply in England.

Regulation 2 sets out the matters to be contained in a penalty notice. Regulations 3 and 4 prescribe the level of the penalty which is to be paid to the local education authority, and what is evidence of its payment or non-payment.

Regulation 5 prescribes 42 days as the period before which no proceedings can be commenced. If the penalty is not paid within that time, Regulation 6 requires the local education authority either to prosecute for the offence under section 444 or to withdraw the notice on one of the grounds set out in Regulation 7.

Regulations 8 to 11 set out details about the issuing of penalty notices.

Regulations 12 to 14 require the local education authority to draw up and consult on a code of conduct for the issuing of penalty notices. Regulations 15 and 16 provide for the Secretary of State to have power to direct a local education authority to draw up a draft code or revisions to a code and for the Secretary of State to approve the draft code or revisions.

Regulations 17 to 19 require records to be kept, a copy of any penalty notice issued to be given to the local education authority, and information to be given to the Secretary of State.

Regulation 20 sets out how penalty notices may be served on the recipient.

Regulation 21 requires local education authorities to use the sums received as penalties to meet the costs of operation and enforcement of the penalty notice scheme.

A full regulatory impact assessment has not been produced for this instrument as it has no impact on the costs of business.

Annex B: Parenting Order Regulations

STATUTORY INSTRUMENTS
2004 No. 182
EDUCATION, ENGLAND

The Education (Parenting Orders) (England) Regulations 2004

Made 29th January 2004
Laid before Parliament 4th February 2004
Coming into force 27th February 2004

The Secretary of State, in exercise of the powers conferred upon him by sections 20(1), 21(4) and 94 of the Anti-social Behaviour Act 2003(**a**), hereby makes the following Regulations:

Citation, commencement and application

1.—(1) These Regulations may be cited as the Education (Parenting Orders) Regulations 2004 and shall come into force on 27th February 2004.
(2) These Regulations apply only in relation to pupils excluded from schools in England.

Interpretation

2. In these Regulations—
'the Act' means the Anti-social Behaviour Act 2003;
'the 2002 Act' means the Education Act 2002(**b**);
'school day' has the same meaning as in the Education Act 1996(**c**).

Prescribed conditions

3.—(1) The following conditions are prescribed for the purposes of section 20(1)(b) of the Act.
(2) In the case of a pupil excluded for a fixed period the exclusion must be the second or subsequent exclusion of the pupil from any school within twelve months from the day on which the previous exclusion began.
(3) The application must be made within the relevant period.
4.—(1) In the case of a pupil excluded for a fixed period, the 'relevant period' is whichever of the following is applicable, and if both are applicable whichever expires the later—
(a) the period of 40 school days beginning with the next school day after the day on which the exclusion was considered by the governing body (or in the case of an exclusion from a pupil referral unit, the local education authority) or, if it was not so considered, the day on which it began;
(b) the period of six months beginning with the day on which a parent of the pupil entered into a parenting contract.
(2) In the case of a pupil excluded permanently, the 'relevant period' is whichever of the following is applicable, and if both are applicable whichever expires the later—
(a) The period of 40 school days beginning with the next school day after—

(a) 2003 c. 38. (b) 2002 c. 32. (c) 1996 c. 56. School days defined by s. 579(1).

(i) the day on which an appeal panel constituted under regulations made under section 52 of the 2002 Act decided to uphold the exclusion, or

(ii) if there was no appeal, the last day on which an appeal could have been made;

or

(b) the period of six months beginning with the day on which a parent of the pupil entered into a parenting contract.

Costs of parenting order

5. The costs associated with the requirements of parenting orders, including the costs of providing counselling or guidance programmes, shall be borne by the local education authority.

Ivan Lewis
Parliamentary Under Secretary of State
Department for Education and Skills

29th January 2004

EXPLANATORY NOTE

(This note is not part of the Regulations)

The conditions are set out in regulation 3. Where the pupil has been excluded permanently, the only condition is that the application must be made within the relevant period. Where the pupil has been excluded for a fixed term, there must have been at least two such exclusions in the last twelve months and the application must be made within the relevant period.

Regulation 4 defines the relevant period, including cases where a parenting contract has been entered into.

Regulation 5 prescribes for the purpose of section 21(4) of the Act that local education authorities are to fund the costs of parenting orders.

A full regulatory impact assessment has not been produced for this instrument as it has no impact on the costs of business.

Annex C: Penalty Notice Proforma

Penalty Notice

S.444A EDUCATION ACT 1996

Please read the notes overleaf carefully.

PART 1

If a child of compulsory school age who is a registered pupil at a school fails to attend regularly at the school, his parent is guilty of an offence under s. 444 Education Act 1996.

To: [Title] ....

[Forenames] ....

[Surname] ....

[Date of Birth (if known)] ....

Of: [address] ....

[postcode] ....

You are a parent of [name and address of child] (called in this notice 'the pupil') who is a registered pupil at [name of school].

On [date]/between [date] and [date] the pupil failed to attend regularly at the school.

This notice gives you the opportunity to pay a penalty fine instead of being prosecuted for the offence given above. The amount of the penalty is £50/£100 in accordance with the table overleaf. If you pay this penalty within the time limits set out below, no further action will be taken against you in connection with the offence as set out in this notice.

Payment should be made within 28 days. If paid after 28 days but within 42 days the penalty is doubled to £100. Payment should be made to [LEA name and address for payment] and can be made in person at [that address] on [office opening hours], or by posting this notice with a cheque or postal order to [that address].

Late or part payments will not be accepted and no reminders will be sent. **If payment is not received by [insert date 42 days from date of issue], you may be prosecuted for the offence and could be subject to a fine of up to £1,000**.

This notice is issued by [name] [official particulars] of [address/employer] [within XXX LEA].

Date of issue: . . . .

PART 2

Please complete the following and return this notice with your payment to [insert LEA address]:

Name: . . . .

Address: . . . .

I attach payment in the sum of £ . . . .

Signed: . . . .

Date: . . . .

NOTES

1. Contact Details.
   If you have any queries about this notice, please contact XXX Local Education Authority at [insert department contact name, telephone number, fax number and address].
2. Amount of penalty.
   The amount of the penalty is as follows:
   When paid
   Within 28 days £50
   Within 42 days £100
3. Code of conduct.
   This notice is issued in accordance with a local code of conduct drawn up by the XXX LEA. Any questions or correspondence about the code should be addressed to the [Education Department] at [address and phone no.].
4. Withdrawal.
   This notice may be withdrawn by the XXX LEA if it is shown that it should not have been issued to you or has not been issued to you in accordance with the local code of

conduct. If you believe that the notice was wrongly issued you must contact the LEA to ask for it to be withdrawn as soon as possible, stating why you believe the notice to have been incorrectly issued. The LEA will consider your request and will contact you to let you know whether the notice is withdrawn. If the notice is not withdrawn and you do not pay, you will be liable to prosecution for the offence that your child has failed to attend school regularly.

5. Payment.
   You should complete the notice above and send or deliver it to the LEA at the address given [insert opening hours of offices etc.].
6. Prosecution.
   If you do not pay the penalty, and the notice is not withdrawn, you will be prosecuted for the offence of failing to ensure your child's regular attendance at school. You will receive a separate summons for this which will give you notice of the time and date of the court hearing. You will be able to defend yourself and you would be advised to seek legal representation; in some circumstances you may be entitled to legal aid.

Annex D: Specimen Application Form for a Parenting Order

Application for Parenting Order
(Anti-social Behaviour Act 2003, section 20)

.... Magistrates' Court
(Code)

Date: ....

Child or young person: ....

Child or young person's address: ....

Child or young person's age: ....

Parent: ....

Parent's address: ....

which is in the area of [ ] Local Education Authority ....

Parent: ....

Parent's address: ....

which is in the area of [ ] Local Education Authority ....

Applicant Local Education Authority: ....

It is alleged that:

(a) the child or young person has been excluded from school on disciplinary grounds; and
(b) the prescribed conditions are satisfied in that [insert details].

[The parent(s)entered into a parenting contract on [date].] [It is alleged that the parent(s) have failed to comply with the parenting contract, a copy of which is attached to this application form.

Short description of alleged failure to comply with parenting contract:

Evidence of this alleged failure to comply is attached.]

[It is alleged that the parent(s) have refused to enter into a parenting contract.]

[The child or young person is under 16. Information as to the family circumstances of the child or young person is attached.]

[It is alleged that:

(a) the attendance of the parent at a residential course is likely to be more effective than their attendance at a non-residential course in improving the child's or young person's behaviour; and
(b) any interference with family life which is likely to result from the attendance of the parent at a residential course is proportionate in all the circumstances.

The court is requested to order that the counselling or guidance programme may include a residential element.]

Short description of the counselling/guidance programme to be attended by the parent(s):

Further requirements to be included in the order:

GUIDANCE ON PART 3: PARENTING CONTRACTS AND ORDERS

(Home Office, DCA and Youth Justice Board Guidance)

Section 1: Scope and status of guidance

1.1. This guidance is about the operation of **parenting orders**[1] and of **parenting contracts.**[2] It is the guidance referred to in sections 25(8) and 27(4) of the Anti-social Behaviour Act 2003 ('the ASB Act 2003'). It is principally technical guidance on the provisions but also aims to reflect good practice. It does **not** offer guidance on the content or quality of parenting programmes or provide advice on engaging with parents and their children. For information on such wider topics, see 1.6 below. It replaces the guidance on parenting orders under the Crime and Disorder Act 1998 ('the CD Act 1998') issued in May 2000. The guidance is mainly intended for youth offending teams (YOTs), responsible officers and the courts but may also be of use to the police, youth offender panels, parenting programme providers, the CPS and defence lawyers.

1.2. The guidance only covers parenting orders and contracts arising from criminal conduct or anti-social behaviour. Separate guidance on parenting orders and contracts arising from truancy and exclusion from school has been published by the DfES.[3]

1.3. Parenting Orders under the CD Act 1998 were implemented across England and Wales on 1 June 2000. Parenting orders and parenting contracts under the ASB Act 2003 and Criminal Justice Act 2003 ('the CJ Act 2003') will be implemented on 27 February 2004.

1.4. This document provides non-statutory guidance only. It should not be regarded as providing legal advice, which should be sought if there is any doubt as to the application or interpretation of legislation. Extracts from the relevant legislation on parenting orders and contracts are included at Annex A. Key terms are defined at Annex B.

1.5. This guidance was first issued for consultation in October 2003 and this version takes into account the comments received. In conjunction with users, the Home Office will update the guidance from time to time and issue amendments to this guidance. The latest version will be held on the Home Office website. If you have any comments or queries about the guidance please contact Anthony Green, Juvenile Offenders Unit, Room 102, Home Office, 50 Queen Anne's Gate, London SW1H 9AT. Email: *anthony.green10@homeoffice.gsi.gov.uk*, Telephone: 020 7273 4182.

---

[1] Under section 8 of the Crime and Disorder Act 1998 (CD Act 1998), sections 18, 26–29 & 85 of the Anti-Social Behaviour Act 2003 (ASB Act 2003) and section 324 of and schedule 34 to the Criminal Justice Act 2003 (CJ Act 2003).

[2] Under s25 of the ASB Act.

[3] To obtain a copy contact the Parental Responsibility (Behaviour and Attendance) Team on 020 7925 5800 or access *www.dfes.gov.uk/behaviourandattendance*.

1.6. **Related material which may be helpful:**

- 'National Standards for Youth Justice Services 2004' have been published by the Youth Justice Board (YJB) for England and Wales. Paragraphs 8.72–8.81 deal specifically with the parenting order. This guidance cross-refers to relevant parts of the National Standards.
- The YJB has also produced various publications on good practice in working with parents of young offenders. See in particular 'Key Elements of Effective Practice—Parenting', 'Key Elements of Effective Practice—Parenting (source)' and the YJB's 'Effective Practice Reader on parenting' in the practitioners' portal at *www.youth-justice-board.gov.uk*.

Section 2: Background to Parenting Programmes

a) Research evidence

2.1. Inadequate parental supervision is strongly associated with offending. For example, a Home Office study[4] showed that 42% of juveniles who had low or medium levels of parental supervision had offended, whereas for those juveniles who had experienced high levels of parental supervision the figure was only 20%. The same research showed that the quality of relationship between the parent and child is crucial. Research also suggests that the children of parents whose behaviour towards them is harsh or erratic are twice as likely to offend.[5]

2.2. In the United States, a study as long ago as 1973 showed that by training parents in negotiation skills, sticking to clear rules and rewarding good behaviour, offending rates among children were halved.[6] Parenting can also be an important protective factor that moderates a child's exposure to risk.[7]

2.3. Parenting programmes are designed to develop parents' skills to reduce parenting as a risk factor and enhance parenting as a protective factor. Throughout this guidance the term 'parenting programmes'[8] is used to refer to the variety of different approaches that may be used by YOTs to help parents address their child's misbehaviour as part of an overall parenting intervention. These include cognitive behaviour programmes, mentoring, parenting advice, individual family based therapy, functional family therapy, solution focussed (brief) therapy, family group conferencing and group based programmes.

---

[4] Graham and Bowling (1995) 'Young People and Crime', Home Office Research Study 145.

[5] 'Family backgrounds of aggressive youths' by DP Farrington (in 'Aggressive and anti-social behaviour in childhood and adolescence' by L Hersov et al. Pergamon Press, 1978. ISBN 0080218105).

[6] 'Short term behavioural intervention with delinquent families: impact on family process and recidivism' by JF Alexander and BV Parsons (in 'Journal of Abnormal Psychology', 81(3) 1973).

[7] See various YJB research about parenting contributing to risk and protective factors including 'Risk and Protective Factors Associated with Youth Crime and Effective Interventions to Prevent it' (2001) (research undertaken by Communities that Care) and 'The evaluation of the validity and reliability of the Youth Justice Board's assessment for young offenders'.

[8] Parenting Programmes are referred to throughout the relevant legislation as 'counselling or guidance programme'.

2.4. Since being introduced through the CD Act 1998, parenting orders have been operating successfully. YOTs have established or commissioned parenting programmes to support court orders and have also worked with parents on a voluntary basis. An evaluation of the Youth Justice Board's parenting programmes by the Policy Research Bureau[9] showed that they have a positive impact both on young people's perception of their parents and on their behaviour.

- Statistically significant positive changes were reported in parenting skills and competencies by the time parents left their programmes.
- 90% of parents said they would recommend the programme to other parents in their situation.
- Court ordered parents benefited just as much as voluntary participants.
- 95% of the young people had committed an offence in the year before their parents began the programme and 89% had been convicted of an offence. Each young person had committed an average of 4.4 offences in that period.
- In the year after their parents completed the programme, reconviction rates had fallen to 61.5% (a reduction of nearly one third), offences resulting in a conviction to 56%, and the average number of offences per young person had dropped to 2.1 (a 50% reduction).[10]

b) Helping parents help their children

2.5. Parenting is a challenging job. Parents need to be able to discipline, guide and nurture their child effectively. Helping parents to develop their skills is an effective way of ensuring that problems in a child or young person's behaviour or development are not allowed to grow unchecked into major difficulties for the individual, the family and the community.

2.6. Help and support for the parents of young people who become involved in crime is part of a wider programme of action to support families. Parents have an important role to play in preventing their children offending: they have a responsibility to the child and to the community to supervise and take proper care of them. Some parents may need help, support, encouragement and direction. Such assistance may be provided at an early stage by or on behalf of social services or a local education authority or by a voluntary agency and could be in the form of group work or one to one counselling. Or there could be work involving the whole family or parents and child. Early advice is also available over the telephone from Parentline Plus on 0808 800 2222.

2.7. If the YOT becomes involved, it could work with the parents on a voluntary basis, possibly using a parenting contract. Where the voluntary approach has failed or is not appropriate YOTs can work with parents through a parenting order. This work with parents should complement work with the child or young person.

---

[9] Ghate D and Ramella M (2002) 'Positive Parenting: The effectiveness of the Youth Justice Board's Parenting Programme', London: YJB (*http://www.youth-justice-board.gov.uk/Publications/Scripts/prodView.asp?idProduct=21&eP=PP*).

[10] These results should be taken as cautiously indicative because parenting programmes contributed to these outcomes in many cases alongside other interventions with the juvenile offender. The contribution of the different programmes is not known.

c) Overview of parenting contracts and orders

2.8. The full detail of parenting contracts and orders is given in section 3 onwards, but essentially a parenting contract is an agreement negotiated between a YOT worker and the parents of the child involved or likely to become involved in criminal conduct or anti-social behaviour. A parenting order is made in similar circumstances by a criminal court, family court or Magistrates' Court acting under civil jurisdiction. However they are made, by reinforcing or securing proper parental responsibility, parenting contracts and orders are intended to prevent offending—which section 37 of the CD Act 1998 established as the principal aim of the youth justice system. Section 37 also requires all those working within the youth justice system to have regard to this aim in addition to any other duties to which they are subject. It therefore helps set the overall framework for work with young offenders and their parents. Following a judicial review, the parenting order has been held to be compliant with the Human Rights Act 1998.[11]

2.9. Parenting contracts and orders can consist of two elements.

(i) The first is a parenting programme designed to meet the individual needs of parents so as to help them address their child's misbehaviour. This is not a punishment but a positive way of bolstering parental responsibility and helping parents develop their skills so they can respond more effectively to their child's needs.

(ii) The second element specifies particular ways in which parents are required to exercise control over their child's behaviour to address particular factors associated with offending or anti-social behaviour. Examples would be ensuring that their child goes to school every day or is home during certain hours.

2.10. Under the CD Act 1998 parenting orders resulting from criminal conduct or anti-social behaviour are available in any court proceedings where:

(a) a child safety order has been made;

(b) an anti-social behaviour order or sex offender order has been made in respect of a child or young person; or

(c) a child or young person has been convicted of an offence.

2.11. The availability of parenting orders has now been extended by the ASB Act 2003 and the CJ Act 2003 to allow them to be made at an earlier stage. Involving parents at an early stage helps to prevent their child's offending or anti-social behaviour from becoming entrenched and leading on to more serious problems. YOTs are now able to apply to Magistrates' Courts to make free-standing parenting orders without the child or young person being required to appear in court for offending. Under the CJ Act 2003, parenting orders—already available alongside most court sentences on a young offender—now also become available when a referral order is made or when a Youth Offender Panel[12] refers a parent back to court for failing to attend panel meetings.

---

[11] R (M) v Inner London Crown Court, [2003] EWHC 30; [2003] 1 FLR 944. *http://www.bailii.org/cgi-bin/ markup.cgi?doc=/ew/cases/EWHC/Admin/2003/301.ht ml&query=[2003]+EWHC+301&method=all.*

[12] When a young offender is made subject to a referral order they are referred to a Youth Offender Panel.

2.12. The ASB Act 2003 has also introduced parenting contracts. These can provide a formal framework for work YOTs carry out with parents on a voluntary basis, encouraging an effective partnership between YOTs and parents. YOTs have a statutory power to make a contract and in return are required to help parents deliver their part of the contract.

2.13. As contracts are voluntary there is no penalty for refusing to enter into or failing to comply with one. However, previous failure to co-operate with support offered through a contract is a relevant consideration for a court when deciding whether to make a parenting order. Therefore contracts provide YOTs with additional authority when attempting to secure voluntary co-operation from parents.

2.14. When parents are unwilling to engage with parenting support on a voluntary basis and a YOT assesses that a parent could be supported to improve the child's behaviour, YOTs can apply for a free-standing parenting order or recommend a parenting order linked to a child's conviction or another order. However, before applying for an order, YOTs should normally have tried to engage with parents on a voluntary basis whether or not through a contract.

Three ways of working with parents.

1) Voluntarily
Many parents want and may even ask for support. YOTs may work with parents on a voluntary basis without using a contract or order.

2) Voluntarily with a parenting contract
If a more formal approach is useful or the parents are unwilling to co-operate, a YOT can suggest a parenting contract. Refusing to enter into a contract can be used as evidence to support an application for an order and may persuade a reluctant parent to engage.

3) Parenting order
If the parent is unwilling to co-operate, the YOT can apply for, or recommend, a parenting order.

2.15. Any parent or guardian of a child or young person may enter into a parenting contract or can be made subject to a parenting order if the relevant conditions apply. Throughout this guidance references to 'parent' include 'guardian' and mean each and every person coming within these definitions. For the definitions of these terms see Annex B.

2.16. Contracts and orders may be made in respect of one or more parents or guardians depending on the circumstances but wherever possible each parent or guardian who could be supported to positively influence their child should be involved. Apart from the mother and father, this could include a step parent, a parent's partner, grandparents or, in some circumstances, another adult significantly involved in a child's upbringing.

2.17. The evaluation of the YJB's parenting programmes has shown that few fathers have been involved in parenting programmes. However, when both parents are participating in the upbringing of a child, even when they live separately, a parenting intervention is likely to be more effective if both the mother and father are involved, unless a parent is estranged, for instance because of domestic violence or abuse (see also 2.20 below). By contrast, working with only one of the parents means that positive results achieved through one of them can be undermined by the influence of the other. Encouraging one parent to set consistent and fair boundaries will have less effect if the other parent continues to be inconsistent and unfair. Whether or not both should go on the same programme should depend on the particular needs of the parents and whether the presence of one parent is likely to reduce the impact of the programme on the other. In some cases a YOT will be able to work with one parent voluntarily but may have to explore using a parenting order to engage the other.

d) Assessment process

2.18. Assessment is needed to form a picture of the child and the family circumstances. This should be informed by information from other agencies. Initially the YOT will complete an ASSET assessment but where this suggests that parenting is a significant factor in the child or young person's misbehaviour a detailed assessment of the parents should be carried out. This should identify:

- parenting risk and protective factors;
- the individual needs and circumstances of the parents;
- whether a programme could support the parents so they can positively influence their child and if so, what form it should take and whether it should involve a parenting contract or an order;
- any cultural, racial, linguistic, literacy, religious or gender specific issues that may affect the kind of programme that will be effective for a particular parent;
- the facts relating to a particular parent or child without invalid assumptions relating to culture, race or gender;
- whether the parent has any disability, special educational need or mental health problem that would affect the parent's ability to participate in a programme and if so, how it can be accommodated;
- any other issue that could affect a parent's ability to participate (such as transport or child care).

2.19. The parenting assessment and the ASSET assessment should be linked and may be presented in court if a YOT applies for, or recommends, a parenting order. The assessment should be updated in light of any significant new information and should be regularly reviewed.

2.20. Any intervention must be in accordance with any existing Child Protection Plan or care plan and be responsive to issues that emerge during the intervention process, such as serious mental health problems, personality disorder, domestic violence or child abuse. Practitioners should follow Area Child Protection Committee procedures. **Parenting practitioners have a duty to protect children and young people. Information that emerges during the intervention or assessment process about domestic violence or abuse will need to be passed on to police and social services for action. Information about other risks may also need to be referred to the appropriate agency.**[13]

[13] For further information the Youth Justice Board's 'Effective Practice Reader on Parenting' includes detailed guidance and 'Working Together to Safeguard Children', DOH HMSO 1999 is the key reference document for inter-agency working (*http://www.doh.gov.uk/quality5.htm*).

2.21. Practitioners should also establish with other agencies, including the police and social services, whether they have information regarding the family about child abuse or domestic violence. If this is the case then there must be discussion with the agencies already involved with the family to establish a joint agency approach. Protocols must be drawn up to ensure that satisfactory information and data sharing is achieved in any joint working arrangements between agencies.[14]

e) Co-ordinating parenting support

2.22. Parenting work can be carried out by or on behalf of a local education authority (under an educational parenting contract or order), social services, health services or by voluntary organisations. The YOT must identify any work with the child or parents by other agencies and co-ordinate any further intervention. Other agencies may also be able to provide useful information about the child or young person's behaviour or the nature and extent of parental supervision. For instance a young person may be playing truant from school and the parent might therefore already be subject to an 'educational' parenting contract or order. This should be included in the YOT assessment. When a parent is taking part in a programme it is important to inform other agencies so they are able to relate to the child and family consistently.

2.23. When arranging a contract or applying for or recommending an order, YOTs should consider whether this should also cover poor behaviour inside school and/or truancy and, if so, who should be the lead agency. Truancy and misbehaviour at school can both be risk factors associated with offending and therefore a YOT parenting intervention can address educational issues. On the other hand, educational parenting orders and contracts cannot address criminal or anti-social behaviour outside school. Therefore it will usually be appropriate for YOTs to lead in cases where the YOT and LEA both wish to work with the parents of a child or young person. However there will be cases where it will be more appropriate for the LEA to take the lead. Local protocols will need to be agreed about co-operating and supplying resources in such cases.

2.24. Local co-ordination in the delivery of parenting programmes may also help target effort where it can be most effective.

f) Looked after children

2.25. 'Looked after' is a term used in the Children Act 1989 to describe all children subject to a care order under section 31, or who are provided with accommodation on a voluntary basis for more than 24 hours under section 20 of the Act. Social services will already have a Care Plan for all their looked after children and will already be working with the family. A parenting order or contract should only be used after consultation with the local authority and where it is consistent with, and forms part of, the child's Care Plan. This is likely to be most appropriate where a child is

---

[14] See YJB 'Guidance for Youth Offending Teams on Information Sharing' (2001) (*http://www.youth-justice-board.gov.uk/Publications/Scripts/prodView.asp?idproduct=74&eP=YJB*) and 'Sharing Personal and Sensitive Information in Respect of Children and Young People at Risk of Offending. A Practical Guide' issued by the YJB and Association of Chief Police Officers (2003) (*http://www.youth-justice-board.gov.uk/PractitionersPortal/News/NewsArchive/InfoSharing.htm*).

placed with his or her parents, or the aim of a Care Plan is for the child to be reunited with them.

g) Feedback to courts

2.26. It would be helpful if YOTs inform all courts able to make parenting orders about parenting programmes available locally, what they can achieve, when they are likely to be effective and what is carried out voluntarily and under parenting orders.

h) Race and diversity

2.27. The PRB evaluation[15] found that the percentage of black and minority ethnic ('BME') parents on parenting programmes is close to the percentage of BME parents in the overall population (that is 8% as against 9% in the general population[16]). Relatively few services, however, are currently targeted specifically at BME parents. YOTs must plan how they can support the delivery of parenting programmes to BME parents and should take into account voluntary sector organisations which have expertise in supporting BME parents.

2.28. Direct or indirect discrimination against parents on grounds of race, colour, nationality (including citizenship), or ethnic or national origin by criminal justice agencies including YOTs is unlawful under the Race Relations Act. YOTs have a duty to consider the promotion of racial equality in carrying out their work. YOTs will be aware of the need to guard against racial stereotyping and assumptions based on race or irrelevant references to race, and make due allowance for different cultural norms or customs. In parenting interventions, equal treatment will be particularly important in assessing parents and their children, making recommendations to courts and deciding whether to pursue a parent for breach of an order.

i) Disability, mental health and special educational needs

2.29. YOT staff will of course be well aware that special educational needs, disability and mental health problems of a child (and of his or her parents) will be highly relevant to the child's (and parent's) behaviour.

2.30. Where a child (or parent) has a disability, mental health problem or special educational needs, the YOT will need to communicate with practitioners who have specialist knowledge of the child and parents in order to determine whether a parenting intervention is appropriate and if so what form it should take, depending on the needs of the child and parents. A specialist involved in the assessment process will therefore inform the nature of any subsequent parenting intervention.

2.31. Parenting programmes will need to be tailored to address specific needs. A child's (or parent's) disability, special educational needs or mental health problem will also have a bearing on any requirements set out in a parenting contract or order, if it has been found appropriate to make one.

2.32. The parenting programme should be designed to ensure that parents with disabilities, mental health problems or special educational needs are not excluded or

---

[15] Ghate D and Ramella M (2002) 'Positive Parenting: The effectiveness of the Youth Justice Board's Parenting Programme', London: YJB.

[16] 2001 census figures.

discriminated against and are able to access the same quality and level of support and have their parenting support needs met.

Section 3: Parenting contracts

a) Description of a parenting contract

3.1. A parenting contract is a voluntary written agreement between a YOT worker and the parents or guardians of a child or young person. A contract consists of two elements:

(a) a statement by the parents or guardians that they agree to comply for a specified period with requirements specified in the contract; and

(b) a statement by the YOT agreeing to provide support to the parents or guardians for the purpose of complying with the contract.

3.2. The requirements in (a) may include, in particular, a requirement to attend a parenting programme.

b) When would a parenting contract be made?

3.3. Parenting contracts are not intended to replace all voluntary work with parents but to provide an additional option backed by statute. As many parents want support, YOTs will often be able to work effectively with them without using a contract. Where a parent is reluctant to engage or would benefit from a more formal arrangement, a YOT may wish to negotiate a parenting contract.

3.4. The purpose of a parenting contract is to prevent the child or young person from engaging or persisting in criminal conduct or anti-social behaviour. Whether a parenting contract will serve this purpose will be determined by the YOT in light of the assessment.

3.5. A YOT worker may negotiate a parenting contract when a child or young person has been referred to the YOT and he or she has reason to believe that the child or young person has engaged, or is likely to engage, in criminal conduct or anti-social behaviour. Whether or not they accept that their child's behaviour is criminal or anti-social, the phrase 'is likely to engage' allows for work with parents without giving the child or young person a reprimand or final warning or charging them with a view to court proceedings.

3.6. The phrase also allows early supportive work with parents who have consented to be referred to a YOT as their child has been identified as being at risk of engaging in criminal conduct or anti-social behaviour. Where a child has not engaged in criminal conduct or anti-social behaviour, the referral to the YOT and any subsequent intervention must be on a voluntary basis.

3.7. Children referred to a YOT, when a parenting contract may be suitable, will include:

- a child convicted of an offence;
- a child who is referred to the YOT in connection with a reprimand or a final warning;
- a child under 10 that a member of the YOT has reason to believe has committed an act, which if the child had been older, would have constituted an offence;
- a child identified as being at risk of offending by a Youth Inclusion Support Panel.

c) Negotiating a contract

3.8. If a YOT considers a parenting contract would be useful, the YOT worker should first consult with other agencies working with the child or young person or with the parents or guardians, to establish both how a parenting contract would fit in with any existing interventions and whether other agencies should be involved in the work on the contract.

3.9. It will be for the YOT worker to decide how best to engage the parents in discussions leading to a contract depending on the circumstances. Usually both parents or guardians should be involved and, subject to age, maturity and understanding, the child or young person as well.

3.10. The parents and where appropriate their child should be asked to outline their views on the misbehaviour, how they believe it should be tackled and what they think of the idea of a parenting contract. The YOT worker should outline what a parenting contract is and why one may be appropriate. The parents and YOT worker will also be able to discuss support the parents would like and what the YOT is able to provide. The aim should be to work in partnership to improve the behaviour of the child or young person.

3.11. All efforts to engage the parents using a contract should be recorded as this would be a relevant factor in any subsequent application for a parenting order.

3.12. If a contract is negotiated, the specified requirements for the parents under s25(3)(a) of the ASB Act 2003 will need to be designed to prevent criminal conduct or anti-social behaviour or further criminal conduct or anti-social behaviour. Parents should be asked about any requirements they would find helpful in addition to those the YOT suggest.

3.13. Examples are:

- to ensure their child stays away unless supervised from a part of town where he or she has misbehaved;
- to ensure their child is effectively supervised at certain times;
- to ensure their child avoids contact with certain disruptive individuals;
- to ensure their child avoids contact with someone he or she has been harassing;
- to ensure their child attends school regularly;
- to ensure that they (the parents) attend all school meetings concerning their child.

3.14. Where there is separate work being carried out with the child it may be helpful for the contract to support this or bring together work involving parents and child. For instance the requirements of a parenting contract could mirror requirements agreed in an Acceptable Behaviour Contract.[17]

3.15. Contracts should normally include a parenting programme, arranged by the YOT and based on an assessment of the parents' needs.

3.16. The contract will need to be written in language the parents can understand (including a translation where appropriate) and should balance specific and general requirements (specific requirements are normally clearer about what parents or guardians should actually do while general requirements are normally clearer about aims).

---

[17] See 'Guide to Anti-social Behaviour Orders and Acceptable Behaviour Contracts', Home Office, 2002 (*www.crimereduction.gov.uk/asbos9.htm*).

3.17. A YOT may include more than one parent or guardian in a contract or negotiate separate contracts with different parents or guardians of a child. Considerations should include whether the parents or guardians have agreed to the same specific requirements, whether the contracts will cover the same period and the preference of the parents or guardians.

3.18. The YOT's side of the contract must include a statement that it agrees to provide the parents with support for the purpose of complying with the requirements. This statement should detail the specific support the YOT has agreed to provide, such as the parenting programme. The YOT can also include any other action it has agreed to take.

3.19. The parents and a representative of the YOT (preferably the person who will deliver the YOT's part of the contract) must sign the contract and they should each be given a copy. It may also be helpful to give a copy to other agencies working with the family. Where the parents are unable to read, the contract should be explained to them and they should be asked to sign and keep a copy.

d) Length of contracts

3.20. The ASB Act 2003 does not specify a time limit for contracts so duration is a question of what is reasonable and effective. A contract should end at the same time as a parenting programme if it includes no other requirements.

e) Delivering the contract

3.21. A particular YOT worker must be responsible for delivering the YOT's part of the contract and for helping to manage its overall outcome. This will require regular contact with the parents to discuss progress and any problems in meeting the contract's requirements; and contact with other interested agencies such as the provider of a parenting programme or, where truancy is an issue, the school authorities.

f) Parents who refuse to enter into a parenting contract or with whom it is impossible to agree a contract

3.22. Parenting contracts are designed to be voluntary. If a parent refuses to enter into one the YOT worker should seek constructively to meet all legitimate concerns and ensure that a written record is kept of all efforts to negotiate a contract. This should include whether the parents were at least willing to meet to discuss the possibility and if so what was said. If the conditions at s26(3) are met and a parent or guardian refuses to enter into a contract or fails to agree to an appropriate contract to try to secure agreement, the YOT worker may wish to warn of the intention to apply for a free-standing parenting order and that the court will take into account the refusal to enter into a parenting contract (s27(1)(a) of the ASB Act 2003).

g) Non-compliance by parents

3.23. The YOT should work with the parents to gain their co-operation and compliance with the contract but will have to judge whether any failure to comply is reasonable and whether the contract remains useful and should continue. There is no penalty for failing to comply with a parenting contract but it would be a relevant consideration for a YOT in deciding whether to apply for, and a relevant consideration for a court in deciding whether to make, a parenting order.

3.24. Any failures to comply must therefore be recorded and acted upon. The YOT worker should contact the parents to seek an explanation. If it is reasonable and overall the contract is still proving useful then the non-compliance and reasons should all be recorded and the contract should continue as normal. If the explanation shows that the contract is proving difficult to comply with through no fault of the parents, the YOT worker should meet the parents to review and, if appropriate, amend the contract.

3.25. If no explanation is given or the YOT worker is not satisfied with the explanation, they should serve the parents with a warning and keep a record of it. If repeated failures to comply are seriously undermining the contract's effectiveness, the YOT worker should meet the parents or guardians to discuss how the contract can be made to work. If the conditions at s26(3) of the ASB Act 2003 are met, the YOT worker should remind them that if the contract fails, the YOT would be able to apply for a free-standing parenting order and that a court would take account of how far the parents had complied with the contract. In light of this meeting, the YOT worker should decide whether the non-compliance is undermining the contract to the extent that the YOT needs to apply for a parenting order or whether to persevere with the contract. The YOT worker must record the decision and reasons. This can be used in any future application for a parenting order.

h) Non-compliance by YOTs

3.26. The YOT worker responsible for the contract should ensure that the parents receive all the support that the YOT agreed to provide. Where for any reason the YOT fails, or will clearly fail to meet one of the contract's requirements, the YOT worker should contact the parents and provide a full explanation. As with non-compliance by parents, this should be recorded on file. The YOT worker should also encourage the parents to voice any concerns they have about the delivery of the YOT's side of the contract and explain how they can make a complaint to the YOT manager if concerns cannot be addressed.

Section 4: Parenting orders

4.1. The procedure for making free-standing parenting orders set out in section 5 is different from that for orders linked to a conviction or order on the child, set out in section 6. The content and operation of the actual order will be the same, as in sections 7–9.

Section 5: Free-standing parenting orders

a) Availability of the order

5.1. YOTs should form a view about the suitability of a parent for a parenting order following assessment of the child and family circumstances. YOTs can apply to the Magistrates' Court for a parenting order in respect of a parent or guardian of a child or young person who has been referred to them.

5.2. The intention is to steer the child away from criminal conduct or anti-social behaviour. Free-standing orders require parents to co-operate to tackle early patterns of offending or anti-social behaviour.

5.3. A YOT should normally only apply for a free-standing order after a parent has failed to co-operate in a parenting contract.

5.4. The YOT could apply after failed attempts to gain parental co-operation on a voluntary basis without attempting a contract but a court might well require evidence of refusing to enter into or non-compliance with a contract.

5.5. To make a free-standing parenting order, a Magistrates' Court needs to be satisfied of two conditions:
   (a) that the child or young person has engaged in criminal conduct or anti-social behaviour; and
   (b) that making the order would be desirable in the interests of preventing further criminal conduct or anti-social behaviour.

5.6. The first condition requires Magistrates to make a finding about alleged criminal conduct or anti-social behaviour by the child or young person. The legislation does not specify a standard of proof for this, but courts might in practice insist on a criminal standard of proof.[18] The second condition is a judgement, so does not involve a standard of proof. Note sections 7 and 8 of this guidance which will have a bearing on evidence.

b) Evidence that the child or young person has engaged in criminal conduct or anti-social behaviour

5.7. A child referred to a YOT will generally have been involved in criminal conduct or anti-social behaviour and may have already received a police reprimand or final warning. If parents deny past involvement by their child, YOTs will need to present evidence and ensure any witnesses or agency workers involved are able to attend. If a YOT is not sure whether there is sufficient evidence it should seek legal advice before applying.

5.8. The supporting evidence could include witness statements of officers who attended incidents or of people affected by the behaviour, evidence of complaints recorded by the police, statements from professional witnesses, video or CCTV evidence, previous convictions, reprimands and final warnings and copies of custody records of previous arrests relevant to the application.

c) Evidence that making the order would be desirable in the interests of preventing further criminal conduct or anti-social behaviour

5.9. The court has discretion to consider all the circumstances of the case in deciding whether it is desirable to make a parenting order, including the evidence of parents and other witnesses in court. The YOT's assessments of the child or young person and the parents or guardians and details of its ability to provide the parenting programme should be presented in a report supporting the application.

5.10. The YOT should also provide evidence of any experience of trying to engage with the parents through a parenting contract. Magistrates are obliged to take into account any refusal by a parent or guardian to enter into, or failure to comply with, a parenting contract. The YOT needs to be clear what evidence there is of this. If

[18] See for instance the case of McCann where the House of Lords held that anti-social behaviour orders are civil orders to which the criminal standard of proof applies to the past acts of anti-social behaviour.

parents or guardians are ready to engage fully with voluntary support, a parenting order would not usually be desirable.

d) Application form and time limits

5.11. Applications should be by complaint to the adult Magistrates' Court. A form is attached at Annex D.

5.12. Under Section 127 of the Magistrates' Courts Act 1980 a complaint must be made within six months of the criminal or anti-social behaviour concerned. If that is done, a summons may be issued later, but not so late as to cause unreasonable delay to the prejudice of the parents.

Section 6: Parenting orders linked to conviction or other order

a) Availability

6.1. A court can make a parenting order in any proceedings where:
(a) a child safety order has been made;
(b) an anti-social behaviour order or sex offender order has been made in respect of a child or young person;
(c) a child or young person has been convicted of an offence; or
(d) a referral order has been made or when a parent is referred back to court by a Youth Offender Panel after failing to attend panel meetings.[19]

6.2. This means that parenting orders can be made in any of the following courts:
(i) a Family Proceedings Court;
(ii) a Magistrates' Court acting under civil jurisdiction;
(iii) all criminal courts, i.e. a Youth Court, an adult Magistrates' Court or the Crown Court.

6.3. The parenting order is made under the court's own motion (suggested forms for the order are at Annex E). The consent of the parent or guardian is not required.

6.4. There are conditions, one of which must apply before the court can make a parenting order. They are that the order would be *desirable* in the interests of preventing:
(a) a repetition of the kind of behaviour which led to a child safety order, an anti-social behaviour order or a sex offender order being made; or
(b) the commission of further offences, where the child or young person has been convicted of an offence or issued with a referral order.

6.5. There is an additional condition when a Youth Offender Panel refers a parent back to court. The court would only be able to make a parenting order if it is proved to its satisfaction that the parent has failed without reasonable excuse to attend panel meetings ***and*** that the order would be desirable in the interests of preventing the commission of further offences. The Home Office will publish revised guidance on referral orders.

6.6. The court has discretion to consider all the circumstances of the case in deciding whether it is desirable to make a parenting order. The court may wish to consider, for example, how much help, support and encouragement the parent or guardian has offered the child, and whether they are willing to receive assistance and support

---

[19] As a result of the CJ Act 2003.

from the YOT or other provider on a voluntary basis. Where the parent is fully co-operating or willing to co-operate voluntarily a parenting order will not usually be desirable. If the parent has attended a programme without changing his or her behaviour, then an order might be called for.

6.7. The suitability of a parent or guardian for a parenting order is normally determined by an assessment process carried out by a practitioner from a YOT. If the assessments provide evidence that parents could be supported to positively influence their child's behaviour and the parents are not willing to engage with support voluntarily it will usually be appropriate to recommend a parenting order to the court. A judgement about the suitability of a parenting intervention and recommendations are usually made in a pre-sentence report ('PSR'). The recommendation takes into consideration the potential needs of both the parents or guardians and the child and the likely effectiveness in terms of changing their behaviour.

6.8. When preparing PSRs in cases where a parenting order is inappropriate due to, for example, domestic violence, abuse or continuing civil disputes, practitioners will need to take into account the level of information the court needs to make a decision. It may be that detailed sensitive information will not be necessary and that a general phrase such as 'while family tensions or civil matters are to be resolved' will be sufficient for the purpose.

6.9. Where a child or young person under the age of 16 has been convicted of an offence or made subject to an anti-social behaviour order, the court is obliged to make a parenting order if it is satisfied that it is desirable to do so in the interests of preventing further offending or anti-social behaviour by the child or young person. If it is not so satisfied, the court must state this in open court and explain why. The only exception is that, when a referral order is made, the court retains discretion whether or not to make a parenting order.

6.10. Before making a parenting order with a referral order the court has to consider a report by an 'appropriate officer' because the court needs to have the information necessary to decide whether a parenting order would be desirable. An 'appropriate officer' can be an officer of a local probation board, a social worker or a member of a YOT. The report should say which requirements should be included in the order and why they are in the interest of preventing further offending and, where the child or young person is below 16, give information about the person's family circumstances and the likely effect of the order on them.

6.11. If the court is considering serious offences when a referral order could be made and a PSR is required, in appropriate cases, the court may request a parenting assessment at the same time.

6.12. Parenting orders would normally only be made at the same time as referral orders if there is enough already known about the parents and family circumstances to enable a satisfactory report to be written in the time before the hearing. This would usually be where the YOT has already attempted to engage with parents, for instance where a young person has received a Final Warning with an intervention. In this case the YOT may be able to provide the court with a report describing the attempts to engage the parents, with an update of the original parenting assessment in the time between notification and court appearance.

6.13. Where the parents are not already known to the YOT in this way, the court will want to provide the opportunity for the Youth Offender Panel to engage parents and young people in agreeing a contract which could include provision of parenting support on a voluntary basis or through a parenting order. If the parents do not attend the panel their case can be referred back to court, and the YOT would provide an assessment. The court would then consider whether a parenting order is desirable.

Section 7: Procedural points common to all parenting orders

a) Information about family circumstances

7.1. Before making a parenting order where the child or young person is under the age of 16, the court must obtain and consider information about the parent's or guardian's family circumstances and the likely effect of the order on those circumstances. Where a young person is aged 16 or 17, the court may obtain such information but is not required to do so.

7.2. This recognises that juveniles aged 16 and 17 are at a transitional stage between childhood and adulthood. Their emotional, social, intellectual and physical development and circumstances will vary greatly. Some may have left school, be living independently of their parents and possibly have family responsibilities of their own. Others may be in full-time education and fully dependent upon their parents.

7.3. The YOT's assessment (see section 2d) and subsequent report should cover the family circumstances although the court may decide to obtain further information by questioning the YOT officer in court or the parents or guardians if they are in court.

b) Parental attendance at court

7.4. The Government believes that parents need to be in court when their children appear so as to support them and help take responsibility for tackling their offending behaviour. Magistrates' Courts, including Youth Courts, and Crown Courts, have powers to enforce parental attendance at court where appropriate. It is usually desirable to ensure both parents attend court and are involved in any parenting intervention. **An important exception to this may be where one parent has a history of being violently or sexually abusive towards the child or other parent**.

7.5. In discussions and correspondence with parents before coming to court, whenever possible YOTs will wish to encourage them to attend court. However, parents, particularly single parents, will sometimes find it difficult to attend court hearings. YOTs should explain that if a parent cannot attend court, reasons should be communicated to the court and that if valid reasons are not provided, any parent who does not attend will risk being made subject to a parenting order. YOTs will also wish to consider whether a non-resident parent should be encouraged to attend. The courts can adjourn to secure attendance and have power to require attendance if thought necessary. But against this they will also weigh up the desirability of completing proceedings.

(i) In a criminal court or a Magistrates' Court acting under civil jurisdiction

7.6. Section 34A of the Children and Young Persons Act 1933 provides that, where a child or young person is charged with an offence or *is for any other reason brought before a court*, the court *may* in any case and *shall* in the case of a child or young person who is *under the age of 16* require a person who is a parent or guardian to attend the court during all stages of the proceedings, unless the court is satisfied that it would be unreasonable to do so.

7.7. The court can issue a summons to secure the attendance of the parents or guardians.

7.8. Section 34A applies to Crown Courts and Magistrates' Courts when dealing with either civil or criminal proceedings against the child or where the child's actions are the subject of a parenting order application. Because the provision relates not only to offences but to cases where the child or young person is for any other reason brought before the court, section 34A applies in the case of all proceedings in relation to parenting orders where the child or young person is brought before the court and his or her actions act as the trigger for the parenting order. Parents who fail to attend such hearings will be subject to the existing rules of those courts.

(ii) In a Family Proceedings Court

7.9. These courts hear applications for Child Safety Orders. The child is not required to attend, but under the Family Proceedings Courts (Children Act 1989) Rules 1991 the court may require a parent or guardian to attend.

(iii) In an adult Magistrates' Court (where an application is made for a free-standing parenting order)

7.10. When a YOT applies for a free-standing parenting order the parents should be summonsed to attend the proceedings on the laying of a complaint.

(iv) Where a parent fails to attend

7.11. It is important that courts do not simply make an order on the parent who attends court rather than on an absent parent. Often it is just the mother who attends court whereas engaging both the mother and father will be most effective in tackling their child's misbehaviour. In fact where one or both parents do not attend and there is no reasonable explanation, this may lend weight to an existing recommendation for a parenting order. Where there has been no recommendation for a parenting order, particularly if there were a pattern of non-attendance without valid reasons, then the court may consider whether there is now sufficient evidence for an order. Alternatively, the court may consider whether the YOT should be asked to re-assess the need for an order and return to the court at a later date with a recommendation (if proceedings involving the child have not been completed) or an application for a free-standing order (if proceedings have already been completed).

c) Explaining the order to the parent

7.12. Before making a parenting order the court must, as required by s9(3) of the CD Act 1998, explain clearly to the parent or guardian the effect of the order and of its requirements; the consequences which may follow if he or she fails to comply with any of them; and that the court has the power to review the order on the application of the parent or guardian or of the responsible officer. This requirement can be dealt with if the parent or guardian is present in court using an interpreter where appropriate.

7.13. Experience has shown it is crucial how a parenting order is explained to parents or guardians. It should be stressed that parenting orders are not a punishment and emphasis should be placed on building parents' existing strengths and skills.

7.14. It is highly desirable for parents to be present in court but a parenting order can be made in their absence. Where the parent or guardian is not present, the court will need to find a different way to comply with s9(3) before it can make a parenting order. One would be to write to the parents or guardians (provided literacy is not a problem), explaining that the court has decided to make a parenting order on them and when the hearing will be, the effect of the order, the nature of its requirements and the consequences of non-compliance; and to invite the parent or guardian to attend the hearing. The YOT or other agency responsible for the proceedings could deliver the letter. There must be proof that the letter has been served.

7.15. A court may include more than one parent or guardian in an order or issue separate orders to different parents or guardians. Consideration should include whether the parents or guardians are being asked to comply with the same requirements over the same period. All parents or guardians named in an order should be given copies.

Section 8: Requirements of parenting orders

8.1. The requirements in parenting orders or in directions given under them should, as far as practicable, avoid any conflict with the parent's religious beliefs and any interference with the times when the parent normally works or attends educational courses.

a) Parenting programme

8.2. The core requirement of a parenting order is that the parent attends a parenting programme.[20] Details and duration of the programme are specified in directions given by the **responsible officer**. All orders must include this, unless the parent or guardian has previously received a parenting order. The programme can last for up to three months. The arrangements should be as flexible as possible, and take account of programme availability and timing. It may be provided by the responsible officer or for example the local authority social services department or a local voluntary sector organisation working with parents. The local authority youth justice plan should set out the general arrangements for delivering parenting orders.

8.3. The **court** will need to decide the length of the order. This needs to allow sufficient time for:

- assessing parents;
- any individual work needed to prepare the parents for the programme;
- any waiting time before the programme can start;
- the programme itself;
- the time any specific requirements should run (see 8.12 below).

8.4. The responsible officer will need to assess what kind of programme is required, in consultation with the provider. This should cover for example who will provide the sessions; whether they should be group, individually or family-based; and whether there are particular cultural and social factors to be considered.

[20] Referred to in legislation as a counselling or guidance programme.

8.5. During the programme the responsible officer and the programme provider (if different) will need to monitor the parents' progress at suitable intervals.

8.6. The parent might also find it helpful to be involved in some voluntary follow-up work when the order has been completed, such as attending a parent support group.

b) Residential requirement

8.7. A parenting order can include a residential course but only if two conditions are met:
   (a) that the attendance of the parent or guardian at a residential course is likely to be more effective than their attendance at a non-residential course in preventing the child or young person from engaging in a repetition of the behaviour which led to the making of the order; and
   (b) that any likely interference with family life is proportionate in all the circumstances.

8.8. This is designed to ensure that residential requirements are made only where proportionate under Article 8 of the European Convention on Human Rights—right to respect for private and family life.

8.9. A YOT recommending a parenting order with a residential component should provide evidence that these conditions are met. An example would be where the parent's home life is so chaotic that he or she needs a structured setting where sustained counselling and guidance can be undertaken.

8.10. For the court to decide whether any likely interference with family life is proportionate the YOT will need to explain the programme. This need not be continuous; a small number of residential weekends structured within a wider non-residential programme may be suitable. Arrangements for the care of the child (and any siblings and dependants) will be a crucial consideration. Voluntary attendance by the child and siblings may be desirable as intensive family work can be particularly effective.

8.11. Residential parenting support is currently being piloted on a voluntary basis and will be fully evaluated. This will inform the development of residential work and practical guidance. YOTs will need to meet all statutory requirements for such courses (depending on their content and format) covering health and safety, criminal record checks and registration with the National Care Standards Commission.

c) Specific requirements

8.12. The court may also include in a parenting order specific requirements for the parent to comply with for not more than 12 months. These may be what the court considers desirable to prevent any repetition of the particular behaviour which led to the child safety, anti-social behaviour or sex offender order, or any further offence by the child or young person. Although discretionary, it may be helpful to include further requirements such as for supervision.

8.13. These requirements would need to be tailored to address the problems which led to the parenting order and should, if possible, be linked to the requirements of any order imposed on the child or young person. They could include requiring the parent to ensure that the child:

- attends school or other relevant educational activities, such as mentoring in literacy or numeracy or a homework club;
- attends a programme or course to address relevant problems, such as anger management or drug or alcohol misuse;
- avoids contact with disruptive and, possibly, older children;
- avoids unsupervised visits to certain areas, such as shopping centres;
- is at home during certain hours at night and is effectively supervised.

8.14. Failing without reasonable excuse to comply with the order is a criminal offence. Therefore the requirements must be clear enough for a parent or guardian to know when they are breaching them and for the responsible officer to be able to monitor compliance.

Section 9: Managing parenting orders and further court involvement

a) Role of the responsible officer

9.1. A parenting order must specify a responsible officer, who will generally be a member of a YOT or may be a social worker from a local authority social services department, a probation officer or a person nominated by the chief education officer who is working outside the team, such as an education welfare officer or social worker. The responsible officer will need to provide or arrange for the provision of the parenting programme, and supervise any other requirements included in the order.

9.2. Where a member of the YOT is not due to attend court, the relevant social worker or other person who is there will need to consult the YOT before giving advice to the court.

9.3. Where a parenting order is made and the young offender is, or is going to be, supervised by the YOT, it may be appropriate for a member of the team to act as responsible officer under the parenting order, to help ensure a coherent approach to the family situation as a whole. Similarly, where the child is being supervised by a social worker, for instance under a child safety order, it may be appropriate for a social worker from the social services department to act as responsible officer under the parenting order.

9.4. Under paragraph 8.74 of the YJB National Standards for Youth Justice Services 2004 the initial contact between the responsible officer and the parent should take place before the end of the working day after the order is made. This should be an opportunity for the responsible officer to explain further to the parent the nature of the parenting order (and provide him or her with a copy of the order), its purpose and how it will work in practice. The practical details of the requirements will need to be set out, the monitoring arrangements described and the consequences of failure to comply with any requirements explained. Under paragraph 8.75, if the counselling or guidance programme under the order is to be provided by someone else he or she should meet the parent up to two weeks before the programme is due to start.

9.5. The relationship between the parent or guardian and the responsible officer will be vital to the successful completion of the order. During the order, the responsible officer should maintain good contact with the parent or guardian. This should help monitor compliance. If the requirements are proving difficult to comply with through no fault of the parent or guardian, the responsible officer may apply to the court for the order to be varied.

b) Variation and discharge

9.6. During a parenting order, the court which made it may vary or discharge it, on the application of the responsible officer or the parent or guardian. Application is by complaint. These are civil procedures and are governed by sections 51–57 of the Magistrates' Courts Act 1980 and Rules 4 and 98 of the 1981 Rules. These sections and Rules deal with, amongst other things, issuing summonses and parties failing to attend court.

9.7. The order can be varied either by an addition or replacement of any provision that could originally have been included, or by cancelling any provision.

9.8. Parenting orders may be varied for a number of reasons, for example where the family moves to another area or where the original requirements are not proving effective.

9.9. An order may be discharged for instance if the parent has fully complied with the requirements and the behaviour of the child has improved.

9.10. Where an application to discharge a parenting order has been dismissed, no further application may be made without the court's consent. This is largely to prevent spurious or repeat applications.

c) Appeals

9.11. Where a parenting order has been made:

- in the same proceedings as a child safety order, an appeal against it can be made to the High Court (the Divisional Court of the Queen's Bench Division);
- in the same proceedings as a referral order, an anti-social behaviour order or sex offender order, an appeal against it can be made to the Crown Court.

9.12. Appeals against a free-standing order can be made to the Crown Court.

9.13. Where a child or young person has been convicted of an offence, a person subject to a related parenting order has the same right of appeal against it as if he or she had committed the offence leading to the order. For example, if the parenting order were made in a youth court, the appeal would be to the Crown Court and if the parenting order were made in the Crown Court, the appeal would be to the Court of Appeal.

d) Breach and monitoring compliance

9.14. The parenting order is primarily designed to help parents or guardians to address their child's behaviour. The responsible officer should aim to secure and maintain the parent's co-operation and compliance with the requirements of the order to ensure that it is successfully completed, and will need to make a judgement about what is reasonable in all the circumstances of the case.

9.15. If different from the responsible officer, the programme provider should immediately report any failure by the parent to attend the parenting programme so the responsible officer can respond promptly.

9.16. How the responsible officer monitors specific requirements will depend on the circumstances. For example, where attending school is a requirement, the responsible officer should ask the school authorities to inform him or her of any non-attendance. Where the parents are required to ensure their child does not go to a particular area unsupervised, the responsible officer may be informed of a breach after the police receive a complaint about further anti-social or criminal behaviour by the child in that area.

9.17. Where the suspected breach is of a specific requirement, the responsible officer will need to consider the extent to which the parents have tried to meet the requirement and how far they are able to control their child's behaviour. Where the parents have made all reasonable efforts to control the child, even if he or she commits a further offence, this will not constitute a breach of a specific requirement.

9.18. Under paragraph 8.78 of the National Standards, if a parent fails to comply with a requirement of the order the responsible officer should contact the parent within one working day by visit, telephone or letter. If there is no acceptable reason for the failure, the responsible officer should give the parent a written warning and if possible a warning in person. Any important correspondence such as this must be sent by registered post and produced in any subsequent breach hearing.

9.19. If the parent has good reason for the failure to comply with the parenting order, the responsible officer may need to consider applying to the court to vary the terms of the order.

9.20. Under paragraph 8.79 of the National Standards, if there is more than one unacceptable failure to comply within three months the responsible officer should meet the parent to review the order and how it can be made to work. It may be appropriate to draw up a new plan with the parents better suited to their needs and circumstances. If the responsible officer cannot make contact with the parents or agree a positive way forward the responsible officer should consider whether the failure should be reported to the police for investigation. Whatever is decided, the responsible officer should ensure that a written record is kept.

9.21. Failure to comply with a parenting order is not an arrestable offence for the purposes of the Police and Criminal Evidence Act 1984 (PACE). If it is reported to them, the police will give the results of their investigation to the Crown Prosecution Service, which will decide whether or not to prosecute. The CPS will have to satisfy itself that there is sufficient evidence to prosecute, and then consider whether or not it is in the public interest to bring a prosecution, having regard to all the circumstances of the case. If the parenting order was made in the family proceedings court, the CPS will only have access to the court papers with the leave of the relevant justices' clerk or the court.

9.22. If a prosecution is brought and the parent pleads not guilty, there will be a summary trial to decide whether the parent has failed without reasonable excuse to comply with a requirement of a parenting order. This will be heard in the *adult Magistrates' Court*. Where the parent pleads guilty the case will proceed to sentence.

9.23. If the parent is convicted, he or she will be liable to a fine not exceeding level 3 on the standard scale (up to £1,000). The offence is not a recordable offence for the purposes of PACE. The decision on the nature and level of penalty to impose will be a matter for the court following consideration of all the facts of the case, such as the family circumstances and the means of the parents. The court could impose any sentence available for a non-imprisonable offence—that is a fine up to £1,000, absolute or conditional discharge, community order or curfew order.[21] Courts cannot re-issue parenting orders in breach proceedings.

---

[21] These other sentencing options derive from the Powers of Criminal Courts (Sentencing) Act 2000. The Community Order and Curfew Order will be replaced by the new generic community sentence introduced through the Criminal Justice Act 2003. Courts will be notified when this sentence is implemented.

9.24. Under section 127 of the Magistrates' Courts Act 1980 there is a six-month time limit for bringing breach proceedings. They can be brought after an order has expired but early action will allow the Court more options, for instance to vary the order so as to require the parent to attend a new parenting programme and fulfil specific requirements to exercise control over the child.

e) Legal services and representation

9.25. Public funding may be available in some circumstances. Parents may seek advice from a solicitor as to the availability of help, or contact the Legal Services Commission on 020 7759 0000 or at *www.legalservices.gov.uk*.

Enquiries

- Please put any enquiries about this guidance to Anthony Green (Tel. 020 7273 4182) of the Home Office Juvenile Offenders Unit, 50 Queen Anne's Gate, London, SW1H 9AT.
- Please put any enquiries about operational matters and the National Standards on Youth Justice to Roger Cullen at the Youth Justice Board, 11 Carteret Street, London, SW1H 9DL.

Process for dealing with breach of parenting order—summary

1. If a parent fails to comply with a requirement of the order, the responsible officer should make contact with the parent within one working day by visit, telephone or letter.
   - If there is no acceptable reason for the non-compliance, the responsible officer should give the parent a written warning and if possible a warning in person.
   - If the parent has good reason for the failure to comply with the requirements of the parenting order, it may be appropriate for the responsible officer to consider whether to apply to the court for the terms of the order to be varied.
2. If there is more than one unacceptable failure to comply within a period of three months, the responsible officer should meet the parent to review the order and how it can be made to work. A written record is kept.
3. Responsible officer should consider whether the failure to comply should be reported to the police for investigation.
4. If reported to police, police then investigate.
5. Failure to comply with a parenting order is not an arrestable offence. Police will give the results of their investigation to the CPS.
6. CPS will have to satisfy itself that there is sufficient evidence to prosecute and decide whether or not it is in the public interest to bring a prosecution.
7. If decision to prosecute, case is heard in the adult Magistrates' Court. The hearing will determine whether the parent is guilty of failing *without reasonable excuse* to comply with a requirement of a parenting order.
8. Court will determine whether to impose on conviction:
   - a fine not exceeding level 3 on the standard scale **and/or**
   - any sentence available for a non-imprisonable offence, i.e.
     - absolute or conditional discharge
     - community order
     - curfew order

Annex A: Relevant legislation

Sections 8–10 of the Crime and Disorder Act 1998

8. Youth crime and disorder—Parenting orders

(1) This section applies where, in any court proceedings—
   (a) a child safety order is made in respect of a child;
   (b) an anti-social behaviour order or sex offender order is made in respect of a child or young person;
   (c) a child or young person is convicted of an offence; or
   (d) a person is convicted of an offence under section 443 (failure to comply with school attendance order) or section 444 (failure to secure regular attendance at school of registered pupil) of the Education Act 1996.

(2) Subject to subsection (3) and section 9(1) below, if in the proceedings the court is satisfied that the relevant condition is fulfilled, it may make a parenting order in respect of a person who is a parent or guardian of the child or young person or, as the case may be, the person convicted of the offence under section 443 or 444 ('the parent').[1]

(3) A court shall not make a parenting order unless it has been notified by the Secretary of State that arrangements for implementing such orders are available in the area in which it appears to the court that the parent resides or will reside and the notice has not been withdrawn.

(4) A parenting order is an order which requires the parent—
   (a) to comply, for a period not exceeding twelve months, with such requirements as are specified in the order, and
   (b) subject to subsection (5) below, to attend, for a concurrent period not exceeding three months, such counselling or guidance programme as may be specified in directions given by the responsible officer.

(5) A parenting order may, but need not, include such a requirement as is mentioned in subsection 4(b) above in any case where a parenting order under this section or any other enactment has been made in respect of the parent on a previous occasion.

(6) The relevant condition is that the parenting order would be desirable in the interests of preventing—
   (a) in a case falling within paragraph (a) or (b) of subsection (1) above, any repetition of the kind of behaviour which led to the child safety order, anti-social behaviour order or sex offender order being made;
   (b) in a case falling within paragraph (c) of that subsection, the commission of any further offence by the child or young person;
   (c) in a case falling within paragraph (d) of that subsection, the commission of any further offence under section 443 or 444 of the Education Act 1996.

(7) The requirements that may be specified under subsection (4)(a) above are those which the court considers desirable in the interests of preventing any such repetition or, as the case may be, the commission of any such further offence.

---

[1] This subsection was previously amended by Youth Justice and Criminal Evidence Act 1999 and later the Powers of Criminal Courts (Sentencing) Act 2000 to preclude making a parenting order with a referral order. The CJ Act 2003 removes this restriction and restores the original wording to the subsection.

(7A) A counselling or guidance programme which a parent is required to attend by virtue of subsection (4)(b) above may be or include a residential course but only if the court is satisfied—
(a) that the attendance of the parent at a residential course is likely to be more effective than his attendance at a non-residential course in preventing any such repetition or, as the case may be, the commission of any such further offence, and
(b) that any interference with family life which is likely to result from the attendance of the parent at a residential course is proportionate in all the circumstances.[2]

(8) In this section and section 9 below 'responsible officer', in relation to a parenting order, means one of the following who is specified in the order, namely—
(a) an officer of a local probation board;
(b) a social worker of a local authority social services department;
(c) a person nominated by a person appointed as chief education officer under section 532 of the Education Act 1996; and
(d) a member of a youth offending team.[3]

9. Parenting orders: supplemental

Where a person under the age of 16 is convicted of an offence, the court by or before which he is so convicted—
(a) if it is satisfied that the relevant condition is fulfilled, shall make a parenting order; and
(b) if it is not so satisfied, shall state in open court that it is not and why it is not.

(1A) The requirements of subsection (1) do not apply where the court makes a referral order in respect of the offence.[4]

(1B) If an anti-social behaviour order is made in respect of a person under the age of 16 the court which makes the order—
(a) must make a parenting order if it is satisfied that the relevant condition is fulfilled;
(b) if it is not so satisfied, shall state in open court that it is not and why it is not.[5]

(2) Before making a parenting order—
(a) in a case falling within paragraph (a) of subsection (1) of section 8 above;
(b) in a case falling within paragraph (b) or (c) of that subsection, where the person concerned is under the age of 16; or
(c) in a case falling within paragraph (d) of that subsection, where the person to whom the offence related is under that age,

---

[2] Subsection 7A allows a parenting order to include a residential course and was inserted by the ASB Act 2003.

[3] This subsection was amended by the Criminal Justice and Court Services Act 2000 to allow a person nominated by a chief education officer to act as responsible officer and also renames a probation officer as an officer of a local probation board.

[4] This subsection was initially inserted by the Powers of Criminal Courts (Sentencing) Act 2000 and has now been amended by the CJ Act 2003 to give courts discretion to make a parenting order when they make a referral order.

[5] This subsection was inserted by the ASB Act 2003 and strengthens the link between anti-social behaviour orders and parenting orders.

a court shall obtain and consider information about the person's family circumstances and the likely effect of the order on those circumstances.

(2A) In a case where a court proposes to make both a referral order in respect of a child or young person convicted of an offence and a parenting order, before making the parenting order the court shall obtain and consider a report by an appropriate officer—
 (a) indicating the requirements proposed by that officer to be included in the parenting order;
 (b) indicating the reasons why he considers those requirements would be desirable in the interests of preventing the commission of any further offence by the child or young person; and
 (c) if the child or young person is aged under 16, containing the information required by subsection (2) above.

(2B) In subsection (2A) above 'an appropriate officer' means—
 (a) an officer of a local probation board;
 (b) a social worker of a local authority social services department; or
 (c) a member of a youth offending team.[6]

(3) Before making a parenting order, a court shall explain to the parent in ordinary language—
 (a) the effect of the order and of the requirements proposed to be included in it;
 (b) the consequences which may follow (under subsection (7) below) if he fails to comply with any of those requirements; and
 (c) that the court has power (under subsection (5) below) to review the order on the application either of the parent or of the responsible officer.

(4) Requirements specified in, and directions given under, a parenting order shall, as far as practicable, be such as to avoid—
 (a) any conflict with the parent's religious beliefs; and
 (b) any interference with the times, if any, at which he normally works or attends an educational establishment.

(5) If while a parenting order is in force it appears to the court which made it, on the application of the responsible officer or the parent, that it is appropriate to make an order under this subsection, the court may make an order discharging the parenting order or varying it—
 (a) by cancelling any provision included in it; or
 (b) by inserting in it (either in addition to or in substitution for any of its provisions) any provision that could have been included in the order if the court had then had power to make it and were exercising the power.

(6) Where an application under subsection (5) above for the discharge of a parenting order is dismissed, no further application for its discharge shall be made under that subsection by any person except with the consent of the court which made the order.

(7) If while a parenting order is in force the parent without reasonable excuse fails to comply with any requirement included in the order, or specified in directions given by the responsible officer, he shall be liable on summary conviction to a fine not exceeding level 3 on the standard scale.

---

[6] Subsections 2(A) and 2(B) have been inserted by the CJ Act 2003 and require courts to consider a report before making a parenting order with a referral order.

(A)7 In this section 'referral order' means an order under section 16(2) or (3) of the Powers of Criminal Courts (Sentencing) Act 2000 (referral of offender to youth offender panel).[7]

10. Appeals against parenting orders

(1) An appeal shall lie—
  (a) to the High Court against the making of a parenting order by virtue of paragraph (a) of subsection (1) of section 8 above; and
  (b) to the Crown Court against the making of a parenting order by virtue of paragraph (b) of that subsection.
(2) On an appeal under subsection (1) above the High Court or the Crown Court—
  (a) may make such orders as may be necessary to give effect to its determination of the appeal; and
  (b) may also make such incidental or consequential orders as appear to it to be just.
(3) Any order of the High Court or the Crown Court made on an appeal under subsection (1) above (other than one directing that an application be re-heard by a Magistrates' Court) shall, for the purposes of subsections (5) to (7) of section 9 above, be treated as if it were an order of the court from which the appeal was brought and not an order of the High Court or the Crown Court.
(4) A person in respect of whom a parenting order is made by virtue of section 8(1)(c) above shall have the same right of appeal against the making of the order as if—
  (a) the offence that led to the making of the order were an offence committed by him; and
  (b) the order were a sentence passed on him for the offence.
(5) A person in respect of whom a parenting order is made by virtue of section 8(1)(d) above shall have the same right of appeal against the making of the order as if the order were a sentence passed on him for the offence that led to the making of the order.
(6) The Lord Chancellor may by order make provision as to the circumstances in which appeals under subsection (1)(a) above may be made against decisions taken by courts on questions arising in connection with the transfer, or proposed transfer, of proceedings by virtue of any order under paragraph 2 of Schedule 11 (jurisdiction) to the Children Act 1989 ('the 1989 Act').
(7) Except to the extent provided for in any order made under subsection (6) above, no appeal may be made against any decision of a kind mentioned in that subsection.

Schedule 1, Part 1A[8] of Powers of Criminal Courts (Sentencing) Act 2000

Referral of parent or guardian for breach of section 20 order

Introductory

9A

(1) This Part of this Schedule applies where, under section 22(2A) of this Act, a youth offender panel refers an offender's parent or guardian to a youth court.
(2) In this Part of this Schedule—

[7] This subsection was inserted by the CJ Act 2003.

[8] Part 1A was inserted by the CJ Act 2003 to allow courts to make parenting orders where a parent fails to attend meetings of a Youth Offender Panel.

(a) 'the offender' means the offender whose parent or guardian is referred under section 22(2A);
(b) 'the parent' means the parent or guardian so referred; and
(c) 'the youth court' means a youth court as mentioned in section 22(2A).

Mode of referral to court

9B

The panel shall make the referral by sending a report to the youth court explaining why the parent is being referred to it.

Bringing the parent before the court

9C

(1) Where the youth court receives such a report it shall cause the parent to appear before it.
(2) For the purpose of securing the attendance of the parent before the court, a justice acting for the petty sessions area for which the court acts may—
  (a) issue a summons requiring the parent to appear at the place and time specified in it; or
  (b) if the report is substantiated on oath, issue a warrant for the parent's arrest.
(3) Any summons or warrant issued under sub-paragraph (2) above shall direct the parent to appear or be brought before the youth court.

Power of court to make parenting order: application of supplemental provisions

9D

(1) Where the parent appears or is brought before the youth court under paragraph 9C above, the court may make a parenting order in respect of the parent if—
  (a) it is proved to the satisfaction of the court that the parent has failed without reasonable excuse to comply with the order under section 20 of this Act; and
  (b) the court is satisfied that the parenting order would be desirable in the interests of preventing the commission of any further offence by the offender.
(2) A parenting order is an order which requires the parent—
  (a) to comply, for a period not exceeding twelve months, with such requirements as are specified in the order, and
  (b) subject to sub-paragraph (3A) below, to attend, for a concurrent period not exceeding three months, such counselling or guidance programme as may be specified in directions given by the responsible officer.
(3) The requirements that may be specified are those which the court considers desirable in the interests of preventing the commission of any further offence by the offender.
(3A) A parenting order under this paragraph may, but need not, include a requirement mentioned in subsection (2)(b) above in any case where a parenting order under this paragraph or any other enactment has been made in respect of a parent on a previous occasion.
(3B) A counselling or guidance programme which a parent is required to attend by virtue of subsection (2)(b) above may be or include a residential course but only if the court is satisfied—
  (a) that the attendance of the parent at a residential course is likely to be more effective than his attendance at a non-residential course in preventing the commission of any further offence by the offender, and

(b) that any interference with family life which is likely to result from the attendance of the parent at a residential course is proportionate in all the circumstances.

(4) Before making a parenting order under this paragraph where the offender is aged under 16, the court shall obtain and consider information about his family circumstances and the likely effect of the order on those circumstances.

(5) Sections 8(3) and (8), 9(3) to (7) and 18(3) and (4) of the Crime and Disorder Act 1998 apply in relation to a parenting order made under this paragraph as they apply in relation to any other parenting order.

Appeal

9E

(1) An appeal shall lie to the Crown Court against the making of a parenting order under paragraph 9D above.

(2) Subsections (2) and (3) of section 10 of the Crime and Disorder Act 1998 (appeals against parenting orders) apply in relation to an appeal under this paragraph as they apply in relation to an appeal under subsection (1)(b) of that section.

Effect on section 20 order

9F

(1) The making of a parenting order under paragraph 9D above is without prejudice to the continuance of the order under section 20 of this Act.

(2) Section 63(1) to (4) of the Magistrates' Courts Act 1980 (power of Magistrates' Court to deal with person for breach of order, etc) apply (as well as section 22(2A) of this Act and this Part of this Schedule) in relation to an order under section 20 of this Act.

Sections 25–29 of the Anti-Social Behaviour Act 2003

[See Appendix 1.]

Annex B: Definitions

'Child' means a person under the age of 14 but any reference in this guidance to a child should be taken as including a young person unless the context indicates otherwise.

'Young person' means a person who has attained the age of 14 and is under the age of 18.

'Parent' Any reference to 'parent' includes a reference to 'guardian' and the term 'parent' has the same meaning as that contained in section 1 of the Family Law Reform Act 1987. That is either of the child or young person's natural parents whether or not they were married to each other at the time of the child or young person's birth. Throughout this document references to 'parent' include 'guardian' and mean each and every person coming within the definitions and should not be taken to mean that provisions only apply to 'parent' in the singular.

'Guardian' is defined with reference to section 107 of the Children and Young Persons Act 1933, and includes any person who, in the opinion of the court, has for the time being the care of the child or young person. This is not the same as a guardian appointed under section 5 of the Children Act 1989, but may include people who may not have parental responsibility for the child or young person as defined by the 1989 Act, such as step parents.

'Criminal conduct' is conduct that constitutes a criminal offence and in the case of conduct of a person under the age of 10, conduct that would constitute an offence were they not under that age.

'Parenting Programmes' refers to counselling or guidance programmes.

Annex C: Example parenting contract

Copy for Parent/Carer and YOT

Personal details

Name .... YOT ID ....

Youth Offending Team ....

date ....

Main objective

We are going to support you to prevent your child from engaging in criminal conduct and/or anti-social behaviour, by working on:

....

....

Major targets for the next three months

What are our targets? How is this going to be done? Who is going to do it?

1. ....

2. ....

3. ....

4. ....

5. ....

Future targets

....

To achieve these targets

I/We (the parent/s) agree to:

(Please detail)

....

....

The YOT agrees to:

(Please detail)

....

....

Consent—Parent or Carer

I/We also understand and agree that information about me/us has been and will continue to be collected for the purpose of assessing and providing appropriate Youth Justice Services. The Youth Offending Team (YOT) may also use this information for service planning, monitoring and research purposes. This information may also be shared with external agencies and providers of relevant services that the YOT needs to consult and work with to ensure that I/we are provided with the most appropriate services.

I/We understand that this information will be stored either electronically or in the manual records by the YOT for case management purposes for the length of the programme and for (x) months following, to monitor and evaluate the effectiveness of the plan. The YOT will keep the information updated and notify all recipients of any changes to ensure corrections are made

Complaints procedure provided and understood ☐ Date:

Information exchange policy provided and understood ☐ Date:

Legal rights and responsibilities information provided and understood ☐ Date:

Important dates

When are we next going to meet? . . . . How often do we meet? . . . .

Are there any other important dates? . . . .

Date of review/plan: . . . .

End of contract: . . . .

Contact details

Parenting Support practitioner's name . . . .

Practitioner's tel. No: . . . . If unavailable contact: . . . .

Agreeing the intervention plan/contract:

I/We have agreed the parenting support plan and will work with the YOT as detailed above to prevent our child from engaging in criminal conduct and/or anti-social behaviour.

I/We also agree to the information sharing under the Data Protection Act.

Signed (Parent/s) . . . . Date:

The YOT will provide the support detailed above and has provided and explained the relevant information as indicated.

Signed (Practitioner) . . . . Date:

Annex D: Suggested form to apply for free-standing parenting orders

Application for Parenting Order (Anti-Social Behaviour Act 2003 section 26)

[See Appendix 2, s. 26 = p. 264.]

Annex E: Suggested forms of parenting orders

A) Parenting Order (Anti-Social Behaviour Act 2003 section 26)

[See Appendix 2, s. 26 = p. 265.]

B) Parenting Order (Crime and Disorder Act 1998 section 8)

[See Appendix 2, s. 8 = p. 266.]

C) Parenting Order (Powers of Criminal Courts (Sentencing) Act 2000 Schedule 1 paragraph 9D)

[See Appendix 2, Sched. 1, para 9 = p. 267.]

Index

Note: references in italics indicate the text of the Anti-Social Behaviour Act 2003 as well as related guidance notes and regulations